Praise for *Re-Imag*

CW00797870

"Encounter this book with enormous respect.
judicious, audacious, and perceptive. Setting the .... , ,
an historical context, he weaves together an account of natural theology that is
innovative, powerful, and intriguing. Critics and advocates for natural theology alike
will have their worldview changed as they encounter this remarkable argument."

Ian S. Markham
Dean and President of Virginia Theological Seminary

"This theological book emerges from a deep and integrating vision of creation – the
natural world appreciated through the Christian *imaginarium*. Composed in crys-
talline prose, McGrath explores the complexity of *theologia naturalis* in a way that is
both insightful and erudite. He enriches the particularities of place with a spirituality
always and only historically and culturally localised. In a time of global ecological
concerns, this is a much needed labour. Christians *need* to engage these concerns,
rooting them profoundly in a thick account of reality and what it is to be alive. There's
a promise of transformation in doing this, and McGrath knows it. This book is an
exciting testimony to the imaginative power behind that promised potential."

Graham Ward
University of Oxford

"In this game-changing book, Alister McGrath develops a thick theology of nature
from a distinctly Christian point of view. He expertly tackles topics that are under-
explored in traditional natural theology, such as the moral and aesthetic ambiguity of
nature, emphasising the importance of both rational and imaginative ways of
engaging with nature."

Helen de Cruz
Oxford Brookes University

"Being informed about natural theology is essential to any substantive understanding
of the relationship of science and theology. The present book nicely sums up and
carries further his indispensable contributions to the topic."

John F. Haught
author of *Science and Faith: A New Introduction*

"In contemporary theology, the project of natural theology has many opponents. In
his latest book, *Re-Imagining Nature*, McGrath presents an ambitious vision for
retrieving a holistic Christian understanding of natural theology that goes beyond the
rationalistic proofs of God's existence of the nineteenth century. By stressing the
imaginative powers of human beings and not just rational ones, McGrath defends a
thick and contextual but at the same time traditional model of Christian natural
theology as a way of seeing the world. A stellar addition to the contemporary literature
on natural theology."

Aku Visala
University of Helsinki

Also by Alister E. McGrath from Wiley-Blackwell

The Christian Theology Reader, 5th edition (2016)

Christian Theology: An Introduction, 6th edition (2016)

Darwinism and the Divine (2011)

Theology: The Basic Readings, 2nd edition (2011)

Theology: The Basics, 3rd edition (2011)

Science and Religion: An Introduction, 2nd edition (2010)

The Open Secret: A New Vision for Natural Theology (2008)

Christianity: An Introduction, 2nd edition (2006)

The Order of Things: Explorations in Scientific Theology (2006)

Luther's Theology of the Cross, 2nd edition (2005)

Dawkins' God: Genes, Memes and the Meaning of Life (2004)

A Brief History of Heaven (2003)

The Blackwell Companion to Protestantism (ed., with Darren C. Marks, 2003)

The Intellectual Origins of the European Reformation, 2nd edition (2003)

The Future of Christianity (2002)

Christian Literature: An Anthology (2000)

Reformation Thought: An Introduction, 3rd edition (2000)

Christian Spirituality: An Introduction (1999)

Historical Theology: An Introduction to the History of Christian Thought (1998)

The Foundations of Dialogue in Science and Religion (1998)

The Blackwell Encyclopedia of Modern Christian Thought (1995)

A Life of John Calvin (1993)

For a complete list of Alister E. McGrath's publications from Wiley-Blackwell, visit our website at http://www1.alistermcgrathwiley.com/

Re-Imagining Nature

The Promise of a Christian Natural Theology

Alister E. McGrath

WILEY Blackwell

This edition first published 2017

© 2017 John Wiley & Sons Ltd

Registered Office
John Wiley & Sons Ltd, The Atrium, Southern Gate, Chichester, West Sussex,
PO19 8SQ, UK

Editorial Offices
350 Main Street, Malden, MA 02148-5020, USA
9600 Garsington Road, Oxford, OX4 2DQ, UK
The Atrium, Southern Gate, Chichester, West Sussex, PO19 8SQ, UK

For details of our global editorial offices, for customer services, and for information about
how to apply for permission to reuse the copyright material in this book please see our
website at www.wiley.com/wiley-blackwell.

The right of Alister E. McGrath to be identified as the author of this work has been asserted
in accordance with the UK Copyright, Designs and Patents Act 1988.

Library of Congress Cataloging-in-Publication Data

Names: McGrath, Alister E., 1953- author.
Title: Re-imagining nature : the promise of a Christian natural theology /
    Alister E. McGrath.
Description: Hoboken : Wiley, 2016. | Includes bibliographical references and
    index.
Identifiers: LCCN 2015046827| ISBN 9781119046301 (cloth) | ISBN 9781119046356
    (pbk.)
Subjects: LCSH: Nature–Religious aspects–Christianity. | Theology.
Classification: LCC BT695.5 .M4437 2016 | DDC 231.7–dc23 LC record available at
http://lccn.loc.gov/2015046827

A catalogue record for this book is available from the British Library.

Cover image: Hans Gude: *From Hardanger*, 1847. Photo © O. Væring

Set in 10/12.5pt, GalliardStd-Roman by Thomson Digital, Noida, India.

Printed and bound in Malaysia by Vivar Printing Sdn Bhd

1   2017

Contents

Introduction

Natural theology has never lost its deep appeal to the human imagination. Might the beauty and wonder of the natural world point to a deeper order of things, even if this is only partially glimpsed rather than fully grasped? Does nature point us toward – to use the imagery of Dante – a "hidden path" leading to a "shining world"?[1] Does the idea of God continue to provide a "repository for our awestruck wonderment"[2] at life itself, or the natural world around us? A natural theology is both a response to and an expression of a real experience of the world of nature, which seems to call for further exploration.

This book sets out to explore what a properly Christian approach to natural theology might look like, and how this relates to alternative interpretations of our experience of the natural world. Although I interact with contemporary theological debates about the nature and scope of natural theology, my more fundamental concern is to demonstrate the potential of natural theology in enabling a productive and significant interaction between Christianity and a wider culture, including the natural sciences.[3]

Re-Imagining Nature opens by offering a genealogical account of the six main divergent senses in which the term *theologia naturalis* has been understood in the western intellectual tradition since late classical antiquity. Does such a plurality of construals point to the incoherence of natural theology? Or is there some grander vision of natural theology which is able to accommodate and colligate these six approaches? Exploring the genealogy of

---

[1] Dante, *Inferno*, 34, 133–5.
[2] Rushdie, *Is Nothing Sacred?*, 8. See also Mancini, *Filosofia della religione*, 41–2, 129–30; Tallis, *In Defence of Wonder*, 1–22.
[3] As I have already dealt recently at some length with the interaction between natural theology and recent theoretical developments in the physical and biological sciences, including an engagement with the substantial research literature in these fields, only minimal reference will be made to these matters in this work: see A. E. McGrath, *A Fine-Tuned Universe*, 111–216; A. E. McGrath, *Darwinism and the Divine*, 185–276.

Re-Imagining Nature: The Promise of a Christian Natural Theology, First Edition.
Alister E. McGrath.
© 2017 John Wiley & Sons, Ltd. Published 2017 by John Wiley & Sons, Ltd.

natural theology discloses its rich and complex history on the one hand, and subverts narrow and inadequate conceptions of the project on the other.

The recognition of the social construction of such notions as "nature," "science," and "religion," particularly during the early modern period,[4] indicates that there is no predetermined essential form of nature or natural theology; it is rather open to cultural revision and ideological reconstruction, reflecting the social and cultural location of its practice.[5] As C. S. Lewis often remarked, the latest is not always the best; furthermore, "a genuinely new perspective often means embracing and developing an old insight."[6] I argue that a "Christian natural theology project" may be developed which holds together a variety of understandings of the notion as aspects or elements of a coherent greater whole. Such a "thick understanding" of natural theology resonates with some of the fundamental themes of Christianity, allowing a retrieval of forgotten or suppressed approaches to these issues.

Given the impossibility of articulating a natural theology "from nowhere," this work makes a case for developing a specifically Christian approach to natural theology, and exploring how this correlates and connects with its alternatives. The modernist dogma of a single way of understanding the world has, largely due to its lack of evidential warrant, given way to the recognition of multiple perspectives of reality – including an important family of perspectives which are grounded and shaped by the Christian faith. I argue that a "Christian natural theology project" may be developed which holds together these six historical articulations of natural theology *as aspects of a single coherent project*. The form that natural theology takes is critically dependent on its context; my approach allows the marked phenomenological diversity of natural theology to be accommodated within a distinctively Christian theological vision of its grounds and possibilities.

I then turn to consider the critically important issue of the interplay of the imagination and reason in a Christian natural theology. Many writers use the term *sensorium* to designate the amalgam of natural human cognitive capacities, cultural webs of meaning, and accessible evidence which shapes human concepts of rationality in any given situation. Although this notion is important in criticizing naïve notions of a "universal rationality," it lacks the capacity for imaginative engagement that is of critical importance for theology in general, and natural theology in particular. I thus introduce the critical concept of an *imaginarium*, which provides a conceptual

---

[4] See Demeritt, "What Is the 'Social Construction of Nature'?"; Evernden, *The Social Creation of Nature*, 37–104; P. Harrison, *The Territories of Science and Religion*, 1–19; Gerber, "Beyond Dualism"; A. E. McGrath, *A Scientific Theology:* vol. 1, *Nature*, 81–133.

[5] See Greider and Garkovich, "Landscapes"; Escobar, "After Nature"; C. M. Harrison and Burgess, "Social Constructions of Nature."

[6] Antognazza, "The Benefit to Philosophy of the Study of Its History," 165.

framework for exploring the interplay of the reason and imagination within a Christian natural theology, offering a way of looking at things in which "a creative imagination is wedded to an acute intellect."[7] A purely rational or ideational construal of natural theology – such as that found in many works of systematic theology – will inevitably fail to do justice to the richness of the notion.[8] Vestiges of the modernist suppression of the imagination still haunt the practice of systematic theology, and impoverish our conception of *theologia naturalis.*

Particular attention is paid in this important chapter to the concept of *metanoia* – traditionally translated as "repentance," but more fundamentally designating a graceful re-orientation of the mind, through which the self and the world are seen in a new and more satisfying manner. Natural theology is one of the outcomes of this process of mental renewal and imaginative transformation, in that we come to imagine the natural world in a new manner.

So how does a Christian natural theology cope with the ambiguity and complexity of the natural world? The third chapter notes the difficulties for a natural theology arising from the moral and aesthetic ambiguity of nature, and explores three interpretative strategies that are based on conceiving nature as a book to be read, a picture to be appreciated, and a sign to be understood. Each of these has a long history of use within the Christian tradition, but is capable of further development in dialogue with recent explorations of their potential.

I then move on to deal with questions of motivation and context, noting how the context within which natural theology is undertaken shapes its forms and construals. Among the themes to be considered are the role of industrialization in creating a desire to reconnect with the natural world, the role of a sense of wonder at the beauty and majesty of nature as a gateway to understanding it, and the human quest for an existentially satisfying "big picture" of life, which embraces the world of nature.

The fifth chapter addresses six major concerns about natural theology, identified in conversation and dialogue with critics, including both fundamental protests about the theological legitimacy of the approach (such as that famously articulated by Karl Barth), and wider concerns about the intellectual and cultural viability of the notion in general, and the particular approach that I develop in this study. In each case, I try to give a fair summary of the concern, before offering a response to the issues being raised. This chapter is placed late in this book, thus allowing some of these concerns to be engaged during the exposition of my approach to a Christian natural theology.

[7] Barfield, *Poetic Diction*, 178.
[8] Cf. Barfield, *Poetic Diction*, 28: "Only by imagination therefore can the world be known."

The final chapter explores the promise of a Christian natural theology, and sets out how this "re-imagination of nature" offers the promise of an enhanced and enriched vision of theology itself, as well as enabling a principled and productive dialogue with other intellectual and cultural stakeholders.

This work builds on three earlier interventions in contemporary discussions about the nature and scope of natural theology, based on major academic lecture series in the United Kingdom: the 2008 Richardson Memorial Lectures at the University of Newcastle upon Tyne; the 2009 Gifford Lectures at the University of Aberdeen; and the 2009–10 Hulsean lectures at the University of Cambridge. These were published as *The Open Secret: A New Vision for Natural Theology* (2008); *A Fine-Tuned Universe: The Quest for God in Science and Theology* (2009); and *Darwinism and the Divine: Evolutionary Thought and Natural Theology* (2011). These three volumes laid the deep foundations for this new study, which is essentially a free-standing essay exploring the promise, potential, and problems of a Christian natural theology. Given my substantial level of engagement with the natural sciences in *A Fine-Tuned Universe* and *Darwinism and the Divine*, the present volume focusses on other themes, while noting the importance of a Christian natural theology in challenging the inadequacies of "scientism."

In those three earlier works, I suggested that Christian discussion about natural theology required retrieval of older understandings of the notion needlessly neglected as a result of controversy. There is a clear need for a reconceptualization of the identity and strategy of a Christian natural theology, and for it to be emancipated from polemical agendas which cast a long shadow over any serious discussion of its nature and scope. In particular, I identified four areas in which a refocussing of the concept of natural theology was appropriate for Christian theology:

1   A dogmatic relocation of the concept of natural theology from the domain of "the natural" to that of "the revealed";
2   A replacement of the fundamentally Deistic concept of God associated with the approaches to natural theology which developed in England during the long eighteenth century (1688–1815)[9] with a distinctively Christian vision of God;
3   A fuller recognition of the theological and philosophical significance of the basic psychological truth that the human observer is an active interpreter of the natural world, not its passive spectator;

---

[9] Black, "Britain and the 'Long' Eighteenth Century, 1688–1815"; O'Gorman, *The Long Eighteenth Century*.

4 An acknowledgment of the importance of the imagination in any Christian encounter with the natural world, particularly in relation to its beauty. John Keats's notion of the "truth of the imagination"[10] may be an imperfect realization of this insight, but it articulates the potential of the human imagination as a truth-bearer.

These four motifs remain embedded within the vision of natural theology which is set out in this volume. Yet my conversations with my critics, subsequently expanded through detailed historical research, has persuaded me of the importance of a fifth theme, hinted at but not fully developed in these three earlier works, which needs to incorporated into an informed discussion of the project of a natural theology:

5 Natural theology is situationally embedded, so that a theology of *nature* exists in an interactive relationship with a theology of *place*.[11] The theory and practice of natural theology in any given historical and cultural context are shaped by its present preoccupations and presuppositions, and its memories of the past.

My study of the perspectives from which nature has been "read" during the last two millennia has made it clear that different cultural locations have developed different "protocols of reading" nature,[12] making it impossible to reflect on the changing shape of natural theology without a sustained engagement with the cultural location of the reader of the "book of nature." Although this work is rich in historical analysis, its ultimate object is not the exploration of how natural theology has developed in various cultural places in the past, but how such past developments might illuminate and inform its theory and practice in the present.

It remains for me to thank my many colleagues at Oxford and beyond who have helped me develop my ideas on natural theology over many years, often by challenging the integrity and propriety of the notion in the first place. Theology is always at its best when undertaken in critical and respectful dialogue, and I owe more to my critics than I can adequately express.

Alister McGrath
Oxford, December 2015

---

[10] See his letter to Benjamin Bailey, dated November 22, 1817: "I am certain of nothing but of the holiness of the Heart's affections and the truth of Imagination." Keats, *Letters*, 67. For comment, see Sallis, *Force of Imagination*, 15–21.

[11] For the basic themes of such a "theology of place," see Sheldrake, *Spaces for the Sacred*; J. Inge, *A Christian Theology of Place*, 59–122.

[12] For this important notion, see Scholes, *Protocols of Reading*.

1

Natural Theology

Questions of Definition and Scope

The heavens declare the glory of the Lord.
(Psalm 19: 1)

Many have experienced a sense of awed wonder at the beauty and majesty of nature, evoked by a stunning verdant landscape, a majestic mountain range, or the cold and clear beauty of the sky at night.[1] But might such an experience be a portal to something still greater? Might this evoke our curiosity, in the deepest sense of that word – a "respectful attentiveness" to the beauty and complexity of the world around us?[2]

Such an attentiveness allows nature to act as a gateway, a threshold to ways of imagining the world, and our place within it. The journey of exploration that is precipitated by a sense of wonder in the presence of nature leads to "a new way of looking at things," in which we see things as if they were new and unfamiliar,[3] bathed in "a sense of the 'newness' or 'newbornness' of the entire world."[4] Both science and religion can be argued to be a response to a sense of wonder at the world around us and within us.[5]

Yet there is another possible outcome, which intersects and interconnects the domains of science and religion, the sacred and secular, in a manner that is perhaps easier to describe than to define. It is often articulated most clearly by

---

[1] Hesse, *"Mit dem Erstaunen fängt es an,"* 7–10; Falardeau, "Le sens du merveilleux." Evans uses the term "cosmic wonder" to refer to a range of such experiences: Evans, *Why Believe?*, 32.

[2] See Gadamer, *Werke*, vol. 4, 37–42; quote at p. 41: *Curiositas* "ist von *cura*, der Sorge und rühmlichen Sorgfalt, abgeleitet."

[3] H. Miller, *Big Sur and the Oranges of Hieronymus Bosch*, 25.

[4] Scarry, *On Beauty and Being Just*, 22.

[5] Haralambous and Nielsen, "Wonder as a Gateway Experience"; Crowther-Heyck, "Wonderful Secrets of Nature"; Dawkins, *An Appetite for Wonder*; Tallis, *In Defence of Wonder*, 1–22. These are not necessary *outcomes*, in that some are led to one, some to both, and some to neither.

Re-Imagining Nature: The Promise of a Christian Natural Theology, First Edition.
Alister E. McGrath.
© 2017 John Wiley & Sons, Ltd. Published 2017 by John Wiley & Sons, Ltd.

those natural scientists who sense that their research is opening up deep questions about meaning, truth, and beauty which lie beyond the capacity of science to answer, and by those theologians who realize that the rich imaginative and conceptual framework of the Christian faith makes it possible to understand the achievements and limits of the scientific enterprise in an informed and enriched manner.[6] This is traditionally known, however inadequately and provisionally, as "natural theology."[7]

Natural theology can broadly be understood as a process of reflection on the religious entailments of the natural world, rather than a specific set of doctrines.[8] In its most general sense, it can be undertaken from a variety of viewpoints, secular and religious, and has no "essential" core, other than an engagement with the question of the relationship of nature (including the human observer) and the divine or transcendent. There are many insights to be quarried and questions to be explored at this rich interface – including the question of whether the natural world is able to signify, intimate, or disclose, no matter how provisionally, a transcendent reality which lies beyond it.

Yet perhaps the most important question to be explored in this work is whether there is a specifically Christian understanding of natural theology, and what form this might take. In 1934 Emil Brunner challenged his theological generation to "find its way back to a right *theologia naturalis*,"[9] believing that something had been lost, which was in principle capable of being retrieved. Brunner, however, never believed he had solved his own challenge.

Brunner's challenge remains open and important, especially in the light of new debates about the rationality and integrity of faith, and its relation to other areas of human inquiry, particularly the natural sciences. This volume is an attempt to "find our way back" to such a natural theology, conscious that Christian history is rich in approaches that have been sidelined and suppressed by dominant theological voices and institutions, yet which may be of service to the theological community today, especially by encouraging theologians to "think outside the box of the latest philosophical orthodoxies or commonly held beliefs."[10]

---

[6] See, for example, Polkinghorne, "Where Is Natural Theology Today?"; B. H. Smith, *Natural Reflections*, 95–120.
[7] For a thorough survey of the field and issues, see the essays gathered in Re Manning, ed., *The Oxford Handbook of Natural Theology*.
[8] J. J. Collins, "Natural Theology and Biblical Tradition," 3.
[9] Brunner, "Natur und Gnade"; in *Ein offenes Wort*, vol. 1, 374–5: "Es ist die Aufgabe unserer theologischen Generation, sich zur rechten *theologia naturalis* zurückzufinden."
[10] Antognazza, "The Benefit to Philosophy of the Study of Its History," 165.

The Aim of This Work

In this work, I argue that a Christian natural theology allows us to re-imagine nature. In speaking of such an act of intellectual permissiveness, I do not mean that it encourages a spurious inflation of our understanding of nature, or a descent into intellectual vacuity or irrationality.[11] Rather, I mean that we are provided with an informing intellectual and imaginative framework which both *warrants* and *enables* us to visualize the everyday natural world in a new way,[12] as if an intellectual sun had illuminated it so that we could see its colors, textures, and details in a manner that had hitherto eluded us. This book is an invitation to enter into such a theological re-imagining of nature,[13] alert to both its risks and its rewards.

Such a re-imagining encourages us to develop a principled attentiveness toward the details of the natural world that enables us to see what might otherwise be missed, to appreciate more fully its beauty and wonder, and to grasp its fundamental interconnectedness. Heidegger famously contrasted the openness of the classic Greek notion of "wonder" with the modern temptations to predatory possessiveness and calculating self-interest in what was observed.[14] Yet this impulse can be challenged and resisted, allowing us to recover a deeper level of engagement with the natural world. Elaine Scarry points to the transformative capacity of beauty, which "ignites the desire for truth" which renders us susceptible to new competencies and imaginative possibilities.[15]

Something of the approach that I have in mind can be seen from John Ruskin's reflections on a "monotonous bit of vine-country" north of Lac Leman in Switzerland. In his diary entry for June 3, 1849, Ruskin noted how his attitude toward an unpromising scene of "sticks and stones" and a "steep dusty road" was transformed through an act of aesthetic imagination, driven

---

[11] For an assessment of New Age approaches to the natural order, which are widely regarded as vulnerable to such criticisms, see Spangler and Thompson, *Reimagination of the World*.

[12] Cf. Pieper, *Was heißt Philosophieren?*, 65–82, especially 66–7: "*Im* Alltäglichen und Gewöhnlichen das wahrhaft Ungewöhnliche und Unalltägliche, das *mirandum*, zu gewahren – das also ist der Anfang des Philosophierens" (emphasis in original).

[13] For the importance of making explicit such an invitation, see Brock, "The Puzzle of Imaginative Failure." For further reflections on why re-imagining can meet resistance, see Gendler, "The Puzzle of Imaginative Resistance"; Liao, Strohminger, and Sripada, "Empirically Investigating Imaginative Resistance."

[14] Kavanagh, "The Limits of Visualization," 70.

[15] Scarry, *On Beauty and Being Just*, 52. For some concerns about such a comprehensive appeal to beauty, see Leib, "On the Difficulty of Imagining an Aesthetic Politics."

by a determination to see the scene afresh through an active application of his mind:

> I had a hot march among the vines, and between their dead stone walls; once or twice I flagged a little, and began to think it tiresome; then I put my mind into the scene, instead of suffering the body only to make report of it; and looked at it with the possession-taking grasp of the imagination – the true one; it gilded all the dead walls, and I felt a charm in every vine tendril that hung over them. It required an effort to maintain the feeling: it was poetry while it lasted, and I felt that it was only while under it that one could draw, or invent, or give glory to, any part of such a landscape.[16]

This act of imaginative reconceptualization goes beyond the purely rational reconfiguration of natural philosophy advocated by writers such as Francis Bacon in the early modern period.[17] The French poet Paul Claudel (1868–1955) wrote critically of the "starved imagination (*imagination à jeun*)" of rationalism, in which a cold rational dissection of things becomes disconnected from a joyful imaginative embrace of reality.[18] Wordsworth made the same point, in emphasizing the aesthetic coherence of nature, grasped by the imagination yet fragmented by reason:[19]

> Sweet is the lore which Nature brings;
> Our meddling intellect
> Mis-shapes the beauteous forms of things: –
> We murder to dissect.

Natural theology invites us to see things with new eyes, to develop a heightened perceptual acuity in the expectation that we will see aspects of nature that we had hitherto missed, or heal our theoretical blindness which prevents us from seeing what is really there on account of our metaphysical prejudices and precommitments. These points will be developed and amplified as our analysis proceeds.

[16] Ruskin, *Complete Works*, vol. 5, xix. See the extended discussion of this theme in Finley, *Nature's Covenant*, 136–53. For Ruskin's views on the "innocence" of the eye, see Wettlaufer, *In the Mind's Eye*, 197–239, especially 231–6. A similar urge to go beneath the outward appearance of landscapes is found in the works of the influential American conservationist Aldo Leopold (1887–1948): see Callicott, "The Land Aesthetic."

[17] Dear, *Revolutionizing the Sciences*, 56. Such a "reimagination" of nature must not be confused with some of the more esoteric approaches to nature which emerged around this time: Coudert, *Religion, Magic, and Science in Early Modern Europe and America*, 153–72.

[18] Claudel, "Introduction à un poème sur Dante," 429. Cf. Borella, *The Sense of the Supernatural*, 31–43.

[19] Wordsworth, "The Tables Turned" (1898), lines 25–8. For comment, see Midgley, *Science and Poetry*, 47–58.

Yet any attempt to explore and advocate a natural theology raises a fundamental question of definition. How is natural theology to be understood? And who has the right to make such a normative decision? Any discussion about whether natural theology is helpful or destructive, proper or improper, wise or foolish, authentically Christian or inherently pagan, is critically dependent on how the notion is defined, and the ideational framework within which it is located. Orthodox theologians, for example, have been critical of western tendencies to impose an unnecessary and improper separation between natural and supernatural revelation. Orthodoxy holds that "natural revelation is understood fully in the light of supernatural revelation," and rejects any scholastic or modernist tendency to ignore divine influence on human theological reflection on the world, seeing humanity as "the only active agent" in this process of reflection.[20]

During the twentieth century, particularly within Reformed Protestantism, discussion of "natural theology" has become entangled with polemical concerns which have disrupted and confounded any serious attempt to offer an objective account of its theological legitimacy and potential.[21] This is perhaps to be expected; George MacDonald is a classic example of a Calvinist writer who struggled to reconcile his theology and his love of the imagination.[22] During the twentieth century, the Reformed tradition temporarily seems to have submitted to Karl Barth's withering criticism of natural theology, with some even falling into what Eberhard Jüngel termed a "sterile Barth-scholasticism" which refused to countenance any misjudgment on Barth's part, or consider alternatives to it;[23] happily, a more attentive reading of the Reformed tradition has demonstrated that alternative approaches to, and understandings of, natural theology lie to hand, with a distinguished history of use.[24] Yet these shadows of past controversies about natural theology are now fading and receding, making possible a reconsideration and re-evaluation of its place in theology in general, in the broader cultural dialogue about the beauty of nature and its representations, and in the more specific dialogue between science and religion.

Ludwig Wittgenstein once quipped that certain expressions need "to be withdrawn from language and sent for cleaning" before they can be "put

---

[20] Stăniloae, *The Experience of God*, 1–36. See further Lemeni, "The Rationality of the World and Human Reason."

[21] Kapper, "'Natürliche Theologie' als innerprotestantisches und ökumenisches Problem"; Kock, *Natürliche Theologie*, 1–16; 391–5; Jüngel, "Das Dilemma der natürlichen Theologie und die Wahrheit ihres Problems."

[22] Dearborn, *Baptized Imagination*, 9–14; 67–94. For reflections on the deficiencies of syllogistic theologies, see Guite, "Through Literature."

[23] Jüngel, "Unterbrechung des Weltlebens," 135.

[24] See, for example, A. E. McGrath, *Emil Brunner*, 228–9.

back into general circulation."[25] It is hard not to appreciate the wisdom of his remark for our topic. So can the term "natural theology" be cleaned up, and put back into circulation? Or do we need to confront and come to terms with its ineluctable multiplicity of meanings?[26] Or might we hope to find some richer understanding of the notion, which helps us understand why it is understood in so many ways, and lend coherence to its plurality?

In this study, we shall offer a careful assessment of how natural theology might be understood and applied, what criticisms and challenges it might face, and what benefits it might bring. The best point at which to start this discussion is clearly to explore how the notion of *theologia naturalis* might be conceived, deploying a genealogical approach which seeks to identify how the idea has been understood, rather than allow others to define the concept in a manner that suits their vested interests.

A Brief Genealogy of Natural Theology

Concepts have histories, and for this reason, they have genealogies which have to be traced in order to deepen our understanding of those concepts and the rationalities which formed them.[27] It is not acceptable to offer a contemporary definition of natural theology which has gained acceptance within some particular community of discourse, as if that settled the matter, or become locked into a "metahistorical deployment of ideal significations" capable of delivering clear and crisp answers.[28] Studying the genealogies of core concepts – such as "rationality" – is one of the most effective (although not unproblematic) means of subverting the vested interests of intellectual power groups, and allowing the retrieval of suppressed or marginalized notions which remain nonetheless live intellectual options for contemporary theological discussion.[29]

The genealogy of natural theology, like so many other critical terms in the history of human thought, is "gray," not black and white. The history of use

[25] Wittgenstein, *Culture and Value*, 44.
[26] Hutchinson, "The Uses of Natural Theology."
[27] Oliver, "Analytic Theology," 466–7. Note his conclusion that "history is determinative of concepts, or at least indicative of the meaning of concepts." For a similar emphasis on studying the history of philosophy, see the well-argued studies of Antognazza, "The Benefit to Philosophy of the Study of Its History"; Garber, "What's Philosophical about the History of Philosophy?"
[28] See Foucault, "Nietzsche, la généalogie, l'histoire," passim: "La généalogie est grise . . . [elle s'oppose] au déploiement métahistorique des significations idéales" (145). The genealogical method adopted by Foucault eschews developmental or progressive accounts of history in favor of an emphasis on historical contingency. For further comment, see Lightbody, *Philosophical Genealogy*, 133–89.
[29] Owen, "Criticism and Captivity"; Dean, *Critical and Effective Histories*, 7–23; Lightbody, *Philosophical Genealogy*, 7–56.

of the notion indicates that it has had, and still has, multiple associations and meanings, with the cultural context influencing which of a range of possible interpretations or implementations achieves dominance in that location. The clarification of the meaning of this notion in any given context must be determined by active engagement with that community of discourse in the empirical, not by ahistorical or purely theoretical argument.

Debate about what we now know as "natural theology" – although this term does not seem to have been generally used at the time – can be traced back to classic Greek philosophers, where it was often framed in terms of a rational or scientific quest for an *archē* – a first principle. The assumption of the rationality of both the empirical world and belief in gods was commonplace, although the pre-Socratic tradition showed little interest in developing arguments in support of the existence of the gods – for example, through an appeal to nature.[30] "Natural theology, taken as a scientific search for an ultimate *archē*, is virtually identical with the activity of a search for wisdom as the Greek philosophers understood it."[31] For the Ionian philosophers, a natural theology interpreted the world as an ordered whole – that is, as a *kosmos* – and therefore was, at least to some degree, transparent to the human intellect.[32] Pythagoras is often credited with being "the first to call the containing of all things the *kosmos*, because of the order which governs it."[33] The Greek term *kosmos* thus developed overtones of order and intelligibility. The universe is something that we can *understand*, however partially and imperfectly.

The Latin term *theologia naturalis* – which could arguably be translated as either "a natural theology" or "a theology of nature"[34] – was coined in the pre-Christian classical world to describe a general mode of reasoning which ascended from the natural world to the world of the gods.[35] It could be seen as a variant on a *philosophia perennis*, which locates humanity's "final end in the knowledge of the immanent and transcendent Ground of all being."[36] Despite writing his treatise in Latin, the philosopher Varro used

[30] E.g., see Lesher, *Xenophanes of Colophon*, 114–19; Enders, *Natürliche Theologie im Denken der Griechen*, 47–73.

[31] Gerson, *God and Greek Philosophy*, 82; Naddaf, "Plato." See also Pelikan, *Christianity and Classical Culture*, 90–106.

[32] Gerson, "Metaphysics in Search of Theology," 1–2.

[33] Brague, *The Wisdom of the World*, 17–25.

[34] See Topham, "Natural Theology and the Sciences." Padgett argues constructively for interpreting *theologia naturalis* philosophically as "natural theology" and theologically as "a theology of nature": Padgett, "*Theologia Naturalis*: Philosophy of Religion or Doctrine of Creation?" There are important parallels here with the "thick" natural theology project I develop in this work.

[35] Klauck, "Nature, Art, and Thought."

[36] Huxley, *The Perennial Philosophy*, vii.

three Greek adjectives (*mythicon, politicon,* and *physicon*) to designate the *tria genera theologiae,* which strongly suggests that this categorization had been borrowed from a philosopher of the Hellenistic age.[37] In Roman religion, *theologia naturalis* was seen as part of a tripartite approach to religion, supplementing *theologia civilis* and *theologia mythica.*[38] The phrase was picked up by some early Christian theologians, such as Augustine,[39] who tended to treat it as little more than a pejorative way of referring to the inferior theologies of pagan philosophers. The term, however, did not find wide acceptance within the western theological tradition. As C. C. J. Webb rightly noted, it was rarely used during the patristic and medieval periods, and only came into wider use in the sixteenth century, mainly through the influence of the Catalan scholar Raymond de Sebonde (*c.* 1385–1436).[40]

Although historians and theologians tend to use the term "natural theology" retrospectively – for example, in speaking of the "natural theology of Thomas Aquinas" (meaning "Thomas Aquinas on what many would now call 'natural theology'") – the general acceptance and wide use of the term *theologia naturalis* within the western theological tradition is actually a relatively late development, and reflects the influence of Sebonde's *Liber naturae sive creaturarum* (later known, partly through the influence of the Renaissance philosopher Michel de Montaigne (1533–92), simply as *Theologia Naturalis*).[41] Montaigne's French translation of Sebonde's work, published as *La théologie naturelle de Raymond Sebon* (1569), did much to popularize Sebonde's approach in the later Renaissance, particularly in affirming the intrinsic rationality of faith and the use of analogies in

---

[37] See Augustine, *de Civitate Dei*, VI.v.12.

[38] Rüpke, *Die Religion der Römer*, 121–5; Heinze, *Virgil's Epic Technique*, 233–4.

[39] Dihle, "Die *Theologia Tripertita* bei Augustin." More generally, see Pelikan, *Christianity and Classical Culture*, 22–39; 184–230.

[40] Webb, *Studies in the History of Natural Theology*, 1–83. Various spellings of this name are found in the literature, including the Catalan form "Raimundo Sibiunda."

[41] Simonin, "La préhistoire de l'Apologie de Raimond Sebond." There is some confusion about the original title of Sebond's treatise. The manuscripts held in leading European libraries have quite different titles: *Liber Naturae sive Creaturarum* (Paris), *Scientia Libri creaturarum seu Naturae et de Homine* (Toulouse), and *Liber Creaturarum sive de Homine* (Clermont-Ferrand). The critically important subtitle *Theologia naturalis* was only added to the second printing (1485) by the publishers, half a century after Sebonde's death. The use of this subsequent subtitle has misled some as to the character and intentions of the book. See further Guy, "La *Theologia Naturalis*: Manuscrits, éditions, traductions." The work was originally written in Sebonde's native Catalan, and circulated in manuscript form.

theological reasoning.[42] Yet Montaigne's influential translation also served to establish the phrase *théologie naturelle* or *theologia naturalis* as a generic way of referring to a way of doing theology that engaged the natural world – intellectually, aesthetically, and morally. By the close of the sixteenth century, the phrase *theologia naturalis* was generally assumed to mean a kind of theology that focussed on the contemplation of nature.

Like most thinkers of the Renaissance, Sebonde did not define natural theology in agonistic terms – for example, in contradistinction to divine revelation – seeing the "book of creatures" as itself being constituted as a species of revelation through which God chose to convey knowledge (both cognitive and affective) to human observers. On the basis of Sebonde's approach, it is difficult to provide a clear distinction between natural theology and natural philosophy.[43] Nor does Sebonde interpret *theologia naturalis* in purely cognitive terms; he clearly understands it to involve an *affective* engagement with or approach to the natural order. Sebonde's treatise, while including sections dealing with dogmatic theology, is as much a work of spirituality as of theology.[44] He lacks the over-intellectualization which impoverished some more recent accounts of the idea, particularly those to have emerged during the period of the Enlightenment.

[42] Note the subtle modifications of Sebonde's original ideas which Montaigne introduced through his translation – such as the heightened importance of the imagination: Habert, *Montaigne traducteur de La Théologie Naturelle*, 198; 237. For Montaigne's use of analogical reasoning, see the masterly study of Carraud, "L'imaginer inimaginable." Sebonde's original work was placed on the *Index Librorum Prohibitorum* in 1559 and 1564 on account of some unwise statements in its preface concerning the sufficiency of Scripture; Montaigne judiciously "corrected" these passages; as a result, his translation of Sebonde attracted no official censure.

[43] See further Blair, "Mosaic Physics and the Search for a Pious Natural Philosophy in the Late Renaissance." Blair suggests that natural theology is more characteristic of early Protestantism than of Catholicism. Although I concede the importance of certain forms of natural theology for Protestantism (particularly in England during the eighteenth century), historical research is uncovering a neglected Catholic exploration of the theme, especially in the Renaissance – for example, in the writings of Raymond Lull. Yet Catholicism tended to see natural theology as confirmatory of *Catholicism*, rather than a generic Christianity. The "three truths" affirmed in works such as Pierre Charron's *Les trois Véritez* (1593) are that God exists; that Christianity is the true religion; and that the Catholic Church is the only true Church.

[44] Révah, *Une source de la spiritualité péninsulaire au XVIe siècle*. As Jean Balsamo notes, Sebonde's work – especially as translated by Montaigne – is best thought of as "a manual of private piety": Balsamo, "Un gentilhomme et sa théologie," 110. The affective aspects of some later forms of natural theology may be noted here: Crowther-Heyck, "Wonderful Secrets of Nature"; Ogilvie, *The Science of Describing*, 87–138.

While Sebonde's later interpreters – such as Montaigne – suggested that his approach to theology could be helpful in challenging atheists and skeptics,[45] Sebonde himself tended to see it as enhancing the rational credentials, the imaginative richness, and the moral commitment of religious believers.[46] The clarity and accessibility of the "book of nature" was contrasted with the inaccessibility of scholastic theology and the Bible.[47] Unlike some later writers, Sebonde does not argue the case for Christianity on the basis of first principles which are independent of Scripture and Church tradition, but rather anticipates (and at points even presupposes) basic Christian ideas, which are then shown to be consonant with the natural world. In the hands of their less accomplished advocates, such "proofs" for the existence of God tend to be rationally questionable and imaginatively dull: "Les preuves fatiguent la vérité" (Georges Braques).

There is a long tradition of linking natural theology with the demonstration of the rationality of faith. Although Montaigne suggested that Sebonde's *Theologia Naturalis* could serve to confute atheists, we find little interest in this topic on the part of Sebonde himself. The rise of atheism was a later development; Sebonde was more concerned to reassure his readers of the trustworthiness of their faith, and to draw them into a deeper understanding of themselves and the natural world within which they live. Yet his approach both expresses and ultimately depends upon Christian presuppositions. This is clear at several points, particularly this important passage dealing with the actuality of sin and necessity of divine grace:

> No one can see this wisdom, or read this said open Book [of Nature and Creatures] by themselves, unless they are enlightened by God (*a Deo illuminatus*) and cleansed from original sin. And therefore none of the ancient pagan philosophers could read this science.[48]

For Sebonde, natural theology was thus helpful and important – yet inadequate, without the illumination of divine grace.

---

[45] It is not clear that atheism was a significant issue at this time. The atheist positions engaged in French apologetic works of this age tend to treat atheism as a hypothetical possibility, allowing clarification of the Christian position: see Kors, "Theology and Atheism in Early Modern France."

[46] Guy, "La *Theologia Naturalis* en son temps."

[47] Printing was still in its infancy at this time, so that it was both impractical (and expensive) for lay people to gain access to such texts, let alone to understand them. Sebonde's point is that nature is publicly available, accessible, and intelligible – even if Sebonde reads the "book of nature" in the light of an informing Christian perspective.

[48] Sebonde, *Theologia naturalis seu Liber creaturarum*, fol. A3. The context indicates that Sebonde intends the term *scientia* to be understood here as *theologia naturalis*.

Many today assume that *theologia naturalis* means something like "the enterprise of providing support for religious beliefs by starting from premises that neither are nor presuppose any religious beliefs."[49] Some scholars thus suggest that Sebonde develops an idiosyncratic or unorthodox notion of natural theology[50] which is out of line with modern thinking on the matter. Yet this judgment results from allowing an understanding of natural theology that became prevalent in a later cultural context to determine what is normative for the notion in earlier periods. A more realistic approach might be to see Sebonde's broader understanding of natural theology as normative, with later formulations of the notion representing a restriction or narrowing of its scope.

This specific notion of natural theology as "providing support for religious beliefs by starting from premises that neither are nor presuppose any religious beliefs" gained the ascendancy during the Enlightenment, and appears to have its roots in the English Deism of the early eighteenth century.[51] Both Samuel Clarke's *Demonstration of the Being and Attributes of God* (1706) and George Cheyne's *Philosophical Principles of Religion, Natural and Revealed* (1715) set out trajectories of reasoning which would now be described as "natural theology,"[52] and were both cited as significant sources by Johann August Eberhard (1739–1809) in his important 1781 lecture "Vorbereitung zur natürlichen Theologie," which influenced Kant's account of the topic.[53]

Yet this rational natural philosophy is to be seen as one specific formulation of the notion of natural theology which assumed hegemony for cultural reasons, reflecting the historical contingencies of the "Age of Reason."[54] This formulation of natural theology is not present in Sebonde's work, nor in

---

[49] Alston, *Perceiving God*, 289.

[50] For example, see the comments of Hartle, *Michel de Montaigne*, 141.

[51] It is historically problematic to assert that "the environmental niche in which natural theology evolved was the competition of ideas within early modern science and philosophy": Schults, "Wising Up," 547. Yet Schults is surely right, if we interpret him to mean that a *certain form* of natural theology emerged as culturally significant at that time, and that this partly reflected tensions between science and philosophy.

[52] For the intellectual context, see Pfizenmaier, *The Trinitarian Theology of Dr. Samuel Clarke*, 29–85. See also Khamara, "Hume versus Clarke on the Cosmological Argument"; Guerrini, *Obesity and Depression in the Enlightenment*, 72–88.

[53] Reprinted in Kant, *Gesammelte Schriften*, vol. 20, 491–606. For comment, see D'Aniello, "Von der Religion zur Theologie," 168–72; Hanke, "Kein Wunder und keine Instruktion," 18–21.

[54] For the concept of "natural philosophy" in the eighteenth century, see Gascoigne, "Ideas of Nature: Natural Philosophy." Haakonssen, ed., *The Cambridge History of Eighteenth-Century Philosophy*; Irving, "Public Knowledge, Natural Philosophy, and the Eighteenth-Century Republic of Letters."

most seventeenth-century Protestant works of systematic theology. For example, the Reformed dogmatician Johann Heinrich Alsted's influential *Theologia naturalis* (1615) seems to treat natural theology as a theology of nature – something quite distinct from philosophy, especially metaphysics.[55] We must resist any suggestion that this rationalized natural theology of the "Age of Reason" is a definitive or normative account of natural theology, against which other approaches are to be judged and found wanting. From the outset, *theologia naturalis* was a conceptually fluid notion, shaped by the apologetic and dogmatic needs of the moment, and possessing multiple derivative meanings and associations.[56]

It is simply not possible to offer an essentialist definition of "natural theology," as if there exists or existed some correct or normative understanding of the notion which is necessary to its identity and function, and grounded in its intrinsic nature.[57] Its relationship to both kindred and rival intellectual enterprises – such as "natural philosophy" – is frustratingly difficult to define.[58] Rather, we find a series of constructed interpretations and applications of the notion, often developed or appropriated in response to cultural situations and challenges. Precisely the same issue arises with the even more contested notion of "natural religion,"[59] and possibly even with the notion of "religion" itself.[60]

Yet if we cannot define what natural theology is, or ought to be, we can at least describe how it has been understood, and reflect on the implications of these observations, not least whether these various construals point to something more fundamental as their ultimate base and norm. When seen in the light of its history, the phrase "natural theology" designates a plurality of possibilities, raising the question of whether the notion is fundamentally incoherent, or whether there exists some overarching notion

---

[55] Lohr, "Metaphysics and Natural Philosophy as Sciences," 290–3.

[56] Casserley, *Graceful Reason*, 2–4; Fergusson, "Types of Natural Theology"; G. L. Murphy, *The Cosmos in the Light of the Cross*, 8–25; Re Manning, ed., *Oxford Handbook of Natural Theology*, passim. For the contested notion of "natural revelation," often elided with "natural theology," see Welker, *Schöpfung und Wirklichkeit*, 42–55.

[57] For the problems of such an approach, see H. C. Barrett, "On the Functional Origins of Essentialism."

[58] The natural philosophy of the seventeenth century implicitly assumed some aspect of natural theology, such as a religiously motivated engagement with nature: Gaukroger, *The Emergence of a Scientific Culture*, 129–54; Calloway, *Natural Theology in the Scientific Revolution*. For the concept in general, see Dear, *The Intelligibility of Nature*, 1–14.

[59] Pailin distinguishes eleven different meanings of the term "natural religion," noting that "the complex variety of ways" in which the term has been understood raises questions about the coherence of the notion: Pailin, "The Confused and Confusing Story of Natural Religion."

[60] Boyer, *The Fracture of an Illusion*, 96. For Boyer, the idea that there exists "some special domain of thought and action that is 'religion'" is a modern delusion.

of natural theology that is capable of accommodating its multiple implementations. I argue that a Christian *imaginarium* allows these multiple
conceptions of natural theology to be seen as culturally localized adaptations
of a grander and richer vision of the concept, which is capable of accommodating its multiple historical instantiations.

Natural Theology: Six Approaches

Six main understandings of the notion of natural theology can be identified
within the western theological tradition.[61] None can be considered as
definitive, and each is open to development beyond the somewhat narrow
scope which I shall outline below.[62] Each can be seen as a construction or
interpretation of a broader and richer underlying concept, reflecting the
needs or opportunities of the particular context within which it is embedded.
In what follows, I shall offer a brief account of these approaches.

  1 Natural theology is the "branch of philosophy which investigates what
human reason unaided by revelation can tell us concerning God."[63] It is here
understood as an attempt to demonstrate the existence or determine the
characteristics of God without recourse to divine revelation.[64] For many, this
has become the default understanding of natural theology. This approach
does not depend upon or express any specifically Christian ideas,[65] and thus
has considerable apologetic appeal within a secular cultural context. It
does not make an appeal to the natural world itself, but rather to a priori

---

[61] For other accounts of the conceptual diversity of "natural theology," see Casserley, *Graceful Reason*, 2–4; Fergusson, "Types of Natural Theology"; A. E. McGrath, *Darwinism and the Divine*, 15–18.

[62] For example, a "ramified" natural theology appeals to a range of considerations, some intrinsic to nature and reason (a "bare" natural theology), others to the Christian tradition – such as the notion of the fulfilment of biblical prophecy, or the resurrection of Christ (a "ramified" natural theology. For an influential statement of this approach, see Swinburne, *The Resurrection of God Incarnate*, especially 204–16. For reflection and comment, see Langtry, "Richard Swinburne," 292–6.

[63] Joyce, *Principles of Natural Theology*, 1. Note also Joyce's comment that "the Natural Theologian bases his conclusions purely and solely on the data afforded by natural reason." For reflections on the role of deductive arguments in such an approach to natural theology, see McGrew and DePoe, "Natural Theology and the Uses of Argument." For theological concerns about such approaches, see A. Moore, "Should Christians Do Natural Theology?"

[64] Clavier, *Qu'est-ce que la théologie naturelle?*; Mascall, *The Openness of Being*, 36–74; Weidemann, *Die Unverzichtbarkeit natürlicher Theologie*, 44–7.

[65] Peterfreund, *Turning Points in Natural Theology from Bacon to Darwin*, 41–58. For an assessment of the various arguments for God's existence associated with this approach to natural theology, see Craig and Moreland, eds., *The Blackwell Companion to Natural Theology*.

ideas which might be considered "natural," and explores their theistic entailments. Natural theology thus designates a theology that comes "naturally" to the human mind.

2 Natural theology is a demonstration or affirmation of the existence of God on the basis of the regularity and complexity of the natural world. This specific formulation of natural theology appears to have emerged in Protestant contexts during the early modern period primarily for apologetic reasons.[66] It is often referred to as "physico-theology,"[67] on account of its appeal to an a posteriori discernment of the regularity of nature which is held to entail or imply divine existence, rather than to a priori ideas of God, such as those traditionally held to underlie the ontological argument.[68] Because of its appeal to the public world of nature, this approach avoids the "scandal of particularity," which arises from modernism's insistence that knowledge of the divine must be universally accessible, not historically or culturally particular.[69]

Within Catholicism, this approach to natural theology became increasingly significant in the nineteenth century, as secularism became a pressing concern in western Europe.[70] This move is reflected in the First Vatican Council's declaration that God "can be known with certainty from the consideration of created things in the natural light of human reason."[71] For the purposes of this classification, we may leave open the question of whether a natural theology adopts a deductive or inferential mode of reasoning in defending a theistic outlook.[72] Although there are obvious similarities

---

[66] Freedman, "'Professionalization' and 'Confessionalization,'" 335.

[67] See P. Harrison, "Physico-Theology and the Mixed Sciences"; Ogilvie, "Natural History, Ethics, and Physico-Theology."

[68] Abbruzzese, "The Structure of Descartes' Ontological Proof." For the quite distinct approach adopted by Anselm of Canterbury in the eleventh century, see Schumacher, "The Lost Legacy of Anselm's Argument."

[69] O. Anderson, "The Presuppositions of Religious Pluralism and the Need for Natural Theology," 206–7. For the broader issues, see Clayton and Knapp, *The Predicament of Belief*, 80–92.

[70] For the impact on Catholic higher education, see Hütter, "University Education, the Unity of Knowledge – and (Natural) Theology."

[71] "Si quis dixerit, Deum unum et verum, creatorem et Dominum nostrum, per ea, quae facta sunt, naturali rationis humanae lumine certo cognosci non posse: anathema sit": Denzinger, *Enchiridion Symbolorum*, #3043. This is not to be understood as entailing that the existence of God could be proved by rational argument: see Kerr, "Knowing God by Reason Alone"; White, *Wisdom in the Face of Modernity*, 6–9; Echeverria, "The Reformed Objection to Natural Theology." For the historical context of this statement, see Menozzi, "Antimodernismo, secolarizzazione e cristianità."

[72] Gagnon, "Raymond Ruyer, la biologie et la théologie naturelle," 159–62; Koons, "A New Look at the Cosmological Argument"; A. E. McGrath, "New Atheism – New Apologetics," 102–8.

between this approach and the first, noted above, their point of departure is significantly different: one proceeds from pure reason, the other from engagement with the world of nature.

3 Natural theology is the intellectual outcome of the natural tendency of the human mind to desire or be inclined toward God. This approach traditionally makes an appeal to the "natural desire to see God," developed by Thomas Aquinas,[73] although more recent developments in the cognitive science of religion have opened up alternative ways of developing this theme.[74] Other theologians have developed this notion in important ways – most notably, Bernard Lonergan's reformulation of this principle as an innate tendency of the human intellect, equivalent to the unrestricted desire to understand being.[75]

4 Natural theology is the exploration of an analogy or intellectual resonance between the human experience of nature on the one hand, and of the Christian gospel on the other. This approach to natural theology often limits itself to establishing the possibility of coherence or congruence between the specific claims of Christian faith and a knowledge of the world derived from other disciplines or areas of life.[76] Natural theology thus articulates and expands the notion of an "isomorphism between our reason and the structure of reality."[77] Variants of this approach are found in Joseph Butler and John Polkinghorne.[78] We might also include in this category those who see natural theology as affirming the rationality of an existing faith, rather than as demonstrating the necessity of that faith in the first place, providing an intellectual "framework for articulating one tradition's existing beliefs about ultimacy in a plausible and faith-nurturing way."[79]

5 Natural theology is an attempt to demonstrate that "naturalist" accounts of the natural world and the achievements of the natural sciences are intrinsically deficient, and that a theological approach is required to give a comprehensive and coherent interpretation of the natural order.[80] This approach involves engaging what now seems to be the culturally dominant

---

[73] Ashley, "What Is the End of the Human Person?"; Feingold, *The Natural Desire to See God According to St. Thomas and His Interpreters*; Kerr, *Immortal Longings*, 159–84; Haldane, "Philosophy, the Restless Heart, and the Meaning of Theism"; Hütter, "*Desiderium naturale visionis Dei*"; Wang, "Aquinas on Human Happiness and the Natural Desire for God."

[74] J. L. Barrett, "Exploring the Natural Foundations of Religion"; J. L. Barrett, *Born Believers*.

[75] Stebbins, *The Divine Initiative*, 142–82; Himes, "Lonergan's Position on the Natural Desire to See God."

[76] See the discussion in M. M. Adams, *Christ and Horrors*, 1–28.

[77] Wasmaier-Sailer and Göcke, "Idealismus als Chance für die natürliche Theologie," 9–10.

[78] Penelhum, *Butler*, 89–112; Irlenborn, "Konsonanz von Theologie und Naturwissenschaft?"; Steinke, *John Polkinghorne: Konsonanz von Naturwissenschaft und Theologie*, 57–82.

[79] Wildman, "Comparative Natural Theology," 180–1; Macquarrie, *In Search of Deity*, 12–13.

[80] This approach is found in Plantinga, *Where the Conflict Really Lies*, 168–74.

belief that intellectual reflection on nature is presently more likely to lead to a "natural atheology" rather than a "natural theology,"[81] while avoiding the theologically questionable notion of the "god of the gaps."[82]

This approach to natural theology is particularly important in contemporary debates about the metaphysical implications of science, in that it challenges the idea that a naturalist account of nature is epistemologically privileged or "neutral." While being open about its own metaphysical assumptions and narrative precommitments, it challenges naturalism to acknowledge its own implicit foundations and assumptions.[83] In particular, this approach to natural theology holds that a "scientistic" account of reality – which in effect reduces reality to a single stratum or perspective – is simply inadequate to account for the complexities of human experience of the world.[84] We shall return to consider the problems of such a flat account of the world later in this work (pp. 161–3).

6 Natural theology is to be understood primarily as a "theology of nature" – that is, as a specifically Christian understanding of the natural world, reflecting the core assumptions of the Christian faith, which is to be contrasted with secular or naturalist accounts of nature.[85] The movement of thought here is from within the Christian tradition toward nature, rather than from nature toward faith (as in the second approach, noted above). Such a theology of nature is often framed primarily in terms of a doctrine of creation.

Given this plurality of interpretations, some might be tempted to conclude that the concept of "natural theology" is incoherent, open to such a wide variety of interpretations that it has ceased to be a legitimate or meaningful

[81] Lustig, "Natural Atheology"; Sosa, "Natural Theology and Naturalist Atheology." Caution needs to be exercised here, in that an "atheological" reading of nature (or other texts) may represent a novel form of discourse, which avoids the assumptions and language of traditional theologies. but which is not necessarily atheistic or anti-theological: see T. Dixon, "Theology, Anti-Theology and Atheology."

[82] A notion criticized by Charles Coulson: see A. Hough, "Not a Gap in Sight." For a response, see Larmer, "Is There Anything Wrong with 'God of the Gaps' Reasoning?"

[83] For the basic issues, see Draper, "God, Science and Naturalism." For theism as the most "natural" explanation of experience and a critique of naturalist accounts, see Visala, *Naturalism, Theism and the Cognitive Study of Religion*, 85–193.

[84] This is often developed in terms of a cumulative account of theistic explanation, perhaps best seen in Tennant's *Philosophical Theology*. For comment, see Bertocci, *The Person God Is*, 159–71. Tennant is one of the few philosophers of this era to develop theistic arguments based on the beauty of nature: see Tennant, *Philosophical Theology*, vol. 2, 89–93.

[85] Barbour, *Issues in Science and Religion*, 452–63; Morley, *John Macquarrie's Natural Theology*, 97–120; Gunton, "The Trinity, Natural Theology, and a Theology of Nature," 98–103.

concept. Some have responded to this plurality of interpretations by asserting the intellectual or historical hegemony of one way of conceiving natural theology, insisting that rival construals of the notion are defective, possibly even degenerate. Yet this diversity of modes of discourse about natural theology can more plausibly be argued to reflect the multi-layered nature of a richer vision of "natural theology," which we shall explore in the following section.

The Natural Theology Project: Thick and Thin Descriptions

As will be clear from the above analysis, the fluidity of the notion of *theologia naturalis* raises a concern about its coherence. It is a simple matter of observation that there are several very different projects that have been designated "natural theology" by their advocates or critics in different historical contexts. Explanations may, of course, be given as to why these different projects chose to designate themselves as "natural theology," or why they were designated as such by others. So is there sufficient "family resemblance" between them to allow us to suggest that there is a plausible "meta-project" that unifies or gives some fundamental cohesion to these very diverse projects? Or are they essentially disconnected and independent projects, with at best tangential connections and correlations? Or is there a Platonic *synoptikon*, a "view from somewhere," that allows these to be seen as different aspects or levels of the same reality?

These are not new questions, and are frequently revisited when considering other potentially complex and incoherent notions, such as that of "religion" itself.[86] In 1912, James H. Leuba found his attempt to develop a psychology of religion hindered somewhat by the fact that he encountered at least 50 definitions of the term "religion." "Religion" is often understood as a category of *genus*, which enfolds a series of *species* (individual religions). Yet the category of religion is a social construction, reflecting a specific tradition of interpretation,[87] which cannot be reified in this manner. If we cannot resolve the question of the identity of natural theology in a rationally compelling manner, we may have to agree to live with definitional plurality.

Yet virtually every major term used in philosophical, theological, or cultural discourse shows at least some degree of definitional elusiveness

---

[86] E.g., see Fitzgerald, "Religion, Philosophy and Family Resemblances"; B. Saler, "The Definition of Religion in the Context of Social-Scientific Study"; Nongbri, *Before Religion*, 15–24.

[87] See especially Masuzawa, *The Invention of World Religions*, 2–29.

or ambiguity. Terms such as "ontology" and "ideology," widely encountered in the scholarly literature, are open to multiple – and often widely diverging – interpretations.[88] Such polyvalence can be accommodated without undue difficulty, so long as it is understood what an author means when using the term, and how this might be related to other understandings of the notion.

The analysis presented in the previous section suggests that natural theology requires, to use Gilbert Ryle's term, a "thick" description, in that it is a "many-layered sandwich, of which only the bottom slice is catered for by the thinnest description."[89] Ryle's approach has been developed by social anthropologists to highlight the difference between a surface-level "thin account" of cultural phenomena that are directly observed with a "thick account" which included reference to the intentions of social actors, and the perceived meaning of events. Although it is not without its difficulties,[90] Ryle's model of description has obvious potential for enabling a richer exploration of the history of ideas.[91]

The concept of *theologia naturalis* ultimately requires and merits a thick description, not a thin definition. The six approaches to natural theology noted earlier are best seen as interconnected "slices of a sandwich" (Ryle). Each can be seen as an enactment of an aspect of natural theology, rather than as defining in itself what natural theology actually is. Natural theology has been a "thick" concept from the outset, finding expression in "thinner" forms in response to specific cultural opportunities or challenges – such as the rise of the "Age of Reason," which led some to accentuate its potential to demonstrate the rationality of faith.[92] Others, however, would challenge this as representing an excessive intellectualization of faith, suggesting that we must learn to live without any ultimate or definitive resolution of these issues.[93]

---

[88] Think, for example, of the radically different understandings of "ideology" in Quine's writings of the 1950s, and Althusser's writings of the 1970s, or the supplementation of traditional philosophical debates about "ontology" with the more recent use of the term within the knowledge engineering community as "explicit specifications of conceptualizations." See Knight, "Transformations of the Concept of Ideology in the Twentieth Century"; Corcho, *A Layered Declarative Approach to Ontology Translation*, 1–24.

[89] Ryle, "The Thinking of Thoughts." For the application of this notion to descriptive ethnography, see C. Geertz, "Thick Description."

[90] Noted by Cyrenne, "Is Thick Description Social Science?"

[91] See, for example, Darnton, "Intellectual and Cultural History," 327; McMahon, "The Return of the History of Ideas?," 15–17; Kaiser, *Toward a Theology of Scientific Endeavour*, 2–5.

[92] Wolterstorff, "The Migration of the Theistic Arguments"; A. E. McGrath, *A Fine-Tuned Universe*, 21–34.

[93] For example, Meister Eckhart's emphasis on living "without a why": see Yamazaki, "Leben ohne Warum."

A "thick" description of natural theology could take the form of an intuited link between the everyday world of natural human experience and a transcendent reality, which arises within human experience in general, yet is capable of being accommodated within various religious traditions, including Christianity. This approach is given added significance on account of recent work in the field of the cognitive science of religion, which has reinforced the perception that religious belief is natural. This "thick" description of natural theology extends to include intuitions and inferences that seem natural to human beings, occurring naturally or spontaneously on beholding a beautiful landscape or the night sky.[94]

Natural theology thus designates – without being limited to – ways of thinking, both rational and imaginative, that arise naturally within human minds on account of innate cognitive processes,[95] and which might subsequently be developed or enriched within a given tradition of interpretation such as that expressed by a *sensorium* or *imaginarium* (pp. 41–61). Natural theology is rooted in the natural ways in which human beings cognize the natural world, while being capable of being enhanced and redirected by the specific way of seeing the world which is endorsed and mandated by a specific tradition-mediated rationality. As we shall see, this opens the way to speaking about a "Christian natural theology," distinguished in at least some respects from other interpretations or implementations of the notion.

Natural theology might thus be best conceived as a certain *way of thinking* about the natural world and God, or a *way of seeing* the natural order, rather than any specific explanatory or normative theory about the world or God. It could be seen as a set of what R. G. Collingwood termed "absolute presuppositions" (even if, paradoxically, these are conceded to be provisional) that govern how we are to engage and understand the natural world, rather than a distinctive set of propositions about it.[96] It is an angle of approach to the natural world, framed as much in terms of imaginative engagement as rational comprehension – a new way of seeing its landscapes, given added depth and resonance by the reflections of those who have discovered and applied it.[97]

Yet while conceding this point, some will still want to press the issue: is there a "natural meta-theology" – so to speak – which itself provides

[94] De Cruz and de Smedt, *A Natural History of Natural Theology*, 41–60.

[95] J. L. Barrett, *Why Would Anyone Believe in God?*; J. L. Barrett, *Born Believers*; Bloom, "Religion Is Natural."

[96] Collingwood *An Essay on Metaphysics*, 408–9. See further Connelly, "R. G. Collingwood, Analytical Philosophy and Logical Positivism."

[97] Proust, *La prisonnière*, 69. "Le seul véritable voyage, le seul bain de Jouvence, ce ne serait pas d'aller vers de nouveaux paysages, mais d'avoir d'autres yeux, de voir l'univers avec les yeux d'un autre, de cent autres."

justification and resourcing for each of these six implementations of a natural theology? Is there a "Grand Theory" or metanarrative which creates space for these diverse notions of natural theology, and allows us to position and correlate them on a conceptual map? In this work, I shall argue for a "Christian natural theology project," by which I mean an approach to and understanding of natural theology which is grounded in the specifics of the Christian tradition, and suggest that this enables us to hold together the various strands of the notion as a coherent whole, rather than as competitive and unrelated strategies, seeing them as specific historically situated and culturally embedded implementions of a more general natural theology project.

This position will be defended and expounded in the remaining chapters of this work. In the following section, I shall outline the reasons for believing that this is both possible and necessary, providing a sketch map of the themes that will be explored later in this work.

In Defense of a "Christian" Natural Theology Project

Despite postmodern chastenings, the appeal of a "Grand Theory" has never disappeared.[98] Indeed, many would now argue that postmodernity "has died in a kind of *fin de siècle* despair at its inability to interrogate the consequences of its own provisionality and indecipherability."[99] In disciplines as diverse as sociology and theology, there is growing interest in retrieving the notion of a "big picture" – a way of seeing things which aims to frame and hold together the elements of our experience and observation.[100]

The capacity of Christianity to offer such a "big picture" of reality has been affirmed since the earliest of times. Although the early Pauline letters tend to stress the coherence of the future age, when all has been reconstituted and renewed in Christ, later New Testament writings affirm that Christ is the ground of coherence within the present age: "in him all things hold together" (Colossians 1: 17).[101] More recently, C. S. Lewis affirmed the

---

[98] For postmodern concerns about such theories, see especially Straus, "Grand Theory on Trial." These concerns focus especially on the abuse of power that is associated with such claims to ultimacy or hegemony.

[99] Wall, "Ethics, Knowledge, and the Need for Beauty," 757.

[100] For the importance of this idea in sociology, see J. H. Turner and Boyns, "The Return of Grand Theory." Note especially their comments about how such a theory might hold together the "macro- and micro levels of reality" (353).

[101] Kooten, *Cosmic Christology in Paul and the Pauline School*, 106–34; Tanzella-Nitti, "La dimensione cristologica dell'intelligibilità del reale."

importance of this "big picture" in one of his most widely cited remarks: "I believe in Christianity as I believe that the Sun has risen, not only because I see it, but because by it, I see everything else."[102] Lewis held that the Christian *imaginarium* allows the beauties of nature to be correlated with an "indescribable something of which they become for a moment the messengers."[103]

If natural theology is understood as the "branch of philosophy which investigates what human reason unaided by revelation can tell us concerning God," it would seem to be somewhat problematic to speak of a "Christian natural theology" (although it might be possible to speak of a natural theology which ultimately leads to Christianity). Yet this philosophical understanding of natural theology accentuates its independence of any religious tradition and its eschewal of dependency upon revelation. It envisages human reason operating autonomously, without any theological or religious precommitments.

Yet it is questionable whether this approach to natural theology can, in fact, be sustained as an independent project. Four serious concerns need to be noted about the viability of this "traditional" approach (which in fact dates from the early modern period, and reflects so many its core assumptions and preoccupations). These four concerns are:

1 it assumes a culturally invariant notion of human reason;
2 it fails to recognize the constructive activity of the human mind in the process of observation;
3 it fails to appreciate the importance of tradition-mediated rationalities; and
4 it is inattentive to the aesthetic, moral, and intellectual ambiguity of nature.

We shall consider each of these concerns in detail in what follows.

1 *It assumes a culturally invariant notion of human reason.* The "scandal of particularity" is avoided by positing a universal mode of human reasoning, accessible to all peoples at all times and in all places. It is no accident that this assumption lay at the heart of the Enlightenment project, with its foundational notion of a universal reason, independent of the historical and cultural location of the thinker. Yet this judgment can no longer be maintained, except in the specific domains of mathematics and logic. It is a "view from

---

[102] Lewis, *Essay Collection*, 21. For further analysis, see A. E. McGrath, "The Privileging of Vision."
[103] Lewis, "The Weight of Glory," in *Essay Collection*, 103.

nowhere," which fails to recognize the critical role of values and judgments that are embedded within the social context of the thinker.[104] Thomas Nagel has shown that every viewpoint is actually a "view from somewhere."[105] We "cannot escape the condition of seeing the world from our particular insertion in it"; however much we may aspire to conditions of absolute cultural detachment, we are forced to settle for a view that is "incurably open to bias and limitation."[106]

Some writers, especially within the New Atheist movement, adopt the unreconstructed view of rationality characteristic of *bien pensants* of the eighteenth century. A. C. Grayling, for example, believes that religious arguments – for example, in defense of theism – are unpersuasive because they are elaborated within "the premises and parameters" of their own system.[107] Yet this concern applies to any discipline other than logic and mathematics – including the natural sciences. The methods of natural sciences cannot evade an entanglement of theory and observation, making it impossible to reflect scientifically outside "the premises and parameters" of their system.[108] The discovery of the structure of DNA, for example, depended on theory-driven interpretations of observations, particularly the theory of "helical diffraction."[109] Likewise, estimates of the age of the universe are dependent on estimates of the speeds and distances of galaxies – which are then interpreted within "the premises and parameters" of contemporary physical theories to yield the age of the universe. Furthermore, the speeds and distances of those galaxies are not observed directly, but are inferred on the basis of "the premises and parameters" of additional physical theories – such as the correlation between velocity and the Doppler red-shift.[110]

As these examples indicate, the exercise of human rational judgment is an activity carried out within a particular theoretical context (whether this is recognized or not), and is essentially dependent on it. We cannot overlook Karl Marx's opinion (originally framed in terms of ideas as the outcomes of underlying socio-economic realities) that reason is both embedded within and shaped by its cultural context, particularly power groups.[111] Later in this

---

[104] For comment and reflection, see Kim, "Ideology, Identity, and Intercultural Communication"; Larrain, *Ideology and Cultural Identity.*
[105] Nagel, *The View from Nowhere,* 67–89.
[106] Weinstein, "The View from Somewhere," 85.
[107] Grayling, *The God Argument,* 66.
[108] See, for example, Machamer, "Feyerabend and Galileo"; Chang, *Inventing Temperature,* 159–219.
[109] S. Schindler, "Model, Theory, and Evidence in the Discovery of the DNA Structure."
[110] E. Harrison, "The Redshift-Distance and Velocity-Distance Laws."
[111] P. Smith, *Cultural Theory,* 6–9.

work (pp. 42–7), we shall return to consider the importance of the *sensorium* – a term which has come to be used to designate the sensory environments within which individuals are located, which shape they understand themselves and their world, and which are determined by both the natural abilities of individuals, and the cultural environment in which they are embedded.[112]

A central theme of this work is that both the forms which a natural theology takes and its cultural plausibility are shaped by their historical and social location (pp. 101–5). It is no accident that the historical emergence of forms of natural theology which sought to demonstrate the existence of God by pure reason, or rational reflection on the world, dates from the seventeenth and eighteenth centuries, when the influence of rationalism was at its height. Earlier demonstrations of the rationality of belief in God – such as those developed by Anselm of Canterbury and Thomas Aquinas – were more concerned to affirm the resonance or convergence of reason and faith, avoiding the inflated notions of reason that became characteristic of some elements of the Enlightenment.[113]

2 *It fails to recognize the constructive activity of the human mind in the process of observation.* The mechanical philosophy of the early Scientific Revolution appears to have encouraged the idea that perception was "another process in a mechanistic universe" involving "the passive reception of impressions from the external world."[114] The Enlightenment's emphasis on the objectivity of judgment was surprisingly inattentive to the question of how the human mind processes experience of the world, perhaps reflecting the lingering influence of Aristotelian conceptions of passive perception into the seventeenth century.[115] The "scopic regime" of modernity is embedded within a specific cultural understanding of both vision and visuality, which shapes both what we see, and what we *expect* to see.[116]

Yet even within a modernity that was characterized by an attempted homogenization of experience,[117] there was a realization, however reluctantly conceded, that there was more than "one unified 'scopic regime' of the modern."[118] Multiple "scopic regimes" entail multiple visions of reality.

---

[112] See Ong, "The Shifting Sensorium."

[113] See Schumacher, "The Lost Legacy of Anselm's Argument"; Schumacher, "The Logic of Faith."

[114] C. Taylor, *Philosophical Arguments*, 3–4.

[115] See the important collection of material in Knuuttila and Kärkkäinen, eds., *Theories of Perception in Medieval and Early Modern Philosophy*.

[116] See the discussion in Metz, *Le signifiant imaginaire*.

[117] Elder, *Body of Vision*, 162.

[118] Jay, "Scopic Regimes of Modernity," 3.

"There is no privileged vantage point outside the hermeneutic circle of sight as perceptual experience, social practice, and discursive construct."[119]

Passive approaches to perception – famously criticized by John Dewey as "spectator theories of knowledge" – fail to appreciate the activity of the human mind in constructing representations of the external world, or the engagement of the observer with what is observed.[120] Like the narrator in John Fowles's *French Lieutenant's Woman* (1969),[121] or the artist in Ford Maddox Brown's *Hayfield* (1855), the observer is now recognized to be part of what is being observed, and cannot be detached or dissociated from such involvement. Many would now argue that a failure on the part of theorists to recognize their own cultural embeddedness amounts to narcissism.[122] Theorists and theories emerge and exist within a cultural matrix, whose covert influence requires acknowledgment and evaluation. Dewey himself argued for a participatory notion of knowledge based on the integration of theory and practice.

Yet the issues here go deeper than the recognition of the cultural embeddedness of the human observer. The human process of perception itself involves interpretation. The heavens might indeed declare the glory of the Lord; yet, as the Cambridge Platonist John Smith (1618–52), argued, "though the whole of this visible universe be whispering out the notions of a Deity," we "cannot understand it without some interpreter within."[123] Early experimental psychologists, such as Hermann von Helmholtz (1821–94), drew a distinction between "sensation" – the taking in of data by the individual senses (such as sensing heat against one's skin) – and "perception" – the combining and making sense of those data (perceiving that one's hand is resting on a hot-plate). While the basic notion of perception as "making sense" of sensory input remains helpful, contemporary cognitive psychology has shown that the simple conceptual distinction between sensation and perception is unsustainable.

The process of perception involves the creation of representations, which are often referred to as *schemas* (or occasionally *schemata*). These can be

[119] Jay, *Downcast Eyes*, 587.
[120] For an assessment and extension of Dewey's concerns, see Pratt, "Two Cases against Spectator Theories of Knowledge"; Kulp, *The End of Epistemology*; Kulp, "Dewey, the Spectator Theory of Knowledge, and Internalism/Externalism." Hannah Arendt's notion of "spectatorial vision" should also be noted here: see Birmingham, "Hannah Arendt: The Activity of the Spectator."
[121] For comment on this device in relation to the literary environment of this era, see Onega, "Self, World and Art in the Fiction of John Fowles."
[122] Altman, *Analyst in the Inner City*, 156.
[123] J. Smith, *Select Discourses*, 136. For reflections on Smith's notion of an "interpreter within," see Micheletti, "'Some interpreter within': l'ermeneutica religiosa di John Smith, platonico di Cambridge."

thought of as mental maps of the world, as sets of rules for negotiating the world, or as schemes for classifying the world. While some schemas or their components are largely "culture-free," it is important to note that others (especially those which incorporate pre-existing verbal classification systems) are culturally dependent.[124]

We thus see and interpret the world through existing mental maps. A phrase in the writings of the great nineteenth-century philosopher of science William Whewell (1794–1866) expresses an idea that is fundamental to any Christian natural theology. There is, Whewell declared, "a mask of theory over the whole face of nature."[125] What some see as naïve facts about nature are recognized by others to be theoretical interpretations of nature. Observation and interpretation were found to be interconnected in a seemingly inescapable circularity. "A fact under one aspect is a theory under another." It is a point that has been made more recently by N. R. Hanson, who argued that the process of observation was inexorably "theory-laden."[126] We do not merely "see" nature; we understand it in a certain way, seeing it *as* something.

Observation is not a neutral process, but is a theory-laden process which involves implicit conceptual schemas, even though these are open to challenge and change.[127] We thus approach an engagement with nature with an implicit set of assumptions or expectations which create a degree of perceptual bias. Our perceptual schemes often lead us to overlook or disregard evidence because it does not fit with our existing mental schemes. For example, it is now known that many observations of the planet Uranus were made before its "discovery" by William Herschel in 1781; while Uranus was indeed "seen" by earlier observers, it was not seen *as a new planet*.[128]

These considerations have clear implications for natural theology. William Paley's classic *Natural Theology* (1802) worked so well partly because it resonated with the cultural assumptions and biases of his day;[129] today, it is generally regarded as discredited. Most people in western culture would now approach nature from the perspective of an "immanent frame,"[130] which inclines them not to expect the natural world to point beyond itself to a

---

[124] Lillard, "Ethnopsychologies"; Tomasello, *The Cultural Origins of Human Cognition*, 13–55.
[125] Whewell, *The Philosophy of the Inductive Sciences*, vol. 1, p. 1. For comment, see Yeo, *Defining Science*, 9–13.
[126] Hanson, *Patterns of Discovery*.
[127] Adam, *Theoriebeladenheit und Objektivität*, 51–97.
[128] Forbes, "The Pre-Discovery Observations of Uranus."
[129] Eddy, "The Rhetoric and Science of William Paley's *Natural Theology*"; Topham, "Biology in the Service of Natural Theology"; Gates, *Kindred Nature*, 39–40.
[130] C. Taylor, "Geschlossene Weltstruktur in der Moderne."

transcendent domain – an issue which we shall consider in greater detail later in this work (pp. 138–43).

Once it is appreciated that we approach the observation of the natural world from an theoretical perspective, the question of the role of communities in shaping our perceptions of reality becomes increasingly important – a matter to which we now turn.

3 *It fails to appreciate the importance of tradition-mediated rationalities.* In an important discussion, the American theologian John Cobb points out that any natural theology is freighted with precommitments.

> Every natural theology reflects some fundamental perspective on the world. None is the pure result of neutral, objective reason. Every argument begins with premises, and the final premises cannot themselves be proved.[131]

Cobb himself offers a definition of both theology and natural theology which excludes any reference to God, which nevertheless recognizes that both arise within a community, and reflects its specific perspectives. Theology, he argues, may be understood as "any coherent statement about matters of ultimate concern that recognizes that the perspective by which it is governed is received from a community of faith."[132] Yet this informing and controlling "perspective" is specific to that tradition. If natural theology is understood as emerging from within such a community, it is already laden with presuppositions, whether these are explicitly acknowledged or implicitly assumed.

The force of Cobb's point would be significantly weakened if the implicit assumptions of any natural theology were universal, shared by all peoples at all times. This, of course, was the implicit presupposition lying beneath and behind the Enlightenment "natural theology" project, which held that a universal human reason reflected on a universal nature, and reached conclusions that were universally binding. Yet this belief can no longer be maintained.

Human rationality is increasingly recognized to be shaped and delineated, at least in part, by cultural forces.[133] Recent studies have highlighted how the "voyager" literature of the sixteenth and seventeenth centuries exposed a diversity in human patterns of reasoning that were difficult to reconcile with the notion of a "universal rationality."[134] Alasdair MacIntyre, one of the more perceptive critics of the flawed core assumptions of the "Age of Reason," argues that the Enlightenment aspired to confront the world in

[131] Cobb, *A Christian Natural Theology*, 175.
[132] Cobb, *A Christian Natural Theology*, 165.
[133] See Nisbett, *The Geography of Thought*; Sauer-Thompson and Smith, *The Unreasonable Silence of the World*.
[134] Carey, *Locke, Shaftesbury, and Hutcheson*, 14–97.

an empirical, presuppositionless way, believing that it was possible to ground public debate in objectified standards of rational justification, using "principles undeniable by any rational person and therefore independent of all . . . social and cultural particularities."[135] This project must now be recognized as having failed, in that it adopted "an ideal of rational justification which it has proved impossible to attain."[136] In place of this deficient innovation, MacIntyre urged the recognition of the role of tradition and communities in rational discourse.[137] We have to recognize that "there is no standing ground, no place for enquiry, no way to engage in the practices of advancing, evaluating, accepting and rejecting reasoned argument apart from that which is provided by some particular tradition or other."[138]

A similar conclusion is reached by Michael Polanyi, as a result of his reflections on the scope and limits of the natural sciences. Scientific knowledge is not generated infallibly by a mechanical process, but involves our personal, provisional, and ultimately *fallible* judgment that certain beliefs are to be trusted.

> We must now recognize belief once more as the source of all knowledge. Tacit assent and intellectual passions, the sharing of an idiom and of a cultural heritage, affiliation to a likeminded community: such are the impulses which shape our vision of the nature of things on which we rely for our mastery of things. No intelligence, however critical or original, can operate outside such a fiduciary framework.[139]

Engagement with the natural world thus takes place from "somewhere," reflecting a specific "point of view," whether this is concealed, implied, or explicitly acknowledged. As we noted earlier, the seemingly neutral process of observation is shaped by covert fiduciary frameworks, which are linked to traditions of inquiry and reflection. There is no neutral standpoint, no universal viewpoint, from which a tradition-independent "natural theology" can be undertaken. Natural theology – unlike mathematics or logic – always arises within, and is informed by, a tradition of rationality.

4 *It is inattentive to the aesthetic, moral and intellectual ambiguity of nature.* Belief in a good, loving creator God could be defended through an

---

[135] MacIntyre, *Whose Justice? Which Rationality?*, 6. For some of the cultural issues which confirm MacIntyre's analysis, see Shore, *Culture in Mind*, 75–187.
[136] MacIntyre, *Whose Justice? Which Rationality?*, 6. Note also his comment that "progress in rationality is achieved only from a point of view" (144).
[137] See especially Herdt, "Alasdair MacIntyre's 'Rationality of Traditions' and Tradition-Transcendental Standards of Justification"; Porter, "Tradition in the Recent Work of Alasdair MacIntyre."
[138] MacIntyre, *Whose Justice? Which Rationality?*, 350.
[139] Polanyi, *Personal Knowledge*, 266.

appeal to the attractive aspects of the natural world, such as beautiful sunsets or alpine meadows. Yet at times, this "scopic regime" seems indefensibly selective. What about nature's more ugly and distressing aspects? What of a "rotten carcass of an elk full of maggots" in the midst of an otherwise beautiful landscape?[140]

In part, the issue is that of taste. The idea that natural landscapes are beautiful is quite recent; earlier generations sought to transmute natural landscapes into constructed gardens, supplementing any natural virtues with those of structure, form, regularity, and symmetry, and filtering out less seemly aspects of the natural world – such as death, decay, and pain. A wild nature could be made to be beautiful; until quite recently, there were few who regarded it as possessing aesthetic merit without recourse to human intervention.[141] The aesthetic complexity of nature, when set alongside the subjectivity of human judgment,[142] makes any attempt to allow nature to *determine* its own interpretation highly problematic.

Nature is intellectually, morally, and aesthetically ambiguous – a point which is of such importance that we shall return to it at several points in this work. Nature does not coerce us evidentially into any specific "clear and distinct ideas" (Descartes) concerning its meaning or significance. It can be argued to be consistent with atheism, agnosticism, and theism – but entails none of them. The meaning of nature must be unlocked using a key which nature itself does not supply.

In his criticism of Paley's *Natural Theology*, John Henry Newman argued that our epistemic situation was such that we had to approach the natural world in the light of an informing "mental map" derived from revelation, rather than try to derive a mental map from an amorphous and ambiguous natural world: "I believe in design because I believe in God; not in God because I see design."[143]

These four sets of considerations seriously, probably fatally, undermine any attempt to construct a "neutral" or "tradition-free" natural theology. We are socially embedded creatures, and cannot escape the particularities of our social and cultural contexts. Every natural theology is a "view from somewhere."

---

[140] Saito, "The Aesthetics of Unscenic Nature."

[141] Parsons, *Aesthetics and Nature*, 6–11.

[142] As noted by Ross, "Landscape Perception: Theory-Laden, Emotionally Resonant, Politically Correct."

[143] Newman, letter to William Robert Brownlow, April 13, 1870; in *The Letters and Diaries of John Henry Newman*, vol. 25, 97. For further comment on Newman and arguments from design, see Roberts, "Newman on the Argument from Design"; Mongrain, "The Eyes of Faith."

This conclusion does not in itself justify a specifically Christian under-standing of natural theology. It does, however, neutralize any concern that this might be tainted by its particularity by creating a context which is intellectually permissive of a specific way of seeing nature, based on a particular tradition of interpretation. A Christian natural theology represents a "view from somewhere"; yet since there is no allegedly objective "view from nowhere," such as that optimistically yet mistakenly advocated during the "Age of Reason," this observation cannot reasonably be considered to be subversive of this enterprise.

Modernity assumed that there was a universal rational framework which was authoritative in all matters of human reasoning. All other positions were dismissed as forms of "fideism," based on local accounts of rationality which were held to be inferior to a universal rationality. From an Enlightenment perspective, describing a system to be "fideist" was framed as a legitimate criticism, even though this is now seen to be an "evasive manoeuvre";[144] from a postmodern perspective, it is simply an acknowledgment of the epistemic situation of humanity, describing the predicament of every system of thought and value. There is no longer any "scandal of particularity" or objectionable "fideism" implicit within the notion of a "Christian natural theology."[145] Like every other perspective on the world, it amounts to a view from somewhere (pp. 26–82).

Some might object, following Heidegger, that speaking of a "Christian natural theology" is as meaningless as speaking of a "Protestant mathematics."[146] If natural theology is treated as analogous to mathematics, the point is fair. Yet the analogy is flawed. Mathematics and logic belong in a class of their own, transcending the boundaries of history and culture. As Stephen Toulmin pointed out, the attraction of pure mathematics to rationalist writers lay partly in the fact that it was seen to be the only intellectual activity whose problems and solutions are "above time."[147] Everything else is embedded in an historical and cultural context, with indeterminate yet significant implications for their patterns of reasoning. This extends to the natural sciences, which deploy at least some culturally conditioned criteria of assessment to determine whether a theory "makes sense."[148] To speak of a "Christian natural theology" is both to recognize this cultural

---

[144] M. M. Adams, *Christ and Horrors*, 5.

[145] For recent philosophical reflections on defensible approaches to fideism, see especially Evans, *Faith beyond Reason*, 1–54; J. Bishop, *Believing by Faith*, 1–25.

[146] Heidegger makes this observation in relation to "Catholic phenomenology": see Heidegger, *The Basic Problems of Phenomenology*, 20.

[147] Toulmin, *The Uses of Argument*, 118.

[148] Dear, *The Intelligibility of Nature*, 194: The history of science shows "how 'making sense' depends on who is doing the judging, and in what cultural circumstances."

embeddedness, and to be explicit about the perspective from which this project is being undertaken.

My concern in this work is not to demonstrate the truth of the Christian faith, but to explore what approaches to natural theology emerge from within the Christian narrative.[149] What ways of seeing reality arise from immersion in this narrative, and the process of reframing and reviewing that results from this? Stanley Hauerwas rightly argues that we can only see the world rightly "by being trained to see," which results from the acquisition of "disciplined skills" which result from "initiation into a narrative."[150] Yet this is true more widely; the "naïve eye" needs to be trained if it is to know what to look for, and what it might see.[151]

This approach to natural theology does not interpret it as an autonomous discipline or tradition of inquiry, but rather provides an informing context which both stimulates and directs it. From the standpoint of a Christian way of looking at things, natural theology is to be framed and pursued as a specific aspect of the theological enterprise as a whole.[152]

So does this specifically Christian point of view allow us to develop a broader vision of natural theology, which holds together the multiple elements noted earlier in this chapter? Can a specifically Christian natural theology project create conceptual space for the classical notion of natural theology as "the enterprise of providing support for religious beliefs by starting from premises that neither are nor presuppose any religious beliefs"?[153] In the next section, we shall explore this important issue.

The Christian Accommodation of Classic Natural Theology

The grand themes of the Christian faith provide an interpretative framework by which nature may be seen in profound and significant ways. The web of Christian theology is the elixir, the philosopher's stone, which turns the mundane into the epiphanic, the world of nature into the realm of God's creation. Like a lens bringing a vast landscape into sharp focus, or a map helping us grasp the features of the terrain around us, the Christian vision of reality offers a new way of understanding, imagining, and behaving. It invites

---

[149] See also Kärkkäinen, *Trinity and Revelation*, 108–22.
[150] Hauerwas, "The Demands of a Truthful Story," 65–6.
[151] Varnelis, "The Education of the Innocent Eye." The important study of de Bolla, *The Education of the Eye*, further develops these themes, especially in relation to the adoption of "regimes of looking" at visual objects.
[152] Polkinghorne, "The New Natural Theology," 42.
[153] Alston, *Perceiving God*, 289.

us to see the natural order, and ourselves within it, in a special way – a way that might be hinted at, but cannot be confirmed by, the natural order itself.

In a brief discussion of Dante's *Divine Comedy*, C. S. Lewis noted its powerful imaginative vision of a unified cosmic and world order. For Lewis, works such as the *Divine Comedy* reflected a "unity of the highest order," because they were able to cope with "the greatest diversity of subordinated detail."[154] So does the intellectual map that might be offered by the Christian tradition fit in the classical notion of natural theology as a religiously uncommitted reflection on the natural order – "the enterprise of providing support for religious beliefs by starting from premises that neither are nor presuppose any religious beliefs"? It is my belief that the Christian *imaginarium* – a notion we shall explore in more detail in the following chapter – offers an imaginative and cognitive framework which is able to *accommodate* and *position* this classic notion of natural theology. By this, I mean that it is able to show that this approach to natural theology can be seen to be part of a greater vision of reality, and that by understanding its position within that vision, its distinct strengths and weaknesses may be appreciated.

Analogies lie to hand within many disciplines. A good example can be found in narratology, an increasingly important player in the field of literary theory. What theoretical model can be developed to give coherence to this field, given that there are so many ways of understanding the concept of narrative itself, as well as its various themes – such as the place and role of the narrator in the narrated world?[155] Classical approaches to the theme have been displaced by alternatives, such as those influenced by Gérard Genette's notion of focalization, allowing a distinction to be drawn between the questions of "who sees?" and "who speaks?"[156] (The idea of a "natural narratology" has also been proposed,[157] with some interesting potential connections with at least some formulations of natural theology.) Postclassical narratology is characterized by "a plurality of models for narrative analysis"; yet, crucially, it incorporates classical narratology as one of its "moments."[158] The larger theory thus creates conceptual space for an earlier iteration or articulation, which is now seen to be one possibility among others, rather than a defining moment or normative formulation.

What is probably the best analogy for conceptualizing the multiple instantiations of natural theology *within a single narrative* comes from the development of scientific theories, specifically the all-important

---

[154] Lewis, *Allegory of Love*, 142. See also the points made by Claudel, "Introduction à un poème sur Dante."

[155] Nünning, "Narratology or Narratologies?"

[156] Pier, "Gérard Genette's Evolving Narrative Poetics."

[157] Fludernik, *Towards a "Natural" Narratology*, 1–67.

[158] Herman, "Introduction: Narratologies."

transition from classical Newtonian mechanics to relativistic quantum mechanics, which took place during the first few decades of the twentieth century.[159] In the eighteenth and nineteenth centuries, classical mechanics was seen as a self-sufficient area of theory, capable of accounting for what could be observed in nature. Based on the extensive earlier observational and analytical work of individuals such as Nicolas Copernicus (1473–1543), Johann Kepler (1571–1630), Galileo Galilei (1564–1642), and Isaac Newton (1643–1727), classical mechanics was widely regarded as a fundamental theory, capable of mathematical formalization.[160] It did not require to be positioned within a richer intellectual framework to be understood, but was seen as an autonomous and essentially complete theory.

Yet following the work of Max Planck (1858–1947), Albert Einstein (1879–1955), and Niels Bohr (1885–1962) in the early twentieth century, it was realized that there was a more fundamental theory, of which classical mechanics was a special, limiting case. As the theory of quantum mechanics developed in response to a growing body of evidence which older theoretical models simply could not accommodate, it became clear that relativistic quantum mechanics was the more fundamental theory, capable of far greater explanatory capacity. And, perhaps most importantly of all for our purposes, this more fundamental theory was able to account for both the successes and the failures of classical mechanics, by identifying its limited sphere of validity. The "correspondence principle," first identified by Niels Bohr in 1923, sets out, clearly and elegantly, how quantum mechanics reduces to classical mechanics under certain limits.[161]

Neither relativistic quantum mechanics nor quantum field theory invalidated classical mechanics; they were able to position it within a wider and more comprehensive context, which indicated that it possessed validity in some circumstances – but not all. The classical model was not autonomous and complete in itself, but was a special case of a more comprehensive and complex theory.[162] In effect, classical mechanics was seen as a special case of relativistic quantum mechanics, applying to large bodies moving at low speeds – in other words, the everyday world that we experience, and which classical mechanics mistakenly (though understandably) assumed to amount to the totality of things. The classical model was thus accounted for on the

---

[159] This topic is covered in standard textbooks, such as Tang, *Fundamentals of Quantum Mechanics*, Wachter, *Relativistic Quantum Mechanics*, Pilkuhn, *Relativistic Quantum Mechanics*. For some accessible reflections on the theological relevance of such developments, see Polkinghorne, *Quantum Physics and Theology*, 48–72.

[160] Illiffe, "Newton, God, and the Mathematics of the Two Books."

[161] For comment, see Pais, *Niels Bohr's Times*, 192–6.

[162] See, for example, Landsman, *Mathematical Topics between Classical and Quantum Mechanics*, 7–10; Gross, *Relativistic Quantum Mechanics and Field Theory*, 18–22.

basis of the greater explanatory capacity of the relativistic model, and the limits of their correspondence established. And, perhaps more importantly, the relativistic approach explained why the classic theory worked in certain situations, and not in others. Its validity was affirmed within certain limits.

We see here an important and well-understood insight from the world of scientific theory development: that a better theory is able to accommodate all the valid insights of an earlier theory, while at the same time expanding its horizons and identifying the basis of its plausibility.[163] A theory with considerable explanatory capacity is able to create conceptual space, valid under certain limiting yet significant conditions, for a theory which might, at first sight, appear to be quite independent, yet, on closer examination, turns out to be a special case of the higher-order theory. A robust Trinitarian theology of creation is able to create conceptual space for the traditional mode of natural theology, limited to a specific domain – in this case, the perception of someone outside the Christian faith, viewing nature without its distinctive conceptual framework.

To appreciate this point, consider James Barr's oft-cited description of natural theology:

> Traditionally, "natural theology" has commonly meant something like this: that "by nature," that is, *just by being human beings*, men and women have a certain degree of knowledge of God and awareness of him, or at least a capacity for such awareness; and this knowledge of awareness exists anterior to the special revelation of God made through Jesus Christ, through the Church, through the Bible.[164]

It is important to note that Barr's definition of natural theology explicitly includes anthropological elements – that is to say, an understanding of what it means to "just" be a human being, along with any capacities or inclinations that this entails. When Barr speaks of thinking in certain ways "by nature," he opens up major questions of the impact of nature and culture on our patterns of thinking, which invites critical exploration in terms of the impact of social and cultural embodiment on what is considered to be a "natural" line of thought and what is not.[165] For Barr's somewhat limited purposes, this is perhaps not necessary. For others, it cannot be overlooked, not least because

---

[163] For a discussion of the "progress as incorporation" dimension of the development of scientific theories, see Losee, *Theories of Scientific Progress*, 5–61.
[164] Barr, *Biblical Faith and Natural Theology*, 1 (my emphasis).
[165] See for example Kimmel, "Properties of Cultural Embodiment"; R. M. Frank, "Sociocultural Situatedness"; Shore, *Culture in Mind*.

it subverts any notion of culturally universal patterns of thinking, save outside the specific realms of mathematics and logic.

As Emil Brunner rightly noted, any approach to natural theology ultimately rests upon a prior *theological* understanding of human nature.[166] For Brunner, a Christian understanding of human nature, especially the all-important insight that humanity bears the image of God, when set alongside the doctrine of God as creator (so that the created order bears a "permanent capacity for revelation"), creates the intellectual matrix from which the classic project of natural theology emerges. It is not enough to suggest that God is disclosed through nature; human beings must have the capacity to recognize this disclosure as such, whether through their natural capacities, or through the healing of those capacities through grace.[167] The doctrine of the *imago Dei* represents a theological formulation of the "preparedness" of humanity for divine disclosure.[168]

A Christian theological framework – such as those articulated in different ways by Athanasius, Augustine, Aquinas, Calvin, and Brunner – thus enables us to account for the existence of the natural human activity of seeking to find God within or through the world of nature.[169] For Athanasius, a Christian anthropology leads directly into a natural theology: God created humanity bearing the "image of God" in order that God might be known through the "works of creation."[170] The *Catechism of the Catholic Church* summarizes this consensus: "The desire for God is written in the human heart, because man is created by God and for God; and God never ceases to draw man to himself. Only in God will he find the truth and happiness he never stops searching for."[171] For Bernard Lonergan, any account of nature which omits discussion of the phenomenon of human *attentiveness* toward nature is necessarily deficient.[172] A Christian vision of reality provides an account of human capacities and inclinations on the one hand, and God's relationship with the created order on the other, which make it *natural* for human beings to want to undertake natural theology, and achieve some degree of success in doing so.

---

[166] For what follows, see A. E. McGrath, *Emil Brunner*, 90–148.

[167] For this theme in Augustine, see Couenhoven, *Stricken by Sin, Cured by Christ*, 19–105.

[168] For the concept of "preparedness" in the cognitive science of religion, see Barrett and Richert, "Anthropomorphism or Preparedness?"

[169] See, for example, Feingold, *The Natural Desire to See God*; Dowey, *The Knowledge of God in Calvin's Theology*; Sudduth, *The Reformed Objection to Natural Theology*, 60–5.

[170] Athanasius, *de Incarnatione*, 3.12. See further Bienert, "Zur Logos-Christologie des Athanasius von Alexandrien in *Contra Gentes* und *De Incarnatione*."

[171] *Catechism of the Catholic Church*, §27.

[172] Lonergan, *Insight*, xvii–xxx. For further development of this point, see the "richer empiricism" proposed by Haught, *Is Nature Enough?*, 119–25.

Yet – and the importance of this point must not be understated – that success is limited. For Calvin, any knowledge of God derived from nature will be fragmentary and incomplete; the clearer way of seeing nature, provided through the biblical narrative, is required if the partial insights about divinity available within the created order are to be supplemented and integrated into a coherent whole.[173] Humanity thus – to draw on the analysis in *The Catechism of the Catholic Church* – "stands in need of being enlightened by God's revelation" to grasp the true significance of nature.[174] Just as relativistic quantum mechanics helped clarify the boundaries of classical mechanics, so Christian theology clarifies the limits of a classic natural theology, helping us grasp its potential for apologetics and other forms of cultural engagement, while appreciating its limits as a resource for systematic theology.

Most importantly, a Christian approach offers a framework which enables the proposed "thick" description of natural theology to be seen as a coherent intellectual option.[175] It proposes a web of interconnected conceptualities – including specific notions of creation, human nature, and divine activity and presence – which allows the six broad approaches noted in this chapter to be seen as intrinsically coherent and interrelated, rather than as a artificially constructed and superficially colligative "meta-project" which amounts to little more than an opportunistic aggregation of essentially disparate and possibly disconnected possibilities.[176]

In this chapter, we have set out the case for a Christian – as opposed to a generic – natural theology. Where some hold that "natural theology" is an attempt to articulate the religious dimension of common human experience independently of special revelation and to relate this experience to the received tradition,[177] I take the view that it is an attempt to interpret and appreciate common human experience of the natural world – including ourselves as observers of nature and participants within nature – in the light of the received Christian tradition. In the following chapter, we shall develop this approach further, exploring the notion of a Christian *imaginarium* and considering its outcomes.

---

[173] Husbands, "Calvin on the Revelation of God in Creation and Scripture." For related concerns about such a fragmentary knowledge in Spinoza, see den Uyl, *God, Man, and Well-Being*, 107–10.

[174] *Catechism of the Catholic Church*, §38.

[175] A. E. McGrath, *The Open Secret*, 171–216.

[176] On these issues, see A. N. Williams, *The Architecture of Theology*, 23–78.

[177] J. J. Collins, "The Biblical Precedent for Natural Theology."

2

Natural Theology and the Christian *Imaginarium*

Plotinus once remarked that the task of seeing demanded an eye that was adapted to what needed to be seen.[1] A Christian natural theology concerns how nature is to be imagined from a Christian viewpoint. It is the imaginative and rational outcome of seeing the world through the distinctive conceptual framework of the Christian tradition[2] – a process of beholding nature that involves the *imagination*, recognizing that this human faculty is capable of making connections and correlations which are difficult to express in the pure language of logic.[3] Such an approach was commonplace during the Middle Ages. Dante's *Divina Commedia* presents theology primarily as an imaginative, rather than a cognitive, activity, recognizing the limits placed on verbal attempts to represent a reality that is fundamentally something that is meant to be *seen*.[4]

> From that moment onwards my power of sight exceeded
> That of speech, which fails at such a vision.

---

[1] Plotinus, *Enneads*, I.vi.9. See further Hadot, *Plotinus, or, the Simplicity of Vision*, 60–3.

[2] For example, see Farrer, *The Glass of Vision*; Lynch, *Christ and Apollo*; Viladesau, *Theological Aesthetics*; Green, *Imagining God*. Green's concept of an "imaginative paradigm" is important here. Although Green is particularly concerned with the disturbing imaginative deficit of leading theologians of the Yale School (such as George Lindbeck), his comments have wider relevance. For the role of the imagination in Jewish theology, see Wolfson, *Through a Speculum that Shines*, 13–51.

[3] See the discussion in Rapport, "Imagination Is the Barest Reality." There are clear affinities between the approach that I will develop here and that developed by C. S. Lewis: see Holyer, "C. S. Lewis on the Epistemic of the Imagination."

[4] Dante, *Paradiso* XXXIII, 55–6: "Da quinci innanzi il mio veder fu maggio, che'l parlar mostra, ch'a tal vista cede." For Dante's appeal to the imagination, see especially Hollander, "Dante's 'Paradiso' as Philosophical Poetry."

Re-Imagining Nature: The Promise of a Christian Natural Theology, First Edition.
Alister E. McGrath.
© 2017 John Wiley & Sons, Ltd. Published 2017 by John Wiley & Sons, Ltd.

Important aspects of Dante's *imaginarium* are picked up in the writings of C. S. Lewis – especially the notion that words or theological concepts are incapable of grasping or communicating the deepest truths, which are best captured and held by the imagination. Lewis's appreciation of the importance of the *imaginarium* dates from early in his life, and emerged as a result of his reading of George MacDonald's *Phantastes.* Lewis spoke of his Christian *imaginarium* in a number of ways – such as a "baptized imagination," which was capable of "transforming all common things" while remaining unchanged itself.[5] It was, Lewis recalled, "as if I had died in the old country and could never remember how I came alive in the new. For in one sense the new country was exactly like the old . . . But in another sense all was changed."[6] Lewis suggests that we must develop a respectful attentiveness toward nature, if we are to see it properly: "The only imperative that nature utters is, 'Look. Listen. Attend.'"[7]

Sensorium and *Imaginarium*: Christianity and the Re-Imagination of Nature

John Ruskin longed for a clarity of vision that could not be diminished by, or reduced to, words or conceptual schemes. "To see clearly is poetry, prophecy and religion – all in one."[8] Ruskin finally came to the conclusion that such an *imaginarium* required the observer to abandon or by-pass schema-driven modes of perception in order to see things in these ways.[9] Ruskin sought (and believed he had, at least in some respects, *found*) a means of transcending the limits of the *sensorium*, without lapsing into irrationality or conceptual inflation.

I here use the term *imaginarium* to accentuate the limits of the human *sensorium*. Although strictly referring to the human sensual apparatus, this latter term is often used in a developed sense to designate the distinct and shifting sensory environments within which individuals are located, determined by both natural capacities and cultural influences, which shape how we understand ourselves and our world.[10] The manner in which we sense, perceive, and interpret information about the world around us is determined

---

[5] Lewis, *Surprised by Joy*, 209. See further Carnell, *Bright Shadow of Reality*, 60–76. On the "baptized imagination" in MacDonald, see Dearborn, *Baptized Imagination.*

[6] Lewis, *Surprised by Joy*, 207.

[7] Lewis, *The Four Loves*, 29.

[8] Ruskin, *Complete Works*, vol. 6, 333. For a helpful discussion of this point, see Hersey, "Ruskin as an Optical Thinker."

[9] Collicutt, *The Psychology of Christian Character Formation*, 133–4.

[10] See Ong, "The Shifting Sensorium."

by both biological and social influences. The capacities and outlook of human observers of nature reflect their embodiment in a natural and cultural world.[11] It is therefore important to identify the embedded cultural assumptions which shape a culture's reading of texts and interpretations of the natural world,[12] partly to subvert any claims of ultimacy, but more fundamentally to understand the critical role of a specific cultural context in interpreting human experience.

Yet the *sensorium* is a human resource which can easily become an intellectual prison. Cultural anthropology has liberated intellectual analysis from the ethnocentrism of the Enlightenment, showing how thinkers embedded within the western philosophical tradition were "prisoners of their own sensorium."[13] From a Christian theological perspective, we could understand sin as a fundamental redirection of vision and thought away from the invisible God to the self and the sensible objects of the world, as determined and limited by the human *sensorium*. Through inhabitation of this *sensorium*, human beings come to limit reality to what can be known "naturally." To break free from this limiting framework requires a realization of its limits and flaws, leading to an openness to a greater vision of reality – a vision that is better (and more positively) articulated by the imagination as it reaches out toward God, than by a negative deconstruction of the capacities of the *sensorium* leading us to wonder if there are viable alternatives.[14]

There is an "inextricable link between imagination, narrative, and embodiment" which cannot be ignored in theological reflection, and must find expression in an authentically Christian natural theology.[15] The Christian *imaginarium* is the divinely transformed capacity of seeing and understanding reality that results from *metanoia* (see pp. 50–4), which enables us to grasp reality at a deeper level, using both reason and imagination, rendering us susceptible to new competencies, new functions, and new possibilities.[16]

The role of the imagination in representing reality has recently been given a new momentum through the rise of the "social imaginary," particularly in the writings of Cornelius Castoriadis and Charles Taylor. Both point to the need for an "originary structuring component," the "source of that which

---

[11] See R. M. Frank, "Sociocultural Situatedness"; Kimmel, "Properties of Cultural Embodiment," especially 91–5.

[12] For a detailed analysis, see Avrahami, *The Senses of Scripture*, 4–64.

[13] Avrahami, *The Senses of Scripture*, 10.

[14] A classic exploration of this theme is found in C. S. Lewis's 1941 sermon "The Weight of Glory," in *Essay Collection*, 96–106. Cf. A. E. McGrath, "Arrows of Joy."

[15] On this point, see J. K. A. Smith, *Imagining the Kingdom*, 39–41.

[16] For the important connection between seeing and wisdom, see the perceptive discussion in Fiddes, *Seeing the World and Knowing God*, 167–217. Kant's notion of the *ens imaginarium* may be noted here: Milz, *Der gesuchte Widerstreit*, 184 n. 224.

presents itself in every instance as an indisputable and undisputed mean-ing."[17] This *imaginary* is not predetermined by ontology, but is a novel element which emerges within a society, and shapes its apprehension and comprehension of its world and its situation. Within a traditional ontology of determinacy, the imaginary dimension is seen as secondary and derivative, a mere reflection of "the real."

For Castoriadis, the "imaginary" is constitutive of meaning, in that it provides an *eidos*, a means of seeing and structuring reality, which allows us to conceive of – or re-imagine – the real in the first place.[18] "Each society is a construction, a constitution, a creation of a world, of its own world."[19] For Castoriadis, this free act of creation is essential for the articulation of meaning and value. "The imaginary is the subject's whole creation of a world for itself." It is impossible to overlook the theological potential of this approach, which offers a fresh perspective on something that the Christian tradition has always known to be true, even if it occasionally struggles to give it proper expression – that the gospel offers an *imaginarium fidei*, a manner of apprehending and grasping reality which is not limited to the intellect, but demands an "imaginative embrace."[20]

There are clearly concerns that need to be addressed here, including Castoriadis's interpretation of Freud's account of the imaginary constitution and the fabrication of individual subjectivity.[21] Yet Castoriadis provides an important counterargument to those – such as Richard Rorty – who adopt a thoroughly determinist ontology which they believe ultimately renders "liberty of imagination" illusory.[22] The internal contradictions of Rorty's position have often been noted. Roy Bhaskar, for example, highlights the implicit contradictions within Rorty's "irrealist ensemble," particularly the contradiction between the belief that we are fully determined as material bodies but free as discursive subjects who can redescribe and re-invent the world and ourselves as we please. Rorty's anthropomorphism is not capable of sustaining an adequate account of either human agency or freedom.[23] As

---

[17] Castoriadis, *The Imaginary Institution of Society*, 145. For a good introduction, see Gaonkar, "Toward New Imaginaries," especially 4–10. Castoriadis developed his approach in response to the failure of Marxist determinism to account properly for social development: Castoriadis, *The Imaginary Institution of Society*, 9–70.

[18] For a good collection of assessments of Castoriadis's approach and significance, see Chihaia, "Das Imaginäre bei Cornelius Castoradis," 70–5; Arnason, "Castoriadis im Kontext."

[19] Castoriadis, *World in Fragments*, 5.

[20] Lewis, "Myth Became Fact," in *Essay Collection*, 141.

[21] For detailed discussion of this and other issues, see Elliott, "The Social Imaginary."

[22] R. Williams, *The Edge of Words*, 37–42.

[23] E.g., Bhaskar, *Philosophy and the Idea of Freedom*, 3–136. This is a substantially expanded version of a shorter essay originally written in 1989. See further Cashell, "Reality, Representation and the Aesthetic Fallacy."

Rowan Williams points out, Rorty seems to think that we are free to offer whatever imaginative rendering of reality we please, so that there is "no difference between 'telling a story' and 'reflecting the world'."[24] Castoriadis's "social imaginary" offers us a way of approaching an engagement with the natural world, partly through a validation of the enterprise of reconceiving and re-imagining the world, rather than merely registering our perceptions concerning it.[25]

Such an imaginatively compelling and intellectually enriching vision of reality is mediated by the Church, understood as an "interpretive community" of faith which is called into being by this God-given and God-grounded vision of reality.[26] Faith thus entails that the community of faith sees the world in a manner which differs strikingly from what Charles Taylor describes as the prevailing "social imaginaries," a term which he uses to designate "the ways people imagine their social existence, how they fit together with others, how things go on between them and their fellows, the expectations that are normally met, and the deeper normative notions and images that underlie these expectations."[27] Such a concept of a "social imaginary" moves away from what might be called a "third-person" or "objective" point of view, in favor of first-person subjectivities. These can be considered to be "imaginary" in two senses: first, they exist "by virtue of representation or implicit understandings," even when these achieve social dominance; and second, they act as the means by which "individuals understand their identities and their place in the world."[28] As Taylor points out, the "way ordinary people 'imagine' their social surroundings" is often "not expressed in theoretical terms, but carried in images, stories, and legends."[29]

Theories of the "social imaginary" – such as Taylor's – aim to explain the way in which the human imagination, not merely reason, plays such a significant role in the construction of social institutions, representations, and practices.[30] Taylor's recognition of the importance of images and stories in creating and sustaining such "imaginaries" fits in well with the classic idea of the Christian Church as the community which crystallizes around what

[24] R. Williams, *The Edge of Words*, 41.

[25] Note Williams's formulation of the issue: *The Edge of Words*, 42–5.

[26] For this phrase, see Fish, *Is There A Text in This Class?*, 147–74. Note also Josiah Royce's concept of a "community of interpretation," to be discussed later in this work (pp. 96–7).

[27] C. Taylor, *Modern Social Imaginaries*, 23.

[28] Gaonkar, "Toward New Imaginaries," 4.

[29] C. Taylor, *Modern Social Imaginaries*, 23.

[30] See, for example, Gaonkar, "Toward New Imaginaries"; Castoriadis, *The Imaginary Institution of Society*, 115–220; B. R. Anderson, *Imagined Communities*, 1–8; Naranch, "The Imaginary and a Political Quest for Freedom."

Rowan Williams styles "the one focal interpretive story of Jesus"[31] – a particular interpretation and imaginative rendering of the texts of Scripture, history, and nature, understood in terms of the life, death, and resurrection of Jesus Christ, or a Trinitarian economy of salvation of creation, redemption, and consummation.

To think of the Church as a "social imaginary" is to recognize our need to imagine – that is, to *see* – the world afresh, rejecting limiting categorizations and over-intellectualized accounts of reality which ultimately impoverish our understanding of the world and ourselves.[32] If we think of a social imaginary as a "world-forming and meaning-bestowing creative force,"[33] we can conceive of the Church as a community which, in the first place, is shaped by this imaginative vision, and, in the second, offers this imaginative lens to the world, in order that it may see itself as it really is. This "imaginary" is not to be reduced to a Kantian conceptual net, but rather is to be seen as an active empowering capacity to see things in a fresh and compelling manner.

The Church transmits both this schema and the outcomes of its application to the world. It proclaims, exhibits, and embodies its own "social imaginary," deeply rooted in the Christian faith on the one hand, and with the capacity to transform reflection and practice on the other. Natural theology is thus to be seen as an integral aspect of the Church's "social imaginary," which reflects and expresses the way in which the Christian community understands its relation to the natural world.

The Christian Church functions as an "ecclesial imaginary,"[34] in that it embodies and exhibits certain ways in which people might imagine their social existence and relate to others, and the deeper controlling or influencing notions and images that undergird these expectations of attitudes and behavior. A fundamental question concerns how the Christian Church can express its ideas and values in the language of, and using the canons of, argumentation which are acceptable in a wider public sphere.[35] For the purposes of this work, the most important question is how the way in which the natural world is imagined and understood by the Christian community of

[31] R. Williams, *Resurrection*, 61–2.

[32] Kelly, "Public Theology and the Modern Social Imaginary."

[33] Gaonkar, "Toward New Imaginaries," 6.

[34] For comment, see Kelly, "Public Theology and the Modern Social Imaginary." I prefer to speak of an "ecclesial imaginary," rather than a "theological imaginary," taking the term "ecclesial" to include "theological," but aligning this with a community of people who consider the Christian "originary structuring component" as persuasive, and see the Christian community as embodying, narrating, and proclaiming this vision of reality.

[35] For the general issues on the role of the "imaginary" in democratic discourse and debate, see Wolin, *Democracy Incorporated*, 17–40.

faith is correlated with the quite distinct approaches found in secular society and in other religious traditions. In using the term *imaginarium* – which I set in an agonistic relation with *sensorium* – I am focussing on the way in which the Christian tradition sees the world, rather than the social factors which help consolidate and transmit this.

Yet some today are resistant to such an imaginative embrace of reality, holding that it represents a retreat into an imaginary world or our own fabrication. We must therefore consider this concern in more detail, and reflect on how it may be addressed and developed.

Modernity and the Suppression of the Imagination

Modernity's demands for clear, unambivalent ideas were inimical to the rich imaginative medieval vision of the world.[36] Descartes can be seen as initiating the Enlightenment's suppression of the imagination, seeing this as a source of error and falsehood.[37] Perhaps the most familiar statement of this "common-sense" rejection of the role of the imagination in critical reasoning is found in Samuel Johnson's 1751 essay "The Rambler," in which he dismisses the imagination as a "licentious and vagrant faculty, unsusceptible of limitations and impatient of restraint."[38] Johnson can be seen as representative of his rationalist age, suspicious of any speculative departures from the secure deliverances of experience and reason.[39]

Yet by the end of the eighteenth century, many had concluded that this rationalist marginalization of the imagination was indefensible and inadequate. Whitehead's famous criticism of a "one-eyed reason, deficient in its vision of depth,"[40] highlights both the shallowness of a rationalist account of reality, and its need for imaginative supplementation.

---

[36] For reflections on this development, see Lewis, *The Discarded Image*. For the strongly imaginative and affective appeal of some early conceptions of natural theology, see Crowther-Heyck, "Wonderful Secrets of Nature"; Ogilvie, *The Science of Describing*, 87–138. Aquinas's concept of the imagination may lack the depth of Dante's, but its theological importance is clear: see Bauerschmidt, "Imagination and Theology in Thomas Aquinas," especially 175–7.

[37] Buchenau, *The Founding of Aesthetics in the German Enlightenment*, 75. For reflections on the importance of the imagination in Pascal, see Maguire, *The Conversion of Imagination*, 17–69. Maguire's reflections on the importance of the imagination for French-speaking *philosophes* of the eighteenth century are relevant to our discussion: Maguire, *The Conversion of Imagination*, 221–3.

[38] Johnson, *Rambler*, no. 125, May 28, 1751; in *Works*, vol. 4, 300.

[39] Sallis, *Delimitations*, 1–5.

[40] Whitehead, *Science and the Modern World*, 59.

Romanticism's renewed appeal to the power of the imagination,[41] and Kant's explicit affirmation of its positive role in philosophical reflection,[42] are telling signs of the growing appreciation of the importance of the imagination in reflection on the natural world,[43] hinted at in Paul Claudel's perceptive criticism of the "starved imagination" of rationalism.[44] The Romantic tradition, partly reacting against what it perceived to be a desiccating rationalism which sucked the life and joy out of religion, emphasized the importance of the retrieval of a theology which recognized the imagination as an "inner power that unites the living self to a living outer world."[45]

While questions may be raised about the theological *orthodoxy* of Coleridge's appeal to the imagination, there is no doubt of its theological *utility*, especially in its capacity to hold together thought, feeling, and emotion.[46] Retrieving the imaginative dimensions of theology addresses one of its most worrying blind spots – a failure to recognize that the theological landscape extends beyond the constrained and constraining domains of the cognitive and rational on the one hand, and the experiential and existential on the other.[47] There remains an importance place for the Coleridgean tradition of natural theology as contemplation rather than argumentation – perhaps best developed in the works of C. S. Lewis – which holds that the coherence of reality is better grasped by a visual imagination than dissected by a cold logic.[48] Seamus Heaney made a similar point, arguing that poetry – rather than logic – is better adapted to catch a "fleeting glimpse of a potential order of things."[49] The human imagination is part of our endowment as those who bear the "image of God," enabling us to "see" the fundamental

---

[41]   Abrams, *Natural Supernaturalism*, 117–22, 169–95; J. R. Barth, *The Symbolic Imagination*; Geldhof, "Romantische Metaphysik als natürliche Theologie?"

[42]   For this suspicion, see Lyons, *Before Imagination*, 251; Terrall, "Metaphysics, Mathematics, and the Gendering of Science in Eighteenth-Century France," 265–7. On Kant, see Kneller, *Kant and the Power of Imagination*, especially 38–59. On Romanticism, see Vallins, *Coleridge and the Psychology of Romanticism*.

[43]   For Hume's concerns about the role of the imagination in scientific induction, see Millican, "Hume's Sceptical Doubts Concerning Induction." Peter Medawar's emphasis on the role of the imagination in scientific theory development should be noted here: see Calver, "Sir Peter Medawar." More generally, see Beveridge, *The Art of Scientific Investigation*, 53–67.

[44]   Claudel, "Introduction à un poème sur Dante," 429.

[45]   Abrams, *Natural Supernaturalism*, 266–7. For a more thorough analysis, see Dürbeck, *Einbildungskraft und Aufklärung*, 256–316.

[46]   Vallins, *Coleridge and the Psychology of Romanticism*, 25–87; J. R. Barth, *The Symbolic Imagination*, 12–14.

[47]   George Lindbeck designates such approaches as "cognitive-propositionalist" and "experiential-expressivist" understandings of doctrine: Lindbeck, *The Nature of Doctrine*, 16.

[48]   Contrast this with Hume's non-imaginative approach to coherence as something that is to be rationally inferred from observation: Schnall, "Constancy, Coherence, and Causality."

[49]   Heaney, *The Redress of Poetry*, xv.

interconnectedness of the world,[50] no matter how difficult this may be to express in words. Coleridge spoke of the need for a "focus of all the rays of intellect which are scattered throughout the images of nature," and located this in the imagination, rather than reason.[51]

Part of the Enlightenment's unease about taking the imagination seriously was its concern that this might lead to a retreat into an imaginary world. Yet, as Iris Murdoch rightly notes, a distinction is easily drawn between an "egoistic fantasy," which is mechanical, egoistic, untruthful, and a "liberated truth-seeking creative imagination," which freely and creatively explores the world, seeking to discern and embrace "what is true and deep."[52] While Kant was committed to the idea that there are strict limits to what human beings could know, he nevertheless retained a conviction that there was some "ineliminable, natural human drive to surpass those limitations."[53] This creates conceptual space for an imaginative natural theology, through a creative reworking of our concept of nature, in the light of this drive to transcend the limits of reason. "Through imagination we are capable, in thought at least, of taking up what nature gives us and working it up into 'another nature'."[54]

The dilemma that can lead to such an approach was famously articulated by C. S. Lewis, who found himself caught up in a tension between his "imaginative life" and the "life of [his] intellect." He experienced a disturbing tension between his "glib and shallow rationalism" and a richer imaginative vision of reality (which he knew to be true) as "a many-islanded sea of poetry and myth,"[55] which demands a new language if we are even to begin to represent it. Lewis gradually came to see reason and imagination as existing in a potentially collaborative relationship, with important implications for apologetics.[56] Reason without imagination was potentially dull and limited; imagination without reason was potentially delusory and escapist. Lewis thus develops a notion of "imagined" – not imaginary – reality, which is capable of being grasped by reason and visualized by the imagination.[57] For Lewis, the artist is one who tries to "embody in terms of his own art some

[50] Green, *Imagining God*, 83–104.
[51] Coleridge, *Biographia Literaria*, vol. 2, 257–8.
[52] Murdoch, *Metaphysics and Morals*, 321.
[53] Kneller, *Kant and the Power of Imagination*, 27–8.
[54] Kneller, *Kant and the Power of Imagination*, 52.
[55] Lewis, *Surprised by Joy*, 197.
[56] There are hints of a similar approach in the writings of Joseph Addison (1672–1719), who offered both rational and imaginative renderings of arguments from design: see Zeitz, "Addison's 'Imagination' Papers and the Design Argument."
[57] See A. E. McGrath, "The Privileging of Vision."

reflection of eternal Beauty and Wisdom."[58] Lewis's approach opens the way to thinking of natural theology in terms of an imaginative enhancement and enrichment of the limited self-disclosures of nature, allowing us to see things in a way that resolves nature's ambiguity through a discernment of its fundamental coherence.[59]

So is there a way of framing nature that allows things to be seen afresh, a conceptual scheme that offers a justified selectivity of attention, or a lens that brings the world into sharper focus? How might we see things as they really are? We shall consider these points in more detail in Chapter 3, when we shall focus on ways of framing the natural world from a Christian perspective, which help us cope with its complexity and ambiguity. Yet we must first consider the origins of such a distinctive way of seeing things, classically expressed in terms of *metanoia*.

Metanoia: Seeing Things as They Really Are

Human nature is haunted by an inability to see things as they really are. An illuminating example of this failure is provided by a block of stone in Canford School, in the southern English county of Dorset. The school was founded in 1923 when an old country manor house was purchased and renovated for educational use. The house had previously been owned by Sir Henry Layard (1818–94), a prominent Victorian archeologist who had spent much of his time excavating archeological sites in Mesopotamia, and was credited with the discovery of the "lost" city of Nineveh in 1845. One of its rooms contained a slab of stone which was assumed to be a copy of an ancient Assyrian carving.

In 1994, John M. Russell, professor of art history at Columbia University, visited Canford School while researching the life of Layard.[60] While exploring the premises, he identified the stone slab as a genuine 3,000-year-old carved panel that Layard had brought back to England from the throne room of the Assyrian King Assurnasirpal II (883–859 BC). It was sold at auction later that year for $11.8 million. A new informing perspective allowed the piece of stone to be seen for what it really was. The stone itself had not changed in any way; it was rather seen in a radically new way, being

---

[58] Lewis, "Christianity and Literature," in *Essay Collection*, 416.
[59] For an extension of Lewis's general approach, see Viladesau, "Natural Theology and Aesthetics." Lewis's use of the imagination should be compared with that of Newman: Hammond, "Imagination in Newman's Phenomenology of Cognition."
[60] J. M. Russell, *From Nineveh to New York*, 179–93.

recognized as an ancient treasure, not a modern replica. The auction valuation reflected a discernment of its true significance.

A Christian natural theology enables us to see the natural world in a new way, which is also considered to be a right way. Our eyes are healed; a veil is removed; the scales fall from our eyes, so that we can see the world in a way that corresponds to its true nature. The Greek term *metanoia* – traditionally and inadequately translated as "repentance" – means something like "a radical change of mind," or "a fundamental intellectual re-orientation," through which we turn away from older habits of thought and action and embrace a new way of thinking and living.[61] "Repentance means 'not primarily a sense of regret,' but 'a renunciation of narrow and sectarian human views which are not large enough for God's mystery.'"[62] It is about a "transformed metaphysical vision" of reality.[63]

The New Testament uses the technical term *metanoia* to refer to a process of spiritual and intellectual re-orientation and re-alignment, in which the believer comes to share in the "mind (*nous*) of Christ."[64] The notion of *metanoia* as "remorse" or "regret" is well attested in the classical world;[65] however, the term acquires new semantic associations in the New Testament, which speaks of the need for believers to be "transformed (*metamorphousthe*) by the renewal of [their] minds," rather than being passively "conformed to the world" (Romans 12: 2). A wide range of images are deployed to describe this change, many of which suggest a change in the way in which we see things (Acts 9: 9–19; 2 Corinthians 3: 13–16).[66] Christianity does not collude in an imaginative conformity to prevailing cultural paradigms, but mandates an imaginative re-alignment through which the world is seen as if with new eyes.

Patristic reflections on the New Testament tended to emphasize that this fundamental change of the human mind and heart was brought about by grace, not by human wisdom or achievement.[67] In his reflections on the significance of the concept of *metanoia* in early Christianity, Michel Foucault noted how it was fundamentally regarded as a movement "towards the light,"[68] in which the soul turned away from a world of shadows and

---

[61] See the essays in Boda and Smith, eds., *Repentance in Christian Theology*.
[62] Norris, *Dakota*, 197.
[63] Tyson, *Returning to Reality*, 196–8.
[64] For a collection of essays on *metanoia*, see Boda and Smith, eds., *Repentance in Christian Theology*. On this specific point, see Ramelli, "Forgiveness in Patristic Philosophy," 209–11.
[65] See the careful study of Fulkerson, *No Regrets*, 32–3.
[66] Chidester, *Word and Light*, 54, 62–4; A. E. McGrath, *The Open Secret*, 3–7; Moroney, *The Noetic Effects of Sin*, 10–12.
[67] For a good account of this, see Ramelli, "Forgiveness in Patristic Philosophy."
[68] Foucault, *Du gouvernement des vivants*, 125.

appearance in order to discover true reality. This transition towards the light allowed the soul to see what had hitherto been hidden from it, as well as knowing itself properly. Light dispels illusions, and leads to truth.

The complexity of the notion of *metanoia* was brought out by Tertullian in his important treatise *de Baptismo*. Although retaining the traditional Latin term *paenitentia* to translate *metanoia*, Tertullian linked this with the ministry of John the Baptist.[69] The fuller baptism offered by Jesus of Nazareth offered the illuminating gift of the Holy Spirit, and was not merely a *baptismus paenitentiae*. Thomas F. Torrance (1913–2007) picked up on this theme in some of his early writings, framing *metanoia* in terms of a fundamental re-alignment of human reason in which it "becomes determined by its object, its proper object, God in Christ, whom reason was made to apprehend."[70] Where secular philosophy emphasizes the place of autonomous reason, Christianity instead recognizes the need for a "heteronomous reason," in that Christian reflection is bound to its object and determined by it. Torrance is representative of a way of thinking, particularly important within the Reformed theological tradition, which conceives *metanoia* in cognitive terms, partly as a result of its implicit rationalizing assumptions. Others, however, have developed the idea of a "*metanoia* of the imagination,"[71] framing conversion in terms of a re-imagining of reality in a manner that is consonant with the Christian faith.

This notion of *metanoia* as a transformed or healed faculty of vision played a significant role in catalysing the emergence of a Christian poetic vision – as, for example, in the writings of George Herbert.[72] It can be argued to underlie both the conversion of C. S. Lewis, and his first published work as a Christian: *The Pilgrim's Regress* (1933). The novel's central character is the pilgrim – "John," generally regarded as a surrogate for Lewis himself – who has momentary visions of an idyllic Island which evokes a sense of intense yet transitory longing on his part. After finally reaching this goal, the pilgrim experiences a transformation of his visual capacity. As he journeys home from the Island – the "regress" of the work's title – the pilgrim discovers that the appearance of the landscapes through which he passes seems to have changed. He sees it in a new way. His accompanying Guide explains that he is now "seeing the land as it really is." The pilgrim's vision has been healed. "Your eyes are altered. You see nothing now but realities."[73]

---

[69] *De Baptismo*, 10. For the context, see Ferguson, *Baptism in the Early Church*, 336–50.

[70] Torrance, "Reason in Christian Theology," 29–30.

[71] García-Rivera and Scirghi, *Living Beauty*, 129–30. C. S. Lewis's notion of the "baptized imagination" is perhaps the most familiar example of this approach: Lewis, *Surprised by Joy*, 209.

[72] Read, *Eucharist and the Poetic Imagination in Early Modern England*, 98–126.

[73] Lewis, *Pilgrim's Regress*, 176–7. See further Wheat, "The Road before Him."

A similar approach is developed and expanded imaginatively in the writings of many early Christian theologians, particularly Augustine of Hippo, whose "illuminationism" can be seen as an attempt to formulate a coherent Christian epistemology of divine enlightenment.[74] For Augustine, God is the intelligible sun who gives light to the mind and therefore brings intelligibility to what we see.[75] At times, Augustine suggests that God illuminates the mind itself; at others, that God, like a sun, illuminates the extra-mental reality which is to be understood. "Both the earth and light are visible; yet the earth cannot be seen unless it is illuminated by light . . . In the same way, things cannot be understood unless they are illuminated by something else as their own sun."[76]

Charles Taylor's analysis of the influence of Augustine on shaping western perceptions of the self and its capacities highlights the importance of such an approach to an imaginative rendering of the world:

> God is not just the transcendent object or just the principle of order of the nearer objects, which we strain to see. God is also and for us primarily the basic support and underlying principle of our knowing activity. God is not just what we long to see, but what powers the eye which sees. So the light of God is not just "out there," illuminating the order of being, as it is for Plato; it is also an "inner" light. It is the light "which lighteth every man that cometh into the world." It is the light in the soul.[77]

The metaphysics of divine illumination have been explored extensively by Christian writers. Both Bede (673–735) and Alfred the Great (849–99), for example, developed the vocabulary and conceptualities of seeing with the "mind's eye" in Anglo-Saxon England.[78] It is easy to see why the image of the "mind's eye" should be so imaginatively productive and theologically illuminating.[79] The most productive and critical exploration of such visual models of knowledge took place during the Middle Ages, as result of which

[74] Schumacher, *Divine Illumination*, 25–65.

[75] For this Christianized version of Platonism, see Cary, *Augustine's Invention of the Inner Self*, 63–76. For the image in Philo, see Chidester, *Word and Light*, 30–43.

[76] Augustine of Hippo, *Soliloquies*, i.viii.15.

[77] C. Taylor, *Sources of the Self*, 129, citing John 1: 9 in the King James translation.

[78] Wilcox, "Alfred's Epistemological Metaphors"; Noble, "The Vocabulary of Vision and Worship in the Early Carolingian Period," especially 219–20. For the close association between "knowledge" and "sight" in Indo-Germanic languages, see S. A. Taylor, "The Vision Quest in the West, or What the Mind's Eye Sees."

[79] C. Collins, *The Poetics of the Mind's Eye*, 1–19. This theme remains important in contemporary discussion of issues such as "artistic depth," as can be seen from Maurice Merleau-Ponty's late essay "Eye and Mind": see Mazis, "Merleau-Ponty's Artist of Depth."

most concluded that it was incapable of supporting the epistemological pressures that came to be placed upon it.[80] The theme of "illumination" was particularly important to some metaphysical poets of the seventeenth century, such as Henry Vaughan, who longed for this "mist-obscured mortal life" to be illuminated by God.[81]

"Illumination" is perhaps best seen as a fertile image, possessing a rich and suggestive imaginative potential, rather than as a precise formula or theory of knowledge.[82] Its potential theological utility is perhaps best seen in the writings of C. S. Lewis (1898–1963), whose apologetic demonstration of the rationality of faith was designed to appeal to the imagination rather than to the more critical faculty of reason.[83] Lewis's commendation of the intellectual and imaginative virtues of the Christian faith reflects his belief that it offers a capacious and deeply satisfying vision of reality – a way of looking at things that simultaneously allows both discernment of its complexity and affirmation of its interconnectedness. The human imagination plays a leading role in grasping this "big picture," in that it is more easily perceived than understood.[84] Lewis advocated and adopted a "way of living, seeing and making,"[85] grounded in the Christian vision of reality, which lends coherence to the whole picture of existence.

These reflections on the concept of *metanoia* help us to see how natural theology can be framed as an *imaginarium*, a way of seeing things which appeals to the imagination as much as to the reason, reflecting the signifying practices and conventions of the Christian faith.[86] This Christian "way of living, seeing and making" is affirmed, enacted, embodied, and transmitted by the Christian community. In what follows, we shall reflect on the role of the Church in the articulation of a Christian natural theology.

---

[80] See, for example, Karnes, *Imagination, Meditation, and Cognition in the Middle Ages*, 78–82; Schumacher, *Divine Illumination*, 181–216; Marrone, *The Light of Thy Countenance*; Connolly, "Henry of Ghent's Argument for Divine Illumination Reconsidered."

[81] Pettet, *Of Paradise and Light*, 156–7. Note especially the analysis of Vaughan's "light-obsessed imagination."

[82] For Pindar's striking use of metaphors of vision, see Adorjáni, *Auge und Sehen in Pindars Dichtung*; for the theme in Thomas Mann, especially in relation to Old Testament characters, see Tingey, *Seeing Jaakob*.

[83] A. E. McGrath, "The Privileging of Vision."

[84] For the importance of such a "big picture," see Hicks and King. "Meaning in Life and Seeing the Big Picture."

[85] Castoriadis, *The Imaginary Institution of Society*, 145.

[86] For the general issues, see Hall, *Representation*.

Imaginative Transformation: The Church as an Interpretive Community

As we noted in the previous section, Augustine of Hippo saw God as the ultimate enabler of the process of healing and renewal which allows us to see things as they really are. But how is this process of transformation *mediated*? Augustine sees the Christian community as playing a critical role in this process by reinforcing this way of seeing things by its proclamation and sacramental ministries, which both narrate and enact this vision of reality, correlating it with human experience.

> Our whole business in this life is to heal the eye of the heart in order that that God may be seen [*sanare oculum cordis unde videatur Deus*]. It is for this reason that the holy mysteries are celebrated and the word of God is preached, and it is towards this goal that the moral exhortations of the church are directed.[87]

Augustine's telling phrase "healing the eyes of the heart" (cf. Ephesians 1: 18) suggests that the acquisition of such new habits of thought can be compared to a blind person being enabled to see the world for the first time. The Christian way of "seeing" reality is neither naturally acquired nor naturally endorsed. It comes about through the Christian revelation, which brings about a transformation of our perception of things. And that revelation is mediated through the proclamation of the Christian Church – including its preaching and sacraments.

Some might wish to raise an objection against speaking of such habits of thought. Surely faith is a divine gift, not an acquired habit?[88] Yet this fails to make the critical point that faith is a divine gift which requires to be developed through a discipleship of the mind. Habituation results from an embrace of, and immersion within, the divine gift of faith, in order to ensure that it has been fully grasped, understood, and applied. When the New Testament speaks of the gift of faith, it does not mean that the entire intellectual body of the Christian faith is given in an instant of illumination. Growth in faith and understanding is an integral part of the Christian journey of faith,[89]

---

[87] Augustine of Hippo, *Sermo* LXXXVIII.v.5.

[88] See, for example, Wisse, "*Habitus Fidei*," 175–6. The traditional distinction between *fides qua creditur* and *fides quae creditur* is helpful in avoiding this misunderstanding (see Augustine, *de Trinitate* XIII.ii.5).

[89] 2 Thessalonians 1: 3 (on which see Furnish, *Thessalonians*, 145–6); Mark 4: 26–9 (on which see Becker, *Jesus of Nazareth*, 123–4).

not something that is received in its totality from God at its moment of bestowal. Rather, faith arises from a regeneration or transformation of the human mind,[90] and is developed through a process of discipline and reflection, as an athlete might hone her natural gifts through practice and exercise.

A similar point is made by Stanley Hauerwas, who stresses the importance of developing and maintaining a distinctively Christian approach to ethics. Once more, we find an emphasis upon the distinctiveness of the Christian way of seeing (and hence evaluating) the world. We need a framework or lens through which we may "see" the world of human behavior. This is provided by sustained, detailed, extended reflection on the Christian narrative, which is articulated and enacted in the life and witness of the Church.[91] The Christian Church is a community which is generated, sustained, and transmitted by its vision of reality – its way of seeing the world, reflected in its controlling words, images, and actions. This habit of thought is something that must be acquired and then developed. There is an obvious correlation here with Alasdair MacIntyre's insights on how communities maintain their identity through "habits" of thought and action which are mediated through traditions.[92] We are thus called upon to see the world in its true light, by adopting a Christian *schema*, a "mental map" which enables the world to be illuminated and brought into focus, so that it may be seen as it really is. Hauerwas thus insists that "the church serves the world by giving the world the means to see itself truthfully."[93]

Earlier, we noted the multiple meanings of the term "natural theology." In particular, we identified two seemingly divergent conceptions of natural theology, and offered an account of how they might be seen as two distinct yet interconnected aspects of the same meta-project (pp. 22–5). The first of these two approaches understands natural theology as the demonstration or exhibition of the rational plausibility of theism by exploring what human reason can discover about God, unaided by revelation; the second views natural theology as a specifically Christian understanding of the natural world, grounded in and expressing core assumptions of the Christian faith.

---

[90] This insight is characteristic of most Christian spiritual traditions, and is of particular importance within Pietism and Puritanism: see, for example, Matthias, "Bekehrung und Wiedergeburt," 79.

[91] Hauerwas, "The Demands of a Truthful Story," 65–6. See also Hauerwas, *Vision and Virtue*. Stephen Fowl's idea of "word-care" should be noted here: Fowl, *Engaging Scripture*, 161–9.

[92] See here Herdt, "Alasdair MacIntyre's 'Rationality of Traditions'"; Porter, "Tradition in the Recent Work of Alasdair MacIntyre."

[93] Hauerwas, *The Peaceable Kingdom*, 101–2.

The model of their relationship I offered was based on the distinction between classical and quantum mechanics. It is, however, possible to develop a second way of holding these two conceptions of natural theology together, by appealing to the two main audiences which Christian communities are called to engage.

In its preaching, the Christian community of faith is called to engage both internal and external audiences.[94] On the one hand, it is called to develop and enrich the faith of believers, in terms of both nourishing the *fides qua creditur*, and expanding and deepening the *fides quae creditur*. On the other, it seeks to reach out beyond the community of faith, and engage *extra muros ecclesiae* on the basis of a wider set of assumptions.[95] This apologetic ministry might take the form of explicit criticism of prevailing worldviews,[96] or a commendation of the intellectual and imaginative plausibility of faith. What is essentially the same body of beliefs can thus be translated and presented in two quite distinct modalities, reflecting the different assumptions and goals of preaching to a Christian community, and offering an apologetic defense and commendation of the Christian faith for a secular audience. This model allows us to conceptualize a "thick" description of natural theology in terms of the multiple audiences of Christian engagement, which necessitate both an apologetic and a dogmatic mode of engagement. Both of these are based on the same fundamental set of beliefs; the difference between them concerns the core assumptions and concerns of the two audiences thus being engaged.

Throughout this section, the language of "seeing" has been used extensively, without critical reflection. In the next section, we shall consider this imagery in more detail, and reflect on its importance for natural theology.

Theōria: Imaginative Beholding and Rational Dissection

Much has been made of the "hegemony of vision" – the seemingly ineluctable commitment of western philosophical discourse to ocularcentric modes

---

[94] For this issues in relation to early Christian preaching, which often intermingled apologetic and kerygmatic elements, see Dulles, *History of Apologetics*, 1–7. See also C. Harrison, "Typology of Listening"; Forde, "The Word that Kills and Makes Alive," 6–7.

[95] For Calvin's legacy on this point, see Husbands, "Calvin on the Revelation of God in Creation and Scripture." For reflections on this theme in the theology of Karl Barth, see Chestnutt, *Challenging the Stereotype*, 87–168. Brunner's analysis of the witness of the Church should also be noted here: Brunner, *Offenbarung und Vernunft*, 134–61.

[96] See the classic statement of this position in Brunner's 1929 essay "Die andere Aufgabe der Theologie"; Brunner, *Ein offenes Wort*, vol. 1, 171–93.

of discourse, leading to a privileging of metaphors of sight and vision in philosophical and cultural reflection.[97] In works such as his "Era of a World-Picture (*Weltbild*)" (1938), Martin Heidegger argued that the "hegemony of vision" had its origins in classical Greece, and was linked with an ocularcentric metaphysics, which inevitably led to the reductive objectification and instrumentalization of the natural world. Heidegger deliberately avoided using the term *Weltanschauung* ("worldview"), preferring instead to speak of a "world-picture." For Heidegger, a *Weltbild* is generally a theoretical view of the external world, whereas a *Weltanschauung* is essentially a view of life, which includes but is not limited to a *Weltbild*.[98] A *Weltbild* is only one constituent element of a *Weltanschauung*. Heidegger thus observes that while communists, fascists, and liberals have different worldviews, they nevertheless share the same world-picture.

At one level, Heidegger was highly critical of the Greek notion of *theōria*, which he held to entail a notion of "spectatorial vision" which distances the knowing subject from the known object, and thus needlessly and improperly leads to their mutual estrangement.[99] Yet in other respects, Heidegger nuances this criticism of *theōria*. His concern was not so much its emphasis on vision which, in several respects, he replicates in his own writings. His concern focussed rather on the degeneration of this notion of vision, which failed to grasp and respect a sense of wonder on beholding nature on account of a preoccupation with a "will to power" over nature, and an improper and unnecessary entanglement with modernist metaphysics. In principle, Heidegger suggested, it was possible to

---

[97] See especially Blumenberg, "Licht als Metapher der Wahrheit"; Jonas, "The Nobility of Sight"; Potestà, *Gli occhi, il sole, la luce*; Adorjáni, *Auge und Sehen in Pindars Dichtung*; Debray, *Vie et mort de l'image*. For more detailed studies of this notion in classical antiquity, see Deonna, *Le symbolisme de l'oeil*; Simon, *Le regard, l'être et l'apparence dans l'optique de l'Antiquité*; A. M. Smith, "Saving the Appearances of the Appearances." For these ideas in the Middle Ages, see Meier, "Malerei des Unsichtbaren"; Schleusener-Eichholz, *Das Auge im Mittelalter*.

[98] Heidegger, "Die Zeit des Weltbildes," 86–7. This essay was originally entitled "Die Begründung des neuzeitlichen Weltbildes durch die Metaphysik," which makes its basic approach more explicit.

[99] The best study is Levin, "Decline and Fall." There are, of course, other ways of construing spectatorial vision: see, for example, Franz and Kalisch, "Tertius Spectans." For the religious origins of a "sacral beholding," see Rausch, *Theoria*, 148–52; Nightingale, *Spectacles of Truth in Classical Greek Philosophy*, 14–92.

renew this notion of vision, and divorce it from such inappropriate associations.[100]

A Christian natural theology provides an imaginative and conceptual framework for the disentanglement of proper vision from covert metaphysical assumptions and innate human tendencies toward domination and exploitation of the natural world. It offers the possibility of an imaginative beholding of the natural world which denies nothing of or about its beauty, save its ultimacy, and declines to reduce reality to what – to use Heidegger's terms – is merely capable of mental representation (*Vorstellen*) and construction (*Herstellen*), so that human beings in effect become the arbiters and artificers of what is deemed to be real. That, many would argue, is the fundamental failing of the modernist project itself – most notably, in its program of "disenchantment."

Many have seen the historical process of the disenchantment of nature as being coextensive with that of "Enlightenment" (*Aufklärung*), understood as "a series of related intellectual and practical operations which are presented as demythologizing, secularizing or disenchanting some mythical, religious or magical representation of the world."[101] There are good historical reasons for making this judgment, which correlates scientific advance with a growing intellectual tendency to think in terms of the rational cognition and mastery of nature, thus reducing nature to what could be observed, measured, and exploited for human ends.[102] In liberating humanity from mystery and magic, the Enlightenment de-spiritualized and de-animated the world, reducing it to raw material to be shaped by human designs through "instrumental rationality" and "social engineering." Yet the category of magic has survived this "disenchantment" of the world,[103] partly because of the failure of modernity to capture the imagination of a wider culture, and partly because the category proved capable of being retooled and re-imagined.

While the Romantic critique of an imaginatively impoverished rationalism can be accepted in several respects, it must be asked whether "disenchantment" may in reality have purged our understanding of nature of

---

[100] For Heidegger's appreciative reading of Aristotle on *theōria*, see McNeill, *Glance of the Eye*, 17–54. For the highly critical evaluation of a metaphysics of vision characteristic of much twentieth-century French philosophy, see Jay, *Downcast Eyes*, especially 263–380. Wittgenstein's analysis of "seeing-as" is important here: note especially the reflections of Voltolini, "The Content of a Seeing-as Experience."

[101] Jarvis, *Adorno*, 24.

[102] For example, see Isambert, "Le 'désenchantement' du monde"; Séguy, "Rationalisation, modernité et avenir de la religion."

[103] Bukow, "Magie und fremdes Denken"; Hanegraaff, "How Magic Survived the Disenchantment of the World."

unhelpful esoteric and mystical ideas of dubious theological merit – such as those which Carl Sagan spoke of in terms of a "demon-haunted" universe.[104] It is certainly true that something of the mystery and magic of the natural world characteristic of earlier periods, such as the Middle Ages, has been lost through the rationalism and objectification of the scientific project. Yet it must be conceded that some of this was probably just irrational nonsense that needed to be purged in the first place.

It is helpful to consider Augustine of Hippo's vision of the natural world, which avoids any suggestion that the world is mysteriously enchanted or animated by various embodied spirits.[105] For Augustine, the world was created, contingent, and rational, capable of being understood, at least in part, by human beings on account of their bearing the *imago Dei*. Nature was not capricious or random, but subject to God's hidden power and agency.[106] Yet this rationalization – in Augustine's sense – was not about the reduction of nature to the limiting categories of human reasoning, but an uncovering of the divine rationality of the ordering of the creation, capable of imaginative articulation in terms of the category of beauty.[107] Augustine's reconceptualization of the natural world in terms of God's contingent creation may indeed "disenchant" it, eliminating any notion of a world inhabited by embodied agencies; nevertheless, the closing of this door is accompanied by the opening of another, leading into a recognition of the capacity of the created order to echo and embody the rationality and beauty of its creator.

It is not difficult to point to the obvious intellectual and imaginative deficiencies of "scientism," which is best understood as "an attempt to *subdue* what it does not understand" through the use of scientific language and concepts to create a scientific semblance to fundamentally unscientific ways of thinking.[108] Yet scientism represents an overstatement of the capacities of the sciences, and an under-evaluation of the merits of other intellectual disciplines. It is perfectly possible to construct narratives in which theology and the natural sciences enrich each other's vision of reality – not

---

[104] Sagan, *The Demon-Haunted World*, 113–33. For early modern versions of these ideas, see Coudert, *Religion, Magic, and Science in Early Modern Europe and America*, 153–72. Classic Greek cosmogonic mythology might also be considered here: Naddaf, *The Greek Concept of Nature*, 37–62.

[105] S. P. Rosenberg, "Forming the *Saeculum*."

[106] *De Genesi ad litteram* v.xx.41.

[107] C. Harrison, *Beauty and Revelation in the Thought of Saint Augustine*, 97–139. This theme is particularly important in the theology of Thomas F. Torrance – note, for example, Torrance, *Reality and Evangelical Theology*, 10–11. On the theme of "ordering" in the development of the natural (especially biological) sciences, see Farber, *Finding Order in Nature*.

[108] See the important analysis in Scruton, "Scientism in the Arts and Humanities."

through an arbitrary or improper embellishment of these visions, but by seeing them as part of a bigger picture, which each discloses only partially.[109]

It is neither necessary nor inappropriate to impose an artificial separation between the "imaginative beholding" and the "rational dissection" of nature. Both can be affirmed by and contained within a Christian *imaginarium*; both are part of the same Christian picture of reality, whose complexity requires engagement and representation at multiple levels and through multiple modalities.

Nature as *logikos*: Reflections on the Doctrine of Creation

One of the outcomes of a Christian natural theology is that nature is seen through a *Trinitarian* (rather than Deist or theist) lens,[110] which recognizes that a rational (*logikos*) divine creator is both disclosed in the work of creation, and embodied in the person of Jesus of Nazareth. I follow Stanley Hauerwas in rejecting any artificial distinction between natural theology and revealed theology: "the God who moves the sun and the stars is the same God who was incarnate in Jesus of Nazareth."[111] A Christian natural theology both mandates and enables a way of imagining the world which is informed by a rich Trinitarian understanding of the economy of salvation.

So how does a Trinitarian articulation and beholding of the world allow us insights that would otherwise be denied to us?[112] It is important to note here that the natural theologies which were developed in England during the late seventeenth and eighteenth centuries make little appeal to the doctrine of the Trinity, probably because the rationality which such natural theologies wished to affirm for apologetic reasons seemed to be denied or tainted by this apparently illogical doctrine.[113] Most leading English theologians of the "Age of Reason" seem to have held on to the doctrine of the Trinity out of respect for tradition, while privately conceding that it appeared irrational in the light of the growing emphasis upon the "reasonableness of Christianity,"

---

[109] See, for example, Tanzella-Nitti, "Le rôle des sciences naturelles dans le travail du théologien"; Florio, "Las ciencias naturales en la elaboración de la teología"; A. E. McGrath, *Inventing the Universe*, 1–43, 181–204.

[110] A. E. McGrath, *A Fine-Tuned Universe*, 61–82.

[111] Hauerwas, *With the Grain of the Universe*, 15–16.

[112] For an influential defense of this position, see Gunton, *The Promise of Trinitarian Theology*, 4.

[113] Babcock, "A Changing of the Christian God."

and provided little in the way of spiritual or theological benefits.[114] While simplifications are potentially dangerous, defense of this doctrine seems to have been seen as being little more than a formal expectation on the part of orthodox theologians. John Donne's famous characterization of the doctrine as "bones to Philosophy, but milk to faith" met with few supporters in the long eighteenth century.[115]

It is not my intention at this point to engage in any detail with contemporary debates about the doctrine of the Trinity. For the limited purposes of this section, I shall echo Emil Brunner's cautious formulation of the doctrine of the Trinity as a "theological safety doctrine [*eine theologische Schutzlehre*]" which is intended to safeguard "the core faith of the Bible and of the church."[116] If my Trinitarianism appears minimalist, it is simply because of the limited agenda of this discussion. Like Brunner, I shall treat the doctrine of the Trinity as a safety doctrine, colligating the essential elements of a Christian doctrine of God, while leaving the question of the precise manner of their interaction open.

Deism, theism, and Trinitarianism alike affirm the divine creation of the universe – that the world around us is not autonomous or self-generating, the product of a human mind, but owes its origins and nature to God. Stanley Jaki captured this point well in his Fremantle Lectures at Oxford: "since the world was rational it could be comprehended by the human mind, but as the product of the Creator it could not be derived from the mind of man, a creature."[117] This theme is found, in various forms, in most of the classic formulations of Anglican natural theology from Newton to Paley. Newton might have been an Arian in his Christology, and anti-Trinitarian in his doctrine of God,[118] yet neither of these theological shortcomings prevented him from affirming the dependence of the creation on God, or its capacity to confirm the rationality of belief in God.[119]

William Paley's *Natural Theology* (1802) speaks of God as an "artificer" – that is, someone who designs and creates – but pointedly declined to allow

---

[114] See Lim, *Mystery Unveiled*, 69–123; Antognazza, *Leibniz on the Trinity and the Incarnation*, 91–110.

[115] P. Dixon, *Nice and Hot Disputes*, 5–28.

[116] Brunner, *Dogmatik I*, 209. See further M. A. Schmidt, "Der Ort der Trinitätslehre bei Emil Brunner."

[117] Jaki, *The Origin of Science and the Science of Its Origin*, 21.

[118] See especially Snobelen, "To Discourse of God"; Mandelbrote, "Eighteenth-Century Reactions to Newton's Anti-Trinitarianism"; Wiles, *Archetypal Heresy*, 77–92. For reservations about such judgments, see Pfizenmaier, "Was Isaac Newton an Arian?"

[119] See, for example, Force, "Providence and Newton's Pantokrator." It remains an open question as to whether the doctrine of creation *ex nihilo* entails a Trinitarian concept of God: for the importance of this notion for a natural theology, see A. E. McGrath, *A Fine-Tuned Universe*, 72–4.

any further divine involvement with the natural order, even if this seemed to evacuate the concept of providence of any meaning.[120] Paley was fascinated with the intricate structures of the human body and other biological organisms;[121] nevertheless, he interpreted this in terms of God's past activity, which was taken to imply God's continuing existence. Paley's lack of interest in the concept of the Trinity – which, it must be noted, was characteristic of his age – denied him access to a concept of God which affirmed ongoing divine presence and activity within the world.

A Trinitarian natural theology, however, proposes a connection between the natural world and the life, death, and resurrection of Jesus of Nazareth. For Brunner, the "mystery" at the heart of the New Testament is not the "intellectual paradox" of the doctrine of the Trinity, but the proclamation that "the Lord God became incarnate and endured the cross for our sake."[122] Classic formulations of natural theology – such as those of Newton's circle and Paley – make little, if any, reference to the incarnation or atonement, despite Jesus of Nazareth's frequent appeal to the natural world, particularly in the "parables of the Kingdom."[123] It is, however, unthinkable for a specifically *Christian* natural theology to consider such an omission. A Christian natural theology simply cannot avoid explicitly engaging Christological themes, not least because it is already implicitly shaped by Christological considerations.

The doctrine of the incarnation relates to both the rationality of the created order and the human capacity to discern and represent this. Although this theme is clearly of importance within the Alexandrian theological tradition,[124] playing a particularly significant role in the theology of Athanasius, it has been developed more recently by writers with a particular concern for both the dialogue between science and religion, and the formulation of a viable natural theology.

Thomas F. Torrance developed his concept of "theological science" which was grounded in the core assumption that God created the world as an expression of the divine rationality, and that this rationality is enfleshed in Jesus of Nazareth. "We direct our minds to the self-giving of God in Jesus Christ and allow our minds to fall under the power of the divine rationality that becomes revealed in him."[125] Christian theology seeks to grasp and

[120] A. E. McGrath, "Chance and Providence in the Thought of William Paley."

[121] Vidal, "Extraordinary Bodies and the Physicotheological Imagination."

[122] Brunner, *Dogmatik I*, 229–30.

[123] A. E. McGrath, *The Open Secret*, 117–26. For the general issue, see Jüngel, "Das Dilemma der natürlichen Theologie und die Wahrheit ihres Problems."

[124] Bienert, "Zur Logos-Christologie des Athanasius von Alexandrien in *Contra Gentes* und *De Incarnatione*"; Rohls, *Offenbarung, Vernunft und Religion*, 99–114.

[125] Torrance, *God and Rationality*, 45.

express the "rationality inherent in the reality of the incarnate Word." If the divine *logos* is indeed incarnate in Christ, then access to the inner divine rationality – and hence the rationality of all that God has created – comes through Christ:

> If God's *logos* inheres in his own Being eternally, and that *logos* has become incarnate in Jesus Christ, then it is in and through Christ that we have cognitive access into the Being of God, into his inner divine intelligibility or *logos*. There is a parallel to this, as we have had cause to see, in the way we now seek to understand nature, or the universe, in accordance with its internal rational order or intrinsic intelligibility.[126]

Torrance thus sees a correlation between the divine rationality, the incarnation, and the deep structure of the universe – including the human capacity to make sense of the world. Both the natural sciences and defensible forms of natural theology reflect this fundamentally Trinitarian insight.[127] Although Torrance is critical of natural theology, when understood as an enterprise which "starts from the same premises and the same phenomena as natural science and seeks to move toward God,"[128] his later works commend an understanding of natural theology as an enterprise undertaken from within the Christian tradition:

> Natural theology cannot be undertaken apart from actual knowledge of the living God as a prior conceptual system on its own . . . Rather must it be undertaken in an integrated unity with positive theology in which it plays an indispensable part in our inquiry and understanding of God.[129]

Yet perhaps the most significant aspect of the Christological dimension of natural theology is the connection between the suffering and pain of the natural order on the one hand, and of Jesus of Nazareth on the other. No Christian natural theology can fail to realize the importance of natural suffering, or to make such a connection.[130] During the late 1510s, Martin Luther famously articulated a *theologia crucis* – a "normative centering" of

---

[126] Torrance, *Ground and Grammar of Theology*, 151.

[127] For discussion of Torrance on natural theology, see Molnar, "Natural Theology Revisited"; Holder, "Thomas Torrance"; McMaken, "The Impossibility of Natural Knowledge of God in T. F. Torrance's Reformulated Natural Theology." For Torrance's important assessment of Barth's position on natural theology, see Torrance, "The Problem of Natural Theology in the Thought of Karl Barth."

[128] Torrance, *Theological Science*, 102–3.

[129] Torrance, *Space, Time and Incarnation*, 69–70.

[130] For reflections, see Luz, "*Theologia Crucis* als Mitte der Theologie im Neuen Testament."

Christian thought on the cross of Christ,[131] which is seen as the focus and foundation of authentically Christian ways of understanding the enigmas of the world. Luther retains the traditional emphasis upon the cross as a symbolic focus of the Christian faith, seeing it as a lens through which the enigmas of faith may be brought into focus. Yet Luther understands the cross as far more than an instrument of theological illumination, linking it with the deep existential anxieties of humanity in the face of suffering, and the radical ambiguity of a shadowy world.

A *theologia crucis* does not offer an explanation of suffering; indeed, it is arguably a form of theology which challenges the meaningfulness of explanation in the first place,[132] pointing instead to the need for an intellectual, relational, and existential re-alignment to be able to cope with suffering in a messy and ambivalent world, within which God remains as a hidden yet loving presence. If nature is read through a "natural" lens, as David Hume demonstrated in his *Dialogues concerning Natural Religion*, pain and suffering point to an incoherent and meaningless world.[133]

Yet, as we shall note later in this work (pp. 135–8), Hume's criticisms are dependent upon the thin interpretative framework of a morally ambivalent natural world provided by either naturalism or Deism. In place of the three weak forms of "liminal" natural theology that Hume is prepared to permit,[134] it is important to realize that a Christian natural theology allows the natural world to be seen through a richer interpretative lens, which frames or positions the empirical reality of suffering in such a way that it is seen in a different way, and is open to new ways of interpretation and engagement. Both naturalism and Deism fail to provide any means for seeing pain and suffering against a more complex background; a Trinitarian vision of God allows suffering to be positioned both redemptively and existentially. As we shall indicate in the following chapter, an appeal to the *signum crucis* offers a way of framing reflections on the place of suffering in the world of nature (pp. 98–100).

Other aspects of a Trinitarian theological framework could be explored here; however, my intention is to be illustrative, not exhaustive. The essential point is that the Christian theological tradition makes available a powerful toolset for the investigation and inhabitation of a complex and ambiguous world.

---

[131] For this theme, see A. E. McGrath, *Luther's Theology of the Cross*, 201–28. See also G. L. Murphy, *The Cosmos in the Light of the Cross*, 26–44.

[132] Rolf, "*Crux sola est nostra theologia,*" 236–9.

[133] Holden, *Spectres of False Divinity*, 145–79.

[134] On which see Holden, *Spectres of False Divinity*, 28–44; Demeter, *Conflicting Values of Inquiry*, 190–6.

Metaphors of Beauty and Order: Harmony and the Dance

The Christian understanding of nature as *logikos*, touched on briefly in the last section, affirms the rationality of the created order, both as something that is intrinsic to the natural world and as something that is capable of being discerned and represented mathematically by the human mind. The beauty and order of the natural world can be expressed at the level of both observation and mathematical representation. Truth is beautiful – not simply as something that is apprehended by the imagination, but as something that engenders elegant theories.[135] Yet how are order and beauty to be grasped by the Christian *imaginarium*, not merely by the theologically informed reason? Both aspects of the creation are too important and complex to be reduced to cold logical analysis; they call out for imaginative expression and expansion, and deployment by a Christian natural theology.

This has long been recognized by Christian poets, such as Dante and George Herbert, both of whom had a remarkable gift for transposing the cognitive truths of theology into the imaginative language of poetry.[136] The forging of theological metaphors – including the development of those already used in the Bible, and those found to be appropriate for the imaginative communication of its fundamental themes – was a commonplace in the patristic age, even if it arguably reached its most creative expression in the Renaissance.[137] Two of these are of especial significance for a Christian natural theology: the metaphors of "harmony" and "dance."

The musical metaphor of harmony has long been used to express the ideas of coherence, order, and beauty.[138] The harmony of the natural world – evident in both the regular movements of the planets, and the capacity of mathematics to represent them – was echoed in the harmony of music.[139] Pythagoras, for example, held that human music was modeled on the "music of the spheres." Medieval discussion of the planets made extensive use of the musical metaphor of "harmony" in emphasizing the regularity of patterns

---

[135] Chandrasekhar, *Truth and Beauty*, 59–73; McAllister, *Beauty and Revolution in Science*, 39–104; Sikka, "On the Truth of Beauty."

[136] G. B. Stone, "Dante and the 'Falasifa'"; Todd, *The Opacity of Signs*; Clarke, *Theory and Theology in George Herbert's Poetry*, 52–3.

[137] See the comprehensive study in Plett, *Rhetoric and Renaissance Culture*.

[138] Spitzer, "Classical and Christian Ideas of World Harmony."

[139] Stephenson, *The Music of the Heavens*, 16–46; Prins, *Echoes of an Invisible World*, 5–13.

disclosed by the observation of the heavens – a tradition extended in the writings of Kepler, especially his *Harmonice mundi* (1619).[140] The Scientific Revolution of the seventeenth century made extensive appeal to such a "harmony," seeing musical and other auditory metaphors as a means of expressing the physical regularities of the natural world in mathematical form.[141] In recent years, there has been growing appreciation of the place of musical motifs and imagery in the scientific writings of Isaac Newton (1643–1727), a pioneer of the Scientific Revolution.[142]

It is important to be clear that nobody believes we can "hear" the harmonies of the universe, which clearly lie beyond the auditory range of the human ear. Music is here being proposed as an analogy for the orderedness and beauty of the world, allowing us to render our experience of the world "under concepts."[143] Music offers a similar way of framing these cosmic virtues,[144] which are clearly of importance to a Christian natural theology. The "music of the spheres" is a powerful metaphor for the beauty, symmetry, and orderedness of the universe, which invites us to discover and appreciate its deeper meaning and significance, and above all to deploy the faculty of the imagination in grasping the depths of the natural world, which simply cannot be expressed adequately in words.

Our second image is that of the dance. Some writers of the seventeenth century – such as Sir John Davies (1569–1626) in his poem "Orchestra, or a Poem of Dancing" – considered the beauty and form of a dance as a means of expressing both the regularity and elegance of the cosmos.[145] At the same time as John Donne expressed anxiety about the lack of coherence of the world – "'Tis all in pieces, all coherence gone"[146] – Davies reaffirmed it in powerfully imaginative terms, seeing the dance as both "heav'ns true figure" and "th'earths ornament."[147] Davies deploys the metaphor of the dance in his imaginative rendering of God's creation of the world through the subjugation of the forces of chaos:

---

[140] Stephenson, *The Music of the Heavens*, 90–241. See also Lindberg, "The Genesis of Kepler's Theory of Light."

[141] Haase, *Aufsätze zur harmonikale Naturphilosophie*; Gouk, *Music, Science, and Natural Magic in Seventeenth-Century England*, 66–111.

[142] McGuire and Rattansi, "Newton and the Pipes of Pan"; Jackson, "Music and Science during the Scientific Revolution."

[143] J. F. Rosenberg, *One World and Our Knowledge of It*, 6.

[144] Scruton, *The Aesthetics of Music*, 80–96.

[145] Thesiger, "The *Orchestra* of Sir John Davies and the Image of the Dance"; Plett, *Rhetoric and Renaissance Culture*, 393–5.

[146] John Donne, "The First Anniversarie: An Anatomy of the World," line 213; in *The Epithalamions, Anniversaries, and Epicedes*, 28.

[147] Davies, *Orchestra*, 38.

> Like this, he fram'd the Gods eternal bower,
> And of a shapeless and confused mass
> By his through-piercing and digesting power
> The turning vault of heaven framed was:
> Whose starry wheels he hath so made to pass,
>   As that their movings do a music frame
> And they themselves, still dance unto the same.[148]

Davies suggests that the order of the created world and that of human society are both based on the order of the dance, seen as an order of moving but constant spatial relationships, capable of development without losing either its elegance or orderedness.

The image of the dance has subsequently been used widely – think, for example, of T. S. Eliot's use of the metaphor in *The Four Quartets* to speak of the human experience of timelessness.[149] Perhaps its most significant recent deployment is to be found in C. S. Lewis's theologically ambitious novel *Perelandra*. Lewis here explores the metaphor of the "Great Dance" as an imaginative vehicle of theological analysis, elucidating God's relation to the world, and particularly to human beings. This rich image, which has been widely used by theologians since about 1980 to explore aspects of both extra-Trinitarian and intra-Trinitarian relationships, was originally formulated by Lewis as an imaginative gateway to aspects of the Christian doctrine of God. The universe which may seem "planless to the darkened mind," yet – when seen rightly – reveals the exquisite patterns of the Great Dance, which disclose both the subordinate orderedness and beauty of the cosmos, and the greater beauty and wisdom of God.

> Set your eyes on one movement and it will lead you through all patterns and it will seem to you the master movement. But the seeming will be true. Let no mouth open to gainsay it. There seems no plan because it is all plan: there seems no centre because it is all centre.[150]

In this chapter, we have made a case for the re-imagination of nature. Yet many questions remain to be answered, including the question of how nature can be "seen" in an authentically Christian manner. In the following chapter, we shall explore three methods for "framing" nature, as a means of achieving focus on what is centrally important for our experience on the natural world, and reflections on its deeper significance.

---

[148] Davies, *Orchestra*, 19.
[149] S. Jones, "At the Still Point"; Hargrove, "T. S. Eliot and the Dance."
[150] Lewis, *Perelandra*, 218.

3

Text, Image, and Sign

On Framing the Natural World

The world is a mirror of infinite beauty, yet no man sees it.[1]

For the English poet Thomas Traherne (1636–74), the human eye all too often fails to penetrate the depths of nature. It skims the surface of reality, failing to penetrate deeper, lacking commitment and discernment.[2] To discern this beauty requires the development of a particular way of seeing things – a heightened perceptiveness and disciplined alertness, which is already embedded within the Christian faith but requires development through a "discipleship of the mind."[3] As Stanley Hauerwas put it, "we can only see the world rightly by being trained to see" – which in turn demands "disciplined skills developed through initiation into a narrative."[4]

Natural Theology as a *Habitus*

Hauerwas here articulates an idea that is central to the natural theology project developed in this work. Theology is an acquired habit of thought and intellectual vision. The Christian community comes into being as a result of an act of divine self-disclosure in Jesus of Nazareth, which is both intellectually illuminating and personally transformative, forcing revision of natural human ways of thinking about the world and ourselves. This "transformation of the mind" (Romans 12: 2) is not instantaneous; it is a process which requires reflection, discernment, and practice. It demands a discipleship of

---

[1] Thomas Traherne, *Centuries of Meditation*, I, 31.
[2] For Traherne's approach, see B. C. Lane, "Thomas Traherne and the Awakening of Want."
[3] McGrath, *The Passionate Intellect*, 7–16.
[4] Hauerwas, "The Demands of a Truthful Story," 65–6.

Re-Imagining Nature: The Promise of a Christian Natural Theology, First Edition.
Alister E. McGrath.
© 2017 John Wiley & Sons, Ltd. Published 2017 by John Wiley & Sons, Ltd.

the mind and imagination, which is rooted in the Christian faith and sustained by grace. The "mind of Christ" – to use an important Pauline concept – can be interpreted in a number of ways,[5] but is perhaps most naturally understood as a settled way of thinking, still capable of expansion and consolidation, which allows our experience of the world to be structured and consolidated.[6]

Natural theology results from a *habitus* of the mind and the imagination, through which the Christian comes to see the natural world in a specific way.[7] Although this can be framed in purely intellectual ways as a "habit of thought," it is better seen in terms of social context and practices which enable us to see things in a particular manner. Pierre Bourdieu's formulation of such a *habitus* as a "principle of the generation and structuring of practices and representations"[8] has considerable potential for natural theology, in that it recognizes that the practice of seeing nature is communally embedded.

> [Practice] is the product of a dialectical relationship between a situation and a *habitus*, understood as a system of durable, transposable dispositions which, integrating all past experience, functions at every moment as a *matrix of perceptions, appreciations, and actions*, and makes possible the achievement of infinitely diversified tasks, thanks to analogical transfers of schemes which permitting problems of the same form to be resolved.[9]

Bourdieu's approach to a *habitus* gives intellectual formalization to the Christian insistence on the central role of both theology and practice in shaping the Christian *imaginarium*, in shaping and reconstructing our desires and affections, and in animating and directing our emotional existence. Such a *habitus* can be thought of as a disposition – or, to use Bourdieu's terms, "systems of durable, transposable *dispositions*," which are to be understood as "structured structures that are predisposed to function as *structuring structures*, that is to say, as principles which generate and organize practices and representations that can be objectively adapted to

---

[5] Healy, "Knowledge of the Mystery."

[6] E.g., see K. Barth, *Church Dogmatics* IV/3.1, 185; IV/3.2, 538–49. Cf. Torrance, *The Mediation of Christ*, 39: "It is the alienated mind of man that God had laid hold of in Jesus Christ in order to redeem it and effect reconciliation deep within the rational centre of human being."

[7] Cf. Congar, *La foi et la théologie*, 192: "La théologie est le plus élevé des habitus intellectuels du Chrétien."

[8] Bourdieu, *Esquisse d'une théorie de la pratique*, 256. For a critical evaluation of this approach, see A. King, "Thinking with Bourdieu against Bourdieu"; Sapiro, "La formation de l'habitus scientifique."

[9] Bourdieu, *Esquisse d'une théorie de la pratique*, 261; emphasis in original.

their outcomes."[10] Bourdieu's notion of the *habitus* is perhaps slightly unclear at points; it nevertheless provides a convenient intellectual framework for consolidating a fundamental theme of Christian theology – namely, the role of the Christian vision of reality as a "structuring structure," correlating theory and practice, and enabling a deeper level of engagement with empirical reality.

So what conceptual tools might enable the proper "seeing" of our world? How might we "enjoy" – and not merely understand – this world? How might we see past and through ambiguity and fuzziness, and discern coherence and intelligibility? In this chapter, we shall consider the interplay of ways of conceiving and interpreting the natural world which make use of the three categories of word, image, and sign. Some historians have argued that the transition from the Middle Ages to the modern period is characterized by a shift from "an image culture" to "a word culture";[11] others that postmodern culture represents a transition in precisely the opposite direction. In reality, the interplay of word, image, and sign has been a feature of western culture down the ages – including the medieval period – with important debates about their mutual relationship and interaction.[12]

In recent years, the idea of "framing" has begun to emerge as a way of achieving focalization on a text or image, allowing and encouraging a heightened attentiveness on the part of the observer to certain of its aspects. In the case of the theory of art, attention has focussed primarily on the physical liminality of frames and their capacity to direct interpretation. Frames help simplify complex issues by attaching greater weight to certain considerations and arguments than to others,[13] thus achieving a degree of focus that is hindered by complex issues and structures. The "frame" of a picture places a boundary around the object of our aesthetic contemplation, thus allowing us to focus on aesthetic characteristics as determined by the object's internal structure.[14] This raises certain difficulties in dealing with the alleged "framelessness" of the natural world,[15] which we shall consider later in this chapter.

---

[10] Bourdieu, *Le sens pratique*, 88; emphasis in original.

[11] E.g., L. Stone, "Literacy and Education in England, 1640–1900," 78.

[12] Müller, "Writing – Speech – Image"; Schroeder, "Looking with Words and Images"; Martinengo, "From the Linguistic Turn to the Pictorial Turn."

[13] The concept plays an important role in contemporary debates about climate change: see Nisbet, "Communicating Climate Change." There is an important debate within the scientific community – of obvious theological relevance – about whether communicating science in this "framed" manner damages its capacity to explain complex scientific issues.

[14] See the seminal study of Schapiro, "On Some Problems in the Semiotics of Visual Art."

[15] Clark, "Contemporary Art and Environmental Aesthetics," 364–7; Hepburn, "Contemporary Aesthetics and the Neglect of Natural Beauty," 46.

Erving Goffman and others have developed the concept of a frame to emphasize its role as a mental map, enabling us to organize our experience of the world. For Goffman, a "frame" is an ensemble of concepts and theoretical perspectives that organize experiences and guide the actions of individuals, groups and societies[16] – an idea which, in some ways, parallels Bourdieu's notion of a *habitus*. For Goffman, frames are fundamentally mental schemas, organizing devices which help individuals and communities structure their experience of reality, and respond appropriately. Goffman's approach allows for frames or perspectives to be deployed as investigative tools – for example, in understanding how drama functions, particularly in connecting with audiences.[17]

The notion of a frame offers a Christian natural theology a helpful way of both understanding and sustaining a distinctively Christian way of engaging the natural world, which highlights the importance of God. One of the most common misunderstandings of any form of theism – such as Christianity – is that it proposes God simply as a supplementary item in the inventory of the universe.[18] Yet for a theist, God is the ultimate ground of the universe, not one of its components. William Inge (1860–1954) rightly argued that God is not something that we prove by direct observation, but is rather the ground of our existence and understanding in the first place.[19] For Inge, the Christian faith offers a *frame* for our "picture of the world" – a conceptual framework, a mental map, a canvas which can accommodate the world around us, and our experiences within us, supporting and holding together a richly textured vision of reality.

In this chapter, I shall consider three ways of approaching or "framing" nature, each of which has something to offer a Christian natural theology. Each of them engages, in its own distinct way, the problem of the ambiguity of nature, and offers ways of discerning a deeper yet fragile understanding of things, which so easily eludes us. This coherence in the midst of apparent ambiguity is best achieved through refocussing our gaze on the complex image of nature. "In order to make the image coherent, the viewer has to find a conceptual focus, as it were, which harmonises all the elements."[20] As we have emphasized throughout this work, following Coleridge and C. S. Lewis, this coherence is best grasped through the imagination, rather than through logical dissection.

---

[16] Goffman, *Frame Analysis*. See further Johnston, "A Methodology for Frame Analysis."
[17] Richards, "Shaking the Frame," 70.
[18] McCabe, *Faith within Reason*; Cottingham, "The Lessons of Life," 217.
[19] W. R. Inge, *Faith and Its Psychology*, 197.
[20] Gaver, Beaver, and Benford, "Ambiguity as a Resource for Design," 236.

We begin by considering the problem of the ambiguity of nature, and the difficulties this raises for a natural theology.

The Intellectual Challenge of the Ambiguity of the World

"Nature by itself speaks only ambiguously of God."[21] Thomas F. Torrance's dictum has much to commend it. For example, early medieval attitudes to the natural world were distinctly ambivalent. On the one hand, nature seemed to bear witness to the beauty and ordering of God's creative power; on the other, it seemed chaotic and lawless, threatening to overwhelm human beings through its unpredictable forces.[22] Where some saw nature as expressing the beauty and form of a dance (pp. 67–8), others saw it as moving randomly, lacking any pattern or meaning.[23] While ambiguity is seen as a virtue by few,[24] it nevertheless seems to be a defining characteristic of the natural world, which obstinately refuses to fit neatly into our preconceived categories of good and evil, or beauty and ugliness.[25]

Sometimes this sense of unease about nature reflects precommitment to certain aesthetic norms, which color our judgment. Many theologians of the seventeenth century, for example, were disturbed by the irregular shape of mountains. Surely God would have constructed the natural order in accord with classical geometric notions of elegance and beauty?[26] It was not until the eighteenth century that the rugged mountains of the Alps – such as the precipitous slopes of Chamonix – were seen as reflecting a deeper concept of beauty, given fuller articulation in Ruskin's concept of natural order.[27]

---

[21] Torrance, *Space, Time and Incarnation*, 59.

[22] See the thorough analysis in Foot, "Plenty, Portents, and Plague," especially 15–17.

[23] For the image of the dance as symbol of natural beauty, order and motion, see John Davies's poem "Orchestra, or a Poem of Dancing." See Thesiger. "The *Orchestra* of Sir John Davies and the Image of the Dance." C. S. Lewis uses the image of the dance for this purpose in *Perelandra*.

[24] See, for example, Caputo, "In Praise of Ambiguity." For the ability of the human mind to cope with (and represent) ambiguity, see Zeki, "The Neurology of Ambiguity," especially 183–92.

[25] L. C. Edwards, *Creation's Beauty as Revelation*, 103–5; Crosby, *Living with Ambiguity*, 21–41; Fiddes, *Seeing the World and Knowing God*, 284–90 (focussing on the theme of the "elusiveness of the world"). For the ambiguity of the notion of the "natural world," see Neville, *Representations of the Natural World in Old English Poetry*, 99–101. On the importance of the ambiguity of nature for any form of natural theology, see A. E. McGrath, *The Open Secret*, 115–39.

[26] The view of Thomas Burnet: Nicolson, *Mountain Gloom and Mountain Glory*, 196–7.

[27] Nicolson, *Mountain Gloom and Mountain Glory*, 5–6. The fourth volume of Ruskin's *Modern Painters* was devoted to "Mountain Beauty."

Instead of bringing a priori notions of beauty to bear about nature, Ruskin suggested that nature itself disclosed certain "types" which were "stamped upon matter" as artistic outworkings of God's wisdom, giving the informed observer "cause for thankfulness, ground for hope," and an "anchor for faith."[28]

A Christian natural theology must come to terms with an aesthetically and morally complex natural world. The intellectual, moral, and aesthetic ambiguity of nature must be engaged in any responsible attempt to undertaken a Christian natural theology. This is not a new issue, and there is an abundance of potential answers in the rich tradition of western culture, particularly the repository of Christian theology and spirituality,[29] as to how such a "penetrative sight"[30] might be developed and cultivated.

Nature is not uniformly beautiful. So how can a natural theology cope with its darker aspects? Some rely – whether explicitly or implicitly – on certain intuitions. We *feel* disturbed by the presence of suffering in the world. Yet the question of the reliability of these intuitive human judgments about nature cannot be overlooked. It is highly questionable whether any aspect of the non-human natural world can be described as "evil." It is certainly "natural"; yet the judgment that it is "evil" demands a framework of evaluation which ultimately rests on higher-order beliefs and assumptions going beyond nature itself.[31] The point at issue was expressed in the form of a question by J. R. R. Tolkien in his poem *Mythopoeia*:

> Whence came the wish, and whence the power to dream,
> or some things fair and others ugly deem?[32]

Evil is not an empirical notion; it represents the interpretation of empirical observations from the standpoint of a theory.

The moral ambivalence of nature was an important issue in David Hume's critique of natural theology, in that Hume argued that phenomena which embodied both evil and good pointed to an indifferent designer, rendering problematic any analogical inference to the morally perfect deity of traditional theism.[33] Yet others offered more nuanced

---

[28] Ruskin, *Complete Works*, vol. 2, 143, 144–5.

[29] See the different approaches advocated by Viladesau, *Theological Aesthetics*, D. B. Hart, *The Beauty of the Infinite*, Farley, *Faith and Beauty*, L. C. Edwards, *Creation's Beauty as Revelation*.

[30] Ruskin, *Complete Works*, vol. 5, 187. For Ruskin's appeal to the "penetrative imagination" see *Complete Works*, vol. 4, 278, 317.

[31] For discussion, see Messer, "Natural Evil after Darwin."

[32] Tolkien, *Tree and Leaf*, 87.

[33] Bradley, "Hume's Chief Objection to Natural Theology."

responses to the question of moral and aesthetic variegation within nature, rejecting simplistic theistic appeals to the goodness of nature on the one hand, and equally simplistic skeptical appeals to the incoherence of nature on the other.

The aesthetic ambiguity of natural landscapes remains a serious issue in contemporary debate. How does an artist respond to an unscenic landscape?[34] For many, the answer is simple: pass on, and find somewhere more scenic and appealing. Others, however, recognize the need for more committed and perceptive approaches.[35] One significant answer lies in the "the cultivation of an ability to see beauty."[36] Our eyes need to be opened in order to see a beauty that is dulled by false expectations or a failure of vision on our part.

It is not a new concern. John Ruskin was scathingly critical of Christian apologists who ignored the darker and more disturbing aspects of the natural world in defending the idea of the goodness of both creator and the creation. It was all very well to portray an idealized natural landscape, in which everything was "sunshine, and fresh breezes, and bleating lambs."[37] But what about its "shadows"? For Ruskin, both art and theology must acknowledge the darker side of nature, if they are to be true to themselves. "All great and beautiful work has come of first gazing without shrinking into the darkness."[38] In practice, many observers of nature are highly selective, filtering out what they do not wish to see.

Part of the problem in dealing with the moral, intellectual, and aesthetic ambiguity of the natural world is the Enlightenment's predilection for clarity, generally thought to have originated in the writings of Descartes.[39] This demand for clear unambiguous thinking – "mathematical plainness" (John Sprat)[40] – was fundamentally inhospitable to any notion of the intrinsic complexity and ambivalence of the natural world. There can be no doubt that this insistence on the rational transparency of nature, linked with a rejection of the imagination as a tool of inquiry and poetry as a medium of expression for truth, played a significant role in consolidating

---

[34] For the debate, see Saito, "The Aesthetics of Unscenic Nature"; Ross, "Landscape Perception"; Reimer, "Whose Goodness?"; Gorringe, "The Decline of Nature."

[35] See especially the essays in Carlson and Berleant, eds., *The Aesthetics of Natural Environments.*

[36] Gussow, "Beauty in the Landscape," 231.

[37] Ruskin, *Complete Works*, vol. 7, 268. For useful reflections on Ruskin's utility in theological aesthetics, see L. C. Edwards, *Creation's Beauty as Revelation*, 132–79.

[38] Ruskin, *Complete Works*, vol. 7, 271.

[39] On which see K. Smith, "A General Theory of Cartesian Clarity and Distinctness."

[40] Axelsson, *The Sublime*, 165.

the Scientific Revolution in the eighteenth century,[41] with its attempt to establish a pure relationship between words and things, devoid of symbols or other imaginative devices.

Yet in the end, the rationalizing natural theologies of the Enlightenment proved unable to deal with the ambiguity and complexity of the natural world, as well as failing to appreciate their own radical cultural and ideological situatedness.[42] Darwin's expression of despair over the place of suffering in nature is one of many cultural indicators of concern about the simplistic accounts of natural goodness offered during the long eighteenth century.[43] The world that we experience irritatingly resists neat categorization as being fundamentally good or evil, beautiful or ugly. In the end, the Enlightenment was forced to suppress serious reflection on the moral complexity and intellectual complexity of the natural world in an attempt to control it, attempting to shoehorn history into a narrative of continual progress and nature into a rationalized social object, capable of sustaining human civilization.[44]

At a more theological level, the suffering and violence of nature called into question the more simplistic accounts offered by well-meaning Christian apologists of the age focussing on the goodness or beauty of nature.[45] How can the perceived beauty of the created order be set alongside the apparent ugliness of the crucifixion of Jesus of Nazareth, whose body was disfigured, wounded, and broken? How is the cross of Christ to be incorporated within a natural theology?[46] Is there any coherence to the world, when the existence of suffering seems to render

---

[41] Thomas Sprat's famous *History of the Royal Society* embodies this ethos, and treats it as paradigmatic: McGuire, "The Rhetoric of Sprat's Defence of the Royal Society." A similar approach is found in recent works with a "scientistic" outlook: see, for example, Dawkins, *Unweaving the Rainbow*, 114–44; Coyne, *Faith versus Fact.*

[42] A. E. McGrath, *The Open Secret*, 140–70. For discussion of the important notions of sociological situatedness and cultural embodiment, which render classic Enlightenment approaches to rationality so problematic, see R. M. Frank, "Sociocultural Situatedness"; Kimmel, "Properties of Cultural Embodiment."

[43] For the problem, see Messer, "Natural Evil after Darwin"; Southgate, *The Groaning of Creation.*

[44] On such trends, see Gray, *The Silence of Animals*; Lewis, *The Abolition of Man*; Wolloch, *History and Nature in the Enlightenment*, 1–72. The polarization between mechanistic accounts of nature characteristic of the Enlightenment and the *Naturphilosophie* of the Romantic age is perhaps too easily overstated – see, for example, Reill, *Vitalizing Nature in the Enlightenment*, 199–234.

[45] See, for example, Hull, "The God of the Galápagos"; Murray, *Nature Red in Tooth and Claw*, 130–92.

[46] For expressions of this concern, see Hauerwas, *With the Grain of the Universe*, 15–16; G. L. Murphy, *Cosmos in the Light of the Cross*, 21–3; Luy, "The Aesthetic Collision."

it incoherent? And how might the cross offer an angle of approach that limits, if it does not entirely resolve, this concern?[47]

Nature may be rationally transparent at the level of physics, capable of being expressed in equations whose beauty mirrors their capacity to tell the truth.[48] Yet at the biological level, nature loses something of this rational and aesthetic transparency. It is as if ugliness and evil emerge at higher levels of reality, or at later stages of cosmic history. Charles Darwin, for example, considered that the "face of nature" was marred by the biological "struggle for existence," which demanded the destruction of life.[49] He found himself repulsed by the thought of parasitic wasps (*Ichneumonidae*) keeping their prey alive so that they could feed on their living bodies. Surely the idea of eating something alive was both morally and aesthetically repugnant, and hence disconfirming of the existence of a good God? "I cannot persuade myself that a beneficent and omnipotent God would have designedly created the *Ichneumonidae* with the express intention of their feeding within the living bodies of caterpillars."[50] Alfred Lord Tennyson's poem *In Memoriam* (1849), widely regarded as one of the most important English poems of the nineteenth century, argued that a belief in a loving God, grounded in the beauty of nature, did intellectual violence to a morally and aesthetically variegated natural world, fraught with violence, pain and suffering.[51] Nature was "red in tooth and claw," and "shriek'd against" such a simplistic creed. Robert Browning's 1864 poem "Caliban upon Setebos: Natural Theology in the Island," invites us to imagine a solitary, untutored interpreter trying to make sense of a highly ambiguous world of pain and suffering in the absence of any divine revelation.[52] The evidence leads him in multiple directions. Perhaps there is no God at all. Or perhaps there are two gods, one good and the other evil. Or perhaps there is only one God, with questionable capacities and intentions.[53] Browning's point was simple: nature is theologically opaque.

This leads us to explore how such ambiguity or opaqueness might be resolved, using the device of framing. As noted earlier, three ways of approaching this question will be developed in this chapter, focussing on

---

[47] A point explored by M. M. Adams, *Christ and Horrors*. Note also the points made in Bauerschmidt, "Aesthetics."

[48] Chandrasekhar, *Truth and Beauty*, 59–73; McAllister, *Beauty and Revolution in Science*, 39–60; 90–104.

[49] C. Darwin, *Origin of Species*, 62.

[50] F. Darwin, *Life and Letters*, vol. 2, 312.

[51] G. Hough, "The Natural Theology of *In Memoriam*."

[52] Peterfreund, "Robert Browning's Decoding of Natural Theology in 'Caliban upon Setebos'."

[53] A. E. McGrath, *Darwinism and the Divine*, 130–3.

nature as a text, image, and sign. We begin by considering the idea of nature as a book which needs to be interpreted properly if its true meaning is to be grasped.

Nature as a Text: Natural Theology and the Book of Nature

One of the most influential metaphors of the Renaissance is that of the "two books" – the "book of nature" and the "book of Scripture," both originating from God yet taking different forms.[54] As Derrida suggested through his notion of the *brisure*, while these two books are connected, they are clearly distinct. In clarifying their connection, we cannot help but articulate their distinction, even their *dis*connection. Yet their shared authorship opens up possibilities for parallel reading, leading to potential enrichment of our understanding of the natural world.[55]

Both books can, of course, be read in maverick and naïve manners. The narrative of Robinson Crusoe displays an individualist and theologically untutored reading of the book of Scripture, paralleling an identically deficient reading of the book of nature in "Caliban upon Setebos."[56] Yet both books can be read in a theologically informed and alert manner, shaped by the core themes of the community of faith, treating them as interweaving and interconnected narratives of disclosure. The Christian Church is an interpretive community (pp. 55–8) which reads the "book of nature" in its own distinct manner. In what follows, we shall explore some aspects of this "book of nature."

The Origins of the Notion of the "Book of Nature"

We will probably never know who first suggested thinking of the natural world as a text, inviting study and reflection. Although there are hints of such ways of thinking in the Bible – particularly those passages which compare human history to a book or scroll (Revelation 20: 12 speaks of the "Book of Life") – there are no passages which explicitly use the analogy of a text to refer to the natural world itself. Although the term was widely used in the late Renaissance and early modern age as new geographical and scientific studies

[54] P. Harrison, "The 'Book of Nature' and Early Modern Science."
[55] I defend the idea of an "enrichment of narratives" in A. E. McGrath, *Inventing the Universe*.
[56] McCrea, "The Hermeutics of Deliverance"; Peterfreund, "Robert Browning's Decoding of Natural Theology in 'Caliban upon Setebos'."

opened up new possibilities for biblical interpretation,[57] the idea can be traced back much further.[58]

One theme that is encountered in a number of patristic writers is that nature is to be seen as God's "first book," given to humanity in its state of innocence as a means by which God could be known.[59] As a consequence of sin, God supplemented this with disclosures "written in ink" or embodied in Christ, as God incarnate.[60] Yet although Augustine speaks of a "book of nature," he does little to develop this image in theologically interesting or significant ways,[61] other than noting that the book of nature discloses God to the unlearned, whereas the wise know God more fully through Scripture. Some scholars seem to have misunderstood Augustine's reference to *liber creaturae caeli et terrae* as implying a "book of nature" beyond Scripture;[62] in fact, Augustine was merely referring to the section of the book of Genesis which describes the creation of the world.[63]

By the Middle Ages, the image of the "book of nature" had found wide recognition and acceptance,[64] partly as a result of the new interest in developing a theology of nature.[65] The use of this analogy in the writings of Hugh of St Victor (*c.* 1096–1141) is particularly interesting:

> For this whole visible world is a book written by the finger of God [*quidam liber est scriptus digito Dei*], that is, created by divine power; and the individual creatures are as figures in it, not derived by human will but instituted by divine authority to show forth the wisdom of the invisible things of God. But just as some illiterate person who sees an open book looks at its figures but cannot make sense of its letters, so the foolish natural person who does not perceive what pertains to the Spirit of God sees the form and the external beauty of creatures without understanding their inner

---

[57] See Debus and Walton, eds., *Reading the Book of Nature*; Tanzella-Nitti, "The Two Books Prior to the Scientific Revolution"; Howell, *God's Two Books*. On the changing context of this age and the challenges this raised for biblical interpretation, see Methuen, "On the Threshold of a New Age."

[58] Glacken, *Traces on the Rhodian Shore*, 203–5.

[59] For the phrase, see Isaac the Syrian, *Sermones Ascetici*, 5.

[60] For the importance of the idea of original sin for the interpretation of the "two books," see P. Harrison, "Original Sin and the Problem of Knowledge in Early Modern Europe."

[61] Mews, "The World as Text," 102.

[62] See, for example, Nobis, "Buch der Natur."

[63] Mews, "The World as Text," 102, n. 18.

[64] See the detailed analysis in Mews, "The World as Text"; Ohly, "Neue Zeugen des 'Buchs der Natur' aus dem Mittelalter."

[65] See the classic study of Chenu, "La nature et l'homme."

meaning. In contrast, the spiritual person can judge everything, and when looking at the beauty of the works, soon realizes how the Creator's wisdom is much more admirable.[66]

Hugh's discussion shows no hint of a dialectic or tension between the "two books," which are seen as serving distinct (yet ultimately complementary) pedagogical functions.

Raymond de Sebonde's treatise on natural theology *Liber naturae sive creaturarum*, which dates from the 1430s, treats the "two books" as complementary sources for the knowledge of God, while noting their different levels of engagement. The "book of nature" is *connaturalis*, where the "book of Scripture" is *supernaturalis*.[67] Yet access to the "book of Scripture" is limited. It is written in a language not understood by the people, and requires privileged skills if it is to be understood. The programmatic translation of the Bible into the vernacular would not take place until the early sixteenth century, and was largely the outcome of the theological concerns of the Protestant reformers; partly due to the inaccuracy of some translations, the production of vernacular Bibles was generally prohibited during the Middle Ages.[68] For Sebonde, the "book of nature" was accessible to all, irrespective of status or accomplishments, whereas the Bible required privileged access (the cost of copying manuscripts was prohibitive in the 1430s) and hermeneutical skills for its decipherment.

Perhaps one of the clearest statements of this approach is found in the writings of Sir Thomas Browne (1605–82), particularly his idiosyncratic and controversial work *Religio Medici* (1643).

> Thus there are two Books from whence I collect my Divinity; besides that written one of God, another of His servant Nature, that universal and publick Manuscript, that lies expans'd unto the Eyes of all: those that never saw Him in the one, have discovered Him in the other.[69]

Browne's discussion reflects the Renaissance assumption that there was some "natural language," accessible to all, which allowed nature to be

---

[66] Hugh of St Victor, *de Tribus Diebus*, 3. For comment, see Illich, *In the Vineyard of the Text*, 33; Mews, "The World as Text," 97–100.

[67] Sebonde, *Theologia naturalis seu Liber creaturarum*, fol. A2.

[68] Liere, *An Introduction to the Medieval Bible*, 203–5.

[69] Browne, *Religio Medici*, 39–40. On this unusual and eclectic work, see Preston, *Thomas Browne and the Writing of Early Modern Science*, 42–81. For the "book of nature" in the thought of Francis Bacon, see Serjeantson, "Francis Bacon and the 'Interpretation of Nature' in the Late Renaissance," 695–6.

interpreted transparently and understood unproblematically.[70] A similar idea underlies the "visual language" developed in the writings of the English philosopher George Berkeley (1685–1753),[71] which Berkeley held to reflect a "natural" reading of nature, intended by God, as opposed to the "artificial" readings, framed in terms of human reflections on nature.

Yet the universal *accessibility* of such natural languages was not understood to entail their universal *comprehensibility*. Galileo, for example, was clear that this language had to be *learned*. The universe is indeed a public text; yet although it can be *seen* by everyone, it cannot be *understood* by all.[72] For Galileo, the "capacity to decipher the 'Book of Nature'" is what distinguishes a philosopher from an ordinary person.[73] Yet Galileo was aware that the reading of the "book of nature" was rendered deeply problematic by a series of concerns that could be traced to the relation of complementarity between Scripture and the book of nature.[74] Milton's *Paradise Lost* clearly echoes these concerns about the difficulty of interpreting the "book of nature," drawing on two quite distinct interpretative strategies for understanding the book of the world: the symbolic or analogic hermeneutic that produced an encyclopedic stock of plant lore from antiquity to the earlier Renaissance, and the "experimental reading" strategy developed by advocates of the "new science," such as Thomas Browne, Robert Boyle, and Robert Hooke.[75] Although both reading strategies are present in *Paradise Lost*, the dominant voice is the latter, given added significance to Milton on account of its close relationship with Protestant devotional practices.[76] Yet Milton's approach fails to resolve the fundamental ambiguity of the language of nature, accepting rather than eliminating the difficulties that this raises.[77] Reading the "book of nature" turned out to be more complex than many had thought.

---

[70] For the ideas of this age, see Singer, "Hieroglyphs, Real Characters, and the Idea of Natural Language in English Seventeenth-Century Thought"; Coudert, "Forgotten Ways of Knowing," 91–4.

[71] Bradatan, "George Berkeley's 'Universal Language of Nature.'"

[72] Tanzella-Nitti, "The Two Books prior to the Scientific Revolution," 243.

[73] Palmerino, "The Mathematical Characters of Galileo's Book of Nature," 29.

[74] A point emphasized by Bagioli, "Stress in the Book of Nature."

[75] Armogathe, *La nature du monde*, 37–8; K. L. Edwards, *Milton and the Natural World*, 40–63.

[76] For the relation between a Puritan "experimental faith" and a Baconian "faith in experiment," see Picciotto, *Labors of Innocence in Early Modern England*, 4–5.

[77] K. L. Edwards, *Milton and the Natural World*, 68.

Mathematics as the Language of Nature?

A development of importance for natural theology took place during the seventeenth century, as leading scientists began to identify this "natural language" with that of mathematics.[78] The idea can be seen clearly in the writings of Johannes Kepler (1571–1630), who regarded geometry as the archetype of the cosmos, coeternal with God as its creator.[79] In his work *Harmonices Mundi* (1619), Kepler argued that, since geometry had its origins in the mind of God, it was only to be expected that the created order would conform to its patterns:

> In that geometry is part of the divine mind from the origins of time, even from before the origins of time (for what is there in God that is not also from God?) has provided God with the patterns for the creation of the world, and has been transferred to humanity with the image of God.[80]

A similar theme is found in the writings of Galileo, who spoke of the universe as a book written using the language of mathematics:

> Philosophy is written in that great book [*questo grandissimo libro*] which stands open continually before our eyes (I am talking about the Universe); but it cannot be understood unless one first learns to comprehend the language and interpret the characters in which it is written. It is written in the language of mathematics, and its characters are triangles, circles, and other geometrical figures, without which it is humanly impossible to understand a single word of it.[81]

The growing trend toward the "mathematization of nature," evident in this passage, reflects this belief that mathematics is the natural language in which the "book of nature" is written.[82]

Today, few would agree. Mathematics is seen as a formal, rather than a natural, language.[83] Yet this does not call into question the remarkable – some would say unreasonable – ability of mathematics to represent the deep structures of the universe. The entire process of the "mathematization of

---

[78] Dorato, "Why Is the Language of Nature Mathematical?"

[79] van der Schoot, "Kepler's Search for Form and Proportion," especially 59–61.

[80] Kepler, *Gesammelte Werke*, vol. 6, 233.

[81] Galileo, *Opere*, vol. 6, 232. See further Palmerino, "The Mathematical Characters of Galileo's Book of Nature"; Dorato, "Why Is the Language of Nature Mathematical?"

[82] Fletcher, *Time, Space, and Motion in the Age of Shakespeare*, 12–20; Dorato, "Why Is the Language of Nature Mathematical?"

[83] For the question of how mathematical language relates to natural contexts, see Ilany and Bruria Margolin, "Language and Mathematics."

nature" – which began in earnest in the early seventeenth century,[84] led to an enhanced appreciation of the rational transparency of the natural world, opening the way to its scientific investigation.

This point was made in a classic essay by the theoretical physicist and Nobel laureate Eugene Wigner, who remarked that "the miracle of the appropriateness of the language of mathematics to the formulation of the laws of physics is a wonderful gift which we neither understand nor deserve."[85] When scientists set out to make sense of the complexities of our world, they use "mathematics as their torch." Sometimes abstract mathematical theories that were originally developed without any practical application in mind later turn out to be powerfully predictive physical models.[86] For Wigner, this amounted to a mystery that called for an explanation. Is there an "ultimate truth," understood as "a picture which is a consistent fusion into a single unit of the little pictures, formed on the various aspects of nature"?[87]

John Polkinghorne developed this point further, noting the significant "congruence between our minds and the universe." Why does mathematics (a "rationality experienced within") correspond so closely to the deep structures of the universe (a "rationality observed without")?[88] Furthermore, true mathematical representations of reality are intrinsically beautiful.[89] This should not be taken to imply that aesthetic qualities are determinative of theoretical truth; it is, however, to observe how, in practice, the best theories general turn out to be elegant and beautiful – even though both "truth" and "elegance" are subjective qualities.[90] The epistemic virtues that are generally considered in determining the "best explanation" of a set of observations invariably include highly subjective criteria such as simplicity and elegance.[91]

For a Christian theologian, the beauty both of nature itself and of mathematical representations of nature can easily be accommodated within

---

[84] Yoder, *Unrolling Time*, 1–8; Malet, "Isaac Barrow on the Mathematization of Nature."

[85] Wigner, "The Unreasonable Effectiveness of Mathematics," 14. For further exploration of this point, see Penrose, *The Road to Reality*, 7–23.

[86] For examples and discussion, see Livio, *Is God a Mathematician?*

[87] Wigner, "The Unreasonable Effectiveness of Mathematics," 8.

[88] Polkinghorne, *Science and Creation*, 20–1. For similar arguments in the Victorian age, with explicit connections being made between mathematics and natural theology, see Cohen, *Equations from God*, 14–41.

[89] McAllister, *Beauty and Revolution in Science*, 24–38; Dubay, *The Evidential Power of Beauty*.

[90] The epistemic issues raised by this observation are engaged in de Cruz and de Smedt, "Evolved Cognitive Biases and the Epistemic Status of Scientiific Beliefs." For reflections on the role of subjective creativity in both art and science, see A. I. Miller, *Einstein, Picasso*, 237–53.

[91] Lipton, *Inference to the Best Explanation*, 66–8; Glynn, *Elegance in Science*, 1–17.

the "big picture" of faith.[92] Yet it remains unclear why beauty should be a desirable quality. Is nature beautiful for a reason? Charles Darwin, for example, considered beauty to have no utilitarian value: natural beauty (for example, in animals) served no practical purpose.[93] While conceding that aesthetic judgment might be a driving force within the process of natural selection, Darwin regarded such preferences as essentially arbitrary. One possibility would be to argue that aesthetic judgments are based on what are essentially short-cuts in mental processing, designed to focus attention on informational cues that are likely to enhance survival and reproduction.[94]

Framing the Book of Nature: Gérard Genette

In speaking of nature as a "text," what importance do we attach to the manner in which the text is presented – to verbal and other devices, which might not strictly be considered part of the text itself, but which nevertheless help shape the way in which we understand and interpret the text?[95] For the French literary theorist Gérard Genette, such material constitutes a "para-text"[96] – a series of literary conventions that mediate between the world of publishing and the world of the text, which subtly indicate expectations about how a text is to be received and interpreted, and act as "thresholds" to its world of meaning.[97] Genette explored two aspects of this "paratext." Firstly, he defined as "peritext" material that was conventionally included within a book, such as titles, signs of authorship, dedications, prefaces, which framed the text itself through the use of "liminal devices" on its thresholds. Secondly, Genette used the term "epitext" to designate additional interpretative elements that exist separately from a book itself, such as interviews, reviews, correspondence, and diaries. Taken together, such paratextual material shaped our reading of the text itself.

Texts are thus *framed*, in the sense that they are located within a hermeneutical context by various forms of "paratextual" apparatus which have been developed and elaborated over the centuries, which offer direction or guidance as to how readers approach the text, often amounting to subtle

---

[92] A. E. McGrath, *The Open Secret*, 261–90; Wynn, "Beauty, Providence and the Biophilia Hypothesis." Hugh Miller's critique of William Paley's mechanical approach to nature should be noted here: Brooke, "Like Minds."

[93] See the important study of Menninghaus, "Biology à la Mode."

[94] For this argument, see Barry, "Perceptual Aesthetics."

[95] For the historical development of these features and their theoretical significance, see Finkelstein and McCleery, *An Introduction to Book History*, 7–28.

[96] Genette, *Palimpsestes*, 7–16. For comment on Genette's approach, see Pier, "Gérard Genette's Evolving Narrative Poetics."

[97] A point developed especially in Genette, *Seuils*.

attempts to direct or control the readers' approach to the text, and their construction of its meaning.[98] Genette proposes that such "paratexts" attempt, more or less successfully, to "frame" both positive reception and "accurate" interpretation of a text, particularly from the author's perspective.[99] Although Genette does not use the term "frame" as frequently as might be expected, his analysis of how the presentation of the text influences its interpretation is easily organized around this central category.

Genette's analysis is particularly helpful in understanding how Sebonde's *Liber naturae sive creaturarum* has come to be understood to be a manifesto of natural theology, in the sense of a knowledge of God which is attained without reference to divine revelation. This theme is present only to a minor extent in the text of the work. Yet, as we noted earlier (p. 12 n. 41), later editions of this work included the significant subtitle: *theologia naturalis*.[100] The influential Renaissance scholar Michel de Montaigne (1533–92) produced a French translation of this work, and entitled it *La théologie naturelle de Raymond Sebon*.[101] The reader was thus directed by such "paratexts" to understand or anticipate that the work which followed was a treatise on "natural theology," when its true focus was actually much wider.

A World outside the Text or Nature? Paul Ricœur

A final question which arises from treating nature as a text concerns whether there is a world outside or beyond that text. Is the text complete in itself, or does it point beyond itself? Paul Ricœur is one of a group of writers to note that the reader of a text in effect makes a choice as to how a text is to be read.[102] We can treat the text as "worldless" and "authorless," and focus on its structure and internal relations. In doing this, the reader chooses to enter "the place of the text" and accepts the "enclosure" that this entails – namely, that the "text has no outside," only an "inside," and that it does not point to anything transcendent lying beyond the world of the text itself. We can explore the text's structures, and work out the rules that govern its assembly and function.[103] Ricœur contrasts this with a second approach, which chooses to see the text as having an "outside." There is a world beyond the text – a "new discourse" which the text enables, by "opening out" to disclose something new, lying beyond that text.[104]

---

[98] M. Maclean, "Pretexts and Paratexts"; Berlatsky, "Lost in the Gutter."

[99] For an illuminating example, see Henrot Sostero, "La fabrique du pré-dire."

[100] Guy, "La *Theologia Naturalis*: Manuscrits, éditions, traductions."

[101] See, for example, the edition of Guillaume Chaudière, published at Paris in 1581.

[102] Ricœur, "What Is a Text?"; in *From Text to Action*, 105–24.

[103] Ricœur, "What Is a Text?," 110–11.

[104] Ricœur, "What Is a Text?," 112–13.

Similarly, we may choose to interpret the natural world as a closed system, inviting us only to explore its structures and inner mechanisms – an approach that is generally termed "naturalism." On this reading of nature, there is no *hors-texte*, nothing beyond the natural world that requires exploration or recognition. We can thus treat nature as a closed, self-referential system, in which every "why" question is ultimately answered by a declaration that this is just the way things are. Or we can choose to regard nature as a text with an author and a vision of a world, which the enlightened reader is enabled to discern and enter.

A Christian natural theology frames our experience and appreciation of the natural world. As I argued earlier (pp. 25–35), we do not encounter this world directly, but through a threshold shaped by the specifics of the Christian tradition, expressed and embodied in the proclamation, teaching, and worship of the Christian Church. If the natural world is to be conceived as a text, the Christian Church provides a "paratext" which adorns and supplements this text, creating certain expectations about what this natural world might be. The liturgical reading of the "book of Scripture" thus functions paratextually, creating a framework for approaching and understanding the "book of nature" – for example, by intimating its author, and encouraging the reader of this text to focus on certain of its aspects. The Christian reader of the "book of nature" thus encounters this text through mediated "frames."

In this section, we have noted how thinking of nature as a text allows us to reflect on the importance of the beauty of mathematical representations of nature – rather than our direct perceptions of nature – for a natural theology.[105] Yet the question of how the "book of nature" is to be interpreted remains important, in that this book is open to multiple translations and interpretations.[106] Many would argue, for example, that the most natural interpretation of the world is that there is no God. So why is a natural theology to be preferred over a natural atheology?[107] Which interpretation of nature is right? Or the best?

The approach adopted in this work holds that the "book of nature" can be read and interpreted in the light of an attentive communal reading of the "book of Scripture."[108] The Christian tradition thus represents a tradition-

---

[105] This relationship was noted by Thomas Chalmers (1780–1847) in his "Natural Theology": Chalmers, *Works*, vol. 1, 26–8.

[106] A. E. McGrath, *The Open Secret*, 147–55; P. Harrison, "The 'Book of Nature' and Early Modern Science," 19–25.

[107] See Lustig, "Natural Atheology"; Sosa, "Natural Theology and Naturalist Atheology." See also the cautionary comments in T. Dixon, "Theology, Anti-Theology and Atheology."

[108] The approach I adopt is similar to that offered by Calvin: see E. Adams, "Calvin's View of Natural Knowledge of God."

mediated "view from somewhere" which provides conceptual acuity for reading the "book of nature."

Many, however, will take the view that a textual metaphor for the world of nature is inadequate. Let's turn to look at more visual models of nature, focussing on the idea of nature as an image.

Nature as Image: Natural Theology and Landscapes

There is a long tradition of framing natural theology in terms of the aesthetic appreciation of landscapes.[109] The search for beauty in landscapes in the early modern period often reflected disenchantment with society, or a growing alienation from the political realities of modern cities. Jean-Jacques Rousseau's longing to return to the simplicity and elegance of nature ultimately reflected his alienation from the political and religious life of Geneva in the eighteenth century, culminating in the longing to return to a rationalist paradise.[110] The discovery of Tahiti led to the islands of the South Pacific being depicted by French writers, such as Denis Diderot, as a naturalist paradise, perhaps reflecting a golden age in the history of humanity which could be recovered through social and ethical engineering.[111] Many of these depictions of exotic landscapes were hopelessly idealistic, projecting contemporary concerns onto paradisiacal canvases – such as asserting the superiority of the "Noble Savage in a State of Nature" over the "Pale Dead Male in the Age of Reason."[112]

More recent work in human geography has emphasized the constructive role of human agency in both the fabrication of landscapes and their interpretations. Landscapes are rarely "natural"; they are often the outcomes of human management and intervention.[113] Yet, despite these ideological manipulations of natural landscapes, it lies beyond doubt that they are capable of evoking a sense of awe and mystery, acting as gateways for reflection and intellectual exploration.[114]

---

[109] John Ruskin is a case in point: see Finley, *Nature's Covenant*, 191–226. Note also the implicit (and often explicit) natural theology of the Dutch masters: Bakker, *Landscape and Religion from Van Eyck to Rembrandt*, 55–66.

[110] von Stackelberg, *Jean-Jacques Rousseau*.

[111] Childs, *Vanishing Paradise*; Matsuda, *Empire of Love*, 91–111.

[112] As noted by Weissmann, "Ecosentimentalism," 486.

[113] Greider and Garkovich, "Landscapes"; C. M. Harrison and Burgess, "Social Constructions of Nature."

[114] For the wide variety of human responses and some of their possible motivations, see Ross, "Landscape Perception."

Yet in the eighteenth and nineteenth century, this sense of appreciation was often expressed in terms of the category of the "picturesque" – that is, as conforming to the aesthetic norms of a human work of art.[115] This tendency has been severely criticized by many, in that it inappropriately makes the appreciation of nature dependent on criteria developed for human art forms, and is thus non-autonomous. Furthermore, the analogy with a two-dimensional painting which is implicit to any attempt to project an arts-based aesthetic onto nature fails to do justice to the complex textures of the natural world.[116] Yet, as we shall see, the analogy is helpful in many ways, especially in engaging the question of the ambiguity of the natural world.

The aesthetic and moral ambivalence of natural landscapes simply cannot be ignored. There is an innate tendency, especially within some sections of the environmental movement, to presume such landscapes to be "good" or "beautiful," without any attempt to interrogate what such notions might mean, and what vested interests they might serve.[117] Some less critical environmentalists appear to suspend their faculties of critical judgment in a somewhat forced, artificial, and ultimately unconvincing attempt to persuade their readers that all of nature is – and must be! –beautiful, and would be seen as such if we could set aside intellectual and cultural impediments to such a discernment.[118]

The concept of "framing" a landscape or other natural vista offers an approach which allows certain aspects of a scene to be foregrounded, while subtly removing others from the frame of vision. In what follows, we shall explore the potential of such an approach for the purposes of a natural theology.

Framing a Landscape: On Changing the Observer's Perspective

In his studies on modern painters, John Ruskin offers his readers a classic example of an aesthetically and morally variegated landscape in the Scottish highlands. I shall cite him extensively, and invite my readers to allow Ruskin's prose to help them to form a mental image of the scene. Ruskin opens his description of this imagined landscape as follows:

> It is a little valley of soft turf, enclosed in its narrow oval by jutting rocks and broad flakes of nodding fern. From one side of it to the other winds, serpentine, a clear brown stream, drooping into quicker ripple as it reaches the end of the

---

[115] See the perceptive analysis in Conron, *American Picturesque*.

[116] For a summary of such criticisms and a defense of the category of the "picturesque," see Paden, "A Defense of the Picturesque."

[117] Gussow, "Beauty in the Landscape"; Reimer, "Whose Goodness?"

[118] For a reflective account of the problem, see Saito, "The Aesthetics of Unscenic Nature."

oval field, and then, first islanding a purple and white rock with an amber pool, it dashes away into a narrow fall of foam under a thicket of mountain-ash and alder. The autumn sun, low but clear, shines on the scarlet ash-berries and on the golden birch-leaves, which, fallen here and there, when the breeze has not caught them, rest quiet in the crannies of the purple rock.[119]

Thus far, Ruskin offers what might be taken as a somewhat simplistic, if elegant, affirmation of the majestic beauty of nature, hinting at its capacity to witness to God's goodness. Although the style may be Ruskin's, the ideas he expresses are those of William Paley. Having lulled his readers into a false sense of aesthetic security, Ruskin breaks into a more sombre reflection on the less attractive aspects of that same scene:

Beside the rock, in the hollow under the thicket, the carcase of a ewe, drowned in the last flood, lies nearly bare to the bone, its white ribs protruding through the skin, raven-torn; and the rags of its wool still flickering from the branches that first stayed it as the stream swept it down.[120]

The dead sheep is a potent symbol of the darker side of nature, the seeming irrationality, ugliness, and wastefulness of life, glossed over by Paley – yet demanding to be accommodated within the scope of any viable natural theology. Yet Ruskin has not finished. There are human figures in this landscape – but they represent poverty and illness, not natural beauty.

I see a man fishing, with a boy and a dog – a picturesque and pretty group enough certainly, if they had not been there all day starving. I know them, and I know the dog's ribs also, which are nearly as bare as the dead ewe's; and the child's wasted shoulders, cutting his old tartan jacket through, so sharp are they.[121]

The man is not fishing to create a picturesque landscape for the benefit of onlookers, but because he and his family need the fish as food, if they are to survive.

So how are we to deal with this landscape? How can it be accommodated within a viable Christian natural theology? One strategy is to frame the landscape – allowing the frame to focus our attention on certain aspects of the image, rather than others. A frame serves to both focus and limit our perception, by drawing our eyes preferentially to certain parts of a picture, and either obscuring or marginalizing others. This selectivity of vision might

---

[119] Ruskin, *Complete Works*, vol. 7, 268.
[120] Ruskin, *Complete Works*, vol. 7, 268.
[121] Ruskin, *Complete Works*, vol. 7, 269.

allow the images of natural decay and human poverty to be removed from the picture, creating a more pleasing impression for those in search of the picturesque, rather than a brutally accurate record of the complexity of nature. Yet it is intellectually unacceptable. We must find some other way of framing the landscape.

One artistic approach is suggested by John Constable (whose style, by the way, Ruskin detested).[122] According to Constable, the artist was called upon to develop a way of seeing nature from the standpoint of perspective – a framing device which caused nature to appear to be beautiful:

> I never saw an ugly thing in my life: for let the form of an object be what it may, light, shade, and perspective will always make it beautiful. It is perspective which improves the form of this.[123]

Constable's point is that the artist can beautify the world by judicious choice of the manner in which it is to be represented. His approach does not entail that all aspects of nature are equally or perfectly beautiful; rather, they are all beautiful in some manner and to some extent. So how might this be transposed to a discussion of the ambiguity of nature?

Seeing a Bigger Picture: An Expanded Context of Interpretation

One approach is to argue that our immediate aesthetic response to the natural world – including a perception that some of its aspects are "ugly" – is "provisional, correctable by reference to a different, perhaps wider context or to a narrower one realized in greater detail."[124] This recognition of the "provisional character of aesthetic qualities in nature" thus creates within the human observer a "restlessness" or "alertness," encouraging the exploration of new standpoints of observation and interpretation.

This can be seen in Holmes Rolston's reflections on the aesthetic complexity of the natural world. In place of Ruskin's "carcase of a ewe," Rolston invites us to reflect on our response to encountering the "rotting carcass of an elk, full of maggots" while on a hike.[125] We may find

---

[122] For Ruskin's comments on Constable's "totally flat" depiction of an aspen, see *Complete Works*, vol. 6, 101: "we have arrived at the point of total worthlessness . . . [it is] wholly false in ramification, idle, and undefined in every respect."

[123] Leslie, *Memoirs of the Life of John Constable*, 308. Note that this statement is not found in Constable's writings, but is a recollection of a conversation. For a more detailed analysis (including a critique of Ruskin), see Thornes, *John Constable's Skies*, 93–198.

[124] Hepburn, "Aesthetic Appreciation of Nature," 198.

[125] Rolston, *Environmental Ethics*, 238.

this repulsive. But this, he suggests, is essentially a response conditioned by our evolutionary history, which is intended to enhance our prospects for survival. "Humans, like other animals, will have been naturally selected to find certain things repulsive, those things (rotting carcasses, excrement) that they as individuals need to avoid in order to survive."[126] Our instinctively negative approach to some aspects of nature is, according to Rolston, an evolutionary predisposition; it is not to be confused with a considered and reflective response to the complexity of nature, which situates such observations within a broader context.[127] Rolston uses the language of "framing" to interpret such examples of natural ugliness, developing this in two distinct ways.

1 *Contextualization.* A decaying animal or plant may seem repulsive in the context of unreflective experience, yet becomes beautiful within the holistic context of an ecosystemic perspective. The rotting hulk of a tree may look ugly, but it "provides nesting cavities, perches, insect larvae, food for birds, nutrients for the soil and on and on." Similarly, the rotting carcase of an elk provides nutrients for the soil. Every event is "framed by its environment, and this frame becomes part of the bigger picture we have to appreciate."[128]
2 *An ongoing narrative.* Rolston suggests that we tend to freeze a single frame of an ongoing narrative, failing to realize that this "moment" leads on to something beautiful. "Momentary ugliness is only a still shot in an ongoing motion picture."[129] Freezing the narrative at such a moment fails to deal with the place of such ugliness in a process, in that death and decay unleash transformative forces that lead toward beauty over time. "Ugliness, though present at times in particulars, is not the last word."[130]

On the basis of these two articulations of "framing" the natural world, Rolston suggests that we do not need to find all places to be "equally or perfectly beautiful"; rather, we can grade them on a "scale that runs from zero upward but has no negative numbers."[131] Holmes does not suggest that individual aspects of complex ecosystems cannot be aesthetically appreciated; his point is rather that we additionally appreciate these natural items in the

---

[126] Rolston, *Environmental Ethics*, 241.
[127] For the growing importance of evolutionary considerations in relation to environmental aesthetics, see Paden, Harmon, and Milling, "Ecology, Evolution, and Aesthetics."
[128] Rolston, *Environmental Ethics*, 239.
[129] Rolston, *Environmental Ethics*, 239.
[130] Rolston, *Environmental Ethics*, 241.
[131] Rolston, *Environmental Ethics*, 237.

light of the larger systems of which they are a part. Seen in this light, for example, death and decay can be seen as "the shadow side of the flourishing."[132]

Rolston's concept of framing nature is not without its difficulties. Nor is the use of the metaphor of framing entirely helpful when dealing with natural landscapes, which are intrinsically unbounded. Hepburn, for example, suggests that it is the essential lack of a frame that enables nature to stimulate our imaginations, partly by providing "scope for imaginative play."[133] Carlson argues that the notion of "framing nature" leads to a static engagement with the world, in which meaning is imposed upon nature by its observer.[134] Yet both these criticisms of the notion of framing seem misplaced. To begin with, human beings naturally "frame" nature[135] – not necessarily as an act of control over nature, but rather as a manner of attempting to accommodate nature within our limited capacity to comprehend and represent.[136] And second, a frame can "provide focus without confinement," allowing a concentration of attention which allows the discernment of beauty in a certain domain, without requiring to see nature *in its entirety*.[137] Such a "God's-eye" perspective is simply unattainable, given human cognitive limitations.

So does the framing of nature help achieve interpretative closure? Jacques Derrida's critique of the Kantian *parergon*, coupled with his own distinct approach to "framing," suggests that it leads to indeterminacy and openness.[138] Derrida notes that the frame is both delimiting and enabling. It does not aim to distinguish itself from the work of art, but to disappear into it, thus achieving a transparency which is naturalized on the part of the viewer.[139] The viewer implicitly accepts and enters into a personal conceptual world which is both enabled and limited by the frame, despite the lack of closure and clarity that some might desire. Derrida's analysis provides intellectual

---

[132] Rolston, *Environmental Ethics*, 239. Some recent criticisms of Rolston at this point seem to miss this point: for example, see Saito, "The Aesthetics of Unscenic Nature," 103–4. A more telling criticism concerns the basis of Holmes's understanding of value: see McShane, "Rolston's Theory of Value."

[133] Hepburn, "Contemporary Aesthetics and the Neglect of Natural Beauty," 48. Note also the discussion of the "framing paradox" in R. Moore, *Natural Beauty*, 105–26.

[134] Carlson, *Aesthetics and the Environment*, 35–7.

[135] Stolnitz, *Aesthetics and Philosophy of Art Criticism*, 48.

[136] For the Piagetian insights involved here, see Keltner and Haidt, "Approaching Awe."

[137] R. Moore, *Natural Beauty*, 117–25.

[138] On which see Höpfl, "Frame"; Heller-Andrist, *The Friction of the Frame*; Pirinen, "Parergon, Paratext, and Title on the Context of Visual Art."

[139] Derrida, *La verité en peinture*, 71–2.

and cultural legitimation for the notion of framing, while declaring that no closure is possible on questions of interpretation.[140]

Derrida's approach to "framing" nature seems thus to lead simply to exploring interpretations of interpretations – such as his own reading of Kant's notion of *parerga*.[141] Yet precisely because it subverts any notion of a privileged or "authorized" interpretation of any artifact or performance, it creates a context within which one specific manner of "framing" the natural world – namely, that offered by a Christian natural theology – could be explored and evaluated.

The concept of an "interpretative community" plays an important role in this process. Just as the Church can be seen as such a community which reads texts – including the "book of nature" – in its own distinct manner, so it is also a community of visualization, which *sees* the natural world in certain ways, and frames that act of vision in the light of its agendas and concerns. There is no neutral viewing of nature, in that any act of observation is shaped by theoretical commitments, whether these are acknowledged or not. Every viewing of the world and its attendant practices of focalization and visual neglect (what is central to the picture? and what is marginal?) reflects some such committed perspective. Any interpretive community offers a construction or re-imagination of nature based on certain precommitments and presuppositions; the Church is no exception to this rule, reading and viewing nature in an act of intellectual and imaginative obedience to its fundamental vision of reality.[142]

Nature as a Sign: Natural Theology and Semiotics

The long history of natural theology has seen an extended engagement with the question of the semiotic status of the natural world.[143] Is nature to be seen as something that is closed and self-sufficient, inviting us to probe more deeply into its mysteries as a means of understanding this self-contained system? Or does it in some way point beyond itself to something deeper or greater, behind or beyond it? And if so, is this significatory capacity to be seen as something that is intrinsic to nature, or something constructed by the

---

[140] The contrast with Heidegger's conception of the "truth of the work of art" is striking: see especially Olivier, "Derrida, Art and Truth."

[141] Librett, "Aesthetics in Deconstruction," 330–1.

[142] I have in mind here the points developed by Paul Ricœur in his essay on "Imagination in Discourse and Action": see Ricœur, *From Text to Action*, 164–83.

[143] For the importance of "natural signs" in Renaissance medicine, see I. Maclean, *Logic, Signs, and Nature in the Renaissance*, 276–81.

human mind? And how does such an understanding of nature as a sign relate to the Christian notion of a sacrament?[144]

These questions hover over any discussion of natural theology, and must be considered in any attempt to clarify how a distinctively Christian natural theology seeks to engage and re-imagine the natural world.[145] Although the research literature prior to 2000 generally held that symbols do not naturally occur in species other than humans,[146] recent research has drawn on the account of symbols developed by the American philosopher and scientist Charles Sanders Peirce (1839–1914) to demonstrate their presence and use in non-human species, suggesting that symbolic competence emerges spontaneously from classical associative learning mechanisms when the conditioned stimuli are self-generated, arbitrary, and socially efficacious.[147] It now seems clear that it is not merely human beings who notice and seek to understand signs within the natural world. While some will resist the use of the verb "interpret" to refer to non-human engagement with nature,[148] a strong case can be made for its propriety in this case.

This naturally leads us to reflect further on Peirce's theory of signs, and how this might inform a natural theology.

C. S. Peirce's Theory of Signs

The theory of signs which Peirce develops is not to be seen as some detached and independent element of his thought, but rather interconnects his thought as a whole.[149] Although other approaches to semiotics have gained a following – such as that of the Swiss linguist Ferdinand de Saussure (1857–1913) – Peirce's approach has secured more attention, particularly within the natural sciences.[150] This partly reflects Peirce's recognition of the importance of the acting subject, seen as an active agent of interpretation of the world.[151] For Peirce, a sign is

> something which stands to somebody for something in some respect or capacity. It addresses somebody, that is, creates in the mind of that person

---

[144] Sherry, "The Sacramentality of Things."

[145] Evans, *Natural Signs and Knowledge of God*, 26–46. For the history of the discipline up to the seventeenth century, see Meier-Oeser, *Die Spur des Zeichens*.

[146] For example, see Deacon, *The Symbolic Species*.

[147] See the landmark paper of Ribeiro *et al.*, "Symbols Are Not Uniquely Human."

[148] Hoffmeyer, "A Biosemiotic Approach to the Question of Meaning," 371–2.

[149] The best study is Short, *Peirce's Theory of Signs*. The historical development of Peirce's semiotics is not straightforward, and Pierce's final statements of his theory are a little confusing at points.

[150] For one influential reworking, see Eco, *Le signe*.

[151] Colapietro, *Peirce's Approach to the Self*, xix.

an equivalent sign, or perhaps a more developed sign. That sign which it creates I call the interpretant of the first sign. The sign stands for something, its object.[152]

Medieval and Saussurian semiotics are essentially dyadic, recognizing a relationship between the thing and its sign, or the word and its associated concept. Peircean semiotics, however, is triadic, recognizing the critically important role of the *interpretant*. Peirce thus does not consider signification to be a simple dyadic relationship between a sign and its object.[153] Rather, he identifies three core constituent elements in any theory of a sign: "the ground, the object, and the interpretant."[154] This could be represented diagrammatically as follows:

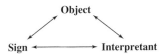

At its basic level, a sign can be conceived as a signifier – for example, smoke as a sign of fire. The object designates whatever is signified – for example, the fire signified by the smoke. The interpretant (generally considered to be the most original and distinctive aspect of Peirce's theory) is best thought of as a translation or development of the original sign, allowing a richer understanding of the object of the sign.[155] The interpretant can be understood as an interpretation in a broader sense of the outcome of an interpretive process, which leads to outcomes which are "emotional, energetic, and logical." A sign may thus lead to an emotional or aesthetic experience, to a specific mode of conduct, or to a new way of understanding things.[156]

Peirce's theory of signs is of considerable interest in itself, and has obvious theological potential, especially on account of the role of the interpretant.[157] Peirce's theory provides a framework which allows the correlation of signs that are transmitted culturally – for example, through a community of discourse – and those which are interpreted instinctively.[158] The role

[152] Peirce, *Collected Papers*, vol. 2, 228. See Short, *Peirce's Theory of Signs*, 29–30. For reflections on how Peirce's semiotics might have theological application, see A. Robinson and Southgate, "Semiotics as a Metaphysical Framework for Christian Theology."
[153] Contrast this with Saussure's definition of a sign as consisting of a "signifier (*signifiant*)" and a "signified (*signifié*)."
[154] Peirce, *Collected Papers*, vol. 2, 229.
[155] Liszka, "Peirce's Interpretant"; Lalor, "The Classification of Peirce's Interpretants."
[156] Short, *Peirce's Theory of Signs*, 345.
[157] See, for example, Power, "Peircian Semiotics, Religion, and Theological Realism"; A. Robinson, *God and the World of Signs*, 15–60.
[158] Nöth, "The Criterion of Habit in Peirce's Definitions of the Symbol," 84–5.

of the interpretant highlights the creative and constructive role of the individual thinker in creating patterns of association between stimuli and outcomes – including certain ways of thinking about the natural world, or experiencing certain emotions in response to it. Although Peirce's reflections on the aesthetic aspects of natural signs are somewhat underdeveloped, they are open to expansion in helpful ways.[159]

So how does this fit into the natural theology project outlined in this volume? For the purposes of this project, Peirce's significance really lies primarily in his proposal that we should think of signs in terms of "habit" rather than convention.[160] We develop a habit of attributing a certain signification to a certain sign in a certain context with which we have become familiar. The interpretant of a symbol is a *habit* – that is to say, a pattern of reflection, or a "generalizing tendency" to enact the same patterns of association on each occasion that an appropriate stimulus is experienced.[161] Peirce's notion of the habit allows him to bridge the two dualisms which have dominated semiotics – namely, the dualism of culture *versus* nature, and the conventional *versus* the innate.

Peirce's approach fits well with the way of interpreting and valuing signs which arises from initiation into, and then inhabitation of, the Christian narrative, and the assimilation of its controlling themes through the formation of habits of association and interpretation in which certain signs within the world elicit certain intellectual and aesthetic outcomes.[162] It is, however, somewhat individualist, focussing primarily on the individual interpreter. Although Peirce does not develop this point, it is clear that his approach opens the way to thinking of the community of faith as *engendering* and *sustaining* a corporate interpretant, offering paradigmatic theological, aesthetic, and moral responses to the natural world.[163]

The need to explore the role of a community in creating and transmitting intrepretations of signs was noted by the Harvard philosopher Josiah Royce (1855–1916). In his influential *The Problem of Christianity* (1913), Royce extended the range of Peirce's semiotics by developing the notion of a "community of interpreters."[164] This development, which some interpreters of Peirce regard as the "single most important contribution" to the extension

[159] Lefebvre, "Peirce's Esthetics" (Peirce regularly used this spelling).

[160] Nöth, "The Criterion of Habit in Peirce's Definitions of the Symbol."

[161] Peirce, *Collected Papers*, vol. 1, 409.

[162] For example, note how the Johannine "I am" sayings develop a rich interpretation of natural signs, which transcend their origins: see A. E. McGrath, *The Open Secret*, 126–33.

[163] Bertilsson, *Peirce's Theory of Inquiry and Beyond*, 135–64, with particular reference to the scientific community.

[164] For a good introduction, see John E. Smith, *Royce's Social Infinite*.

of Peirce's approach,[165] involved the recognition of a social or communitarian dimension to semiotics. The process of interpretation of signs both creates and sustains community: "My life means nothing, either theoretically or practically, unless I am a member of a community."[166] Accepting such interpretative traditions expresses *loyalty* to the community on the one hand, and serves to combat intellectual and imaginative fragmentation on the other.

Royce's notion of a "community of interpretation" could be applied in many ways. One obvious example would be to consider the semiotic function of sacraments, in which the link between "natural" elements – such as water, bread, and wine – is established by a process of social construction, in which the Christian community constructs (on dominical authorization) a semantic link between the elements and spiritual realities.[167] A similar process is at work in the Johannine "I am" sayings, in which natural elements (such as a vine) are given a deeper level of meaning through their association with the symbolic history of Israel.[168]

Yet for the purposes of the present study, the most important outcome is the establishment of a communal interpretation of a sign which is open to multiple readings, none of which is self-evidently authoritative. As we have noted, the moral and aesthetic ambiguity of the natural world is such that it could be held to signify meaninglessness, incoherence, and hopelessness.[169] The classic example of this within the Christian tradition is the *signum crucis* – the "sign of the cross," so central to Christian iconography, to the hope of salvation, and to reflection on the profound ambiguity of the world.[170] This has traditionally been marginalized from discussions of natural theology. It lies beyond the scope of this section to develop a theology of the cross, and explore its bearing on a Christian natural theology.[171] We can, however, begin to note some issues that are illuminated in this way.

---

[165] Apel, *Charles S. Peirce*, 135.

[166] Royce, *The Problem of Christianity*, 357. See further Corrington, "A Comparison of Royce's Key Notion of the Community of Interpretation with the Hermeneutics of Gadamer and Heidegger"; Stikkers, "Royce and Gadamer on Interpretation as the Constitution of Community."

[167] Sherry, "The Sacramentality of Things." Note Sherry's reflections on the limits on natural signs as signifying divine realities.

[168] A. E. McGrath, *The Open Secret*, 126–33.

[169] E.g., Hull, "The God of the Galápagos."

[170] All of these aspects of the cross have been comprehensively studied: see, for example, Dinkler, *Im Zeichen des Kreuzes*; Loo, *Versöhnungsarbeit*; Rolf, "*Crux sola est nostra theologia*."

[171] Martin Luther's interpretation of the *signum crucis* is a classic example of this process of reflection. For detailed exposition of its historical development and theological characteristics, see A. E. McGrath, *Luther's Theology of the Cross*, especially 201–28.

In the following section, we shall consider the place of the "sign of the cross" within a natural theology project.

Natural Theology and the Sign of the Cross

The *signum crucis* affirms that the one "through whom all things were made" is also the one who suffered and died on the cross. The Christian *imaginarium* provides ontological security for an approach to the created order which focusses on the cross as a definitive moment of divine self-disclosure and self-commitment. "The world's pains are God's stigmata."[172] An integral theological connection is established between the creation and the cross.[173] The cross thus provides a point of theological focalization, recognizing both the reality of suffering in natural and human history, and insisting that the God to whom any Christian natural theology bears witness chose to be present in, and be disclosed through, an episode of deliberately inflicted suffering. The natural world is thus more than morally and aesthetically *ambiguous*; it is theologically *opaque*,[174] incapable of disclosing reliable knowledge of God yet capable of being interpreted and accommodated within a revelational framework.

God is thus "hidden" or "concealed" within creation (whether we conceptualize this in terms of our failure to find God, or as an active divine self-concealment).[175] The trajectory of theological reflection is thus from the cross to nature, not the reverse, encompassing both the present analysis of a suffering creation, and the hope of its future transformation and consummation. A natural theology engages nature as it is presently known and experienced; yet this must be set against the eschatological hope of a renewed world, which will displace the broken and damaged reality that we now know, experience, and inhabit.[176] A theology of the cross thus invites us to recognize the penultimacy of the present natural order and our attempts to develop a natural theology based upon it.

---

[172] G. L. Murphy, *The Cosmos in the Light of the Cross*, 87.

[173] T. Peters, "Evolution, Evil, and the Theology of the Cross." For an excellent account of the theological location of evil within a doctrine of creation, see McFarland, *From Nothing*, 111–34.

[174] In using the term "opaque" to refer to nature, I am not denying its potential to refer, but noting the lack of an autonomous clarity on what its referent might be. Cf. Tanner, *God and Creation in Christian Theology*, 11–13.

[175] For Pascal's concerns about natural theology arising from this consideration, see Frigo, "L'evidenza del Dio nascosto." For the idea in Luther, see A. E. McGrath, *Luther's Theology of the Cross*, 219–23. Note Rowan Williams's perceptive comment that the cross is "our central image of the strangeness of God": *A Ray of Darkness*, 101.

[176] G. L. Murphy, *The Cosmos in the Light of the Cross*, 178–95.

Any supposition that nature designates the same entity throughout the economy of salvation is open to question.[177] As Wolfhart Pannenberg (1928–2014) frequently pointed out, the true standpoint from which any aspect of our history is to be viewed must be the end and final goal of that history. The interpretation of nature, as we presently know it, is thus to be framed *eschatologically*, by reminding us that our present endeavors are framed by a view of nature which is both historically situated and theologically relativized. We are invited to undertake a hypothetical experiment, and construct a natural theology based upon the eschatological vision of a renewed nature.

Luther's reflections on the *signum crucis* are perhaps best framed in terms of a semiotic rupture, in which a fractured sign is (mis)interpreted by a sin-darkened human mind. A theory of signs entails the two core elements of the sign itself, and the observer who seeks to interpret it.[178] So what if the former possesses an impaired ability to signify? Or the latter an impaired ability to see? We have already noted how Christian theories of knowledge which make use of the informing metaphors of light and illumination interpret sin partly in terms of a darkening of the human intellect or an attenuated or distorted capacity to see properly.

This point has been discussed throughout Christian history, and we may note one significant contribution in closing. Sir John Davies, in reflecting on the consequences of sin in his poem *Nosce Teipsum* (1599), makes an essentially semiotic point:

> But then grew Reason dark, that she no more,
> Could the fair forms of Good and Truth discern.[179]

Davies here treats the term "form" as equivalent to "sign," lamenting the breaking of the true semantic link between natural signs and their proper meaning.

> What can we know? or what can we discern?
> When Error chokes the windows of the mind,
> The divers forms of things, how can we learn,
> That have been ever from our birth-day blind?[180]

---

[177] A. E. McGrath, *A Fine-Tuned Universe*, 77–82.

[178] See Thomas Aquinas's account of the epistemological processes underlying natural semiotics: Pellerey, "Thomas Aquinas," 90–101.

[179] Davies, *Complete Poems*, vol. 1, 16. For comment on this anthropology in its historical context, see Archdeacon, "The 'Nothing' Trope"; Howard, "Renaissance World-Alienation."

[180] Davies, *Complete Poems*, vol. 1, 18.

For Davies, humanity originally possessed an innate capacity to signify God; yet the capacity of nature to signify, and human beings to discern its signification, having been compromised by sin, requires renewal by grace.

> How can we hope, that through the eye and ear,
> This dying sparkle, in this cloudy place,
> Can recollect these beams of knowledge clear,
> Which were infus'd in the first minds by grace?[181]

Davies himself hoped for the transformation of human vision and the restoration of the semantic link between the natural and the divine – but held that this could only come about by divine transformation, not human learning.[182] Reverting to Josiah Royce's categories, this can be accommodated in the notion of the Church as a "community of interpretation," safeguarding, unfolding and *using* the Christian *imaginarium* to grasp the significance of the world.

This chapter has considered how nature can be considered as a text, image, and sign, and how these may be framed in ways that help us engage with its moral and aesthetical ambiguity. Each of the three approaches noted in this chapter facilitate and focus the process of theological reflection on the natural world, although without entirely resolving some of the more complex issues of interpretation. It has also noted the importance of an engagement with nature – imagined as text, image, and sign – on the basis of explicitly Christian presuppositions, such as the dialectic between sin and grace.

We now turn to reflect on the reasons for developing a natural theology (in the broadest sense of the term), as well as considering how the form of natural theology is shaped by the multiple contexts within which it is embedded, and the motivations which underlie it.

[181] Davies, *Complete Poems*, vol. 1, 18.
[182] For the debate over the role of learning in the English Renaissance, see Block, "Reading Greville's 'Hard Characters.'"

4

Natural Theology
Contexts and Motivations

Why should anyone want to do natural theology, in the broadest sense of the term? There are multiple motivations for the deepened and enriched vision of the everyday world that many see as the goal of a natural theology, whether this is understood as a generalized quest for the transcendent in or through the natural world, or in a more specifically Christian sense of the term, as explored in the present volume. Some of those are cultural; some intellectual; some religious. In this chapter, we shall consider some of these factors, and reflect on how they impact on the promise of natural theology.

Yet alongside these multiple motivations for natural theology we must also recognize the multiple contexts within which these motivations emerge. This chapter offers a brief account of some of these contexts and motivations, noting how they can both stimulate the development of natural theology, and shape the forms which it takes.

The Importance of Cultural Location for Natural Theology

Reflections about natural theology take place within a specific cultural context. So how does the fact that the practice of natural theology is culturally embedded affect its outcomes?[1] The importance of this question had long been recognized in reception history. Both books and their ideas are understood and evaluated in ways that are shaped by the cultural context of those who receive them.[2] The intellectual historian recognizes the

---

[1] For an important analysis, see G. Ward, *Cultural Transformation and Religious Practice*, especially 12–60.
[2] See Withers, *Placing the Enlightenment*, 136–48; Livingstone, "Science, Text, and Space."

Re-Imagining Nature: The Promise of a Christian Natural Theology, First Edition.
Alister E. McGrath.
© 2017 John Wiley & Sons, Ltd. Published 2017 by John Wiley & Sons, Ltd.

"constitutive significance of place in the production of the various meanings" that emerge from a work or set of ideas.[3] A theory or idea thus transmutes as it travels; its place of reception differs from its place of origin, in that they are continually shaped and reshaped according to the local conditions of production, reception, transmission, and resistance.[4] The reception of Darwinism was a culturally embedded enterprise, leading to Darwin's evolutionary theory being understood and evaluated in different ways in different places in the late nineteenth century.[5]

More recently, the celebrated 1934 debate between Karl Barth and Emil Brunner over natural theology (or, more accurately, the epistemic capacities of human nature) took place against a cultural context in which *ideology* – rather than *theology* – was a dominant consideration in framing the terms of the debate.[6] Brunner, located in Switzerland, was simply unable to grasp the *ideological* implications of the rise of Nazi ideology in German following Adolf Hitler's political triumph of 1933, and could not see why these had any bearing on what he considered to be an essentially *theological* debate about the capacity of nature to disclose God as its creator. Barth, alert to the new German political context, saw natural theology as tantamount to intellectual collusion with the Nazi policy of *Gleichschaltung* ("assimilation" or "co-ordination"). For the Church to maintain its distinct Christian identity, it had to seek its norms and foundations in Jesus Christ. With the passing of this cultural moment, many would argue that Barth's ferocious objection to natural theology requires review and revision. Yet the 1934 debate is to be seen as a landmark in the reception of natural theology, in that it demonstrates that cultural, political, and social elements – and not merely theology – shape that reception, sometimes subtly and sometimes decisively. We shall consider other aspects of this 1934 debate in the next chapter.

To the intellectual historian, natural theology has been constructed, interpreted and applied in different manners in different cultural contexts. As we noted earlier (pp. 19–20), the rise of a specific form of natural theology, usually referred to as "physico-theology,"[7] in England during

---

[3] Rupke, "A Geography of Enlightenment," 336. A good example of this can be found in the reception of Einstein's theory of relativity, in which philosophical, cultural, and personal concerns shaped its evaluation: see Glick, "Cultural Issues and the Reception of Relativity."
[4] This was famously argued by Edward Said in his essay "Travelling Theory": see Said, *The World, the Text, and the Critic*, 226–47. For its application, see Secord, "Knowledge in Transit"; M. C. Frank, "Imaginative Geography as a Travelling Concept."
[5] See especially Livingstone, *Dealing with Darwin*.
[6] For a detailed historical and intellectual analysis, see A. E. McGrath, *Emil Brunner*, 90–127.
[7] P. Harrison, "Physico-Theology and the Mixed Sciences"; Ogilvie, "Natural History, Ethics, and Physico-Theology." For the somewhat different approaches which emerged in Germany around this time, see Marcolungo, "Christian Wolff und der physiko-theologische Beweis."

the long eighteenth century is a particularly interesting and illuminating case study illustrating the importance of a social context in shaping attitudes toward natural theology. Physico-theology argued that the regularity and complexity of the natural world – the recognition of which was one of the scientific achievements of this age – affirmed some core themes of the Christian faith, especially the notion of a creator God who governed the world by "laws of nature."[8]

The reasons for this development are relatively well understood. A number of wider cultural factors created a receptivity toward such a form of natural theology in the first half of the long eighteenth century.[9] The political cultural aftermath of the English Civil War and the Glorious Revolution created a climate of suspicion for organized religion – especially Puritanism and Catholicism, both of which were held to be implicated in the religious instability of this period. This led many intellectuals to ask whether there was a way in which knowledge of God might be secured without recourse to ecclesiastical authority. This was linked with a growing concern at this time about the interpretation of the Bible, which came to be seen as problematic, contested, and often opaque. Many in positions of cultural authority and influence thus came to look to the "book of nature" as possessing greater clarity than the "book of Scripture."[10]

The "Age of Reason," which began to take root in England around this time, led some to prefer to think of God in manners that were minimally counterintuitive – especially the "Deist" notion of God as a creator, who avoided further engagement with the created order. Trinitarian notions of God were seen as being at best metaphysically inflated, if not downright irrational. The new emphasis on the "order" and rational transparency of nature, particularly as disclosed by Newtonian mechanics, was seen as confirmatory of the Christian doctrine of creation. The notion of the "laws of nature," which became increasingly accepted at this time, was easily correlated with the idea of God who was the origin and ground of cosmic order.

These developments and others foregrounded one specific notion of natural theology – the idea of a deep resonance between the order of the natural world and the Christian vision of God. Although this was initially framed in terms of the regularity and ordering of the physical world, it was

---

[8] For this important development, see Henry, "Metaphysics and the Origins of Modern Science"; P. Harrison, "The Development of the Concept of Laws of Nature."

[9] See the analysis in Westfall, "The Scientific Revolution of the Seventeenth Century"; A. E. McGrath, *Darwinism and the Divine*, 49–73; Mandelbrote, "The Uses of Natural Theology in Seventeenth-Century England."

[10] The development of the image of the "book of nature" predates the "Age of Reason": see especially Mews, "The World as Text."

soon extended to the complexity of the biological world. This "physico-theology" was not framed in terms of a rational demonstration of the existence of God from first principles, but was generally seen as an affirmation of a resonance or congruence between human observation of the regularities of nature on the one hand, and the intellectual framework provided by the Christian faith on the other.[11]

This strongly rational and cognitive approach to natural theology resonated with the cultural mood of the day, especially within scientific circles. Thomas Sprat's *History of the Royal Society* is widely regarded as a manifesto of the new scientific confidence of the age.[12] Science was about gaining an objective, mathematized knowledge of nature, from which such subjective intrusions as rhetoric or imagination were to be excluded as a matter of principle. In the end, this fiction could not be sustained; the role of the imagination in the development and justification of scientific theories is now widely accepted.[13] Yet during the long eighteenth century, this view of scientific knowledge prevailed, and helped shape the distinctive form of natural theology which emerged from this context.

For reasons such as those noted above, "physico-theology" is to be regarded as a form of natural theology which was adapted to the needs and opportunities of this specific situation; it would not have been possible in England during the sixteenth century (when the natural sciences had yet to emerge fully), nor the later nineteenth century (when the rise of Darwinism was seen to erode the plausibility of the ordering of nature at the biological level).[14] As it traveled across the historical landscape, natural theology assumed different forms as it found different habitats. "Physico-theology" is one of these. But it is not to be regarded as normative or definitive; it is simply the culturally embedded form of natural theology which emerged at that place in history, reflecting specific local conditions.

The reception of natural theology throughout the two thousand years of Christian history suggests that both the manner in which this notion is understood and the evaluation of its legitimacy and merits are shaped by cultural factors which go beyond pure theological reflection. Both the *performer* and the *assessor* of natural theology are culturally embedded. The cultural context can thus, as the rise of "physico-theology" indicates,

---

[11] For the slightly different approaches to "physico-theology" found in Paley's *Natural Theology* (1802) and the *Bridgewater Treatises* of the 1830s, see A. E. McGrath, *Darwinism and the Divine*, 85–127; Topham, "Biology in the Service of Natural Theology."

[12] McGuire, "The Rhetoric of Sprat's Defence of the Royal Society."

[13] Downie, "Science and the Imagination in the Age of Reason"; Calver, "Sir Peter Medawar"; Midgley, *Science and Poetry*, 38–41.

[14] Peterfreund, *Turning Points in Natural Theology from Bacon to Darwin*, 109–29; A. E. McGrath, *Darwinism and the Divine*, 155–71.

provide a motivation for affirming natural theology; it can also, as the Barth–Brunner debate of 1934 suggests, cause it to be viewed with suspicion.

Yet most importantly, the critical role of the context within which natural theology is practiced allows us to understand how substantially the same theological trajectory can take such dissimilar forms in different situations, reflecting the cultural challenges and opportunities arising from specific audiences and environments. A coherent Christian natural theology project designates a *spectrum* of possibilities; the form that it takes is shaped by the context of its articulation and implementation. A Christian natural theology thus exists in an interactive relationship with a theology of *place*,[15] and cannot be presented as some universal ahistorical method, detached from the worlds of place and history.

A New Vocational Space: Natural Theology as a Religious Calling

An important stimulus for the study of natural theology emerged in the sixteenth century, through an erosion of the medieval notion of the "spiritual" and "secular" estates.[16] This development was well under way in the corporate world of European imperial cities in the 1490s; it was, however, given a new momentum by the rise of Protestantism. One of the defining themes of Martin Luther's 1520 reforming manifesto "An Appeal to the Nobility of the German Nation" was that all believers were called to be priests, and to exercise a spiritual ministry in the secular world. Although Luther's program can be argued to have ended up secularizing the sacred, his intention was clearly to sacralize the secular. Believers were called to serve and live out their faith in the secular realm.

The debates about the links between the correlation of Protestantism and secularism in western European cultural history remain unresolved;[17] nevertheless, one thing is reasonably clear. The Protestant Reformation gave a theological justification and stimulus to a process in which Christians set out to explore various spheres of life, each of which they regarded as being governed by God according to its own distinct logic – such as economics, the natural sciences, and politics. Whatever else the Reformation may have brought about, it created new vocational spaces – that is, areas of life in

---

[15] J. Inge, *A Christian Theology of Place*, 59–122.
[16] Elshtain, *Sovereignty*, 82. For a classic analysis of Luther's notion of a secular calling, see Weber, *Gesammelte Aufsätze zur Religionssoziologie*, vol. 1, 63–84.
[17] For a good overview, see A. J. Carroll, *Protestant Modernity*; A. J. Carroll, "Disenchantment, Rationality, and the Modernity of Max Weber."

which an authentically Christian calling could be pursued. Christians felt increasingly drawn to the natural sciences as a means of exploring and appreciating God's created order.

A good example of this is provided by the astronomer Johannes Kepler (1571–1630), who participated in this new vocational space. Kepler openly spoke of the sanctity of his scientific calling, proposing that the world was "the temple of God" and "the book of nature," which allowed new spiritual insights into the wisdom of God.[18] For Kepler, to investigate nature was to engage in the worship of God.[19] John Calvin was one of many Protestant theologians who stressed the religious motivations of the natural sciences: to study God's creation was to gain a deepened appreciation of God's wisdom.[20] The natural order – as God's creation – renders God visible, mirroring his divinity.[21]

It is not difficult to see how such a theological framework created a motivation for the study of nature, which was expressed – although in different ways – in the pursuit of both the natural sciences and natural theology.[22] Scientific investigation of nature on the one hand, and religious contemplation of the natural world on the other, were both seen as theologically legitimate and spiritually enriching projects. The case of England during the seventeenth century is particularly illuminating. Many leading scientists of this age – such as Robert Boyle – saw their research as an expression of their religious devotion.[23] The Christian *imaginarium* provided them with a stimulus for reading the "book of nature" in the pursuit of spiritual wisdom. Boyle himself proposed that experimental philosophy was to be seen as a genuinely religious activity, and that those who investigate nature's structures and operations are "priests of nature."[24] Natural theology served to confirm the rationality of religious belief (a point to which we shall return presently: pp. 173–80), to encourage piety, and to enhance human wisdom. "Boyle believed not only that natural philosophy provided evidence for the existence, power, and wisdom of God,

---

[18] Funkenstein, *Theology and the Scientific Imagination from the Middle Ages to the Seventeenth Century*, 3–9.

[19] Lindberg, "The Genesis of Kepler's Theory of Light," 38–40.

[20] Schreiner, *The Theater of His Glory*; Young, *John Calvin and the Natural World*; Partee, *The Theology of John Calvin*, 78–80.

[21] Zachman, "The Universe as the Living Image of God."

[22] Note also the points made by Vidal and Kleeberg, "Knowledge, Belief, and the Impulse to Natural Theology."

[23] For the best recent survey, see P. Harrison, "Sentiments of Devotion and Experimental Philosophy in Seventeenth-Century England." The classic study remains H. Fisch, "The Scientist as Priest."

[24] H. Fisch, "The Scientist as Priest."

but also that it promoted piety and particular virtues."[25] Although Boyle was aware of certain epistemological challenges in correlating the scientific investigation and religious contemplation of the natural world,[26] he clearly regarded these two enterprises as being interconnected and mutually supportive.

If there was a "Golden Age" of natural theology in England, most would see this as being the long eighteenth century (1688–1815), during which natural theology gradually lost its apologetic appeal, and became increasingly detached from any distinctively Christian outlook.[27] Yet our concern here is not to document the reasons for the decline in the fortunes of English natural theology, but to account for its rise in the first place.[28] One of the factors that clearly played an important role in its rise was the creation of a new vocational space, in which natural theology emerged as a form of theology that could be undertaken by a devotionally motivated and scientifically informed laity, free from ecclesiastical control.

The Wasteland: Natural Theology and the Recovery of a Lost Nature

The period 1790–1830 witnessed dramatic social and political changes across western Europe. The French Revolution of 1789 called into question the stability and permanence of existing social structures, plunging the region into an uncertainty which was only partially resolved with the end of the Napoleonic wars. Yet this political insecurity was accompanied by wider changes in society, particularly through the rise of industrialization and economic modernization which radically altered western culture, leading to emigration from the countryside to urban industrial centers.[29]

Working-class families who settled in industrial cities often found themselves longing for the countryside or seaside, partly as a response to the grim realities of urban life, and partly as an attempt to reconnect with a lost past, so easily idealized. Something of this sense of dislocation and yearning can be

[25] P. Harrison, "Sentiments of Devotion and Experimental Philosophy in Seventeenth-Century England," 127.
[26] MacIntosh, "Robert Boyle's Epistemology."
[27] For some of the reasons, see Odom, "The Estrangement of Celestial Mechanics and Religion"; F. M. Turner, "The Secularization of the Social Vision of British Natural Theology."
[28] See A. E. McGrath, *Darwinism and the Divine*, 49–84.
[29] Groh, *Die Gesellschaftskritik der politischen Romantik*, 52–64.

seen in Coleridge's poem "Frost at Midnight," which contrasts the barren industrial cityscape with the beauty of the night sky:

> For I was reared
> In the great city, pent 'mid cloisters grim,
> And saw nought lovely but the sky and stars.[30]

Nature came to be seen as an aesthetic oasis, to be contrasted with bleak industrial landscapes.

The quest for the seaside mirrors this longing to reconnect with something deeper. The "discovery of the seaside" thus parallels the rise of the Industrial Revolution.[31] Paradoxically, the "excursion trains" laid on to allow urban populations to travel to the seaside to be refreshed by the beauty of nature were themselves one of the most important outcomes of – and contributors to – the Industrial Revolution.[32]

For Karl Marx, this process of industrialization led to the alienation or estrangement (*Entfremdung*) of individuals from core aspects of their basic human nature (*Gattungswesen*) as a result of social stratification.[33] Numerous attempts were made in the nineteenth century to reduce this alienation through a facilitated reconnection with nature, developed in response to the new social realities of the industrial age – such as the construction of "Botanic Gardens," and the rise of the "Garden City" movement.[34]

The rise of the modern age led to both the intellectual reduction of nature to a set of abstractions, and a surge in industrialization which brought about the physical despoliation of nature. Where nature was once seen as a threat to humanity, which could be overcome through the establishment of cities, the "grey, gritty hopelessness"[35] of industrialized urban landscapes created a desire to reconnect with the unspoiled simplicity of nature – partly as a distraction from the harsh realities of urban life, yet mainly for spiritual refreshment.[36]

This occasionally led to some intriguing paradoxes – such as William Paley's appeal to the technology of the Industrial Revolution (most

---

[30] Coleridge, "Frost at Midnight," lines 51–3. Cf. Harter, *Coleridge's Philosophy of Faith*, 151.

[31] Corbin, *The Lure of the Sea*, 57–185.

[32] Pick, *Building Jerusalem*, 169–91.

[33] Ollman, *Alienation*, 171–233.

[34] See, for example, N. C. Johnson, "Grand Design(er)s"; Meacham, *Regaining Paradise*; Livesey, "Assemblage Theory, Gardens and the Legacy of the Early Garden City Movement"; Tabarasi, *Der Landschaftsgarten als Lebensmodell*, 344–474.

[35] Lawrence, *Lady Chatterley's Lover*, 149.

[36] See, for example, Knoepflmacher and Tennyson, eds., *Nature and the Victorian Imagination*.

famously, a watch, but also a stocking-loom and carding-machine) in exploring the notion of the divine design and construction of the world – two ideas that Paley brought together in the single notion of God as "artificer."[37] Paley's natural theology made use of some decidedly technological analogies in securing its intended outcomes.

An interest in natural theology can thus be understood, at least in part, as a response to a decline in human proximity to nature itself.[38] The increasing *distance* from and *unfamiliarity* with nature, coupled with a sense that it was under threat, became a stimulus to reflect further on its significance. A sense of loss of contact with the natural world led to a renewed concern to affirm its importance, and rediscover its deeper significance. Romantic poets such as Novalis and Joseph von Eichendorff saw both the physical process of industrialization and the scientific process of what would later become known as "disenchantment" as robbing nature of its proper meaning and status.[39] For Eichendorff, it was necessary to find *das Zauberwort* – a way of seeing nature which unlocked its hidden meaning, and allowed its suppressed melodies to be heard.[40] In England, John Keats protested against the reduced account of the natural world he held to be entailed by the scientific method, which conquered "all mysteries by rule and line," reducing an awe-inspiring world to a "dull catalogue of common things."[41]

Perhaps these poetic concerns might be overstated or misplaced. Yet they help us grasp the continuing appeal of natural theology, in the broad sense of the term, as a way of grasping and preserving a deeper understanding of the natural world. To note a theme which is significant in Virgil's *Aeneid*, a natural theology can establish a "cosmic setting,"[42] which frames deeper discussions of identity, place, and meaning.

A related longing for natural beauty and purity can be seen emerging in the aftermath of the First World War. The devastation caused by this war in western Europe led to a growing feeling that the industrial processes of modernity created a "wasteland" in a double sense – both in terms of the continuing destruction of the beauty of nature in order to produce industrial commodities, and in the use of such commodities – especially explosive

---

[37] F. M. Turner, "The Secularization of the Social Vision of British Natural Theology."

[38] Gorringe, "The Decline of Nature," 205–8.

[39] Groh, *Die Gesellschaftskritik der politischen Romantik*, 87–140; Tabarasi, *Der Landschaftsgarten als Lebensmodell*, 373–43.

[40] A. E. McGrath, "Schläft ein Lied in allen Dingen?" For further discussion of the theme of longing in Eichendorff, see Löhr, *Sehnsucht als poetisches Prinzip bei Joseph von Eichendorff*. 247–353.

[41] For comment on these lines from "Lamia," see Motion, *Keats*, 431–7; Fisher, *Wonder, the Rainbow, and the Aesthetics of Rare Experiences*, 87–93.

[42] Hardie, *Virgil's Aeneid*, 66–8.

ordnance – in the wartime devastation of cities and rural landscapes. T. S. Eliot's *The Waste Land* (1922) expressed a sense of despair and despondency at the seeming incoherence, fragmentation, and meaninglessness of the modern world.[43] While the work's poetic structure might suggest unity and coherence, the thematic substance emphasizes disintegration and dissonance. Eliot's *Waste Land* helps us to grasp one of the motivations toward returning to nature as a source of wisdom – a collapse of trust in the capacity of "civilization" to deliver a coherent account of reality. Others made the same point in the aftermath of the Great War. In 1926, the great German poet and novelist Hermann Hesse (1877–1962) argued that, where there was once a sense of intellectual and moral coherence to reality, there now seemed to be only a mere aggregation of intellectual fashions and the "transitory values of the day [*vergängliche Tageswerte*]."[44] Where was something deeper and more permanent to be found?

These cultural anxieties might not lead to a fully developed natural theology; they nevertheless initiate a process of questioning and exploring, which opens up some of the great themes of natural theology, most notably that there exists some deeper ordering to the created world which can inform human thinking about truth, beauty, and goodness through a human "attunement" to the divine wisdom embedded within the created order.[45] At this point, a human question might find a Christian answer, in that Christianity provides a web of meaning, a deep belief in the fundamental interconnectedness of things, which holds that there is a hidden web of meaning and connectedness behind the ephemeral and incoherent world that we experience – a matter which needs further discussion.

Wonder and Mystery: Transcendent Experiences

The phenomenon of transcendent experiences is widely believed to represent a stimulus to natural theology.[46] Few have failed to experience a sense of wonder at the beauty of nature or the vastness of the universe. Those who have known such an experience often feel that they have somehow entered into the realm of the extraordinary; that the mundane world has given way to, or acted as a threshold to, something beyond it. William Wordsworth tried to capture this idea in the phrase "spots of time" – rare yet precious moments of

---

[43] G. Smith, "Memory and Desire in *The Waste Land*."

[44] Hesse, "Die Sehnsucht unser Zeit nach einer Weltanschauung."

[45] On this idea, see Fiddes, *Seeing the World and Knowing God*, 116–17.

[46] A. E. McGrath, *The Open Secret*, 23–79; Haldane, "Philosophy, the Restless Heart, and the Meaning of Theism." Note that the phrase "transcendent experiences" is widely used to mean something like "experiences which are interpreted to relate to a transcendent reality."

profound feeling and imaginative strength, in which individuals grasp something of ultimate significance within their inner being. Michael Mayne wrote of this sense of wonder while sojourning in the Swiss Alps:

> My subject is wonder, and my starting point is so obvious it often escapes us. It is me, sitting at a table looking out on the world. It is the fact that I exist, that there is anything at all. It is the *givenness* that astonishes: the fact that the mountains, the larch tree, the gentian, the jay, *exist*, and that someone called *me* is here to observe them.[47]

The poet Goethe suggested that such a sense of wonder, even astonishment (*das Erstaunen*), is to be seen as an end in itself.[48] But for others, it is a starting point for imaginative exploration and aesthetic discovery. Might the mystery of our universe be something that can be unfolded,[49] opening up new ways of thinking and living? Aristotle held that a sense of wonder (*thaumazein*) precipitated a journey of discovery, in which our horizons are expanded, our understanding deepened, and our eyes opened.[50]

The apologetic importance of such experiences has long been known. In his *De orbis terrae Concordia* (1544), Guillaume Postel (1510–81) argued for the truth of Christianity by showing its fundamental congruence with natural human religious instincts and insights. Such "feelings" are widely encountered across human culture, and are generally designated "transcendent experiences."[51] Sometimes, these experiences are triggered by natural wonders such as vast landscapes, or awe-inspiring phenomena such as rainbows.[52] In a review of the theoretical literature on awe, Keltner and Haidt proposed that awe-eliciting stimuli are characterized by two features: perceptual vastness and need for accommodation.[53] The term "vast" is not restricted to great physical size – as in a landscape – but to any stimulus that challenges one's accustomed frame of reference in some dimension. They often evoke a sense of longing to grasp some deeper truths or secrets which

---

[47] Mayne, *This Sunrise of Wonder*, 15. See also Peterson, *Christ Plays in Ten Thousand Places*, 51–129.

[48] Eckermann, *Gespräche mit Goethe*, vol. 2, 50. For Hölderlin's approach, see Kreuzer, "Die Sphäre die Höher ist, als die des Menschen." For the argument that it is a sense of wonder, not of the sublime, that drives scientific investigation, see Fisher, *Wonder, the Rainbow, and the Aesthetics of Rare Experiences*, 1–17.

[49] Evans, *Why Believe?*, 32–60.

[50] Aristotle, *Metaphysics*, 982b. See also Plato, *Theaetetus*, 154b–155c. For useful reflections on this theme, see J. Miller, *In the Throe of Wonder*, 11–52.

[51] Roy, *Transcendent Experiences*; Hay, *Something There*.

[52] Fisher, *Wonder, the Rainbow, and the Aesthetics of Rare Experiences*; Shiota, Keltner, and Mossman, "The Nature of Awe."

[53] Keltner and Haidt, "Approaching Awe."

seem to be intimated in or through the natural world, and are often associated with natural theology. Something *within* nature intimates that there is something *beyond* nature. Implicit within a Christian natural theology is a semiotics of nature, in which nature is understood as a system of natural signs – such as a sense of wonder – intimating the existence of some transcendent reality.[54]

The fundamental inability of the human mind to take in the vastness of nature is one of the underlying causes of a sense of awe in its presence.[55] As Mayne rightly notes, the fundamental irreducibility of nature inevitably subverts the adequacy or ultimacy of any attempts to categorize or represent it. The novelist John Fowles (1926–2005) suggested that the elusiveness of nature calls into question whether science can ever hope to give us a full account of its mystery.

> It, this namelessness, is beyond our science and our arts because its secret is being, not saying. Its greatest value to us is that it cannot be reproduced . . . All experience of it through surrogate and replica, through selected image, gardened word, through other eyes and minds, betrays or banishes its reality.[56]

Such experiences of wonder, though transient and ineffable, are perceived to be enormously significant. As Michael Mayne discovered during his pilgrimage of discovery in the Swiss Alps, such epiphanic "moments" remain as "vivid in my mind as on the day I first felt them."[57] For William James, such an experience could not be described adequately in words. "Its quality must be directly experienced; it cannot be imparted or transferred to others."[58] One of the most familiar descriptions of such transient moments of significance is found in C. S. Lewis's notion of joy – an elusive longing for something of supreme significance, which tantalizingly refused to be satisfied by anything transient or created, and which could not be captured by words.[59] Lewis believed that such experiences shattered the imaginative hegemony of a "glib and shallow rationalism."[60] Similarly, Salman Rushdie suggests that such intuitions of transcendence were to be seen as the "flight of the human spirit outside the confines of its material, physical existence."[61]

---

[54] Evans, *Natural Signs and Knowledge of God*, 26–46.
[55] See the detailed analysis in Keltner and Haidt, "Approaching Awe."
[56] Fowles, *The Tree*, 93–4. See further Barnum, "The Nature of John Fowles."
[57] Mayne, *This Sunrise of Wonder*, 43.
[58] James, *The Varieties of Religious Experience*, 380–1; Otto, *The Idea of the Holy*, 5.
[59] A. E. McGrath, "Arrows of Joy"; Arnell, "On Beauty, Justice and the Sublime in C. S. Lewis's *Till We Have Faces*."
[60] Lewis, *Surprised by Joy*, 197.
[61] Rushdie, *Is Nothing Sacred?*, 8.

Yet although such an "awestruck wonderment" cannot be expressed in words, it nevertheless evokes an intellectual quest for understanding and fulfilment. To rephrase Anselm of Canterbury, it can be thought of as *reverentia quaerens intellectum* or *mysterium quaerens intellectum*. Natural theology may well represent a flawed attempt to capture something of the truth, beauty, and goodness of a complex and fundamentally irreducible nature – but the legitimacy of such an attempt lies beyond doubt.

Re-Enchantment: Sustaining a Sense of Wonder

In the previous section, I noted the sense of wonder that spontaneously results from an encounter with the beauty of nature, often framed in terms of "transcendent experiences." But can such a sense of wonder be sustained? Or is it an ephemeral moment of fleeting insight, which vanishes before we have fully appreciated it? Can we recover such a naïve sense of wonder and the sense of longing or yearning that it so often evokes? Or are we left, as C. S. Lewis once put it, with a world that has "turned commonplace again," or was "only stirred by a longing for the longing that had just ceased"?[62] One motivation for natural theology is the longing to recover or recreate such a lost sense of wonder at the natural world.

One major cause of this imaginative failure is an overfamiliarity with the natural world, which dulls us to its beauty and wonder. An excellent example of this erosion of a sense of wonder through a process of habituation is found in Johanna Spyri's classic *Heidi* (1880), which tells of a young girl's first encounters with the beauty of the Swiss Alps, often in the company of Peter the goatherd. Heidi is amazed when she first sees the *Alpenglühen* – an alpine atmospheric condition observed at sunrise and sunset which leaves the foreground in shadow, while the mountain peaks turn a brilliant red. Excited, she tells Peter that the mountains are on fire.[63] Peter, however, has seen this astonishing phenomenon many times before. "It's always like that." It has lost its sense of wonder, having become routine and unremarkable.

A similar story is told in Mark Twain's 1883 reminiscences of his time as a steamboat pilot on the Mississippi River before the American Civil War, which include one of the finest literary descriptions of the evaporation of a sense of awe and delight in the presence of nature as a result of habitual overfamiliarity. In his early period, Twain found it easy to appreciate the wonder of the Mississippi's depths and raw beauty.

---

[62] Lewis, *Surprised by Joy*, 16.
[63] Spyri, *Heidis Lehr- und Wanderjahre*, 45. For comment on and illustration of this *Alpenglühen*, see Maurer, "Warum wie alle das Heidi lieben."

> The face of the water, in time, became a wonderful book – a book that was a dead language to the uneducated passenger, but which told its mind to me without reserve, delivering its most cherished secrets as clearly as if it uttered them with a voice. . . . There never was so wonderful a book written by man; never one whose interest was so absorbing, so unflagging, so sparkingly renewed with every re-perusal.[64]

Twain's description of a sunset stands out as one of the most lyrical portrayals of the awesome. He stood, spellbound, "like one bewitched," absorbing the sight "in a speechless rapture." This world was new to him, and he had never seen anything like this before.

Yet gradually Twain lost any sense of the "glories and the charms which the moon and the sun and the twilight wrought upon the river's face." His inhabitation of this new world made it overfamiliar and routine. As he "mastered the language" of the great river, and came to "know every trifling feature that bordered the great river as familiarly as I knew the letters of the alphabet," Twain found that he had lost something. "All the grace, the beauty, the poetry had gone out of the majestic river!"[65] Yet, more disturbingly, he found that what he had lost was irretrievable. "I had lost something which could never be restored to me while I lived." The Mississippi had not changed; the change lay within Twain himself, as he slowly changed from being a young apprentice overwhelmed by the beauty of the river to an experienced riverboat pilot concerned to know its currents and avoid its dangers. He found himself unable to recapture or recreate his early naïve sense of wonder, which lingered only as a nostalgic memory.

Twain's concerns are echoed in Shelley's assertion that David Hume's account of causality reduced the level of human engagement with nature to that of "habitual noticing," devoid of any sense of wonder or amazement.[66] So can a "habitual noticing" be transformed into an attentive engagement? A Christian natural theology helps us to re-imagine nature, and develop a visual acuity that allows an imaginative renewal and refreshment of our beholding of the natural world, enabling us to recover at least something of its wonder and beauty. A core theme of any responsible natural theology is attentiveness to the natural world, which is seen – and hence valued – as God's creation. This involves an act of commitment, often expressed in terms of concentration and focus – as in William James's celebrated definition of the notion.

---

[64] Twain, *Life on the Mississippi*, 94. For an analysis of this work, see Hellwig, *Mark Twain's Travel Literature*, 98–115.
[65] Twain, *Life on the Mississippi*, 95. For reflections on this transition, see Coulombe, *Mark Twain and the American West*, 120–1.
[66] Wilson, *Shelley and the Apprehension of Life*, 92.

[Attention] is the taking possession by the mind, in clear and vivid form, of one out of what seem several simultaneously possible objects or trains of thought. Focalization, concentration, of consciousness are of its essence. It implies withdrawal from some things in order to deal effectively with others.[67]

James himself provides an example of his own inability to see something clearly, showing an inattentiveness on his part as he reflected on a landscape in North Carolina. In his perceptive essay, "On a Certain Blindness in Human Beings," James notes how he intuitively reacted against a scene which seemed to him to represent "unmitigated squalor." Poorly constructed log cabins had been made out of felled trees. The stumps of these trees had been burned, rather than uprooted, and new trees planted haphazardly. Yet further reflection caused James to question this initial judgment. He had failed to see that, to those who lived there, this scene "spoke of honest sweat, persistent toil and final reward." His judgment had missed "the root of the matter." A more attentive reading of what might otherwise seem to be "a mere ugly picture on the retina" leads to it being recognized and appreciated as "a symbol redolent with moral memories" and "a very paean of duty, struggle, and success."[68]

A natural theology provides a way of seeing nature which accentuates the importance of *attentiveness*, rather than "habitual noticing."[69] James's first-person view of selective consciousness or awareness has been developed by a number of writers. Simone Weil (1909–43) argued that proper attention leads to a transformation of spiritual vision, opening up new ways of understanding the world and behaving within it. Weil's approach was developed by Iris Murdoch (1919–90), who defined attentiveness as "a just and loving gaze directed upon an individual reality."[70] One of Murdoch's fundamental concerns was to "unself" the perception of reality, thus subverting the hegemony of self-interest that she regarded as being integral to human observation. Beauty challenged such self-interest, offering a means for the "checking of selfishness in the interest of seeing the real."[71] Murdoch's approach is easily adapted to the natural world, encouraging us to pay attention to *it*, rather than to ourselves.

---

[67] James, *The Principles of Psychology*, 403–4.

[68] James, "On a Certain Blindness in Human Beings," 150–2.

[69] Styles, *The Psychology of Attention*, 15–79.

[70] Murdoch, *The Sovereignty of Good*, 34. On Murdoch's development of Weil's approach, see Bowden, "Ethical Attention"; Lovibond, *Iris Murdoch, Gender and Philosophy*, 28–46.

[71] Murdoch, *The Sovereignty of Good*, 63. There are interesting parallels between Murdoch's notion of "attentiveness" and Albert Borgmann's concept of "focal practice": Borgmann, *Technology and the Character of Contemporary Life*, 196–210. For a helpful theological reflection on Borgmann's approach, see Waters, *Christian Moral Theology in an Emerging Technoculture*, 81–101.

Perhaps we must be realistic about what can be achieved. Epiphanic movements, like a bird in flight, can never be frozen or captured. Twain's comments bear witness to the "receding thresholds of wonder,"[72] as routinization, habituation, and the development of automatic or reflexive habits of thought impact negatively on our appreciation of the beauty and wonder of nature.[73] If our loss of wonder in the presence of nature reflects overfamiliarity, perhaps we could retrieve at least something of that experience through the literary technique that we now call "defamiliarization," but which was well known to poets at least as far back as the eighteenth century.[74] Sadly, further discussion of this point must remain beyond the scope of this volume; it does, however, represent an obvious means of expanding this vision of natural theology. In the final chapter of this work, which explores the promise of a Christian natural theology, we shall consider how a natural theology can be developed into a spirituality of nature, picking up on some of these points (pp. 163–8).

We now turn to consider a classic motivation for developing a natural theology – the need to affirm and demonstrate the fundamental rationality of religious faith, especially in intellectual or cultural contexts which are suspicious of religious authorities and institutions.

The Rational Transparency of Nature and Faith

Western culture treats rationality as an intellectual virtue, while conceding that the term can be understood in a multiplicity of manners.[75] That we should be "epistemically responsible" lies beyond dispute;[76] the difficulty lies in articulating and applying the criteria of adjudication which are to be used in achieving this virtue – criteria which might reasonably be said to include coherence, being based on good reasons, and fitting the evidence. The notion of "rationality," however, requires more careful probing.

From the outset, the approaches to natural theology developed during the "long eighteenth century" were predicated on the assumption of the rational transparency of nature – that is to say, a belief in both the rational ordering of the natural world, and the capacity of human reason to discern and represent this.[77] The rational transparency of nature or the contemplation of

---

[72] I borrow this phrase from Kirshenblatt-Gimblett, *Destination Culture*, 72.

[73] See the findings of Miall and Kuiken, "Foregrounding, Defamiliarization, and Affect."

[74] Kareem, *Eighteenth-Century Fiction and the Reinvention of Wonder*, 6–20.

[75] Note especially the comments of Mortimore and Maund, "Rationality in Belief."

[76] See Kornblith, "Justified Belief and Epistemically Responsible Action."

[77] See P. Harrison, *The Fall of Man and the Foundations of Science*, 46; Mandelbrote, "The Uses of Natural Theology in Seventeenth-Century England," 455.

the beauty of nature came to be seen as evidential grounds for some form of belief in God.[78] In one sense, this approach to natural theology reflects the rationalized view of nature characteristic of modernity, characterized by Max Weber as "disenchantment." As Weber noted, this involved seeing religion as the realm of the irrational, and science as that of the rational.

> The general result of the modern form of a thoroughly rationalizing view of the world [*Durchrationalisierung des Weltbildes*] . . . has been that the more this type of rationality has progressed, from the standpoint of the intellectual shaping [*intellektuelle Formung*] of a view of the world, the more religion has been shifted into the realm of the irrational.[79]

Classical forms of natural theology, such as "physico-theology," could be conceived as countering this retreat into the "realm of the irrational" by offering a rationalized intellectual articulation of the world, in which its potentially irrational or non-rational aspects were marginalized.

This motivation for natural theology rests on a belief that the perception of irrationality is destructive for the cultural plausibility of Christianity. Yet while the importance of this point must be noted, the limits of such a rational comprehension of nature must also be conceded. There is a sense in which natural theology forces us to recognize the limits of our knowledge of God. Victor Preller's perceptive and influential reading of Thomas Aquinas suggested that the "human intellect is ordered to a reality it cannot know, and is seeking an intelligibility it cannot understand."[80] God lies outside the realm of intelligibility, as this term is commonly understood.[81]

Furthermore, there are difficulties in articulating a coherent notion of rationality. We have already noted that the patterns and norms of human reasoning have been shaped by historical and cultural factors, and are often embedded within certain traditions of rationality. To be "rational"

---

[78] For example, see Topham, "Biology in the Service of Natural Theology"; Mandelbrote, "The Uses of Natural Theology in Seventeenth-Century England"; Peterfreund, *Turning Points in Natural Theology from Bacon to Darwin*. On the appeal to the beauty of nature in general, see Dubay, *The Evidential Power of Beauty*, 181–207.

[79] Weber, *Gesammelte Aufsätze zur Religionssoziologie*, vol. 1, 253. Note also 564: The growth of "rationalism in empirical science increasingly pushes religion from the realm of the rational into that of the irrational." For an analysis, see A. J. Carroll, "Disenchantment, Rationality, and the Modernity of Max Weber."

[80] Preller, *Divine Science and the Science of God*, 179–80. For the development of Preller's analysis in later accounts of natural theology, see Hauerwas, *Performing the Faith*, 112–20; R. Williams, *The Edge of Words*, 8–9.

[81] Preller, *Divine Science and the Science of God*, 154. For Preller's influence on post-liberal theology at this point, see Cathey, *God in Postliberal Perspective*, 152–6.

often means "conforming to dominant viewpoints," representing a confession of cultural pliability rather than an assertion of intellectual independence. Alvin Plantinga rightly noted how the notion of "rationality" is shaped by controlling presuppositions (not always explicitly acknowledged) about the nature of the world and human beings.[82]

The idea of a single, universal, and omnicompetent human reason may remain an important aspiration; it nevertheless faces considerable difficulties. We have already commented on the diversity of human modes of reasoning; we must now note the large research literature, especially in the field of cognitive psychology, which argues that the human reasoning process can be subject to hidden cognitive biases which shape its outcomes, leading to what are essentially irrational outcomes being seen as if they were rational.[83] We cannot, following some writers of the eighteenth century, use (or presuppose) reason to defend reason, in that the *assumed* functional validity of rational processes is used to *demonstrate* their theoretical validity. In effect, this is a form of fideism, which is locked into a circular set of assumptions which blur the critical lines of demarcation between presuppositions and conclusions.

Yet despite this diversity of understandings of what it means to show that something is "rational," it remains important to be able to identify criteria of judgment by which the rationality of a belief may be assessed. Two of the most important such criteria are correspondence with the external world, and internal theoretical coherence. A Christian natural theology can be seen as affirming the rationality of faith by offering a *theōria*, a manner of beholding and imagining the world, which corresponds to the world as we see it, and whose internal elements are seen to be consistent and coherent.[84]

Some earlier approaches to natural theology suggest that close observation of the natural world leads unproblematically to belief in God. This is certainly the impression left on the reader of William Paley's *Natural Theology* (1802). Paley's approach often focussed on aspects of human anatomy, which was

---

[82] Plantinga, *Warranted Christian Belief*, 190. For a criticism of Plantinga's approach, see Oppy, "Natural Theology." For Bernard Lonergan's discussion of such controlling assumptions, see Lonergan, "The General Character of the Natural Theology of Insight," 6; Mathews, *Lonergan's Quest*, 438–47.

[83] For discussion, see M. A. Bishop, "In Praise of Epistemic Irresponsibility"; Goldman, *Epistemology and Cognition*, 181–369; Stanovich and West, "Individual Differences in Reasoning"; Piattelli-Palmarini, *Inevitable Illusions*, 17–30; Stanovich, *Rationality and the Reflective Mind*, 6–25.

[84] I have explored these issues in relation to both the physical and biological sciences: A. E. McGrath, *A Fine-Tuned Universe*, 51–60; A. E. McGrath, *Darwinism and the Divine*, 185–267.

held to disclose evidence of purpose and design.[85] However, when Paley speaks of offering a "proof" of the existence of a creator, it is clear that he does not mean a *logical* proof, but rather a rhetorical demonstration according to familiar conventions, similar to that then encountered in a court of law.[86] Paley stands within an apologetic tradition going back to Joseph Butler, which argued for a fundamental resonance between human reflection on the created world using experience and reason, and the broader vision of reality revealed in the Christian tradition.[87]

Although natural theology is sometimes presented as deductive – that is, that observation of nature necessarily leads to a theistic conclusion – most forms of natural theology are actually inductive,[88] arguing for a fundamental resonance or congruence between experience of the world and a theistic framework.[89] The observation of fine-tuning within the universe is thus not proposed as a proof of theism, but as what might be expected if theism were true. The capacity of a hypothesis to explain observations or experience is here taken to raise the probability of that hypothesis.[90] However, while such arguments may serve to demonstrate that belief in God is rational, this does not necessarily mean that they would be considered to be convincing by all reasonable non-theists.[91] Such a natural theology is intellectually suggestive, not compelling. It is consistent with observation, but not entailed by observation.

In this section, we have noted that natural theology often resulted from a desire to demonstrate the rationality of faith, and some of the difficulties that arise from this enterprise. Yet the validity and importance of the motivation are not negated by difficulties in its implementation. We shall consider the way in which the project of natural theology developed in this volume relates to Christian apologetics at a later stage (pp. 173–80). We now turn to consider another motivation for natural theology – a longing for a coherent view of reality.

---

[85] For the general approach, see Hitchin, "Probability and the Word of God"; A. E. McGrath, *Darwinism and the Divine*, 85–103. For the cultural interest in anatomy and its apologetic and theological implications, see Vidal, "Extraordinary Bodies and the Physicotheological Imagination."

[86] For the importance of the socially constructed notion of "received opinion" in shaping such perceptions, see Patey, *Probability and Literary Form*, 3–13.

[87] Rurak, "Butler's *Analogy*." For the role of vision and imagination in Jewish tradition, see Wolfson, *Through a Speculum that Shines*, 13–51.

[88] Polkinghorne, "The New Natural Theology."

[89] Polkinghorne, "Physics and Metaphysics in a Trinitarian Perspective."

[90] Swinburne, *The Existence of God*, 133–52.

[91] See Oppy, *Arguing about Gods*, 1: "a successful argument on behalf of [a theistic] claim has to be one that ought to persuade all of those who have hitherto failed to accept that claim to change their minds."

Connectedness: The Human Longing for Coherence

Human beings aspire to integrate the multiple dimensions of life into a coherent and satisfying whole. Instead of thinking of our mental worlds as a series of disconnected and incoherent thoughts and values, we try to weave them, like threads, into a pattern. We long for some reassurance of the *coherence of reality* – that however fragmented our world of experience may seem, there is a half-glimpsed "bigger picture" which holds things together, its threads connecting together in a web of meaning what might otherwise seem incoherent and pointless.[92] The importance of this is brought out with particular clarity in a sonnet by the American poet Edna St. Vincent Millay (1892–1950), who spoke of being bombarded by "a meteoric shower of facts" raining from the sky, which lay "uncombined" on the ground.[93] They were like threads that needed to be woven "into fabric," dots that needed to be joined together to disclose a picture. This theme resonates throughout the poetic and religious writings of the Middle Ages, such as Dante's *Divine Comedy*, which ends with Dante finally catching a glimpse of the unity of the cosmos, in which its aspects and levels are seen to converge into a single whole.[94]

The modern period has raised doubts about the coherence of reality, many arising from the "new philosophy" of the Scientific Revolution.[95] Do new scientific ideas destroy any idea of a meaningful reality? The English poet John Donne (1572–1631) voiced this concern in the early seventeenth century. It seemed to him that radical new philosophies and scientific discoveries eroded any sense of connectedness within the world. "'Tis all in pieces, all coherence gone."[96] More recently, Nancy Cartwright has developed the idea of a "dappled world," in which there exists a multiplicity of orderings, requiring multiple accounts of the natural world and its structures.[97] Where C. S. Lewis argued that "we are not reading rationality into an irrational universe, but responding to a rationality with which the universe has always been saturated,"[98] Cartwright holds that we are

---

[92] See Bernstein, *Progress and the Quest for Meaning*, 14–15; Kekes, *Moral Wisdom and Good Lives*, 129–36; Thagard, "The Emotional Coherence of Religion"; Wiseman, *Theology and Modern Science*, 133–50.

[93] Millay, *Collected Sonnets*, 140.

[94] Dante, *Paradiso* XXXIII, 85–90.

[95] Kleiner, "Explanatory Coherence and Empirical Adequacy."

[96] John Donne, "The First Anniversarie: An Anatomy of the World," line 213.

[97] Cartwright, *The Dappled World*, 23–34.

[98] Lewis, *Christian Reflections*, 65.

imposing a natural order or inventing a cosmic rationality when there may be none to discern in the first place.[99] There are localized patchworks of natural laws, not a universally valid set of laws of nature.

A Christian natural theology affirms the *coherence of reality*, declaring that, no matter how fragmented our world of experience may appear, there is a half-glimpsed "bigger picture" which holds things together, its threads connecting together in a web of meaning what might otherwise seem incoherent and pointless. It provides a web of meaning, a deep belief in the fundamental interconnectedness of things, expressed in the New Testament theme of all things "holding together" in Christ (Colossians 1: 17).[100] Christ is the one who "gives the universe its metaphysical coherence."[101] It affirms that there is a hidden web of meaning and connectedness behind the ephemeral and incoherent world that we experience.

This was the insight which constantly eluded the novelist Virginia Woolf (1882–1941), who occasionally experienced short, stabbing, instances of insight, which seemed to her tantalizingly to reveal – but only for a fleeting instant – "some real thing behind appearances."[102] These transitory and rare "moments of being" (as she called them) convinced her that there were hidden webs of meaning and connectedness behind the world she knew, which constantly eluded her intellectual grasp, even if they captured her imagination while they lasted.

There are significant limits to the extent to which either logic or the natural sciences can discern and stabilize any such vision of coherence.[103] The world may indeed seem to be "dappled" in some sense of the term; yet it can still be governed by pervasive and stable laws on the one hand, and be said to be "coherent" on the other. A Christian natural theology provides an affirmation of the coherence – not merely the intelligibility – of the world. It does this by providing a "big picture," which allows what might otherwise seem disconnected and discontiguous to be seen as integral parts of a coherent whole through an act of penetrative imagination.[104] The *synoptikon* provided by the Christian faith allows individual observations and

[99] See especially Cartwright, "God's Order, Man's Order and the Order of Nature."

[100] For an exploration of this theme, see Tanzella-Nitti, "La dimensione cristologica dell'intelligibilità del reale."

[101] M. M. Adams, *Christ and Horrors*, 171. Adams's discussion of the Christological grounding of metaphysical coherence should be read in its totality, especially as this bears upon the incarnation: M. M. Adams, *Christ and Horrors*, 170–204.

[102] For a full discussion, see Sim, *Virginia Woolf*, 137–59.

[103] Sallis, *Logic of Imagination*, 69. For Newman on the role of imagination in discerning the coherence of faith, see Gallagher, "Newman on Imagination and Faith."

[104] For the psychological importance of such a "big picture" see Hicks and King, "Meaning in Life and Seeing the Big Picture." For the relation between coherence and Christology, see M. M. Adams, *Christ and Horrors*, 170–204.

experiences of nature to be positioned and correlated within an overall framework of meaning and intelligibility. This *synoptikon* is held to be grounded in a deeper order of things, which is revealed and held together in the being of God, disclosed partly in the order of the natural world, but more fundamentally in Christ, as God incarnate.

Meaning: Nature and Ultimate Questions

Human beings are meaning-seeking animals. Unsurprisingly, one fundamental motivation for natural theology is a yearning to discern meaning or significance within the world of nature. What does nature mean? Are the natural sciences capable of discovering this meaning, or does it lie beyond their reach and scope?[105] Some of the most active recent advocates of some form of natural theology are scientists, alert to the limits of their professional disciplines on the one hand, and their concern for what Karl Popper termed "ultimate questions" on the other. Popper argued that the natural sciences were not in a position to "make assertions about ultimate questions – about the riddles of existence, or about man's task in this world."[106]

The question of the limits of the natural sciences has been the subject of debate in recent years, with some arguing that their methods and approaches offer the only reliable source of knowledge about the universe and human identity. Others regard this as an ambitious over-extension of the sciences, which need to acknowledge their limits in order to ensure their distinct identity.[107] Sir Peter Medawar argued that "ultimate questions" lie beyond the scope of the scientific method, and must be acknowledged to require alternative means of engagement and exploration. Medawar insisted that there were important "questions that science cannot answer and that no conceivable advance of science would empower it to answer."[108] He went on to draw a distinction between "transcendent" questions, which he thought were best left to religion and metaphysics, and questions about the organization and structure of the material universe, which were dealt with authoritatively by the natural sciences.

---

[105] The Old Testament speaks of wisdom being concealed within the natural world, rather than open to public inspection: Fiddes, *Seeing the World and Knowing God*, 249–56; VanDrunen, "Wisdom and the Natural Moral Order."

[106] Popper, "Natural Selection and the Emergence of Mind," 342.

[107] See, for example, Stenmark, *Scientism*, 18–33; Olafson, *Naturalism and the Human Condition*.

[108] Medawar, *The Limits of Science*, 66.

Yet although "ultimate questions" might lie beyond science, their importance can hardly be overlooked, in that they relate to the important existential domains of meaning, value, and purpose.[109] One of the major roles of religious belief – which assimilates and integrates each of these domains into a "big picture" – is to enable believers to cope with situations through engaging such "ultimate questions."[110] The Spanish philosopher José Ortega y Gasset (1883–1955) is one of many writers to emphasize that the conceptual precision of the natural science is achieved at a price – namely, in that science engages secondary concerns, while being obliged to pass over questions of ultimate significance. Ortega argues that human beings – whether scientists or not – cannot live without considering and answering such questions, even in a provisional manner. "We are given no escape from ultimate questions. In one way or another they are in us, whether we like it or not. Scientific truth is exact, but it is incomplete."[111]

Recent studies in experimental psychology have confirmed this long-standing view, showing how physical scientists possess "tenacious teleological tendencies."[112] Being a scientist does not suppress the natural human tendency to ask fundamentally theological or religious questions. This natural inclination of human beings to ask such ultimate questions is, of course, no indication of their ultimate legitimacy, nor does it validate the answers that have been given. Yet it does help us understand why it is, so to speak, *natural* for human beings to think about natural theology.

This helps us to understand the "enduring popularity and cross-cultural recurrence of natural theological arguments."[113] They are found within both monotheistic traditions – including Islam and Christianity – and in polytheistic traditions, such as those of India and classical antiquity.[114] Natural theology, in the broadest sense of the term, comes naturally to human beings, on account of intrinsic cognitive biases; it is, so to speak, "meant to be."[115] Natural theology is thus a natural aspect of human inquisitiveness, and an innate desire to make sense of the world. Far from being something

---

[109] Baumeister, *Meanings of Life*, 29–57.

[110] Park, "Religion as a Meaning-Making Framework in Coping with Life Stress"; Hicks and King, "Meaning in Life and Seeing the Big Picture."

[111] Ortega y Gasset, "El origen deportivo del estado," 259–60.

[112] Kelemen, Rottman, and Seston, "Professional Physical Scientists Display Tenacious Teleological Tendencies."

[113] De Cruz, "The Enduring Appeal of Natural Theological Arguments," 147–8; see also Kelemen, "Are Children 'Intuitive Theists'?"

[114] For example, see C. M. Brown, "The Design Argument in Classical Hindu Thought"; R. G. Morrison, "Natural Theology and the Qur'an."

[115] See especially the analysis in Heywood and Bering, "'Meant to Be': How Religious Beliefs and Cultural Religiosity Affect the Implicit Bias to Think Teleologically."

that goes against the grain of normal cognitive processes, it is arguably their natural outcome.[116] So important is this point that it needs further discussion.

Natural Theology as a "Natural" Quest

Thus far, we have tended to focus on natural theology considered as insights into God arising from nature, or into nature arising from God. Yet there is another sense in which we must parse the concept of natural theology – as an enterprise of theological reflection or speculation which *happens naturally*, rather than as something that is artificial or forced. A central theme of much classical theology is that it is *natural* for human beings to desire God. In his *Confessions*, written between 397 and 400, Augustine of Hippo offered a prayer to God which clearly sets out this idea: "You have made us for yourself, and our hearts are restless until they find their rest in you."[117] The idea of some natural desire to know – or see – God played an important role in patristic thought, and is a commonplace in much early medieval theology.[118]

This idea of a "natural desire for God" has been developed in a number of ways within the Christian tradition – such as Pascal's idea of a God-shaped "abyss" within human nature, which is too deep to be satisfied by anything less than God, or C. S. Lewis's idea of a deep sense of yearning for significance, which both originates from and leads back to God.[119] Although the idea is framed in slightly different ways, the basic idea is that, because we are created by God and bear God's image, it is natural for us to yearn for God. Natural theology is thus an intuitive natural instinct within human nature, seen from the standpoint of the Christian tradition.

Although some leading writers of the Enlightenment tended to see religion as something that was imposed on people, recent empirical research suggests that religion is a cognitively natural human activity.[120] The

---

[116] De Cruz and de Smedt, *A Natural History of Natural Theology*, 19–39.

[117] Augustine of Hippo, *Confessions*, I.1.i.

[118] For example, see Feingold, *The Natural Desire to See God According to St. Thomas and His Interpreters*; Kerr, *Immortal Longings*, 159–84; Haldane, "Philosophy, the Restless Heart, and the Meaning of Theism"; Hütter, "*Desiderium naturale visionis Dei*"; Wang, "Aquinas on Human Happiness and the Natural Desire for God."

[119] A. E. McGrath, "Arrows of Joy."

[120] For a good introduction to the issues, see Bloom, "Religion Is Natural."

emerging field of the cognitive science of religion focusses on three key themes, each of which has a strong empirical basis.[121]

1   Religious beliefs and practices are to be seen as products of normal human cognition, so that it does not make sense of speak of any specifically "religious cognition."
2   While religion may be considered as a cultural artifact, it has roots partly in pan-human cognition that constrains this religious expression.
3   Human cognition involves sets of "intuitive knowledge" which function as cognitive defaults and operate without the need for extensive reflective processing.

The "cognitive science of religion" suggests that religion arises *through* normal human processes of thought, not in opposition to these.[122] Religion is natural, in the sense that it arises from human cognitive processes that are automatic, unconscious, and not dependent on culture. This emerging scientific narrative thus speaks of religion as a cognitively natural human activity.

On this approach, natural religion or theology (in some sense of the term) can be understood to reflect cognitively natural intuitions,[123] in that beliefs that give rise to religion are part of the human cognitive architecture. This does not mean that such a natural theology or religion can be discredited simply because it reflects cognitively natural intuitions.[124] We cannot judge the reliability of these intuitions on a metaphysically neutral ground, in that existing views about the plausibility of theism and atheism play a significant (if generally unacknowledged) role in the process of epistemic analysis.

The origins of religious belief do not lie primarily in cultural or social conditions, but in the intuitions that arise from normally developing and

---

[121] There is a large literature, and each of these three elements needs further discussion. See especially the following edited collections: Schloss and Murray, eds., *The Believing Primate*; Dawes and Maclaurin, eds., *A New Science of Religion*; Watts and Turner, eds., *Evolution, Religion and Cognitive Science*; Trigg and Barrett, eds., *The Roots of Religion*. See also Visala, *Naturalism, Theism and the Cognitive Study of Religion*.

[122] For various approaches, see Boyer, *Religion Explained*; Atran, *In Gods We Trust*; J. L. Barrett, *Why Would Anyone Believe in God?* For cautions about potential over-interpretations of the cognitive science of religion at this point, see Jong, Kavanagh, and Visala. "Born Idolaters"; A. W. Geertz, "How *Not* to Do the Cognitive Science of Religion Today."

[123] For the most detailed analysis of this issue to date, see de Cruz and de Smedt, *A Natural History of Natural Theology*, 19–39.

[124] De Cruz and de Smedt, *A Natural History of Natural Theology*, 194–9. For some such "debunking" arguments, see Jong and Visala, "Evolutionary Debunking Arguments against Theism Reconsidered."

functioning human cognitive systems.[125] This strongly suggests that the secular humanist and "New Atheist" visions for a totally secular human world are simply unrealistic, in that religion may be expected to re-emerge naturally, even where it is suppressed. It also suggests that non-religious people possess natural capacities and tendencies which might otherwise lead to religion, but which have either not yet been activated by any triggers in their environment or experience, or have been suppressed by social or cultural pressures.

So does such an innate propensity toward religion lead to a natural theology? Here, we need to make a clear distinction between the ideas of "religion" and "theology," in that the cognitive science of religion suggests that religion (especially when framed in terms of rituals, myths, symbols, and prayer) is natural, where theology is not.[126] There is an important parallel here between theology and the natural sciences, both of which involve abstract formulations that are counterintuitive, and require cultural support. As Robert McCauley has argued, a good case can be made for suggesting that, while religion is a natural outcome of human cognitive processes, the natural sciences are not.[127]

Yet this does not negate the lines of exploration in this section. A "thick" description of natural theology includes intuitive and analytical, imaginative and rational, approaches to nature, with porous boundaries between them. An intuition that the natural world points beyond itself need not be formalized in explicitly theological terms; it nevertheless can become a stimulus to do this, in much the same way as a sense of wonder at the beauty of nature can lead to the natural sciences.

So what kind of natural theology results from such intuitions? Most scholars in the field of the cognitive science of religion argue that religion is natural, whereas both science and theology involve abstract formulations that are seriously counterintuitive, and require cultural support. "Cognitively unnatural" beliefs abound in both the natural sciences and theology – the doctrine of the Trinity being one particularly obvious example. If this line of thought is pursued, it leads to the conclusion that the kind of "natural theology" which results from a human "preparedness" for religion is more intuitive than cognitive,[128] perhaps better formulated in

---

[125] See J. L. Barrett, *Born Believers*; B. H. Smith, *Natural Reflections*, 59–94.

[126] See especially Sosis and Kiper, "Religion Is More Than Belief." The problems encountered in defining "natural religion" are well known: see Pailin, "The Confused and Confusing Story of Natural Religion."

[127] McCauley, *Why Religion Is Natural and Science Is Not*, 212. See further B. H. Smith, *Natural Reflections*, 119–20; Boyer, *Religion Explained*, 321.

[128] On the notion of "preparedness," see Barrett and Richert, "Anthropomorphism or Preparedness?"

terms of the perceived plausibility of belief *in* God than specific beliefs *about* God. Nevertheless, some such beliefs (especially of a teleological nature) are easily developed,[129] and can be woven into such a nascent natural theology.

The field of the cognitive science of religion is relatively new, and it is clear that more work needs to be done. However, it clearly offers grounds for suggesting motivations for natural theology based on natural human cognitive processes, rather than purely cultural factors. Nevertheless, some important questions are beginning to emerge. For example, Robert McCauley has argued that this approach to religion suggests that people with certain cognitive impairments – such as autism or any autistic spectrum conditions – will find religion to be "largely inscrutable" and "cognitively challenging."[130] Such "mentalizing deficits" associated with the autistic spectrum are generally thought to be more common in men than in women. While this clearly needs further investigation, it raises some important questions about the "universal" appeal of natural theology, and suggests that there are some potential limits to its scope.

In this chapter, I have considered a number of issues concerning the development and evaluation of natural theology. In doing so, I have touched on some areas of concern about the viability and coherence of a natural theology project. These concerns clearly deserve fuller treatment. In the chapter which follows, I will set out and respond to some significant criticisms of natural theology, both in the broader sense of the term and as I myself understand the notion, and offer responses to these concerns.

---

[129] De Cruz and de Smedt, *A Natural History of Natural Theology*, 61–84.
[130] McCauley, *Why Religion Is Natural and Science Is Not*, 254–68.

5

Natural Theology

Some Concerns and Challenges

In the final chapter of this work, I shall outline what I consider to be the promise of a Christian natural theology. Yet before doing this, it is clearly important to consider some concerns that might reasonably be raised about the notion of natural theology in general, or the more specific approach which I have outlined and defended in this volume. Some potential difficulties have already been addressed in the course of discussion. This penultimate chapter considers six specific objections that I believe merit careful consideration. The six concerns to be addressed have been identified through a close reading of the substantial literature in the field, as well as conversations with colleagues.

We begin by reflecting on a concern that is often raised about the propriety and legitimacy of a natural theology from the standpoint of the Christian faith.

Natural Theology: Improper and Redundant?

Some will want to raise a major concern from the outset – namely, that the enterprise of natural theology is at best a waste of time, and potentially a subversion of core Christian themes.[1] Such a criticism often depends upon a specific understanding of natural theology – for example, as the attempt to offer demonstrative proof for God's existence based on rational argument, or an appeal to the structure or beauty of nature. It is easy to demonstrate that

---

[1] For a helpful presentation of such concerns, see A. Moore, "Should Christians Do Natural Theology?"

Re-Imagining Nature: The Promise of a Christian Natural Theology, First Edition.
Alister E. McGrath.
© 2017 John Wiley & Sons, Ltd. Published 2017 by John Wiley & Sons, Ltd.

this form of natural theology is not "biblical."[2] I concede immediately that such an approach is open to criticism on several grounds, while insisting that natural theology is a much broader notion than this limited and limiting conceptualization permits. Two concerns seem to me to be of particular importance.

1 *The over-intellectualized concept of God which is the intended outcome of such an argument is theologically and doxologically inadequate.* John Henry Newman reacted against William Paley's anemic idea of God, declaring that it bore little relationship to the actual reality of Christianity itself.[3] Paley's natural theology, Newman suggested, was as likely to lead to atheism as to belief in God.[4] It reduced God to the intellectually manageable and familiar, losing any sense of glory.[5] This criticism has been reinforced by scholarly study of the responses of Christian theologians to the growing skepticism of the early modern age. The "proofs" of God's existence developed in this period were such that they seemed merely to intimate the intellectual superiority of atheism.[6]

Christian Thomasius (1655–1728) remains one of the most important critics of scholastic attempts to "prove" God's existence. Based on his reading of Spinoza, Thomasius declared that any attempt to define the Christian God as an object of philosophical knowledge ultimately led to atheism.[7] William Inge (1860–1954), who drew a similar conclusion, helpfully identified the key error in such an approach as its rationalized notion of God as a constituent part of the world:

> Rationalism tries to find a place for God in its picture of the world. But God, whose centre is everywhere and His circumference nowhere, cannot be fitted into a diagram. He is rather the canvas on which the picture is painted, or the frame in which it is set.[8]

---

[2] See, for example, Spencer, "Is Natural Theology Biblical?" It is, however, fair to suggest that Spencer's definitions of natural theology as "the development of an entire theological system without reference to revelation" or "the establishment of the existence and to some degree the character of God without recourse to revelation" (59–60) predetermine his response to his own question.

[3] Newman, *Fifteen Sermons Preached before the University of Oxford*, 114–15.

[4] For further comment, see A. E. McGrath, *Darwinism and the Divine*, 127–30.

[5] The question of whether such a natural theology needs to be qualified or reframed *apophatically* clearly merits exploration: Pelikan, *Christianity and Classical Culture*, 40–56.

[6] Buckley, *At the Origins of Modern Atheism*. The reliability of this judgment has been called into question: see especially Gaukroger, *The Emergence of a Scientific Culture*.

[7] Hunter, *The Secularisation of the Confessional State*, 71–2.

[8] W. R. Inge, *Faith and Its Psychology*, 197.

The English Dominican theologian Herbert McCabe (1926–2001) argued that Christianity brought about the "abolition" of generic gods, such as those associated with Paley's natural theology. The Christian God cannot be conceived as an object that we can discover or investigate. "God is not an inhabitant of the universe; he is the reason why there is a universe at all."[9] For McCabe, the best that a "natural theology" can hope to achieve is to suggest that there might be a "beyond" that transcends all that we can know. Yet it tells us almost nothing about the Christian God. Deficient forms of natural theology lead to a generic and impersonal notion of God, which may be intellectually interesting, but is nevertheless existentially inadequate. A greater vision of God is required – such as that offered by the Christian faith, which may easily be mapped onto our experience of the world, but which is not ineluctably entailed by that experience.

 2   *The self-revelation of God renders natural theology – in this rationalist sense of the term – irrelevant or redundant.* This concern, often linked with the leading Swiss Protestant theologian Karl Barth, has merit and must be taken seriously. For Barth, sinful humanity prefers to assert its autonomy by finding God in a manner of its own choosing.[10] Natural theology represents an unnecessary, intellectually flawed, and theologically rebellious strategy, designed to allow us to find or invent a God who we find congenial. Why do we need to find God, when God has chosen to find us?

The Yet this is a criticism of one specific form of natural theology, not the Christian natural theology project set out in this volume, in which natural theology is seen as a aspect of revealed theology, legitimated by that revealed theology rather than by natural presuppositions or autonomous human insights. What if the legitimation of natural theology is understood, not to lie in its own intrinsic structures, nor in an autonomous act of human self-justification, but in divine revelation itself? On this approach *theologia revelata* both legitimates *theologia naturalis* and defines its scope, anchoring it within the realm of grace, rather than pure nature. This points to the possibility of a conceptual relocation of natural theology, with important implications for an understanding of its foundations and its scope.

In his reflections on the significance of the theological legacy of Karl Barth, Thomas F. Torrance noted that Barth did not reject philosophical thinking, but rather demanded that theology should follow "a rigorous rational epistemology governed by the nature of the object, namely, God in his self-communication to us within the structures of our human and worldly

---

[9] McCabe, *God Still Matters*, 37.

[10] For an excellent summary of this concern, see Gestrich, *Neuzeitliches Denken und die Spaltung der dialektischen Theologie*; Kock, *Natürliche Theologie*, 23–102.

existence."[11] Despite Barth's hostility toward one specific form of natural theology, it seems to me that his theological epistemology ultimately mandates some form of natural theology, at the very least as some "theology of nature" that is grounded in – not opposed to – divine self-revelation.[12] God's self-disclosure seems to mandate some such engagement with the created order – not to "prove" God's existence, or to subvert the autonomy of divine revelation, but rather to contemplate the creation as a means of enhancing and enriching our appreciation of God's chararacter. Natural theology, as I understand the notion, is not about discovering persuasive grounds of faith outside the bounds and scope of revelation, but is rather a demonstration that, when the natural world is "seen" through the lens of the Christian revelation, the outcome is imaginatively compelling and rationally persuasive. In other words, natural theology *presupposes* the Christian view of the world, and makes an appeal to two audiences.

1   *Those within the Church*, who are invited to see the world as God's creation, and experience the deepened sense of understanding and aesthetic appreciation that is consequent upon this realization. Job, for example, is invited to contemplate the works of creation in order to extend his grasp of God's greatness (Job 38: 1–42: 6).[13] This theme has a long tradition of use within the Christian tradition.[14] The long tradition of natural law within such interpretative communities as Judaism and Reformed Protestantism rests on a solid foundation in the literature of the Old Testament; although the notion is contested, there is little doubt of its importance or impact.[15]

2   *Those outside the Church*, who are invited to see the world through the lens of the Christian *imaginarium*, and appreciate the aesthetic power and rational satisfaction that results. If natural theology leads to faith, it is not primarily through rational persuasion, but through imaginative empathy, in which the audience is asked to imagine a way of seeing things which proves to be deeply meaningful, and then told that this is, in fact, the way things are.

---

[11] Torrance, *Karl Barth*, 122.

[12] This seems to me to be a clear outcome of Barth's unpublished reflections on the *Church Dogmatics*, now published as "§43 Der Schöpfer und seine Offenbarung": K. Barth, *Unveröffentlichte Texte zur Kirchlichen Dogmatik*, 5–304.

[13] Schifferdecker, *Out of the Whirlwind*.

[14] For example, see Harrington, "Creation and Natural Contemplation in Maximus the Confessor's *Ambiguum* 10: 19."

[15] Novak, *Natural Law in Judaism*, 27–61. For Barth's impact on this discussion within Reformed Protestantism, see Grabill, *Rediscovering the Natural Law in Reformed Theological Ethics*, 21–53.

As I emphasized earlier (pp. 102–5), certain approaches to natural theology emerged in response to specific challenges and opportunities, reflecting local factors such as, in the case of English "physico-theology":

1   the rise of biblical criticism, which seemed to call into question the reliability or intelligibility of Scripture, and hence generated interest in the revelatory capacities of the natural world;
2   a growing distrust of ecclesiastical authority, which led some to explore sources of knowledge which were seen to be independent of ecclesiastical control, such as an appeal to reason or to the natural order;
3   a dislike of organized religion and Christian doctrines, which led some to seek for a simpler "religion of nature," in which nature was valued as a source of revelation.

The primary motivation for undertaking natural theology within English Christianity during the late seventeenth and eighteenth century was thus primarily *apologetic*, rather than *dogmatic*. The Church itself did not reject revelation; it realized that it now needed to relate the gospel to a culture which had hesitations in accepting this notion. Natural theology rapidly became an apologetic tool of no small importance, as the English Church attempted to maintain the cultural plausibility of Christianity in an increasingly skeptical context. Within the Reformed tradition,[16] Jean-Alphonse Turretin (1671–1737) developed an apologetic program based on a natural theology that sought to engage skeptics on their own rational territory. Barth may not agree with such a strategy; others, however, considered this (or something like it) to be both legitimate and necessary.[17] This theme emerges as significant in the writings of Emil Brunner, and we shall return to consider this further later in this chapter (pp. 144–9), as we consider the 1934 debate between Barth and Brunner over the natural capacities of humanity.

The genealogical approach to natural theology which I adopt in this work aims to establish how it has been understood throughout its history, allowing us to retrieve alternative theological possibilities, adapted and responsive to the situation of the community of interpretation in the present. Barth's concerns, to the extent that they are legitimate, can be met – not by denying the possibility of natural theology, but by recovering more authentic understandings of the natural theology project in the first place.

---

[16] Klauber, *Between Reformed Scholasticism and Pan-Protestantism*, 69.
[17] Dulles, *A History of Apologetics*, 176–90.

Ontotheology? Natural Theology and Philosophical "First Principles"

A further concern about natural theology arises from a perception that it is merely the intellectual outcome of a presupposed metaphysics, an intellectual enterprise which is in effect determined and supported by philosophical "first principles." For some, natural theology is thus an example of a discredited ontotheology, a preconceived metaphysics of the kind so vigorously criticized by Martin Heidegger.[18] Barth's critique of natural theology, although misplaced in some respects, is entirely appropriate when dealing with any *theologia naturalis* which is shaped by a priori metaphysical assumptions.

Heidegger's criticisms of natural theology at this point have prompted considerable debate, and led to a re-examination of leading thinkers of the Christian tradition – such as Aquinas and Augustine – to determine whether they can legitimately be considered to be open to such a criticism.[19] Some, particularly within the "Radical Orthodoxy" movement, see the origins of such an ontotheology in the writings of Duns Scotus;[20] I have to confess I do not share this judgment, which seems to be inadequately grounded in the primary sources.[21] Nevertheless, Heidegger's concerns seem to require a critical re-appropriation of the western theological tradition, not its abandonment in favor of some "methodological atheism."[22]

Merold Westphal has recently suggested that a defective "ontotheology" emerges from three intellectual or cultural contexts:

1   when the personal God of revelation and worship is displaced by systems of conceptual mastery that strive to be completely self-grounding;
2   when mathematical physics finally replaces theology as our highest science, leaving us with a purely instrumentalist, depersonalized, and human-controlled form of "religion"; and

---

[18] D. Turner, *Faith, Reason, and the Existence of God*, 26–9; Vitiis, "La problematica dell'ontoteologia e la filosofia teologica." On Heidegger's approach see Moran, "The Destruction of the Destruction"; Thomson, "Ontotheology?"; Robbins, "The Problem of Ontotheology."
[19] See, for example, S. McGrath, "Heidegger's Approach to Aquinas"; White, *Wisdom in the Face of Modernity*, 67–100.
[20] See, for example, Boulnois, "Quand commence l'ontothéologie?"; J. Milbank, "Only Theology Saves Metaphysics."
[21] For some concerns about this judgment, see Cross, "Duns Scotus and Suarez at the Origins of Modernity."
[22] For similar judgments and analyses, see White, *Wisdom in the Face of Modernity*, 3–30; D. C. Schindler, *The Catholicity of Reason*, 231–61; Westphal, *Overcoming Onto-Theology*, 1–28.

3   when theology becomes detached from the relationships and the
    practices of worshiping communities which lie at the heart of any
    living faith.[23]

It is my belief that all three of these pitfalls can be avoided, and that the
approach set out in this volume allows us to articulate and practice an
authentically Christian natural theology, well positioned to engage and
inform contemporary debates.

The approach adopted in this book represents a critical re-appropriation of
the Christian tradition, attentive to such concerns, which aims to liberate
theology from past cultural entanglements, and allow the recovery of a
deeper vision of natural theology. It is not grounded in a presupposed
metaphysics, but in a way of thinking and living which is disclosed through
Scripture, and passed down and consolidated through tradition.[24] A Christian natural theology is ultimately grounded, not in philosophical "first
principles," but in a narrative – especially as this focuses on the history of Jesus
of Nazareth. This important insight allows us to engage with one of the
worries that some contemporary writers express about its legitimacy.

Like the natural sciences, Christian theology can open up an implicit or
implied metaphysical landscape; it does not, however, assume such a landscape as a starting point, but rather seeks to unfold it as the process of inquiry
and reflection proceeds.[25] The lens through which Christians view the
natural world need not be based on the metaphysical a priori, but arises
through reflection on the metaphysical implications of a narrative of action
and identity, focussing supremely on the life, death, and resurrection of Jesus
of Nazareth. This approach has important implications for a natural theology, in that it mandates an engagement with pain and suffering, of central
importance to the narrative of Jesus.[26]

It must be conceded that the Christian tradition has made extensive use of
metaphysical categories in its theological elaborations – think, for example,
of the Nicene Creed, which is steeped in the language and conceptual world
of contemporary Greek metaphysics.[27] Yet the approach to natural theology
developed within this volume is grounded in a narrative, not the metaphysical
a priori. Just as there is a linear intellectual trajectory from the

[23] Westphal, *Overcoming Onto-Theology*, 17–18.

[24] For example, see Long, *Speaking of God*; Levering, *Scripture and Metaphysics*.

[25] For a detailed study, see A. E. McGrath, *A Scientific Theology*, vol. 3: *Theory*, 237–94. White's
via inventionis should also be noted here: White, *Wisdom in the Face of Modernity*, 28–30;
117–20.

[26] G. L. Murphy, *The Cosmos in the Light of the Cross*, 8–25.

[27] However, it must be noted that these notions are used in the service of theological exposition,
and do not function as its determinants: see the careful analysis in Ayres, *Nicaea and Its Legacy*.

New Testament's Christological statements to those of the Chalcedonian definition,[28] so the form of natural theology developed here is ultimately grounded in a narrative of divine creation, self-disclosure, and redemption which is open to metaphysical elaboration.

David Hume: The Intellectual Inadequacy of a Deist Natural Theology

Many philosophers routinely dismiss any notion of "natural theology" or "natural religion" on the grounds that this has been shown to be incoherent and implausible by the great Scottish philosopher David Hume (1711–76). Although Hume's general criticism of religion focusses particularly on the question of whether the category of the "miraculous" is defensible, it extends (especially in the *Dialogues concerning Natural Religion*) to include the generic theme of natural theology, understood as an attempt to demonstrate the existence of God, or determine the character of God, from an appeal to the natural world.[29] There is a long-standing debate about whether Hume's critique of natural religion is to be thought of as representing his *naturalism* or his *skepticism*, and the implications of the latter for any attempt to develop human knowledge.[30]

Serious philosophical discussion of this question has been significantly hindered by a failure to engage Hume's ideas in terms of their historical context – in effect, treating them as timeless philosophical ideas – and by omitting discussion of how Hume's ideas were received and assessed by his contemporaries. Simon Blackburn, for example, seems to treat Hume as an essentially ahistorical figure, whose ideas have timeless significance.[31] This is very difficult to defend, since Hume's ideas are historically and culturally situated, reflecting the perceived inadequacies of a specific (and clearly deficient) form of Deist natural theology which gained the cultural ascendancy in the early eighteenth century.[32]

Hume's *Dialogues concerning Natural Religion* involve three interlocutors – Philo, Cleanthes, and Demea – raising the question of which of these correspond to Hume's own views, and whether Hume conceals some of his

---

[28] See the important argument in Hooker, "Chalcedon and the New Testament."
[29] Holden, *Spectres of False Divinity*, 19–47; Bradley, "Hume's Chief Objection to Natural Theology."
[30] For the debate, see P. Russell, *The Riddle of Hume's Treatise*, 3–11.
[31] Blackburn, *Think*, 159–82.
[32] Khamara, "Hume versus Clarke on the Cosmological Argument."

own perspectives.[33] It is a matter for some regret that Hume appears to engage with only one argument for the existence of God, detaching it from the context of interrelated arguments and considerations which constitute a cumulative case for theism.[34] Cleanthes – who is presented as the advocate of a defensible natural theology – only defends one argument for God's existence, based on the order of the natural world. "By this argument a posteriori, and by this argument alone, do we prove at once the existence of the deity and his similarity of the deity to human mind and intelligence."[35] Having proposed to limit such proofs to a single approach, Cleanthes in effect closes off other a posteriori arguments for religious belief, such as those based on an innate sense of divinity, or transcendent experiences. Hume's critique of natural theology thus engages a remarkably "thin" representation of a much richer and greater reality.[36]

Hume's main objections to natural theology are summed up in the following passage, which highlights the main difficulties he believes it faces – namely, the moral ambiguity of the natural world. It is taken from the section in the *Dialogues* in which Philo suggests to Cleanthes that an argument from design does not permit the conclusion that God is infinite, perfect, or one.

> This world, for aught that [Cleanthes] knows, is very faulty and imperfect, compared to a superior standard; and was only the first rude essay of some infant Deity, who afterwards abandoned it, ashamed of his lame performance; it is the work only of some dependent, inferior Deity; and is the object of derision to his superiors; it is the production of old age and dotage in some superannuated Deity; and ever since his death has run on at adventures, from the first impulse and active force, which it received from him.[37]

Hume's argument assumes that it is self-evident that a "superior standard" is available, by which this world may be judged and found to be deficient. Yet this amounts to a hypothetical "view from nowhere," resting on a fundamental human intuition that the world ought to be better than what we

---

[33] For a summary of the issues, see O'Connor, *Routledge Philosophy Guidebook to Hume on Religion*, 214–18.

[34] For this point, see especially Tennant, *Philosophical Theology*; Mitchell, *The Justification of Religious Belief*; Abraham, "Cumulative Case Arguments for Christian Theism"; Geivett, "David Hume and a Cumulative Case Argument."

[35] Hume, *Philosophical Works*, 19. Note that Hume's character Demea defends the view that the existence of God should be proved through a priori reasoning, rejecting Cleanthes's more inductive approach.

[36] For a critical evaluation of Hume's critique of natural theology, see Sennett, "Hume's Stopper and the Natural Theology Project."

[37] Hume, *Philosophical Works*, 46.

experience, rather than a demonstrative evidence-based argument. Yet any attempt to calibrate the aesthetic or moral excellence or deficiency of our world demands a comparator – something with which it may be compared to determine whether this is indeed the case. We know of no other world, and are thus unable to make this comparison.[38]

Hume, in effect, is relying on intuition – a human hunch that things ought to be better than what we actually observe and experience. It is an instinct that makes little sense and has little intellectual grounding within the Deistic framework that Hume critiques. Yet the intuition that there is a better world than this arises naturally within a Trinitarian framework (pp. 38–40). A natural theology based on a Trinitarian vision of God has a significant explanatory advantage over its Deist alternative.

Hume's criticisms are best seen as directed against variants of a Newtonian natural theology, such as that set out by the Scottish writer Colin Maclaurin in 1748,[39] suggesting that more probable naturalist accounts of the regularity of nature might be offered, but not providing a conceptual apparatus by which such probability might be evaluated.[40] In the end, Hume's critique of natural theology cannot be seen as a rational disconfirmation of theism, but an articulation of the belief that it is simpler or more reasonable to account for the structures of the world by naturalist means, than by an appeal to a generic creator God, such as that of Deism. Yet this probability judgment is based on undisclosed and undefended calibrations of possibilities, leading some to suggest Hume is best defended using the notion of a "subjective probability."[41] Yet to its critics, this seems to make the debate about natural theology depend on subjective precommitments, in which judgments are not based on a "conviction that *comes from* experience, but a conviction we are designed to *bring to* experience."[42]

Hume offers a robust challenge to a "thin" natural theology which seeks to prove the existence of a generic god from the natural world, on the implicit assumption that such a god has no connection with the processes of human reasoning or intuition that might lead to such a view in the first place. Hume,

---

[38] This difficulty also applies to Leibniz's assertion that this is "die beste aller möglichen Welten," which requires a similar calibration and comparison. See W. C. Lane, "Leibniz's Best World Claim Restructured."

[39] McLaurin's *Account of Sir Isaac Newton's Philosophical Discoveries* was widely read, and offered a Deistic interpretation of the regularity of natural processes: Markley, "Representing Order," 139–41.

[40] The recent application of Bayesian reasoning to Hume's arguments about miracles should be noted here: see, for example, Holder, "Hume on Miracles."

[41] For the view that the allocation of prior probabilities to theories is a purely subjective matter, see Sobel, *Logic and Theism*. For criticism of this approach, see Swinburne, "Sobel on Arguments from Design."

[42] Sobel, *Logic and Theism*, 311 (emphasis in original).

for example, regarded any form of theistic reasoning based on human experiences as "spectres of false divinity" which were "projected by the restless mind and its wheel of inner passions" onto an illusory first cause of the universe.[43] In the end, however, Hume is prepared to permit certain weak forms of "liminal" natural theology.[44] Thomas Holden argues that Hume develops an important distinction between a "core natural theology" which aims to achieve "knowledge of the deity's distinctive intrinsic character," and a "liminal natural theology" which "stops short of such ambitions."[45] Hume's famous dislike of philosophical speculation about matters that were "beyond the sphere of everyday experience and common life" seems to have been a significant motivation for his rejection of a "core natural theology."

So what are we to make of this? As William Paley's *Natural Theology* (1802) indicates, Hume's criticisms of natural theology were not seen as decisive by his own age.[46] Furthermore, Hume's approach is vulnerable when pitted against cumulative arguments for the existence of God, or the kind of "thick" natural theology project outlined in the present work. Hume's skeptical and naturalizing agenda, however, has contributed indirectly to a growing trend within western culture to see the natural world as self-contained and self-referential.[47] In what follows, we shall consider this important development, which clearly has implications for the public perception of natural theology, in more detail.

Charles Taylor: Natural Theology and the "Immanent Frame"

Many in contemporary western culture might now consider it more appropriate to speak of a natural "atheology" than a natural "theology."[48] This

---

[43] Holden, *Spectres of False Divinity*, 76. C. S. Lewis developed approaches which would seem to fall under Hume's criticisms. For an important assessment of Lewis's approach to the issues raised by Hume, see Wielenberg, *God and the Reach of Reason*, 7–152.

[44] On which see Holden, *Spectres of False Divinity*, 28–44; Demeter, *Conflicting Values of Inquiry*, 190–6.

[45] Holden, *Spectres of False Divinity*, 20.

[46] At points in this work, Paley appears to engage with an imagined Humean critic: see Brooke and Cantor, *Reconstructing Nature*, 196–8. Paley's notion of the watchmaker subtly subverts some of Hume's criticisms of arguments from design: A. E. McGrath, *Darwinism and the Divine*, 95–7.

[47] As Murphy notes, Hume does not really articulate a worldview; the "immanent frame" (Charles Taylor) represents a broader development of Hume's approach. N. Murphy, "Mac-Intyre, Tradition-Dependent Rationality, and the End of Philosophy of Religion," 40–1.

[48] See Lustig, "Natural Atheology."

raises an important question. Why did natural theology, understood in the sense of inferring the existence of God from the beauty and complexity of nature, seem so imaginatively and rationally "natural" to most western Europeans in the past, but now seems equally unnatural to many in western culture? In part, the answer lies in shifting cultural expectations and norms. The philosopher Charles Taylor offers a critical account of how this cultural transition – with significant implications for natural theology – is to be explained. "Why was it virtually impossible not to believe in God in, say, 1500 in our Western society, while in 2000 many of us find this not only easy, but even inescapable?"[49]

Taylor's answer is presented in terms of the social dominance of a cluster of modern prejudices which he designates the "Immanent Frame." This cultural metanarrative weaves together a number of themes, including the disenchantment of the world, an understanding of nature as an impersonal order, the rise of an "exclusive humanism," and an ethic which is framed primarily in terms of discipline, rules, and norms. Taylor notes that this "exclusive humanism" advocates a view of human flourishing which denies or suppresses any notion of a transcendent source of morality, such as God or the Tao, and which refuses to recognize any good beyond this life and world. The outcome of the dominance of this narrative is the cultural exclusion of a transcendent reality in general, particularly the notion of a God who can be considered to act within the world. For Taylor, contemporary understandings of human flourishing, the natural order, and the moral life, and nature are all framed in a self-sufficient, naturalistic, and immanent manner.

> Being rational now comes to mean taking some distance from ordinary, embodied human existence and striving to acquire mastery over the self and the world. The disengagement that this involves is mental or intellectual; the mind tries to prescind from its involvement in ordinary existence and aspires to a more detached, disinterested perspective on the world.[50]

The natural sciences, Taylor notes, articulate a "disenchanted" view of the world which is widely held to force us to "trade in a universe of ordered signs, in which everything has a meaning, for a silent but beneficent machine."[51]

Echoes of Taylor's analysis can be found in older critics of western culture. For example, C. S. Lewis's writings of the 1940s show his growing concern

---

[49] C. Taylor, *A Secular Age*, 25. For assessments of Taylor's approach, see Warner, VanAntwerpen, and Calhoun, eds., *Varieties of Secularism in a Secular Age*; Colorado and Klassen, eds., *Aspiring to Fullness in a Secular Age*. For Taylor's own views on natural theology, see Ormerod, "Charles Taylor and Bernard Lonergan on Natural Theology."
[50] C. Taylor, *Sources of the Self*, 149.
[51] C. Taylor, *A Secular Age*, 98.

over signs that the category of the transcendent was being intentionally sidelined within English intellectual life. His *Abolition of Man* (1943) noted how the educational system of the day seemed designed to eradicate any intuitions of transcendence in morality or religion.[52] The sermon "The Weight of Glory" (1941) develops the theme that people are now held spellbound by a secular and secularizing metanarrative that insists that human destiny and good lie in this world alone. We are told – and come to believe – that the ideas of transcendent realms, of worlds to come, are simply illusions. The educational system, Lewis notes with obvious sadness, has colluded with the modern myth that the sources and goals of human good are "found on this earth."[53]

Lewis declared that the time had come to break free from this "evil enchantment of worldliness." So deeply had this "evil enchantment" saturated English culture that the "strongest spell" was now required if its power was to be broken. Lewis reminded his readers that "spells are used for breaking enchantments as well as for inducing them." For Lewis, Christianity has to show that it can tell a more compelling and engaging story that will capture the imagination of its culture, such as the counternarrative Lewis himself offered in his *Chronicles of Narnia*.

Taylor's point is that the culture of our "secular age" now makes a sharp distinction between the natural and the supernatural, the human and the divine, so that making sense of the world around us now seems to be possible in terms of this world alone. Nature became emptied of the spirits, signs, and cosmic purposes that once seemed a fact of everyday experience. It came to be conceived fundamentally as an impersonal order of matter and force, governed by causal laws, making the notion of special divine action counterintuitive, if not conceptually incredible. Taylor notes the importance of Weber's concept of the "disenchantment of nature,"[54] while offering his own reinterpretation of this in terms of "disengagement."[55]

For Taylor, there has been a marked shift within western culture toward "Closed World Structures" that tacitly accept "the immanent frame" as normative, seen in the fact that most people no longer see natural events

---

[52] See Aeschliman, *The Restitution of Man*, 48–55.

[53] Lewis, *Essay Collection*, 99. Note also Wesley Kort's assessment of Lewis's approach: Kort, *C. S. Lewis Then and Now*, 33: "Lewis was convinced that before modern people can understand what religion is all about, they must change their relation to the world and how they understand their place within it."

[54] On which see M. T. Saler, "Modernity, Disenchantment, and the Ironic Imagination"; A. Stone, "Adorno and the Disenchantment of Nature." Note also Kort, *C. S. Lewis Then and Now*, 33: "Lewis believes that religion can be rightly understood only by people who live in a world that is at least to some degree *enchanted*."

[55] van den Berge and Ramaekers, "Figures of Disengagement."

as acts of God, or discern a divine presence within or beyond nature.[56] Nature has become reduced to the predictable and quantifiable, and evacuated of any transcendent dimension. "Closed World Structures" now function as unchallenged axioms in western culture. For Taylor, this means that the dominant cultural narrative leaves no place for the "vertical" or "transcendent," but in one way or another closes these off, rendering them inaccessible or even unthinkable. The cultural plausibility of natural theology is partly dependent on an unproblematic transition, connection, or association between the horizontal and vertical dimensions of nature. The marginalization or denial of such a transcendent dimension clearly renders the project of natural theology problematic in this cultural context.

Taylor here describes a cultural predisposition, an axiomatic way of seeing and conceiving the world, which simply excludes the notion of special divine action as a matter of principle. This notion is now deemed "unthinkable"; to run counter to this cultural mindset is a symptom of a fundamental irrationality. So what can be done about it? How can this cultural narrative be challenged? Taylor's response is complex, and rests partly on under- standing how this narrative achieved social dominance in the first place. It involves grasping an alternative "master narrative," one of several "broad framework pictures of how history unfolds" which helps us understand how the rise of "disenchantment" led to the gradual erosion of any cultural plausibility for a transcendent dimension to nature.[57]

In exploring these issues, Taylor sets out an account of secularization which has analytical, phenomenological, and genealogical components. Taylor's account of the historical origins of this "master narrative" empha- sizes its historical contingency. "It is a crucial fact of our present spiritual predicament," he declares, "that it is historical; that is, our understanding of ourselves and where we stand is partly defined by our sense of having come to where we are, of having overcome a previous condition."[58]

Taylor's innovative and engaging account of how this cultural mindset developed questions the validity of what he terms "subtraction stories," understood as "stories of modernity in general, and secularity in particular, which explain them by human beings having lost, or sloughed off, or liberated themselves from certain earlier, confining horizons, or illusions, or limitations of knowledge."[59] For those committed to "subtraction stories," the notions of divine presence and transcendence seem to belong

---

[56] For a succinct account of this notion, see C. Taylor, "Geschlossene Weltstruktur in der Moderne."
[57] C. Taylor, *A Secular Age*, 573.
[58] C. Taylor, *A Secular Age*, 29.
[59] C. Taylor, *A Secular Age*, 22.

to the past, and have no place in the present or future. Any sense of the transcendent has been subtracted from the natural world. For Taylor, however, the western mindset remains open to the notions of transcendence and divine action; the problem is that it is not *perceived* to be so. Taylor's account of the emergence of a "secular age" emphasizes the constitutive God-reference that still "haunts" the secular age.

A similar point was made by the Polish philosopher Leszek Kolakowski (1927–2009). "God's unforgettableness," Kolakowski argued, "means that He is present even in rejection." Developing this point further, Kolakowski suggests that the "return of the sacred" is a telling sign of the failure of the *ersatz* Enlightenment "religion of humanity," in which a deficient "godlessness desperately attempts to replace the lost God with something else."[60] Taylor concurs, arguing that this persistence of a God-reference should not be seen as an empty vestige, a dead metaphor, but rather as a sign that interest in the transcendent remains embedded within culture, and has the potential for future development.

Taylor's analysis is intended to hold up a mirror to our present, allowing us to discern its regnant implicit narrative – the "immanent frame" – and grasp that this can be understood as both "closed" and "open." The outcomes of this "immanent frame" are thus not determined by the frame itself, but by how we choose to interpret and apply it. Taylor himself opts for an "open" interpretation of the "immanent frame," where Weber endorses a "closed" reading. Both, he suggests, are defensible interpretations of the "immanent frame"; both, however, must also be seen as acts of faith, in that neither are demanded by this frame.

> The immanent order can, therefore, slough off the transcendent. But it doesn't necessarily do so. What I have been describing as the immanent frame is common to all of us in the modern West, or at least that is what I'm trying to portray. Some of us want to live it as open to something beyond; some live it as closed. It is something which permits closure, without demanding it.[61]

Taylor thus notes that, as a matter of fact, far from being uniformly anti-religious or atheist, western culture displays "a whole gamut of positions, from the most militant atheism to the most orthodox traditional theisms, passing through every possible position on the way."[62]

So where does this leave us? What are the implications of Taylor's reflections on the regnant narrative of western culture for any approach

---

[60] Kolakowski, "Concern about God in an Apparently Godless Age," 183.
[61] C. Taylor, *A Secular Age*, 544.
[62] C. Taylor, *A Secular Age*, 556.

to natural theology? Taylor helps us to grasp that suspicion of the notion of natural theology rests partly on a dominant cultural narrative, rather than specifically philosophical objections. The "immanent frame" has become the default position for contemporary discussion of these issues; it is shaped, in part, by philosophical considerations, but has developed a plausibility which goes beyond its philosophical roots. It is impossible to debate the issue of divine action without taking account of this cultural predisposition against this notion.

> We have here what Wittgenstein calls a "picture," a background to our thinking, within whose terms it is carried on, but which is often largely unformulated and to which we can frequently, just for this reason, imagine no alternative.[63]

If Taylor is right, the plausibility of any project of natural theology is shaped by cultural pressures and imaginative constructions which ultimately transcend the rational arguments which underlie it. Cultural practices thus help "shape our imaginations," effecting both an "education of desire" and a "pedagogy of the heart."[64] The best way of engaging a closed reading of the "immanent frame" would thus seem to be to provide an imaginatively compelling alternative, which is seen to have rational plausibility. Reflecting on his own wrestling with the problem of cultural determinants, Arthur Koestler pointed out that:

> A faith is not acquired by reasoning. One does not fall in love with a woman, or enter the womb of a church, as a result of logical persuasion. Reason may defend an act of faith – but only after the act has been committed, and the man committed to the act.[65]

A deeper level of commitment than pure reason is required – even presupposed. To revert to the language of C. S. Lewis, noted earlier, we need to break the "spell" of a closed world system, and open up alternative readings of our world – and perhaps that is best done, not by rational argument, but by capturing the cultural imagination with a richer and deeper vision of reality – in short, a "re-imagined nature," which is the intended outcome of this volume. This re-orientation will not arise from the cold certainties of closed logical argument, but from the open imaginative embrace of a luminous and compelling vision of truth, beauty, and goodness which stands at the heart of the Christian faith.

[63] C. Taylor, *A Secular Age*, 549.
[64] J. K. A. Smith, *Desiring the Kingdom*, 24–5.
[65] Koestler, *The God that Failed*, 15.

Barth and Brunner: The Debate which Discredited Natural Theology?

During the twentieth century, natural theology became a *Streitbegriff* – a "contested concept" – within German-language Protestantism, causing a degree of polarization and factionalization which now seems more than a little exaggerated and misplaced.[66] At points, it seemed as if the very identity of Protestantism was at stake, as if the rejection of natural theology had become a new benchmark of orthodoxy – an *articulus stantis et cadentis ecclesiae*. As we noted earlier in this chapter (pp. 130–1), one of the more significant factors contributing to this polarization was Karl Barth's hostility toward natural theology, partly reflecting his emphasis on the "otherness" of God, and especially his insistence upon the chasm separating God and humanity which precludes humanity knowing God on their own terms and on their own grounds.[67] However, this critique of human epistemological autonomy was initially framed in terms of *religion*, rather than natural theology.[68]

Yet by the late 1920s, "natural theology" increasingly became a place-holder for a human refusal to accept or submit to divine revelation, or an attempt to secure knowledge of God outside the scope of God's self-disclosure in Christ.[69] Barth understands "natural theology" to designate all forms of theology which do not begin exclusively from the disclosed *ratio* of God.[70] Although prepared during the 1920s to allow that the earlier Reformed tradition saw "natural revelation" as "an enjoyable and useful entrance hall or precursor [*eine erfreuliche und nützliche Vorhalle oder Vorstufe*]" on the way to the true Christian revelation,[71] Barth was concerned that such concessions might subvert the authority of divine revelation, and open the way for idolatrous approaches to nature.

---

[66] For the best account of this development, see Kock, *Natürliche Theologie*, 391–412. For aspects of this debate, see Kapper, "'Natürliche Theologie' als innerprotestantisches und ökumenisches Problem?"; Gestrich, "Die unbewältigte natürliche Theologie."

[67] See especially the discussion in K. Barth, *Der Römerbrief*, 213–55. See further Torrance, "The Problem of Natural Theology in the Thought of Karl Barth."

[68] As pointed out by Szekeres, "Karl Barth und die natürliche Theologie."

[69] Szekeres, "Karl Barth und die natürliche Theologie"; Prenter, "Das Problem der natürlichen Theologie bei Karl Barth"; Kock, *Natürliche Theologie*, 23–86.

[70] K. Barth, *Church Dogmatics*, I/1 36. For useful analysis, see Wüthrich, *Gott und das Nichtige*, 201–15.

[71] K. Barth, *Unterricht in der christlichen Religion*, 111. For these technical terms in the earlier Reformed tradition, especially Calvin and Schleiermacher, see P. Barth, *Das Problem der natürlichen Theologie bei Calvin*, 6; Werner, "Die Reformation geht noch fort!" 195–6. For Barth's engagement with Schleiermacher's natural theology around this period, see Kock, *Natürliche Theologie*, 23–7.

Critics of Barth have focussed on both the substance of his criticism of natural theology, and the seemingly disproportionate intensity of that criticism.[72] In terms of the substance of that critique, it is clear that Barth's concerns relate to the *socially constructed forms of natural theology* which emerged during the modern era, often in response to the apologetic needs of the churches in the late seventeenth and eighteenth centuries.[73] Barth's formulation of natural theology has little, if anything, in common with what we find in Augustine of Hippo, Gregory of Nazianzus, or Thomas Aquinas; it is specifically tied to the paradigms of natural theology which emerged during modernity.[74]

Barth's polemic against the modernity's quest for human autonomy is focussed on a specific conception of natural theology, which is seen to express, and provide intellectual justification for, this fundamental motif.[75] Barth's criticisms are directed against a constricted and culturally located notion of natural theology that limits it to philosophical arguments for the existence or character of God, without recourse to or acknowledgment of divine revelation. While Barth's criticisms of this "thin" concept of natural theology must be taken seriously, his understanding of natural theology must be called into question.[76]

The intensity of Barth's critique is best understood in terms of the political context following the Nazi *Machtergreifung* ("power-grab") in Germany in 1933. Aware of the emerging political crisis in Germany, Barth argued that the construction of a viable theological alternative to the collaborationist "German Christian" movement rested on the unequivocal rejection of natural theology.

> The inevitable controversy about natural theology is a controversy about a right obedience in theology [*unvermeidliche Streit gegen die natürliche Theologie ist ein Streit um den rechten Gehorsam in der Theologie*] . . . It must abandon each and every natural theology and dare, in that narrow isolation, to cling alone to the God who has revealed himself in Jesus Christ.[77]

---

[72] See especially Barr, *Biblical Faith and Natural Theology*.

[73] Marcolungo, "Christian Wolff und der physiko-theologische Beweis"; A. E. McGrath, *The Open Secret*, 140–70; A. E. McGrath, *A Fine-Tuned Universe*, 11–20.

[74] See especially Wissink, *De Inzet van de Theologie*, 311–27; Veldhuis, *Ein versiegeltes Buch*, 15–16.

[75] For this motif, see Macken, *The Autonomy Theme in the Church Dogmatics*, 69–80.

[76] One question, raised with particular acuity in an early essay by Rowan Williams, concerns the problematic character of Barth's understanding of revelation itself, which clearly shapes his views about natural theology: R. Williams, "Barth on the Triune God."

[77] K. Barth, "Das Erste Gebot als theologisches Axiom," 142. For comment, see Gestrich, *Neuzeitliches Denken und die Spaltung der dialektischen Theologie*, 158–9; Demut, *Evangelium und Gesetz*, 281–4; Gorringe, *Karl Barth: Against Hegemony*, 130.

Barth's passionate denunciation of natural theology – as he understood it – can easily be understood against this context, allowing it to be seen as a protest against hegemony. "Over against all self-existent and 'natural' theologies [Barth] sets the reality of the God who loves in freedom – the One who can in no circumstances ever be colonized or be the subject of any hegemony."[78]

As Marquardt argues, Barth's "total negation of natural theology" can be understood in terms of *political* engagement; it is, at one level, a critique of an ideology. Barth was thus able to adopt a more considered and conciliatory approach to natural theology before the rise of Nazism, and after its passing.[79] Barth's criticisms really have validity only in relation to those forms of natural theology (or "physico-theology") which developed during the modern period, reflecting its specific agendas.[80] Barth's critique of the understanding of humanity which emerged during this period includes its associated conceptions of natural theology, which Barth problematically interprets as assertions of human autonomy.[81]

In this section, we shall consider the famous 1934 debate between Barth and Emil Brunner, in which natural theology was a significant element in a broader, essentially anthropological discussion about the relation of nature and grace. This debate is sometimes misrepresented, particularly by those who have failed to read Emil Brunner's theological project in its totality, as a debate about natural theology in which Brunner was defeated by Barth, thus demonstrating the intellectual fragility and theological illegitimacy of natural theology. A more informed approach to this debate, however, allows it to be seen in a somewhat different perspective.[82]

For a start, Brunner was not – and did not consider himself to be – a representative of "natural theology, in the usual sense of the term."[83] Brunner's stated concern was to help the Church to "find the way back to a right *theologia naturalis*,"[84] rooted in the Bible and the theology of the Reformation. Brunner distances himself from any notion of natural theology which affirms the possibility of a general, self-authenticating knowledge of God, which may be had outside the Christian revelation. God's revelation in

---

[78] Gorringe, *Karl Barth: Against Hegemony*, 5.

[79] Marquardt, *Theologie und Sozialismus*, 263.

[80] For an historical analysis of the "anthropocentric" motif in the early eighteenth century, see Brooke, "Wise Men Nowadays Think Otherwise."

[81] These concerns are voiced throughout K. Barth, *Die protestantische Theologie im 19. Jahrhundert*.

[82] See the detailed analysis of the debate against its political and ideological context in A. E. McGrath, *Emil Brunner*, 90–132. For additional historical and theological reflections, see Sauter, "Theologisch miteinander Streiten"; Jehle, *Emil Brunner*, 293–321.

[83] Brunner, *Der Mensch im Widerspruch*, 509.

[84] Brunner, "Natur und Gnade"; in *Ein offenes Wort*, vol. 1, 374–5.

creation, Brunner insists, brings about knowledge of sin, but cannot liberate humanity from bondage to sin. Nevertheless, he also insists that God has bestowed "a permanent capacity for revelation [*dauernde Offenbarungs-mächtigkeit*]" on the natural order.[85] The capacity of humanity to "see" nature as disclosing God's true nature is compromised by sin; it is only when humanity's theological vision is repaired and renewed by divine grace that nature can be seen for what it really is.

> In faith, on the basis of revelation in Jesus Christ, we shall not be able to avoid speaking of a double revelation – of a first in his creation, which can only be recognized in all its greatness by those whose blindness has been healed by Christ [*dem durch Christus der Star gestochen ist*]; and of a second in Jesus Christ, in the full light of which they can clearly see the first, which far surpasses whatever the first was able to show him.[86]

It is clearly a distortion of Brunner's position to represent him as endorsing any notion of natural theology as an independent and autonomous knowledge of God, independent of divine revelation. Brunner insists that such a "natural theology" is an impossibility. On account of sin, humanity is blinded; it is only when our "eyes have been opened" that we are "able to see what God shows us through his revelation in creation." That self-revelation of God is there for all to see; yet sin blinds the created, natural human capacity, as one created in the image of God, to discern the creator in the creation. "Due to the sin of humanity, this meaning has been concealed from them; either they do not see this obvious [*augenfällig*] revelation of God, or they seriously misunderstand it."[87]

Brunner defends a traditional Reformed position – criticized by Barth – which holds that there are two modes of knowing God, one through the natural order, and the second through Scripture, with the second mode being clearer and fuller than the first.[88] This is essentially the substance of

---

[85] Brunner, "Natur und Gnade"; in *Ein offenes Wort*, vol. 1, 345. Barth persistently misrepresents Brunner's notion of *Offenbarungsmächtigkeit*, as a human "capacity for revelation," which is clearly not what Brunner meant by this idea. See Brunner, *Der Mensch im Widerspruch*, 509: "Some twenty times or so Karl Barth quotes from my writing the expression *Offenbarungsmächtigkeit des Menschen* which I not only have never employed at all, but which I heartily detest as heretical as much as he does."

[86] Brunner, "Natur und Gnade"; in *Ein offenes Wort*, vol. 1, 344.

[87] Brunner, *Offenbarung und Vernunft*, 77.

[88] See, for example, *Confessio Gallicana*, 1559, article 2; *Confessio Belgica*, 1561, article 2. Barth's critical comments on these two Reformed confessions should be noted: K. Barth, *Church Dogmatics*, II/1, 127.

Calvin's distinction between the *cognitio Dei creatoris* and *cognitio Dei redemptoris.*[89] For Brunner, Calvin holds that a natural knowledge of God can be had *extra muros ecclesiae*;[90] the important question is how such a notion can function as the basis of a constructive natural theology.

The approach to natural theology set out in this volume echoes some aspects of Brunner's approach, though diverging from him in others – most notably, in the emphasis I place on the theological role of the imagination. A Christian natural theology is a project located within a Christian way of thinking, determined and informed by the self-revelation of God in Christ, which offers a way of seeing the natural world as God's creation without imputing any independent revelational capacity to nature. That was clearly Brunner's position, which has been misunderstood and misrepresented in much Protestant discussion of the issues:

> It is not on the basis of our own reason, but on the basis of the saving revelation of God, that we teach about revelation through creation [*Schöpfungsoffenbarung*]. We do not pursue "natural theology," but, in the context of Christian theology, we teach about this specific form of revelation, which is bestowed on all humanity, yet is not correctly received by all, because all are sinners. Since it is Jesus Christ alone who reopens to us the buried entrance to this source of the knowledge of God that has been given to us, there is no question of minimizing the status of Christ, or diminishing the *sola gratia*, which some have feared from the affirmation of this teaching.[91]

Yet Brunner is himself open to criticism, most notably for failing to understand how the notion of natural theology as an autonomous human activity – which, I must emphasize, Brunner did not himself endorse – had political entailments. At the time of this debate (1934), Brunner was based in the Swiss city of Zurich, with a less than thorough understanding of the massive changes taking place in Germany as a result of the Nazi political victory, and its programs for the Nazification of German culture. Barth, in marked contrast, was located in Germany, and believed – whether rightly or wrongly – that a "natural theology" subverted any viable theological critique of this trend.

As Marquardt and others have noted, the "German church crisis" thus provided the context in which Barth made certain judgments about the

---

[89] For discussion of this tradition within Reformed theology of the sixteenth century and beyond, see Sudduth, *The Reformed Objection to Natural Theology*, 9–40. See also the good general discussion in Horton, *The Christian Faith*, 146–50.

[90] Brunner, "Natur und Gnade"; in *Ein offenes Wort*, vol. 1, 352–67.

[91] Brunner, *Offenbarung und Vernunft*, 78.

political implications and consequences of natural theology. Yet this specific historical context – which shaped Barth's critical approach to natural theology – now lies in the past. If Marquardt is right, this ought to open the door to serious reconsideration of the place and purpose of natural theology in the academy and Church. As we shall see in the concluding chapter of this work, it holds considerable theological promise.

Fideism: Natural Theology as Self-Referential and Self-Justifying?

Some readers will wish to raise a concern about the intellectual credentials of the Christian natural theology project outlined in this work. Surely it is self-referential, locked into self-justifying modes of argumentation, which in effect amount to a form of fideism? This is not an easy question to address, not least because the term "fideism" is often used pejoratively and ahistorically, without noting its multiple meanings or their genealogies.[92] To describe a position as "fideist" can easily become a means of abuse, rather than an instrument of inquiry. In particular, its associations have largely been determined by an outdated dichotomy between "rationalism" and "irrationalism."[93] The term originated in the middle of the nineteenth century, and has come to mean something like this:

> a philosophical and theological doctrine or attitude that minimizes the capacity of the human intellect to attain certitude and assigns faith as a criterion of the fundamental truths. Thus, God's existence, the immortality of the soul, the principles of morality, the fact of divine revelation, and the credibility of Christianity cannot be proved by reason alone, but must be accepted on authority.[94]

In recent Protestant discussions, the term fideism has often been deployed as a criticism of postliberal theologies – such as those of George Lindbeck and

[92] See the important analysis in T. D. Carroll, "The Traditions of Fideism"; Vainio, *Beyond Fideism*.

[93] Vainio, *Beyond Fideism*, 3. The suggestion that Tertullian was a fideist largely rests on a misreading of his works, particularly his non-saying *credo quia absurdum*: see Osborn, *Tertullian*, 48–64, where it is argued that Tertullian's position is better framed as *credible est quia ineptum est*, relating specifically to the paradox of the incarnation, not to a crude dismissal of rational reflection in theology.

[94] Matczak, "Fideism," 711. Note Plantinga's definition of fideism as an "exclusive or basic reliance upon faith alone, accompanied by a consequent disparagement of reason and utilized especially in the pursuit of philosophical or religious truth": Plantinga, "Reason and Belief in God," 87.

Hans Frei – which were held by their opponents to rest on a "Wittgensteinian fideism."[95] A similar criticism is often directed against the ecclesiocentric approach associated with Stanley Hauerwas.[96] This it is argued, locked theology into a textual or confessional ecclesial ghetto, and rendered it incapable of engaging with broader cultural issues of reason, evidence, and argumentation.[97] Jeffrey Stout directs a similar criticism against Karl Barth, suggesting that he is committed to a strategy of cultural isolationism, withdrawing into a private region which is invulnerable to rational criticism, but also incapable of communication with wider culture.[98]

This cultural withdrawal or isolation is perhaps the most significant concern about fideism, as this term has come to be used in this context – its perceived inability to *negotiate* with other viewpoints. Fideism, it is argued, cannot explain why some beliefs, language games, or convictions are to be chosen rather than others. It fails to articulate and defend criteria which would allow someone to determine why one belief should be deemed more reasonable, or more plausible, than another. My own approach might therefore be seen by some critics as an attenuated and idiosyncratic view of nature originating from within an isolated and defended Christian ecclesial ghetto, incapable of engaging with dialogue with other interpretative communities, or the wider culture.

I concede there is a genuine risk here, and share the concerns raised about the approach of "postliberalism," which risks cultivating a theological polity of intellectual isolationism.[99] Yet we need to ask whether the charge of fideism against any system or approach ultimately rests on assumptions about the universality of reason and the foundations of knowledge which were generally unproblematic to modernism, but are now seen as questionable. We noted some of these concerns earlier in this work when rejecting the modernist notion of a universal rational viewpoint (pp. 26–8). This is not to be seen as a lapse into irrationalism, or a failure to use reason in debate and

[95] For this notion and its influence on twentieth-century theology, see T. D. Carroll, *Wittgenstein within the Philosophy of Religion*, 101–45.
[96] Rasmusson, *The Church as Polis*, 175–7; Healey, *Hauerwas*, 17–38. Hauerwas can be defended here: see, for example, Wells, *Into Destiny*, 77–80.
[97] DeHart, *The Trial of the Witnesses*, 35–6. Note particularly DeHart's suggestion that postliberalism "is constructed through a blunt opposition between intratextuality and extra-textuality" (237). A particularly aggressive criticism of the "sectarianism" of fideism, as developed by Stanley Hauerwas, can be found in Gustafson, "The Sectarian Temptation."
[98] Stout, *The Flight from Authority*, 141–8. Such criticisms are plausible for the earlier Barth, particularly in the 1920s; Barth developed strategies that reduced this difficulty in his later works. For comment on Barth's alleged "fideism," see Diller, "Does Contemporary Theology Require a Postfoundationalist Way of Knowing?"
[99] My concerns were set out in my 1990 Bampton Lectures at Oxford University: A. E. McGrath, *The Genesis of Doctrine*, 14–34.

discussion; rather it is to use reason to demonstrate its own limitations.[100] Recent nostalgic attempts on the part of some rationalists to return to the "Age of the Enlightenment" represent a retreat into a mythical "Golden Age of Reason," which Heidegger, Gadamer, and the later Wittgenstein exposed as unsustainable.[101]

The approach I adopt in this work acknowledges and develops a response to the epistemic dilemma of humanity, recognizing both the limits of reason and the "evidential ambiguity" of the natural world,[102] with their important implications for belief entitlement. Reason itself is limited in scope, physically and socially embodied, and contextualized in history, culture, gender, and language. Whatever the leading representatives of the Enlightenment may have thought, reason is never objective, neutral, or free from bias. This raises serious concerns about the grounds for discussion between different communities of discourse, and especially the *criteria* to be employed in assessing the entitlement for belief.[103] It is not – and cannot be – irrational to assert that being situated in history and society makes absolute certainty and the quest for universality impossible. It is simply a recognition of an awkward truth, which should not be seen as an obstacle to true knowledge, but rather as a condition for proper knowledge.

This book cannot offer a defense of Christianity; my concern is rather to explore the vision of nature which Christianity enables and informs.[104] The most telling potential criticism of my approach would be that it at least stifles, and possibly prevents, dialogue with other traditions. If this were true, it would indeed be a cause for considerable concern. However, I do not believe that this is the case. As I hope this volume makes clear, I do not consider Christianity to be intellectually isolationist, but hold that it offers a coherent way of thinking which is capable of engaging and making sense of the world of nature and human experience, and in particular of entering into constructive dialogue with the natural sciences. My approach could be considered fideist only in the sense that it involves commitment to a way of thinking that cannot be *proved* to be true.[105] Yet this is true for most disciplines outside the

---

[100] For this theme in Pascal, see J. R. Peters, *The Logic of the Heart*, 279–80.

[101] The best example of this nostalgia is found in Hitchens, *God Is Not Great*, 277–84.

[102] For this phrase, and the importance of this notion in a defensible form of fideism, see J. Bishop, *Believing by Faith*, 70–1.

[103] Strandberg, *The Possibility of Discussion*, 1–26.

[104] However, it should be noted that some Christian writers – such as Pascal – treat aspects of the Christian "big picture" as empirical hypotheses that function as indirect proofs of the truth of Christianity. His treatment of the Fall is especially interesting in this respect: see Fouke, "Argument in Pascal's *Pensées*."

[105] See especially Buchak, "Rational Faith and Justified Belief"; Wolterstorff, "Entitlement to Believe and Practices of Inquiry."

limited domain of mathematics and logic. Think of Bertrand Russell's candid declaration about philosophy, amply borne out by contemporary debates within the discipline: we need to learn "how to live without certainty, and yet without being paralyzed by hesitation."[106] Or Michael Polanyi's reflections on the need to commit himself to what he believed (scientifically) to be true, while knowing that some of this would later be shown to be false.[107]

The extensive engagement within this volume with wider cultural authorities, issues, and outlooks makes it clear that I regard my construal of the Christian natural theology project to open the way to dialogue and debate with those outside the community of faith, rather than a lapse into some kind of sectarian isolation. In eschewing intellectual isolation as an intellectual option or a cultural strategy, however, I have consistently noted the difficulties in securing dialogue between different interpretive communities. The slow collapse of belief in a universal rationality with secure and uncontested criteria of epistemic adjudication raises fundamental questions about how *any* community or tradition of interpretation can meaningfully converse with another such community or tradition.[108] Every "view from somewhere" experiences some conceptual difficulties in negotiating with a "view from somewhere else."

Yet these difficulties can be engaged and resolved. As Alasdair MacIntyre has argued, it is possible to recognize the inexorable historicity of human experience and our own specific cultural or communal embodiment without abandoning a belief in the objectivity of rationality[109] – thus opening the way to dialogue between traditions, avoiding the stigma of isolationism and disconnection, and creating possibilities for intellectual enrichment. There may exist an incommensurability of truth and justification between traditions; this does not necessarily entail an incommensurability of meaning.[110] When rightly understood, a Christian natural theology has the capacity to become a "public" theology, capable of addressing the multiple traditions which shape the cultural context in which we live, not least because it "understands God as the source of all meaning, all truth, and all goodness, wherever it is found."[111]

[106] B. Russell, *A History of Western Philosophy*, xiv.

[107] See especially Polanyi, *Personal Knowledge*.

[108] For one solution, see Strandberg, *The Possibility of Discussion*, 121–47.

[109] For a development of his approach, see Herdt, "Alasdair MacIntyre's 'Rationality of Traditions' and Tradition-Transcendental Standards of Justification."

[110] For a discussion, see Porter, "Tradition in the Recent Work of Alasdair MacIntyre." See further my discussion of natural theology and the trans-traditional rationality of the Christian faith in A. E. McGrath, *A Scientific Theology*, vol. 2: *Reality*, 55–102.

[111] Ormerod, *A Public God*, 151. For clarification of some of the claims made about God and "truth," see Wood, "Thomas Aquinas on the Claim that God is Truth."

This insight into the scope of natural theology prompts a deeper discussion of its potential. What is the promise of a Christian natural theology? In the concluding chapter, we shall consider this in relation to some major contemporary concerns.

6

The Promise of a Christian Natural Theology

This book has set out a way of construing a natural theology project within a specifically Christian *imaginarium* – an intellectual and imaginative framework which both reaffirms the rational transparency and the inherent beauty of nature, and grounds these in the deeper reality of a Trinitarian vision of God. It affirms and develops a theme of major importance in contemporary criticisms of secularism – the need to reconnect the notions of rationality and transcendence.[1] The "thick" conception of Christian natural theology developed in this work represents a retrieval of much of the wisdom of the Christian theological tradition before the rise of modernity, yet is adapted to engage subsequent cultural and theological concerns. Like theology itself, a natural theology engages multiple audiences, articulating a theology and spirituality of nature to those within the Church, and affirming the rationality and aesthetic adequacy of faith on the other. For this reason, this work has strayed far beyond the traditional boundaries of systematic theology, and explored the borderlands of theology with the arts and sciences. This is not an act of pointless peregrination, but a principled engagement with the wider territory that a Christian natural theology bestrides.

Yet many will feel that the ultimate justification of such a natural theology will lie not in an extended defense of its legitimacy, but in a demonstration of its utility. What promise does a Christian natural theology offer? And to whom is this promise offered? The three main audiences addressed by Christian theology are traditionally understood to be the Church, the academy, and the wider culture.[2] In this final chapter, I will explore four of the areas in which I believe such a natural theology offers an enhancement

---

[1] Agar, *Post-Secularism, Realism and Utopia*, 15–67.

[2] The best known formulation of this threefold audience is found in Tracy, *The Analogical Imagination*, 3–98. The distinction goes back much further. For comment, see Komonchak, "The Future of Theology in the Church," 33–7.

Re-Imagining Nature: The Promise of a Christian Natural Theology, First Edition.
Alister E. McGrath.
© 2017 John Wiley & Sons, Ltd. Published 2017 by John Wiley & Sons, Ltd.

of Christian theological reflection, as well as to the churches' engagement with wider culture, including both the arts and the sciences. Others could easily be added to this list, which is intended to be illustrative of the possibilities rather than definitive.

It is clear that a natural theology offers some important starting points in dialogue between different religious traditions.[3] Most religions have their "books of Scripture"; they all arguably have the same "book of nature." This offers important opportunities to reflect on how different religious traditions *read* nature,[4] opening up angles of approach to a comparative theology. Just as there has been much recent interest in the process of "scriptural reasoning,"[5] in which people of different faith traditions learn how to live with differences in both their "books of Scripture" and how they are interpreted, there is the potential for reflection on how different religious communities "see" nature, and the outcomes of this process.

A Christian natural theology also offers a significant platform for the development of an environmental ethic, in that it articulates and safeguards an ontology of nature which provides a basis for treating the natural order with respect *because of what it really is*. Much thinking in environmental ethics tends to be instrumental, focussing on what will happen to humanity through degradation of the world of nature. A Christian natural theology denies none of these instrumental considerations; it nevertheless insists that nature *is* special, and thus deserves to be treated accordingly. The way we *see* something determines the way we behave toward it.

In part, the promise of a Christian natural theology rests on its innate capacity for interdisciplinarity, in that it opens up important possibilities of intellectual dialogue and conceptual enrichment between theology, philosophy, and – to name the more obvious of its potential interlocutors – literary studies, the visual arts, and the natural sciences. It makes possible an enrichment of scientific and theological narratives, without requiring them to surrender their distinctiveness.[6]

Limits on space mean that I shall have to restrict myself to exploring four areas in which a Christian natural theology has promise for offering an expanded vision of reality, especially as the community of faith engages with the natural sciences, with the world of nature, and with the broader world of culture in which it is located. These four areas are representative of the kinds of wider and deeper engagement that a Christian natural theology sustains,

---

[3] See O. Anderson, "The Presuppositions of Religious Pluralism and the Need for Natural Theology."
[4] For a good example, see Lasher, "Dialogue with Nature and Interreligious Encounter."
[5] See especially Ford, "An Interfaith Wisdom."
[6] For a detailed exploration of this theme of the "enrichment of narratives," see A. E. McGrath, *Inventing the Universe.*

and are intended to be illustrative, not exhaustive. Each of these case studies will be engaged in some detail. I begin by offering some reflections on how a natural theology can enrich the Christian engagement with the natural sciences, while at the same time offering a way of seeing things that challenges scientific overstatement.

The Natural Sciences: Natural Theology and the Subversion of Scientism

The natural sciences are seen by many as embodying the ideals of the Enlightenment, especially in their objectivity, their universality, and their rigorous appeal to evidence in support of their core beliefs. The natural sciences have enormous strengths, in terms of their methodological rigor, their willingness to correct themselves as inquiry progresses, and their careful delimitation of the scope of the scientific method. Yet some, searching for certainty in a complex world, have forced the sciences to answer questions which lie beyond their scope. They privilege the natural sciences, holding that scientific inquiry enables the resolution of conflicts and dilemmas in contexts where traditional sources of wisdom and practical knowledge seemed to have failed.[7] "Scientism" – a contracted version of "scientific imperialism" – has gradually come to be understood as "a totalizing attitude that regards science as the ultimate standard and arbiter of all interesting questions; or alternatively that seeks to expand the very definition and scope of science to encompass all aspects of human knowledge and understanding."[8]

This privileging of scientific inquiry inevitably leads to the rejection of other methodologies as invalid. As the philosopher Mary Midgley, one of most acute critics of scientism, points out, "scientism's mistake does not lie in over-praising one form of [knowledge], but in cutting that form off from the rest of thought, in treating it as a victor who has put all the rest out of business."[9] Scientism remains influential within western culture, finding its

---

[7] For a defense of this position, see A. Rosenberg, *The Atheist's Guide to Reality*. For comment on the notion of "scientism," see Maffie, "Naturalism, Scientism and the Independence of Epistemology"; Code, "On the Poverty of Scientism"; von Hayek, *Mißbrauch und Verfall der Vernunft*. For comment on its cultural location, see Habermas, *Erkenntnis und Interesse*, 13. For the problem with demarcating science from other disciplines, see Pigliucci and Boudry, eds., *Philosophy of Pseudoscience*.

[8] Pigliucci, "New Atheism and the Scientistic Turn in the Atheism Movement," 144. For an important collection of studies of this idea and its cultural influence, see D. N. Robinson and Williams, eds., *Scientism: The New Orthodoxy*.

[9] Midgley, *Are You an Illusion?*, 5.

most recent expression in the implicit epistemology of the "New Atheism,"[10] often expressed in the strapline "reason and science."

The philosopher Bertrand Russell once remarked that, to understand Aristotle and his contemporaries, it was necessary to "apprehend their imaginative background."[11] Russell's point was that our grasp of reality is limited by our "imaginative preconceptions." One of the most distinctive features of "scientism" is its repression of the imagination, echoing the attitudes of some influential Enlightenment thinkers of the eighteenth century (see pp. 47–50). Leading representatives of scientism – such as Richard Dawkins and Peter Atkins – are thus highly critical of poetry and other imaginative endeavors, seeing these as enemies of truth and science.[12] Yet most disagree, believing that the scientistic propensity toward intellectual totalization – which, it need hardly be said, is not part of the mainstream understanding of science – inevitably leads to an impoverished grasp of the world.

There are, of course, valid concerns here – not least the fear that science might be compromised by flights of imaginative invention or fantasy which are devoid of evidential warrant. Yet the exclusion of any possibility of a synergy of reason and imagination overlooks or denies both the historical importance of the imagination in the scientific enterprise and its critical role in the synthesis of cognitively satisfying and existentially meaningful accounts of the world.[13] As the sociologist Max Weber (1864–1920) pointed out in his critique of the rationalization of modern western culture, it was difficult to see how the findings of astronomy, biology, physics, or chemistry could teach us anything about the *meaning* of the world[14] – a question which Weber recognized as fundamental to human existence, even if he was skeptical about the answers offered.

Reinhold Niebuhr argued that western culture as a whole was tainted by a pervasive imaginative failure, lacking any sense of the critical role of the "poetic imagination" in the quest for truth, whether religious or scientific.

> Fundamentalists have at least one characteristic in common with most scientists. Neither can understand that poetic and religious imagination has a way of

[10] See especially Dawkins, *The God Delusion*. For critical comment and analysis, see Pigliucci, "New Atheism and the Scientistic Turn in the Atheism Movement."
[11] B. Russell, *History of Western Philosophy*, 195.
[12] For a detailed assessment and response, see Midgley, *Science and Poetry*.
[13] For an exploration of this theme, see Funkenstein, *Theology and the Scientific Imagination from the Middle Ages to the Seventeenth Century*; Downie, "Science and the Imagination in the Age of Reason"; Beveridge, *The Art of Scientific Investigation*; Medawar, "Science and Literature."
[14] Weber, "Wissenschaft als Beruf," in *Gesammelte Aufsätze zur Wissenschaftslehre*, 524–55.

arriving at truth by giving a clue to the total meaning of things without being in any sense an analytic description of detailed facts.[15]

Especially in his debates with John Dewey, Niebuhr argued that scientism displays precisely the imaginative deficit which prevents us from discerning coherence ("the total meaning of things") and instead locks us into a mere description of the world. A deeper vision of reality was required which transcended the rehearsal of observations.

So how might a Christian natural theology offer a richer vision of reality than that of scientism? Perhaps the most fundamental answer lies in the Christian vision of reality providing ontological stabilization for a richer understanding of nature. Truth, beauty, and goodness are not imaginary, the outcome of our tragic desire to spin webs of meaning, but are rooted in a deeper order of things. They are discerned, not invented. One of the core functions of a *theologia naturalis* is to offer a theology of nature – that is to say, a compelling, comprehensive and fundamentally *religious* vision of the world as God's creation, which can illuminate our minds and excite our hearts.[16] The community of faith is "a people caught and held by a vision of a King, a kingdom, and a consummation – and by the massive contexts of culture, history, and nature, as fields of its holy disturbance."[17] A theology of nature changes the way in which we see the natural world. And, as Iris Murdoch repeatedly emphasized, the essential prerequisite for moral engagement and transformation was a capacity to see things properly.

If we are to see nature properly, we cannot rest content with the reduced, impoverished, and depersonalized account of things proposed by scientism. Reality is richer and deeper than scientism allows. Scientism ends up in a hermeneutical circle, confirming its own judgments by adopting methods that exclude alternative perspectives. Peter de Bolla points out how this problem arises in viewing works of art, in that the viewer becomes locked into "a set of expectations and beliefs – in ideological positions – to such an extent that any reading can only reiterate the grounding ideology."[18] The Christian *imaginarium* breaks this rationalist imprisonment by offering an alternative which captures the imagination and prompts a more critical and radical reassessment of possibilities. Why? Because something about nature has been *seen* which cannot be contained in and by the dogmatic and limiting

[15] Niebuhr, *Leaves from the Notebook of a Tamed Cynic*, 141. Note that the term "fundamentalism" had only entered into general circulation less than a decade earlier.

[16] Macquarrie, "The Idea of a Theology of Nature"; Gunton, "The Trinity, Natural Theology, and a Theology of Nature."

[17] Sittler, *Essays on Nature and Grace*, 119. See further Santmire, "A Reformation Theology of Nature Transfigured."

[18] De Bolla, *Art Matters*, 97.

worldview of scientism – and once it has been seen, the reliability of the worldview which caused it to be invisible is called into question.

The Christian faith is able to enrich a scientific narrative by preventing it from collapsing into what John Keats famously described as a "dull catalogue of common things."[19] How? One of the most important functions of the Christian *imaginarium* is to allow us to develop a theological response to the beauty of nature which is "germane to the aesthetic response evoked, and not to the objects that evoked them."[20] A Christian response to nature is informed by the natural world, but not limited to a scientific account of natural objects. We discern a richer and deeper vision of nature, rooted in the beauty of God. A Christian natural theology allows us to "save the phenomena" of nature (Aristotle), not merely by affirming their particularity, but by refusing to allow these to be reduced to the level of the mundane.[21]

Science offers a reliable yet partial account of reality, which requires supplementation from other sources. Max Weber used the term "disenchantment" to refer to an excessively intellectual and rationalizing way of looking at nature which limited it to what could be measured and quantified.[22] A religious perspective on nature – such as that expressed in a Christian natural theology – does not in any way deny the scientific utility of such a rationalizing approach. It simply insists that there is more that needs to be said, if a full and satisfying account of reality is to be provided, and offers a supplementation of a scientific narrative by which this might be achieved.

To understand both the limits of scientism, and the manner in which a Christian natural theology can counter its deficiencies, we must explore models for understanding the complexity of the natural world. In what follows, I shall briefly explore two ways of framing this question, which allow us insights into both the nature of scientism and the place of a natural theology: approaching nature in terms of "multiple perspectives on reality" and "multiple levels of reality."[23] Both articulate the fundamental insight that the complexity and richness of the natural world demand a corresponding complexity in human representations of nature. Simplification, though helpful heuristically, can lead to distortion, reduction, and intellectual manipulation.

First, we consider how we might think of multiple perspectives on nature. Mary Midgley insists that we need "many maps, many windows," if we are to

---

[19] See Motion, *Keats*, 431–7.

[20] Starr, *Feeling Beauty*, 55.

[21] "See Duhem, *Sozein ta phainomena*, especially 109–40. Cf. A. M. Smith, "Saving the Appearances of the Appearances."

[22] For the process, see Schluchter, *Die Entstehungsgeschichte des modernen Rationalismus*, A. J. Carroll, "Disenchantment, Rationality, and the Modernity of Max Weber."

[23] See A. E. McGrath, *Inventing the Universe*, 21–43.

represent the complexity of reality.[24] Midgley suggests that it is helpful to think of the world as a "huge aquarium" – a complex reality, which is difficult to represent from a single perspective.

> We cannot see it as a whole from above, so we peer in at it through a number of small windows . . . We can eventually make quite a lot of sense of this habitat if we patiently put together the data from different angles. But if we insist that our own window is the only one worth looking through, we shall not get very far.[25]

On this approach, scientism can be understood as the dogmatic insistence that only a scientific perspective on reality has any validity. For Midgley, scientism fails to appreciate that no single way of thinking or research method is adequate to engage, let alone to *explain*, on its own, the meaning of the natural world around us. "For most important questions in human life, a number of different conceptual tool-boxes always have to be used together."[26] If we follow the limit ourselves to the methods of science in general, or one science in particular, we needlessly lock ourselves into a "bizarrely restrictive view of meaning."[27]

In effect, as the philosopher Roger Scruton notes, scientism insists that every human question must be reduced to a *scientific* question, which can be expressed and answered in the language and using the methods of the natural sciences:

> Scientism involves the use of scientific forms and categories in order to give the appearance of science to unscientific ways of thinking. It is a form of magic, a bid to reassemble the complex matter of human life, at the magician's command, in a shape over which he can exert control. It is an attempt to *subdue* what it does not understand.[28]

Midgley's basic principle of using multiple maps to represent a complex reality raises some challenges and some significant questions – such as the need to develop and deploy an appropriate interpretative framework to settle boundary disputes.[29] Yet it also opens up some important possibilities for integration and enrichment of our vision, and helps us understand how a Christian natural theology offers a perspective on the natural world which

---

[24] Midgley, *The Myths We Live By*, 26–8.

[25] Midgley, *The Myths We Live By*, 40.

[26] Mary Midgley, unpublished essay "Dover Beach"; cited in Rivera, *The Earth is Our Home*, 179 n. 21.

[27] Midgley, *Wisdom, Information, and Wonder*, 199.

[28] Scruton, "Scientism in the Arts and Humanities," 46.

[29] As noted by Gieryn, "Boundary-Work and the Demarcation of Science from Non-Science."

subverts the presumed intellectual and existential hegemony of scientism, while enriching legitimate scientific accounts of nature by proposing and enacting additional perspectives on the world.

A second way of engaging scientism's approach to nature is to offer a stratified account of both reality itself, and our representations of that reality, which we find expressed and developed in certain forms of "critical realism." Although this term designates a number of philosophical schools, I am here using the term in the sense developed by Roy Bhaskar (1944–2014). This form of critical realism holds that reality is *stratified*, and that each level of reality thus demands and deserves different modes of investigation and representation, which are developed a posteriori rather than imposed a priori.[30] This rejects the notion of a single universal research method, characteristic of the Enlightenment, which was severely criticized from a theological perspective by Karl Barth and others.[31]

Bhaskar argues that the natural world is stratified, consisting of multiple levels, each of which requires investigation by a research method that is appropriate to that level. Bhaskar's critical realism offers an account of the relation of the natural and social sciences which affirms their methodological commonalities, while respecting their distinctions, particularly when these arise on account of their objects of investigation.

> Naturalism holds that it is possible to give an account of science under which the proper and more or less specific methods of both the natural and social sciences can fall. But it does not deny that there are significant differences in these methods, grounded in real differences in their subject-matters and in the relationships in which these sciences stand to them. . . . It is the nature of the object that determines the form of its possible science.[32]

Each science is determined by the nature of its object, and is required to investigate it in a manner which is appropriate to its distinct nature. For Bhaskar, ontology determines epistemology; what can be known about nature, and the manner in which it is to be known, is determined by nature itself. Thomas F. Torrance and others have explored the theological possibilities opened up by recognizing the "stratified structure of scientific knowledge."[33] Reliable human knowledge of any level of reality is obtained *kata physin* – that is, according to its distinct nature.

---

[30] For the fullest account, see A. E. McGrath, *A Scientific Theology*, vol. 2. *Reality*, 195–244. Note also Archer, Collier, and Porpora, *Transcendence*.
[31] See A. E. McGrath, "Theologie als Mathesis Universalis?"
[32] Bhaskar, *The Possibility of Naturalism*, 3.
[33] Torrance, *The Christian Doctrine of God*, 88–91. For discussion, see Myers, "The Stratification of Knowledge in the Thought of T. F. Torrance."

This way of conceiving reality offers Christian theology some helpful perspectives, not least in allowing "theology" and "religion" to be understood as designating quite different levels of reality, each of which has its own appropriate mode of engagement and expression. Knowledge in any field of inquiry must be developed according to the nature of the reality under study. The distinctive methods and language of theology can be understood (and defended) as resulting appropriately from its distinctive object of investigation. Instead of conforming to the unreasonable modernist demand that all sciences adopt a single research method, theology – like every other science – uses an approach that is adapted to its specific object – namely, the self-revealing God.[34]

On this approach, scientism can be seen as the improper imposition of a research method appropriate for one level of reality onto every aspect of the natural and social world.[35] For Bhaskar, "the nature of the object" determines "the form of its possible science"; scientism, however, insists that everything must be investigated using the methods of the natural science – even when these are not adapted or appropriate for the investigation of certain critical questions, such as issues of meaning or purpose. Scientism thus reduces reality to what can be known through the application of one specific research method. Epistemology thus determines ontology, in that the use of one specific research method determines what is "seen." There is simply no way in which the natural sciences can investigate "ultimate questions" (Karl Popper), as the Spanish philosopher José Ortega y Gasset (1883–1955) noted:

> Scientific truth is characterized by its precision and the certainty of its predictions. But science achieves these admirable qualities at the cost of remaining on the level of secondary concerns, leaving ultimate and decisive questions untouched.[36]

Scientism proves to be blind to these "ultimate and decisive questions" precisely because it operates at a single level of inquiry, which limits what can be "seen" when applied to other levels of reality. Thomas F. Torrance argued that the natural sciences look "at the universe and its natural order"; what he

---

[34] For comment, see A. E. McGrath, "Theologie als Mathesis Universalis?" This approach underlies the approach to theology developed by Thomas Torrance: see especially Torrance, *Theological Science*. For discussion of this approach, see Davis, "Kataphysical Inquiry, Onto-Relationality and Elemental Forms in T. F. Torrance's Doctrine of the Mediation of Jesus Christ."

[35] Bhaskar, *The Possibility of Naturalism*, 2–3. For reflections on the limits of empiricism from a critical realist perspective, see Collier, *Critical Realism*, 70–106.

[36] Ortega y Gasset, "El origen deportivo del estado," 259.

terms "theological science," however, looks "through the rational structures of the universe to the Creator."[37] Both approaches are needed.

A Christian natural theology offers a "thick" account of the many layers of the natural world, avoiding the ontological reductionism implicit within scientism's aggressive methodological naturalism, which in effect prevents any significant engagement with deeper questions of beauty and meaning within the natural world. It offers a vibrant multi-leveled account of reality, creating space for theologically important concepts such as meaning, as well as the idea as God as the ultimate ground of all things.

Now this is a point of no small importance, given the widespread concern that the scientific study of nature alienates humanity from the natural world, on account of its "exclusive pursuit of 'objectivity.'"[38] In what follows, we shall consider how a Christian natural theology offers us a framework for appreciating the beauty of nature – especially natural landscapes – and connecting this with core themes of the Christian faith.

The Affective Imagination: Natural Theology and the Spirituality of Nature

We have already noted that an integral aspect of the project of a Christian natural theology is what might be termed a "theology of nature." Yet this is too easily misunderstood simply as cognitive or analytical reflection on nature, which marginalizes, excludes, or simply overlooks the affective and imaginative aspects of theology.[39] The Christian tradition is rich in examples of the affective and imaginative enhancement of purely "doctrinal" accounts of matters of faith. An obvious example lies to hand in the medieval Augustinian tradition, characterized by a strongly affective understanding of theology which refused to limit reflection on the death of Christ on the cross to logocentric "theories of the atonement" and developed tools for ensuring that its powerful emotional aspects were properly understood.[40]

As a detailed study of the Christian theological tradition makes clear, there is a rich heritage of correlating doctrine and the imagination, which calls out to be used in theological reflection on the natural world.[41] Jonathan Edwards

[37] Torrance, *Reality and Evangelical Theology*, 70.
[38] For this thesis, see Roszak, *Where the Wasteland Ends*; Barfield, *The Rediscovery of Meaning and Other Essays*, 216.
[39] A point stressed in J. K. A. Smith, *Imagining the Kingdom*, 103–49.
[40] See the excellent study of Schuppisser, "Schauen mit den Augen des Herzens."
[41] See, for example, Volpe's critical rereading of Gregory of Nyssa's account of the relation of doctrine and imagination: Volpe, *Rethinking Christian Identity*, 183–221. See also Zahl, "On the Affective Salience of Doctrines."

(1703–58), perhaps America's greatest Christian theologian, developed an approach to theology which at the very least safeguarded the affective aspects of faith (many would say *emphasized* those aspects), especially in his reflections on the world of nature.[42] For Edwards, regeneration "establishes a new vision, radically different from that of natural understanding and sight."[43] As a result, nature is seen in a new way, its beauty being highlighted and exhibited by the new vision of reality resulting from conversion.[44] This is particularly evident in one of Edwards's most lyrical descriptions of nature:

> When we are delighted with flowery meadows and gentle breezes of wind, we may consider that we only see the emanations of the sweet benevolence of Jesus Christ; when we behold the fragrant rose and lily, we see his love and purity. So the green trees and fields, and singing of birds, are emanations of his infinite joy and benignity; the easiness and naturalness of trees and vines [are] shadows of his infinite beauty and loveliness; the crystal rivers and murmuring streams have the footsteps of his sweet grace and bounty.[45]

The Christian vision of reality allows us to see nature in such a way that its beauties "are really emanations, or shadows, of the excellencies of the Son of God."[46]

Much contemporary discussion, however, focusses on a related, though clearly distinct theme – the "spirituality of nature."[47] The term "spirituality" has found widespread acceptance in recent decades, often being used to emphasize the inner aspect of religious traditions, as opposed to their outward or institutional forms, and particularly to avoid the impoverishment which results from an excessively rational approach to religious engagement and reflection.

> The term spirituality as currently used, indicates both the unity at the heart of religious traditions and the transformative inner depth or meaning of those traditions . . . It supplies a term which transcends particular religions and it suggests a non-reductionist understanding of human life. It is more firmly associated than religion with creativity and imagination, with change, and with relationship.[48]

---

[42] McClymond and McDermott, *The Theology of Jonathan Edwards*, 311–20.

[43] Simonson, "Typology, Imagination, and Jonathan Edwards," 28–9. Cf. McClymond and McDermott, *The Theology of Jonathan Edwards*, 373–88.

[44] B. C. Lane, "Jonathan Edwards on Beauty, Desire and the Sensory World"; cf. McClymond and McDermott, *The Theology of Jonathan Edwards*, 93–101.

[45] J. Edwards, Miscellanies, no. 108, in *Works*, vol. 13, 279.

[46] J. Edwards, Miscellanies, no. 108, in *Works*, vol. 13, 279.

[47] For an excellent account, see Santmire, *Before Nature*, 129–84.

[48] A. S. King, "Spirituality," 346. See also Schneiders, "Religion vs. Spirituality." Orthodoxy generally regards western theology as having adopted an excessively rationalist approach, which introduces an unnecessary and improper distinction between "theology" and "spirituality."

As is clear from Edwards's approach, a Christian spirituality is intertwined with and informed by a Christian theology, even if their points of focus are not the same.[49] So how might a Christian natural theology enable or encourage such a "transformative inner depth" in our relationship with the natural world? Once more, the issue of how we *see* nature emerges as being of critical importance. As Iris Murdoch observed, "I can only choose within the world I can see, in the moral sense of 'see' which implies that clear vision is a result of moral imagination and moral effort."[50] The Christian *imaginarium* gives us this way of seeing the world, which enables and informs both reflection and action, and produces "new value in what we see and what we feel."[51]

To explore this point further, we shall focus on one specific issue – the aesthetics of natural landscapes, familiar to all readers of the Romantic poets. For Elaine Scarry, the love of beauty is part of human nature. "No matter how long beautiful things endure, they cannot out-endure our longing for them."[52] We have already touched on some themes of importance relating to this topic (pp. 87–92); there is, however, more that needs to be considered. *Why* are such landscapes seen to be beautiful? And how are we to understand this beauty?[53] Is it an aspect of a self-enclosed system, with no external reference? Or does it point beyond itself, intimating the presence of a transcendent beauty beyond it?

One of the most influential responses to this question is due to the Canadian philosopher Allen Carlson. Objects in the natural world – including landscapes – must not be considered as "works of art," but as natural entities, requiring a "natural" framework of interpretation. For Carlson, there is only one such interpretative framework – that afforded by the natural sciences.[54] "Scientific knowledge is essential for appropriate appreciation of nature."[55] It is a curious suggestion, which raises certain rather difficult questions.

---

[49] Schneiders, "Religion vs. Spirituality," 176–81. Edwards would not, of course, endorse the modern distinction between "theology" and "spirituality."

[50] Murdoch, "Vision and Choice in Morality," 36–7. This point is of central importance to Stanley Hauerwas's theological ethics.

[51] Starr, *Feeling Beauty*, 66. Starr's comments refer specifically to beauty, but can easily be adapted to the vision of truth, beauty, and goodness enfolded within a Christian natural theology.

[52] Scarry, *On Beauty and Being Just*, 50.

[53] Porteous, *Environmental Aesthetics*, 5–41. Porteous rightly notes a frustrating lack of interest in the origins of the aesthetic stimulus: Porteous, *Environmental Aesthetics*, 24.

[54] See especially Carlson, *Aesthetics and the Environment*, 85–95. For further discussion, see Brady, "Imagination and the Aesthetic Appreciation of Nature"; Hepburn, "Contemporary Aesthetics and the Neglect of Natural Beauty."

[55] Carlson, *Aesthetics and the Environment*, 90. Holmes Rolston also adopts such an approach, arguing that our aesthetic evaluation of nature must be based on a recognition of its scientific complexity: Rolston, "Does Aesthetic Appreciation of Landscapes Need to Be Science-Based?"

First, Carlson is a little vague about what he means by science, and shows little interest in questions about potential applications of the scientific method to the human aesthetic appreciation of nature. He tends to think of science as "facts," and thus overlooks the risk of depicting a "big world of facts" with only a "little peripheral area of value."[56] He does not discuss the critically important issue of disenchantment which attends the scientific rationalization of nature. Nor does he deal with the issue of loss of a sense of wonder through overfamiliarity (pp. 113–16), which is a major concern for many scientists engaged with the investigation of nature – for example, astronomers. There is no discussion of aesthetics as an (arbitrary?) outcome of the process of evolution, as suggested by some schools of evolutionary psychology. Carlson's somewhat uncritical adoption of the natural sciences provides him with no protection against a scientism which argues that such an emotional response to nature is simply an evolutionary by-product, without any significant correlate.

Second, it is far from clear why a "scientific knowledge" should be required for a proper appreciation of a landscape. Suppose I stand in a valley, surveying a grand vista of mountains, woods, and streams, which impresses me as beautiful. Do I need to know precisely what sort of trees are there in the woods to experience that sense of beauty? Do I need to know the geological history of the mountains to experience a sense of awe? No. My impression of beauty is evoked by the landscape as a whole, not by meticulous detailed information about its individual components. It is a cumulative experience, not the sum of individual elements. It is possible to argue that science may help me to appreciate something more fully, adding rational comprehension and appreciation to what is essentially an aesthetic experience. But science does not generate that experience in the first place.

Yet there is a third point which is particularly important. Carlson's analysis treats nature as an object without an author. In part, this reflects his decision to eschew any analogy between nature and a human work of art; in part, it reflects his naturalist inclination to dispense with any notion, however construed, of divine creation of the world. Yet the difficulty is clear: "modern aesthetics simply cannot handle objects which have no author."[57] This does not mean that we do not find natural objects beautiful; it is clear that we do.[58] Rather, the point is that many find it difficult to cope conceptually with an object that simply "is" beautiful, rather than one which has been "made" beautiful.

---

[56] Murdoch, *The Sovereignty of Good*, 27.
[57] Porteous, *Environmental Aesthetics*, 23.
[58] See the discussions in Huston *et al.*, eds., *Art, Aesthetics, and the Brain*.

The Christian *imaginarium* offers us a conceptual net that can be thrown over our aesthetic experience of nature, holding together its imaginative and rational elements. The experience of beauty is affirmed, and engaged with a "penetrative imagination" (Ruskin),[59] grounded in the Christian vision of reality, that penetrates to the heart of beautiful objects, and grasps what the uninformed senses would otherwise overlook. This *imaginarium* provides ontological security for the semiotic link between the natural world and God, affirming that nature can be read as a sign of the creator – not as an imposition of an alien meaning, but as a discernment of their true significance. Nature can be seen as a divine work of art – something that is *authored*, even if discernment of its meaning and value requires tutored engagement.[60]

This allows us to make the critical connection between natural theology and a spirituality of the created order. The re-imagination of nature outlined in this volume allows a constant engagement of enrichment of our thoughts about God and creation. It is not a question of a "hermeneutical circle" in which we are locked into certain self-referential modes of thought from which we cannot escape; rather, the Christian *imaginarium* enables an iterative process of ascension – a hermeneutical spiral – in which there is a "circularity of motion" between our thoughts of God and creation, between *significans* and *signum*, leading to an enhanced appreciation and enriched understanding of both God and the natural world.[61]

Already being in possession of a concept of God, the community of faith finds that this is imaginatively enriched and expanded by the beauty and vastness of the created order, such as the night sky. And so it returns to its concept of God, and finds that it has been deepened in an "enriched cognition." This, after all, seems to be the trajectory of thought explored in Psalm 19: "The heavens declare the glory of the Lord." Israel, we must appreciate, already knew about God. There was no question of an unknown God being disclosed through the night sky. Rather, contemplation of the night sky offered an imaginative enrichment of Israel's vision of God.

Part of that process of reflection involves the question of our place within the order of nature. The spiral of reflection on the relation of creation and creator outlined above is clearly significant in developing what Iris Murdoch termed "techniques of unselfing," paralleling Christian contemplative and ascetic practices designed to heighten our attentiveness toward God, and secure liberation from potentially destructive self-preoccupation and self-deception.

---

[59] Ruskin, *Complete Works*, vol. 4, 278, 317.
[60] For connections between natural theology and human works of art, see Monti, *A Natural Theology of the Arts*, 135–74.
[61] I borrow this imagery from R. L. Hart, *Unfinished Man and the Imagination*, 60–3.

In intellectual disciplines and in the enjoyment of art and nature we discover value in our ability to forget self, to be realistic, to perceive justly. We use our imagination not to escape the world but to join it, and this exhilarates us because of the distance between our ordinary dulled consciousness and an apprehension of the real.[62]

Murdoch's reflections open up further possibilities for discussion of the role of a natural theology – such as the role of the imagination in enabling us to "join" the world, and the difficulties that arise from attempting to deploy "our ordinary dulled consciousness" to apprehend reality.

Yet perhaps the greatest transformation that Christianity enabled in our attititudes toward and relationship with the natural world is that noted by William James: "At a single stroke, [theism] changes the dead blank *it* of the world into a living *thou*, with whom the whole man may have dealings."[63] James here uses the language of a "second person relationship" with the natural world, perhaps best known from the writings of Martin Buber, where it is framed in terms of the tension between the world as *Du* and as *Es*.[64] It can also be framed in terms of the more psychological notion of "joint attention,"[65] which allows a deepened theological appreciation of the sense of awe in the presence of natural vastness.

Boundaries and Trespass: Natural Theology and Systematic Theology

There are many legitimate criticisms that could be made of this volume, and one of them is that I have not explored the relationship between natural theology and systematic theology in any depth. It is a fair criticism. The only argument I offer in my defense is the need to clarify what I mean by "natural theology" before entering into this discussion.[66] This, it seems to me, is an entirely appropriate point at which to consider this important relationship in more detail.

---

[62] Murdoch, *The Sovereignty of Good*, 88.

[63] James, *The Will to Believe*, 127.

[64] For an excellent introduction to the origins of this way of thinking and its wider implications, see Casper, *Das dialogische Denken*.

[65] De Cruz and de Smedt, "Delighting in Natural Beauty," 173–83.

[66] It is also important to clarify what is meant by "systematic" theology, particularly the complex question of whether theology is a "science" (*Wissenschaft*) – a question that cannot be resolved here. For an important analysis of this debate in the nineteenth century, see Zachhuber, *Theology as Science in Nineteenth-Century Germany*, especially 27–50. For its counterpart in High Scholasticism, see Chenu, *La théologie comme science au XIIIe siècle*.

Much has been written about the fragmentation of theology, in which a formerly unitary discipline has broken apart into specialist areas, each with its own sense of identity and privilege. In an influential study, Edward Farley argued that the term *theologia* has lost its original meaning as "sapiential and personal knowledge of divine self-disclosure" which leads to "wisdom or discerning judgment indispensable for human living."[67] In part, this is simply due to the expansion of the topic, which is the inevitable result of professional specialization, and can be seen in any intellectual discipline – such as my own field of chemistry, which now consists of myriad specialist subfields, with little sense of belonging to a greater or colligating whole.[68]

The same concern must be expressed in the case of theology, where components of a coherent vision have become research fields in their own right, resulting in both professional autonomy and a sense of independence from any single coordinating vision. Scholars in the field of New Testament studies, spirituality, philosophy of religion, and systematic theology rarely transgress professional boundaries. There is probably little that can be done to reverse this trend. However, it is important to note that the relationship between natural theology and systematic theology is open to exploration in ways that create possibilities for mutual enrichment and dialogue, which might stimulate wider discussion and reflection.

To reiterate a by now familiar point: any account of the relationship between natural theology and systematic theology depends entirely on how "natural theology" is defined. The regnant definition of natural theology within the discipline of the philosophy of religion as "the enterprise of providing support for religious beliefs by starting from premises that neither are nor presuppose any religious beliefs"[69] dates from the early modern period, at a time of conceptual innovation and terminological malleability. Two points need to be made here.

First, the understanding of the meaning of "natural theology" – along with other pivotal concepts, including both "science" and "religion" – is determined by their cultural location.[70] There is no "essential" definition of any of these ideas; they are all subject to social negotiation. "Natural theology" has no "essential" meaning, intrinsic to its nature, and claiming authority on account of its inherent correctness. Rather, the preferred meaning of this term is defined by communities of interest, having a specific meaning within those groups. Raymond de Sebonde's notion of *theologia naturalis* is very difficult to categorize using the professional templates of twenty-

---

[67] Farley, *Theologia*, x, 7.
[68] Reinhardt, "Disciplines, Research Fields, and Their Boundaries."
[69] Alston, *Perceiving God*, 289.
[70] See especially P. Harrison, *The Territories of Science and Religion*.

first-century theology. This, however, does not reflect confusion or incoherence on Sebonde's part, but the subsequent imposition of mental barriers and boundaries that now cannot accommodate his rich and complex approach under a single category.

Second, the concept of "natural theology" is thus open to redescription by other theological stakeholders, who find the restricted meaning associated with other interpretive communities to be inadequate or misleading. The broader Christian theological community needs to retrieve older and wiser ways of conceiving a natural theology, noting that the term *theologia naturalis* was used surprisingly infrequently prior to 1600, and certainly not to designate a proof of God's existence. Some might object that this will lead to the same term being understood in quite different manners by different interpretive communities. This may be inconvenient, but it is normal practice within professional communities, including specialist subject groups within the natural sciences.

If natural theology is understood as an attempt to derive a theological system from natural reason or reflection on the natural world, it clearly stands in a potentially agonistic relationship with systematic theology.[71] As the example of Thomas Aquinas indicates, however, this need not be the case.[72] Aquinas's mature discussion of the relation of faith and reason is not framed using the language of "natural theology," but in terms of the potential complementarity of two distinct forms of wisdom: philosophical reflection on creatures, considered as effects of God; and the revealed truths of Christian doctrine. "The light of faith [*lumen fidei*], which is graciously imparted to us, does not abolish the light of natural reason [*lumen naturalis rationis*], given to us by God."[73]

In the end, however, these discussions ultimately rest on questions of definition. The concerns of Karl Barth are well known, and continue to be represented in contemporary German-language discussions of natural theology.[74] The question of the ground and extent of the capacity of the natural world to be analogous to the divine remains complex and contested.[75] Yet

[71] Tegtmeyer, *Gott, Geist, Vernunft*, 345–63.

[72] See White, *Wisdom in the Face of Modernity*, 69–75. For an important Catholic statement of this position, see Knauer, "Natürliche Gotteserkenntnis."

[73] Aquinas, *Expositio de Trinitate*, q. 2 a. 3. For comment, see Elders, "Le rôle de la philosophie en théologie"; Honnefelder, "Weisheit durch den Weg der Wissenschaft." For a leading Catholic New Testament scholar's reflections on core Pauline texts on this theme, see Kertelge, "'Natürliche Theologie' und Rechtfertigung aus dem Glauben bei Paulus."

[74] See, for example, Ruster, *Der verwechselbare Gott*, who argues that natural theology is unnecessary and improper. On Barth, see Szekeres, "Karl Barth und die natürliche Theologie"; Gestrich, *Neuzeitliches Denken und die Spaltung der dialektischen Theologie*.

[75] Roth, *Gott im Widerspruch?*, 76–81. For the development of this idea in the Middle Ages, see Pannenberg, *Analogie und Offenbarung*, 52–180.

the emerging consensus within Protestant theology since about 1990 is that natural theology, when rightly understood, must be considered an integral part of Christian theology.[76] It is clear, however, that further discussion of the nature and dogmatic location of natural theology is required.

One significant contribution to this discussion merits closer attention. The leading Scottish Reformed theologian Thomas F. Torrance, who played a leading role in disseminating the ideas of Karl Barth in the English-speaking world, rejects the notion of natural theology, understood as a natural knowledge of God originating independently of God's self-revelation.[77] Rather, Torrance argues for a "reformulated natural theology" which amounts to a reconceptualization of natural theology as an integral aspect of systematic theology.[78] Torrance sees – as I do – a "reformulated natural theology" as being a necessary consequence of a properly Christian knowledge of God, rather than a necessary (though not sufficient condition) for our knowledge of God in the first place.

In reflecting on Barth's criticism of natural theology, Torrance stresses that Barth's rejection of the notion is not based on the grounds of rational skepticism or some form of *via negationis* which denies any positive knowledge of God. Rather, the issue concerns the innate human desire to ground theology on anthropocentric foundations, as an assertion of human autonomy.[79] Any claim to a "natural knowledge of God," as Barth understands it, is inseparable from his belief that humanity seeks to assert and justify itself "over against the grace of God," which inevitably leads to a form of natural theology that is "antithetical to knowledge of God as he really is in his acts of revelation and grace."[80]

If all theology proceeds from God's self-revelation in Christ, as Barth insists is indeed the case, then it might seem that there remains no valid place for natural theology. Yet Torrance points out that Barth is not denying the possibility or even the actuality of natural theology. "What Barth objects to in natural theology is not its rational structure as such, but its *independent* character, i.e. the autonomous rational structure which it develops on the

---

[76] See the argument of Irlenborn, "Abschied von der 'natürlichen Theologie'?" Irlenborn notes particularly the following major discussions in drawing this conclusion: Jüngel, "Das Dilemma der natürlichen Theologie und die Wahrheit ihres Problems"; Pannenberg, *Systematische Theologie*, vol. 1, 83–132; Kraus, *Gotteserkenntnis ohne Offenbarung und Glaube?*

[77] See Torrance's discussion of Barth: Torrance, "The Problem of Natural Theology in the Thought of Karl Barth."

[78] For a good discussion, see McMaken, "The Impossibility of Natural Knowledge of God in T. F. Torrance's Reformulated Natural Theology."

[79] Torrance, "The Problem of Natural Theology in the Thought of Karl Barth," 125.

[80] Torrance, "The Problem of Natural Theology in the Thought of Karl Barth," 125.

ground of 'nature alone' in abstraction from the active self-disclosure of the living God."[81]

According to Torrance, Barth's objection to natural theology lies in the perceived danger that such a natural theology will be seen as an independent and equally valid route to human knowledge of God, which may be had under conditions of our choosing. Yet this danger is averted if natural theology is itself seen as a subordinate aspect of revealed theology, legitimated by and grounded upon revealed theology rather than natural presuppositions or insights. The authorization for natural theology does not lie in its own intrinsic structures, but in divine revelation itself, which both legitimates it and defines its scope.[82] Natural theology has a proper and significant place *within the scope of revealed theology.*

> Barth can say that *theologia naturalis* is included and brought to light within *theologia revelata*, for in the reality of divine grace there is included the truth of the divine creation. In this sense Barth can interpret, and claim as true, the dictum of St Thomas that grace does not destroy nature but perfects and fulfils it, and can go on to argue that the meaning of God's revelation becomes manifest to us as it brings into full light the buried and forgotten truth of the creation.[83]

Torrance thus presents his notion of a "reformulated natural theology," not as a *correction* of Barth, but as the unfolding of lines of thought which are implicit in Barth's own theological program.[84] Although Torrance's interpretation of Barth has met with resistance from some Barth scholars,[85] it offers a helpful perspective on how a natural theology can be reconceived in a helpful and productive manner, avoiding some of the legitimate concerns raised by Barth. Some aspects of Torrance's approach can be discerned in the approach developed in this volume.

---

[81] Torrance, "The Problem of Natural Theology in the Thought of Karl Barth," 128.

[82] Torrance, "The Problem of Natural Theology in the Thought of Karl Barth," 128–9.

[83] Torrance, "The Problem of Natural Theology in the Thought of Karl Barth," 128–9. Richard Muller's assessment of the place of natural theology in Protestant Orthodoxy should be noted here: Muller, *Post-Reformation Reformed Dogmatics*, vol. 1, 307–8: Natural theology "exists as a result rather than as a basis for Christian doctrine. The truths of natural theology are not excluded from supernatural theology – they are included in the body of revealed doctrine – not because natural theology is the rational foundation of the system but because its truths belong to the higher truth."

[84] For reflections of Torrance's relation to Barth at this point, see see McMaken, "The Impossibility of Natural Knowledge of God in T. F. Torrance's Reformulated Natural Theology," 337–9.

[85] E.g., Molnar, "Natural Theology Revisited," which, as McMaken points out, misreads Torrance at crucial points.

My approach recognizes that the Christian faith naturally gives rise to a way of looking at the natural world, shaped by the Christian *imaginarium*, which is not seen as the basis for faith or as a source for our knowledge of God, but rather as the *consequence* of that knowledge. As such, it allows a "theory-laden" observation of the natural world which is informed by the distinctive Trinitarian ontology of the Christian faith, which is not limited to cognitive or conceptual analysis, but extends to include affective, relational, and existential issues. It avoids the excessive detachment of attitude and rationalizing style of analysis – sadly, characteristic of certain neo-scholastic approaches to theology, both Catholic and Protestant – which so signally fail to capture the richness of the natural world.

Modernist assumptions have dominated recent presentations of natural theology within works of systematic theology, which tend to reduce natural theology to rationalist categories. Modernity's characteristic instinct to suppress the theological role of the imagination lingers on, impoverishing our vision for an enterprise which is – and ought to be – both rational and imaginative.[86] Neither the academy nor the Church can be trapped within a conceptualization of natural theology that reflects the social and cultural situation of the early modern period, focussing primarily (sometimes, it has to be said, *exclusively*) on the rationality of belief in God. We need to move on, and reclaim a richer vision of natural theology.

Yet, despite such concerns, it remains essential to consider the rationality of the Christian faith. In the final section of this work, we shall consider how a Christian natural theology project relates to the apologetic ministry of the churches.

Apologetics: Natural Theology and Public Engagement

The rise of the "New Atheism" in the period 2006–7 raised fundamental questions about the rationality of the Christian faith, and particularly its relation to the natural sciences. Although this movement soon faded, in terms of both its public profile and the perceived plausibility of its critique of religion, it served to highlight the importance of apologetics to the ministry of the Christian churches. Above all, it raised the question of how Christianity could affirm and defend its core beliefs *extra muros ecclesiae*. This growing appreciation of the importance of a theologically informed public engagement created a new awareness of the potential importance of natural

---

[86] Note the points made in Caldecott, *Beauty for Truth's Sake*, 37–52.

theology to present "a God who is known through a form of publicly accessible reason."[87]

Such a move has met with resistance. For some – such as Karl Barth – apologetics is a bastard child of theology, of questionable legitimacy and spurious utility. Theology is primarily concerned with the unfolding of the truth of the Christian faith. The best apologetics is thus a good dogmatics. Perhaps this may have been true in the settled days of western European Christian hegemony, when few felt the need to defend Christianity against its critics, or attempt an intellectual justification of its leading themes in the face of criticism and misunderstanding. Yet the situation has changed. Western Christianity now needs a theologically informed apologetics if it is to secure its future in an increasingly complex cultural context.

Barth regarded apologetics, as generally understood, as the false task of describing and defending the Christian faith without the fundamental presupposition of faith in the Word of God.[88] In response to those who advocated some form of natural theology, Barth held that creation can only be understood as creation in the light of Jesus Christ. "It is as we know this Father that we know the Creator, and not vice versa."[89] The approach adopted in this work follows a similar trajectory, insisting that the natural world is only *rightly* understood when it is seen in the light of the informing framework of the Christian faith. Yet Barth's dogmatic approach leaves an important question unanswered: what reasons might be given to those outside the community of faith for believing that the Christian framework is right?

This is hardly a new question. Attentiveness to the history of Christianity suggests that an apologetic dimension to theology has actually been the norm, rather than the exception.[90] The major cultural changes in western culture since the Second World War have led most western theologians since about 1950 to recognize the importance of apologetics. For example, Emil Brunner's reflections on the post-war situation led him to emphasize the missionary challenges confronting the western churches, and to ensure that they were resourced theologically as they engaged in this task. Brunner thus included a section entitled "Missionary Theology" in the prolegomena to his *Dogmatics*,[91] which emphasized the role of theology in "removing the obstacles which lie on the road between the gospel and its audience – namely, those obstacles which are amenable to intellectual reflection."

[87] Ormerod, *A Public God*, ix.
[88] K. Barth, *Church Dogmatics*, ii/1, 8; 93–5.
[89] K. Barth, *Church Dogmatics*, iii/1, 39.
[90] See, for example, Dulles, *A History of Apologetics*, Pelikan, *Christianity and Classical Culture*.
[91] Brunner, *Dogmatik I*, 108–9.

Brunner's approach is important, as it demonstrates that there are alternatives available to Barth. By the late 1920s, Brunner had become convinced of the need for theology to be conceived, not merely as the dogmatic enterprise of expounding and correlating key doctrinal themes in the service of the Church, but in terms of engaging and critiquing contemporary culture. Although Brunner initially used the term "eristic" to designate the "second task of theology," it is clear that the general approach he adopted is better understood in terms of "apologetics" – the challenging of prevailing cultural assumptions, and the identification and exploitation of ways in which the Christian proclamation can be brought into contact with contemporary cultural concerns.[92] This led him to inform Barth that he believed that theology was "fundamentally nothing other than a specific form of evangelisation."[93]

As we noted earlier (pp. 102–4), the forms of "physico-theology" which emerged in England during the early modern period were explicitly apologetic in orientation, intended to show that the rational transparency of nature, especially as uncovered and highlighted by Newtonian physics, was consistent with the Christian revelation. Although "physico-theology" was initially concerned as much with providing a religious motivation for the natural sciences as offering confirmation of theistic belief, its primary function – especially in the early Boyle Lectures – was to offer rational support for religious belief.[94] One aspect of the natural theology project has thus been explicitly apologetic. Some of the forms of natural theology that emerged from this period are now seen as being of questionable utility – including, it must be said, William Paley's classic work *Natural Theology* (1802), which achieved the status of a popular classic in England during the early nineteenth century.[95]

There is, however, ample evidence to suggest that there has been renewed interest in recent decades in the apologetic potential of a natural theology project, such as that set out in this work. Although such approaches are adopted by many Christian theologians, it is important to note the stimulus toward its development by natural scientists who are aware of the deeper theological questions raised, yet not answered, by scientific theorization.[96] Although some suggest that a priori proofs of God's existence, such as that

---

[92] Vogelsanger, "Theologie als Apologie des Glaubens"; Kramer, "Die andere Aufgabe der Theologie"; A. E. McGrath, *Emil Brunner*, 66–74.

[93] Letter to Barth, December 13, 1932; *Karl Barth–Emil Brunner, Briefwechsel*, 212.

[94] Dahm, "Science and Apologetics in the Early Boyle Lectures."

[95] Fyfe, "Publishing and the Classics."

[96] Representative examples include Polkinghorne, "The New Natural Theology"; McGrew and DePoe, "Natural Theology and the Uses of Argument"; Ormerod and Crysdale, *Creator God, Evolving World*; A. E. McGrath, *The Open Secret.*

developed in modern versions of Anselm of Canterbury's ontological argument, do not strictly come under the scope of natural theology (in that they make no appeal to the natural world), others would argue that such arguments conform to the basic idea of natural theology as "the enterprise of providing support for religious beliefs by starting from premises that neither are nor presuppose any religious beliefs."[97]

The approach adopted in this volume is similar to that developed by many theologians with interests in the field of science and religion. Robert John Russell, for example, describes his own theological program as

> a project in constructive theology, with special attention to a theology of nature. This hypothesis should be taken not as a form of natural theology, nor one of physical-theology, and most certainly not an argument from design. Instead it is part of a general constructive Trinitarian theology pursued in the tradition of *fides quaerens intellectum*, whose warrant and justification lie elsewhere and which incorporates the results of science and the concerns for nature into its broader framework mediated by philosophy.[98]

I echo many of these themes. Like Russell, I do not set out to prove the fundamentals of Christian belief, but rather to explore the intellectual possibilities and implications of a basic Trinitarian theology – above all, in relation to our understanding of the natural world. I do not consider the "warrant and justification" of such a theology to lie in reflection on nature or innate ideas, although I consider these to be signs and indicators of the greater truth that lies beyond them. I do not see my own approach as a form of physico-theology, as this is traditionally understood; rather, I see the Christian theological tradition as opening up understandings of the natural world which allow a broad or "thick" natural theology project to be developed *retrospectively* – that is to say, the natural theology project here outlined is not to be seen as a *warrant or proof* of the Christian faith, but as its *outcome*.

Yet it is an outcome that is itself evidencing of faith. This theme is echoed in one of C. S. Lewis's most interesting remarks: "I believe in Christianity as I believe that the Sun has risen, not only because I see it, but because by it, I see everything else" – including science, art, and morality.[99] For Lewis, the

---

[97] Alston, *Perceiving God*, 289. For a discussion of Anselm's approach within the rubric of a natural theology, see Tegtmeyer, *Gott, Geist, Vernunft*, 81–121.

[98] R. J. Russell, "Special Providence and Genetic Mutation," 196. For the context to Russell's approach, see T. Peters, "Robert John Russell's Contribution to the Theology and Science Dialogue."

[99] Lewis, *Essay Collection*, 20–1. For further reflection, see A. E. McGrath, "The Privileging of Vision."

Christian *imaginarium* is able to "contain" or "fit in" what might otherwise seem disordered and disconnected, bringing into focus what might otherwise seem blurred or chaotic. The capacity of faith to contain or embrace reality is seen by Lewis as an indication of its truth, in effect defining epistemic value in terms of explanatory virtue.[100]

Although my approach to natural theology is not fundamentally apologetic, it will be obvious that it opens up important apologetic possibilities, along the lines suggested by Lewis. The phenomena do not prove faith; faith, however explains and accommodates the phenomena. In particular, it provides a rational and imaginative framework – an *imaginarium* – to reflect on how experience and observation fit in to a deeper vision of things.[101]

In this section, I will focus on one specific manner in which a "thick" account of natural theology can play an important apologetic role, encouraging an "intellectual conversion" which allows us to discern a deeper structure to the natural world around us.[102] Where some argue that there are certain incorrigible considerations that force us to draw the conclusion that God exists, I suggest that the Christian faith can be considered to be, in some respects, like a good scientific theory: it gathers together or "colligates" observations and experiences in a manner that is plausible, expansive, and productive.[103]

When confronted with a mass of observations, the scientist's fundamental instinct is to try and work out what "big picture" or "theory" makes the most sense of them. Knowing that there are multiple possible theories – in the sense of "ways of beholding" – of such observations, the scientist is then obliged to determine which of these is to be regarded as the best explanation, using a series of epistemic criteria, such as simplicity or comprehensiveness.[104] "We may characterize the best explanation as the one which would, if correct, be the most explanatory or provide the most understanding: the 'loveliest' explanation."[105] The best theory is the one

---

[100] A. E. McGrath, "An Enhanced Vision of Rationality." For a similar theme in G. K. Chesterton's writings, see Oddie, *Chesterton and the Romance of Orthodoxy*, 240–1. We should not exaggerate the similarities between explanatory merit and likelihood: see Iranzo, "Bayesianism and Inference to the Best Explanation," 94–5.

[101] For the importance and potential roles of the imagination in apologetics, see A. Milbank, "Apologetics and the Imagination"; Holyer, "C. S. Lewis on the Epistemic of the Imagination."

[102] The phrase "intellectual conversion" is of particular importance in the later writings of Bernard Lonergan. For its use in relation to the apologetic role of natural theology, see Ormerod, *A Public God*, 53–77.

[103] For this approach, see Polkinghorne, "Physics and Metaphysics in a Trinitarian Perspective."

[104] Lipton, *Inference to the Best Explanation*, identifies such properties as scope, simplicity, unification, mechanism, and precision as means of distinguishing good explanations from bad ones.

[105] Lipton, *Inference to the Best Explanation*, 59.

that is able to fit in observations and experiences most elegantly, most simply, most comprehensively, and most fruitfully.

The apologetic question is thus the following: does the Christian *theōria* – which can be parsed as "a way of seeing things" – make the best sense of what we experience within us, and observe in the natural world around us? Is a *theōria* which is held to be grounded in divine revelation, and does not itself originate from natural reflection, capable of accommodating what is known of the natural world? While there is more to Christianity than making sense of reality, the intellectual capaciousness of faith cannot be overlooked. As the Harvard psychologist William James argued, a core element of a religion such as Christianity is a "faith in the existence of an unseen order of some kind in which the riddles of the natural order may be found and explained."[106]

A concern might be raised at this point. On what grounds is the idea of God proposed in the first place? Charles Peirce used the term "abduction" to refer a search for a way of seeing things that fitted in observations naturally and persuasively. The logic of this approach could be represented as follows:

1   The surprising fact, *C*, is observed.
2   But if *A* were true, *C* would be expected as a matter of course.
3   Hence there is reason to suspect that *A* is true.[107]

For Peirce, a "logic of discovery" led to the formulation of possible explanations; a "logic of justification" was then deployed to determine whether the proposed explanatory frameworks made sense of the world.

William Whewell, one of the greatest early Victorian philosophers of the empirical sciences, wrote of the capacity of a good theory to "colligate" observations, like a string holding together a group of pearls in a necklace. Whewell held that all observation involves what he terms "unconscious inference," in that what is observed is actually unconsciously or automatically interpreted in terms of a set of ideas. Like Bacon before him, Whewell rejected the deficient notion of induction as a mere enumeration of observations. Instead, Whewell developed the idea that induction was an active process of reflection that added something essential to this process of enumeration – namely, some kind of organizing principle. In the process of induction, he suggested, "there is a New Element added to the combination [of instances] by the very act of thought by which they were combined."[108] Whewell held that this "act of thought" was to be understood as a process of "colligation" – the mental operation of bringing together a

---

[106] James, *The Will to Believe*, 51.
[107] Peirce, *Collected Papers*, vol. 5, 189.
[108] Whewell, *The Philosophy of the Inductive Sciences*, vol. 2, 48.

number of empirical facts by "superinducing" upon them a way of thinking which unites the facts. For Whewell, this renders them capable of being expressed by a general law, which both identifies and illuminates the "true bond of Unity by which the phenomena are held together."[109]

One of the points that emerges from Whewell's perceptive analysis is that a good theory should be able to "colligate" observations that might hitherto have been regarded as disconnected. Newton's theory of gravity thus "colligated" observations that had up to that point been seen as unconnected and unrelated – such as the falling of an apple to the ground, and the orbiting of planets around the sun. This idea of explanation as colligation of what might otherwise be seen as unrelated and disparate events underlies Margaret Morrison's notion of unitative explanation,[110] which has obvious importance for Christian apologetics – above all, because it addresses the issue of coherence (see pp. 120–2).

The apologetic strategy resulting from this approach to Christian natural theology does not involve proving God's existence from the perceived ordering, complexity, or beauty of nature; rather, it involves recognizing an intellectual resonance, congruence, or consilience between the Christian vision of reality and what is actually seen and experienced within nature.[111] Christianity provides – but is not limited to – an intellectual framework which allows us to make sense of what we experience and observe. For example, our experience of the beauty of nature itself does not prove God's existence; it is, however, easily shown to be consistent with the greater Christian vision of God.[112] The prevailing scientific hypothesis of the origin of the universe in the "big bang" does not prove the existence of God, nor does it validate the theological notion of creation; both, however, are clearly *consistent* with this scientific hypothesis.

It may, of course, be objected that this is to place too much emphasis on the explanatory capacity of faith. The cultural critic Terry Eagleton is suspicious of those who treat religion as a fundamentally explanatory phenomenon. Christianity was never meant to be an explanation of anything in the first place. "It's rather like saying that thanks to the electric toaster we can forget about Chekhov." Eagleton suggests that believing that religion is

---

[109] Whewell, *The Philosophy of the Inductive Sciences*, vol. 2, 46.
[110] E.g., M. Morrison, *Unifying Scientific Theories*.
[111] Elsewhere, I use the term "resonance" to convey the sense of a theory "chiming in" with what is observed, without entailing demonstrative proof: A. E. McGrath, *The Open Secret*, 15–18. Polkinghorne prefers "congruence" or "consonance": see Irlenborn, "Konsonanz von Theologie und Naturwissenschaft?" Whewell speaks of the "consilience of inductions," which has potential for further development in this context: for a critical assessment, see M. Fisch, "Whewell's Consilience of Inductions."
[112] Viladesau, "Natural Theology and Aesthetics."

a "botched attempt to explain the world" is about as helpful as "seeing ballet as a botched attempt to run for a bus."[113] While Eagleton is right to argue that there is more to Christianity than an attempt to make sense of things, this explanatory capacity is nevertheless part of its rich heritage.

The Christian tradition represents a "view from somewhere" rather than a utopian "view from nowhere." It offers a way of seeing and understanding the natural world that invites public engagement and assessment. That process of evaluation inevitably has strongly subjective aspects, involving personal assessments of a theory's capacity to explain, and the merits of its consequences. This, however, is emblematic of any form of engagement with a complex and variegated reality, such as the natural world.[114] One may offer justification for a belief; yet only in the realms of mathematics and logic can a definitive "proof" be offered.

The epistemic situation of humanity is such that the aspirations of modernists such as Spinoza and Descartes to attain demonstrative knowledge in every domain have now been replaced by a chastened and more realistic pursuit of fiduciary judgments. "In every commitment to the beliefs of a worldview, there is a gap between the evidence/reasons/justification one has for the beliefs, and one's decision actually to hold the beliefs."[115] Both the Marxist and the New Atheist – to mention two intellectual traditions which would probably resist being designated as "faiths" in the first place – have to live with the fact that they cannot prove their core beliefs, even if they believe them to be realistic and justified. A decision to commit to the truth of these beliefs, and to live according to them, is thus a decision of the will, as much as of the intellect.

In all of this, a Christian natural theology presents a coherent vision of the natural world which the community of faith believes is firmly grounded in reality, with the capacity to allow us to see things in a new way. This is about more than demonstrating the rationality of faith. It is an act of "*faithful imagination* – living in conformity to the vision rendered by the Word of God in the Bible."[116] Yet this act of imagination is not arbitrary or uncontrolled; it is grounded in a deeper order of things, which in turn secures its capacity to illuminate and interpret the world around us. There are clear parallels here with the dilemma of a scientist, famously framed by Eddington in terms of the need for fiduciary judgments, set against the context of a deep intuition of order and beauty: "we sometimes have convictions as to the right

[113] Eagleton, *Reason, Faith, and Revolution*, 7.

[114] The issue of subjectivity is of especial importance in Bayesian approaches: see Howson and Urbach, *Scientific Reasoning*, 265–95. While objectivity is the ideal (9–10), this seems impossible to achieve in practice.

[115] Sweetman, "Commitment, Justification, and the Rejection of Natural Theology," 421.

[116] Green, *Imagining God*, 134.

solution of a problem which we cherish but cannot justify; we are influenced by some innate sense of the fitness of things."[117]

Conclusion

"Few new truths have ever won their way against the resistance of established ideas save by being overstated."[118] Readers will have noted my fundamental belief that the "established idea" that needs to be challenged is this: natural theology is simply and exclusively "the enterprise of providing support for religious beliefs by starting from premises that neither are nor presuppose any religious beliefs."[119] History suggests otherwise, opening a doorway to more varied and engaging understandings of natural theology, which I believe to be necessary and proper.

This work has argued that making sense of things is indeed part of the broader overall concept of natural theology, but that it is not in itself determinative or constitutive. It is merely a limited – and hence *limiting* – aspect of the greater project of a Christian natural theology. Perhaps I may overstate my criticisms of this received idea, which is endlessly and uncritically repeated in philosophical textbooks; nevertheless, this restricted concept of natural theology clearly needs revision and review.

This work has developed and explored a richer vision of natural theology, which repositions such arguments within a broader context, allowing them to be seen in a more realistic and responsible manner, in effect offering a "meta-theory" of natural theology which allows the main ways of understanding the notion to be seen as part of a "thick" description of natural theology. The re-imagination of nature goes hand in hand with a reconception of the nature and scope of natural theology – not necessarily by inventing new approaches, but by retrieving and developing those already known to the Christian tradition.

The Enlightenment chose to marginalize any positive role for the imagination, seeing the quest for truth as fundamentally, even exclusively, rational in character. Yet that movement now lies in the past, its *froideur* toward the domain of the imagined superseded by intellectual and cultural approaches which see the quest for truth as being partly governed and nourished by the interplay of reason and imagination. Such approaches are already well

---

[117] Eddington, *The Nature of the Physical World*, 337.
[118] Berlin, "The Philosophical Ideas of Giambattista Vico," 120.
[119] Alston, *Perceiving God*, 289.

established within both the natural sciences and Christian theology,[120] suggesting that their application in the field of natural theology is both appropriate and perhaps somewhat overdue.[121] Even the cold rationalism of the "Age of Reason" could not suppress the role of the human imagination in scientific reflection and advance.[122] As the American theoretical physicist Richard Feynman (1918–88) once remarked, the human imagination finds itself "stretched to the utmost, not, as in fiction, to imagine things which are not really there, but just to comprehend those things which are there."[123]

Christianity offers more than a changed way of thinking about the natural world; it offers a warranted remapping of imaginative possibilities, enabling and encouraging us to imagine nature in a new way through a "conversion of the imagination."[124] A "baptism of the imagination" allowed the Christian Church to re-imagine the history and cultic images of Israel, simultaneously affirming and transforming their significance,[125] just as it opens up ways of re-imagining the natural world through a metamorphosis of the imagination, supplementing that of the mind (Romans 12: 2). This is not to be seen as an "imaginative embellishment"[126] of reality, or as a cold logical response to the "spontaneous overflow of powerful feelings"[127] aroused by the beauty of nature. Rather, it is an imaginative discernment of deeper levels of truth, beauty, and goodness within the natural world, enabled by the informing *imaginarium* of the Christian tradition. This permits a "double vision" or "stereoscopic vision" which allows us to entertain two distinct viewpoints at the same time, and inhabit their liminal space meaningfully and with intellectual integrity.[128]

The last word must be eschatological. Nature, when seen through the Christian *imaginarium*, points beyond itself. A Christian natural theology celebrates the wonder of nature, rightly seeing it as indicative of the greater wonder of God, while at the same time inviting us to see beyond the limits of

---

[120] See Calver, "Sir Peter Medawar"; Avis, *God and the Creative Imagination*, 3–73; D. Brown, *Discipleship and Imagination*.

[121] Avis, *God and the Creative Imagination*, 26.

[122] Downie, "Science and the Imagination in the Age of Reason."

[123] Feynman, *The Character of Physical Law*, 127–8.

[124] For the notion of the "conversion of the imagination," see Utzschneider, *Gottes Vorstellung*, 193–297; Green, *Imagining God*, 66–74; Levy, *Imagination and the Journey of Faith*, 1–18. The concept of "imagination" is, of course, open to multiple interpretations: Stevenson, "Twelve Conceptions of Imagination."

[125] Hays, *The Conversion of the Imagination*, 1–24; Hogeterp, *Paul and God's Temple*, 271–91.

[126] I borrow this striking phrase from Stanbury, *The Visual Object of Desire in Late Medieval England*, 173–4.

[127] Wordsworth, *Lyrical Ballads*, 111.

[128] For these phrases, see Perry, *Coleridge and the Uses of Division*, 35–101; Prickett, *Words and the Word*, 224–7.

the present to a renewed nature that lies beyond, but whose presence is hinted at in our world of signs, and consolidated through the Church, understood as a semiotic "community of interpretation."[129]

For C. S. Lewis, one of the greatest recent exponents of the imaginative dimensions of faith, the Christian hope concerns more than simply *seeing* beauty; it is about the hope of a future immersion in its wonder. We stand on the threshold of something greater, scenting its fragrance on the passing breeze of space and time.

> We do not want to *see* beauty, though, God knows, that is bounty enough. We want something else which can hardly be put into words – to be united with the beauty we see, to pass into it, to receive it into ourselves, to bathe in it, to become part of it.[130]

A Christian natural theology celebrates and articulates the half-grasped rational transparency and oblique beauty of a complex and multifaceted nature, while at the same time proclaiming that a greater beauty lies beyond its horizon. The Christian life is thus a journey in and through the natural world, as we grasp the true meaning of its signs. The promise of such a natural theology does not extend merely to such promissory notes as facilitating intellectual enrichment and imaginative enrichment. Its promise is deeper.

A Christian natural theology is, in its own distinctive way, a theology of *hope* – a means of sustaining us as we travel through this sign-studded world, reassuring us that there is indeed a "big picture," which we presently grasp only in part. As Lewis concluded: "We are summoned to pass in through Nature, beyond her, into that splendour which she fitfully reflects."[131] A bright shadow will finally give way to a radiant reality – the greater glory of which nature is "only the first sketch."[132] A Christian natural theology helps us discern and appreciate the veiled beauty and wisdom of that "first sketch," while engendering hope and longing for what it signifies and promises.

[129] Royce, *The Problem of Christianity*, 7, 22.
[130] Lewis, "The Weight of Glory," in *Essay Collection*, 104.
[131] Lewis, "The Weight of Glory," in *Essay Collection*, 105. See also Harries, *Art and the Beauty of God*, 91–100, especially 95–7.
[132] Lewis, "The Weight of Glory," in *Essay Collection*, 105.

Bibliography

Abbruzzese, John Edward. "The Structure of Descartes' Ontological Proof." *British Journal for the History of Philosophy* 15 (2007): 253–82.

Abraham, William J. "Cumulative Case Arguments for Christian Theism." In *The Rationality of Religious Belief: Essays in Honour of Basil Mitchell*, edited by William J. Abraham and Steven W. Holtzer, 17–37. Oxford: Clarendon Press, 1987.

Abrams, M. H. *Natural Supernaturalism: Tradition and Revolution in Romantic Literature*. New York: Norton, 1973.

Adam, Matthias. *Theoriebeladenheit und Objektivität: Zur Rolle von Beobachtungen in den Naturwissenschafte*. Frankfurt am Main: Ontos Verlag, 2002.

Adams, Edward. "Calvin's View of Natural Knowledge of God." *International Journal of Systematic Theology* 3, no. 3 (2001): 280–92.

Adams, Marilyn McCord. *Christ and Horrors: The Coherence of Christology*. Cambridge: Cambridge University Press, 2006.

Adorjáni, Zsolt. *Auge und Sehen in Pindars Dichtung*. Hildesheim: Georg Olms Verlag, 2011.

Aeschliman, Michael D. *The Restitution of Man: C. S. Lewis and the Case against Scientism*. Grand Rapids, MI: Eerdmans, 1998.

Agar, Jolyon. *Post-Secularism, Realism and Utopia: Transcendence and Immanence from Hegel to Bloch*. London: Routledge, 2014.

Akbari, Suzanne Conklin. *Seeing through the Veil: Optical Theory and Medieval Allegory*. Toronto: University of Toronto Press, 2004.

Alston, William P. *Perceiving God: The Epistemology of Religious Experience*. Ithaca, NY: Cornell University Press, 1991.

Altman, Neil. *The Analyst in the Inner City: Race, Class, and Culture through a Psychoanalytic Lens*. 2nd edn. New York: Routledge, 2010.

Anderson, Benedict R. *Imagined Communities: Reflections on the Origin and Spread of Nationalism*. 2nd edn. London: Verso, 2006.

Anderson, Owen. "The Presuppositions of Religious Pluralism and the Need for Natural Theology." *Sophia* 47 (2008): 201–22.

Antognazza, Maria Rosa. "The Benefit to Philosophy of the Study of Its History." *British Journal for the History of Philosophy* 23, no. 1 (2014): 161–84.

Re-Imagining Nature: The Promise of a Christian Natural Theology, First Edition.
Alister E. McGrath.
© 2017 John Wiley & Sons, Ltd. Published 2017 by John Wiley & Sons, Ltd.

Antognazza, Maria Rosa. *Leibniz on the Trinity and the Incarnation: Reason and Revelation in the Seventeenth Century.* New Haven, CT: Yale University Press, 2007.

Antonaccio, Maria. *Picturing the Human: The Moral Thought of Iris Murdoch.* New York: Oxford University Press, 2000.

Apel, Karl-Otto. *Charles S. Peirce: From Pragmatism to Pragmaticism.* Amherst, NY: University of Massachussets Press, 1981.

Archdeacon, Anthony. "The 'Nothing' Trope: Self-Worth in Renaissance Poetry." *Literature Compass* 11, no. 8 (2014): 549–59.

Archer, Margaret S., Andrew Collier, and Douglas V. Porpora. *Transcendence: Critical Realism and God.* London: Routledge, 2013.

Armogathe, J. R. *La nature du monde: Science nouvelle et exégèse au XVIIe siècle.* Paris: Presses Universitaires de France, 2007.

Arnason, Johann P. "Castoriadis im Kontext: Genese und Anspruch eines metaphilosophischen Projekts." In *Das Imaginäre im Sozialen: Zur Sozialtheorie von Cornelius Castoriadis,* edited by Harald Wolf, 39–62. Göttingen: Wallstein, 2012.

Arnell, Carla A. "On Beauty, Justice and the Sublime in C. S. Lewis's Till We Have Faces." *Christianity and Literature* 52 (2002): 23–34.

Ashley, Benedict M. "What Is the End of the Human Person? The Vision of God and Integral Human Fulfillment." In *Moral Truth and Moral Tradition: Essays in Honour of Peter Geach and Elizabeth Anscombe,* edited by Luke Gormally, 68–96. Blackrock, Co. Dublin: Four Courts Press, 1994.

Atran, Scott. *In Gods We Trust: The Evolutionary Landscape of Religion.* Oxford: Oxford University Press, 2002.

Avis, Paul D. L. *God and the Creative Imagination: Metaphor, Symbol, and Myth in Religion and Theology.* London: Routledge, 1999.

Avrahami, Yael. *The Senses of Scripture: Sensory Perception in the Hebrew Bible.* London: T. & T. Clark, 2012.

Axelsson, Karl. *The Sublime: Precursors and British Eighteenth Century Conceptions.* Bern: Peter Lang, 2007.

Ayres, Lewis. *Nicaea and Its Legacy: An Approach to Fourth-Century Trinitarian Theology.* New York: Oxford University Press, 2004.

Babcock, William S. "A Changing of the Christian God: The Doctrine of the Trinity in the Seventeenth Century." *Interpretation* 45 (1991): 133–46.

Bagioli, Mario. "Stress in the Book of Nature: The Supplemental Logic of Galileo's Realism." *MLN* 118, no. 3 (2003): 557–85.

Bakker, Boudewijn. *Landscape and Religion from Van Eyck to Rembrandt.* Aldershot: Ashgate, 2012.

Balsamo, Jean. "Un gentilhomme et sa théologie." In *Dieu à nostre commerce et société: Montaigne et la théologie,* edited by Philippe Desan, 105–26. Geneva: Droz, 2008.

Balthasar, Hans Urs von. "Der Begriff der Natur in der Theologie." *Zeitschrift für katholischen Theologie* 75 (1953): 452–61.

Balthasar, Hans Urs von. *Herrlichkeit: Eine theologische Ästhetik.* 3 vols. Einsiedeln: Johannes Verlag, 1988.

Barbour, Ian G. *Issues in Science and Religion.* London: SCM Press, 1966.

Barfield, Owen. *Poetic Diction: A Study in Meaning.* Middletown, CT: Wesleyan University Press, 1973.

Barfield, Owen. *The Rediscovery of Meaning and Other Essays.* 2nd edn. San Rafael, CA: Barfield Press, 2006.

Barnum, Carol. "The Nature of John Fowles." In *John Fowles and Nature*, edited by James M. Aubrey, 87–95. Cranbury, NJ: Associated University Presses, 1999.

Barr, James. *Biblical Faith and Natural Theology.* Oxford: Clarendon Press, 1993.

Barrett, H. Clark. "On the Functional Origins of Essentialism." *Mind and Society* 3, no. 2 (2001): 1–30.

Barrett, Justin L. *Born Believers: The Science of Childrens' Religious Belief.* New York: Free Press, 2012.

Barrett, Justin L. "Exploring the Natural Foundations of Religion." *Trends in Cognitive Sciences* 4 (2000): 29–34.

Barrett, Justin L. *Why Would Anyone Believe in God?* Lanham, MD: AltaMira Press, 2004.

Barrett, Justin L., and Rebekah A. Richert. "Anthropomorphism or Preparedness? Exploring Children's God Concepts." *Review of Religious Research* 44, no. 3 (2003): 300–12.

Barry, Ann Marie. "Perceptual Aesthetics: Transcendent Emotion, Neurological Image." *Visual Communication Quarterly* 13, no. 3 (2006): 134–51.

Barth, J. Robert. *The Symbolic Imagination: Coleridge and the Romantic Tradition.* 2nd edn. New York: Fordham University Press, 2001.

Barth, Karl. *Church Dogmatics.* 14 vols. Edinburgh: T. & T. Clark, 1957–75.

Barth, Karl. "Das Erste Gebot als theologisches Axiom." *Zwischen den Zeiten* 13 (1933): 127–43.

Barth, Karl. *Karl Barth–Emil Brunner, Briefwechsel 1911–1966.* Zurich: Theologischer Verlag, 2000.

Barth, Karl. *Die protestantische Theologie im 19. Jahrhundert.* Zurich: Evangelischer Verlag, 1957.

Barth, Karl. *Der Römerbrief.* 2nd edn. Munich: Kaiser Verlag, 1922.

Barth, Karl. *Unterricht in der christlichen Religion.* Zurich: Theologische Verlag Zurich, 1985.

Barth, Karl. *Unveröffentlichte Texte zur Kirchlichen Dogmatik.* Zurich: Theologische Verlag Zurich, 2014.

Barth, Peter. *Das Problem der natürlichen Theologie bei Calvin.* Munich: Kaiser Verlag, 1935.

Barua, Ankur. "The Problem of Criteria and the Necessity of Natural Theology." *Heythrop Journal* 54, no. 2 (2013): 166–80.

Bauerschmidt, Frederick Christian. "Aesthetics: The Theological Sublime." In *Radical Orthodoxy: A New Theology*, edited by John Milbank, Catherine Pickstock, and Graham Ward, 121–43. London: Routledge, 1999.

Bauerschmidt, Frederick Christian. "Imagination and Theology in Thomas Aquinas." *Louvain Studies* 34 (2009–10): 173–88.

Baumeister, Roy. *Meanings of Life.* New York: Guilford Press, 1991.

Becker, Jürgen. *Jesus of Nazareth.* New York: Walter De Gruyter, 1998.

Berlatsky, Eric. "Lost in the Gutter: Within and between Frames in Narrative and Narrative Theory." *Narrative* 17, no. 2 (2009): 162–87.

Berlin, Isaiah. "The Philosophical Ideas of Giambattista Vico." In *Three Critics of the Enlightenment*, 21–121. Princeton, NJ: Princeton University Press, 2000.

Bernstein, John Andrew. *Progress and the Quest for Meaning: A Philosophical and Historical Inquiry.* London: Associated University Presses, 1993.

Bertilsson, Margareta. *Peirce's Theory of Inquiry and Beyond: Towards a Social Reconstruction of Science Theory.* Frankfurt am Main: Peter Lang, 2009.

Bertocci, Peter A. *The Person God Is.* London: Routledge, 2002.

Beveridge, W. I. B. *The Art of Scientific Investigation.* New York: Norton, 1957.

Bhaskar, Roy. *Philosophy and the Idea of Freedom.* New York: Routledge, 2011.

Bhaskar, Roy. *The Possibility of Naturalism: A Philosophical Critique of the Contemporary Human Sciences.* 3rd edn. London: Routledge, 1998.

Bienert, Wolfgang A. "Zur Logos-Christologie des Athanasius von Alexandrien in *Contra Gentes* und *De Incarnatione*." In *Papers Presented to the Tenth International Conference on Patristic Studies*, edited by E. A. Livingstone, 402–19. Louvain: Peeters, 1989.

Birmingham, Peg. "Hannah Arendt: The Activity of the Spectator." In *Sites of Vision: The Discursive Construction of Sight in the History of Philosophy*, edited by David Michael Levin, 379–96. Cambridge, MA: MIT Press, 1999.

Bishop, John. *Believing by Faith: An Essay in the Epistemology and Ethics of Religious Belief.* Oxford: Clarendon Press, 2007.

Bishop, Michael A. "In Praise of Epistemic Irresponsibility." *Synthese* 122 (2000): 179–208.

Black, Jeremy. "Britain and the 'Long' Eighteenth Century, 1688–1815." In *The Practice of Strategy: From Alexander the Great to the Present*, edited by John Andreas Olsen and Colin S. Gray, 155–75. Oxford: Oxford University Press, 2011.

Blackburn, Simon. *Think: A Compelling Introduction to Philosophy.* Oxford: Oxford University Press, 1999.

Blair, Ann. "Mosaic Physics and the Search for a Pious Natural Philosophy in the Late Renaissance." *Isis* 91, no. 1 (2000): 32–58.

Blaser, Klaus-Peter. "Communiquer l'incommunicable révélation. Le conflit Barth–Brunner revisité à la lumière de leur correspondance." *Etudes Théologiques et Religieuses* 78 (2003): 59–67.

Block, Alexandra Mills. "Reading Greville's 'Hard Characters': Metaphor and Ambivalence in *A Treatie of Humane Learning*." In *On Interpretation: Studies in Culture, Law, and the Sacred*, edited by Andrew D. Weiner, Leonard V. Kaplan, and Sonja Hansard-Weiner, 127–40. Madison, WI: University of Wisconsin Press, 2002.

Bloom, Paul. "Religion Is Natural." *Developmental Science* 10, no. 1 (2007): 147–51.

Blum, Lawrence. "Visual Metaphors in Murdoch's Moral Philosophy." In *Iris Murdoch, Philosopher*, edited by Justin Broackes, 307–23. Oxford: Oxford University Press, 2012.

Blumenberg, Hans. "Licht als Metapher der Wahrheit." *Studium Generale* 10 (1957): 432–47.

Boda, Mark J., and Gordon T. Smith, eds. *Repentance in Christian Theology*. Collegeville, MN: Liturgical Press, 2006.

Bolla, Peter de. *Art Matters*. Cambridge, MA: Harvard University Press, 2001.

Bolla, Peter de. *The Education of the Eye*. Stanford, CA: Stanford University Press, 2003.

Borella, Jean. *The Sense of the Supernatural*. Edinburgh: T. & T. Clark, 1998.

Borgmann, Albert. *Technology and the Character of Contemporary Life: A Philosophical Inquiry*. Chicago: University of Chicago Press, 1984.

Boulnois, Olivier. "Quand commence l'ontothéologie? Aristote, Thomas d'Aquin, et Duns Scot." *Revue Thomiste* 95 (1999): 85–105.

Bourdieu, Pierre. *Esquisse d'une théorie de la pratique*. Paris: Editions du Seuil, 2000.

Bourdieu, Pierre. *Le sens pratique*. Paris: Editions de Minuit, 1980.

Bowden, Peta. "Ethical Attention: Accumulating Understandings." *European Journal of Philosophy* 6, no. 1 (1998): 59–77.

Boyer, Pascal. *The Fracture of an Illusion: Science and the Dissolution of Religion*. Vandenhoeck & Ruprecht: Göttingen, 2010.

Boyer, Pascal. *Religion Explained: The Evolutionary Origins of Religious Thought*. New York: Basic Books, 2001.

Bradatan, Costica. "George Berkeley's 'Universal Language of Nature'." In *The Book of Nature in Early Modern and Modern History*, edited by Klaas van Berkel and Arie Johan Vanderjagt, 69–82. Louvain: Peeters, 2006.

Bradley, M. C. "Hume's Chief Objection to Natural Theology." *Religious Studies* 43, no. 3 (2007): 249–70.

Brady, Emily. "Aesthetics in Practice: Valuing the Natural World." *Environmental Values* 15 (2006): 277–91.

Brady, Emily. "Imagination and the Aesthetic Appreciation of Nature." *Journal of Aesthetics and Art Criticism* 56 (1998): 139–47.

Brague, Rémi. *The Wisdom of the World: The Human Experience of the Universe in Western Thought*. Chicago: University of Chicago Press, 2003.

Brock, Stuart. "The Puzzle of Imaginative Failure." *Philosophical Quarterly* 62 (2012): 443–63.

Brooke, John Hedley. "Like Minds: The God of Hugh Miller." In *Hugh Miller and the Controversies of Victorian Science*, edited by Michael Shortland, 171–86. Oxford: Clarendon Press, 1996.

Brooke, John Hedley. "Science and the Fortunes of Natural Theology: Some Historical Perspectives." *Zygon* 24 (1989): 3–22.

Brooke, John Hedley. "'Wise Men Nowadays Think Otherwise': John Ray, Natural Theology and the Meanings of Anthropocentrism." *Notes and Records of the Royal Society of London* 54, no. 2 (2000): 199–213.

Brooke, John, and Geoffrey Cantor. *Reconstructing Nature: The Engagement of Science and Religion*. Edinburgh: T. & T. Clarke, 1998.

Brown, C. Mackenzie. "The Design Argument in Classical Hindu Thought." *Journal of Hindu Studies* 12 (2008): 103–51.

Brown, David. *Discipleship and Imagination: Christian Tradition and Truth*. Oxford: Oxford University Press, 2000.

Brown, Hunter. "Alvin Plantinga and Natural Theology." *International Journal for Philosophy of Religion* 30 (1991): 1–19.

Browne, Thomas. *Religio Medici*. London: Pickering, 1845.

Brunner, Emil. *Dogmatik I: Die christliche Lehre von Gott*. Zurich: Zwingli-Verlag, 1959.

Brunner, Emil. *Der Mensch im Widerspruch: Die christliche Lehre vom wahren und vom wirklichen Menschen*. 4th edn. Zurich: Zwingli-Verlag, 1965.

Brunner, Emil. *Offenbarung und Vernunft: Die Lehre von der christlichen Glaubenserkenntnis*. Zurich: Zwingli-Verlag, 1941.

Brunner, Emil. *Ein offenes Wort: Vorträge und Aufsätze 1917–1962*. 2 vols. Zurich: Theologischer Verlag, 1981.

Buchak, Lara. "Rational Faith and Justified Belief." In *Religious Faith and Intellectual Virtue*, edited by Laura Frances Callahan and Timothy O'Connor, 49–73. Oxford: Oxford University Press, 2014.

Buchenau, Stefanie. *The Founding of Aesthetics in the German Enlightenment: The Art of Invention and the Invention of Art*. Cambridge: Cambridge University Press, 2013.

Buckley, Michael J. *At the Origins of Modern Atheism*. New Haven, CT: Yale University Press, 1987.

Bukow, Wolf-Dietrich. "Magie und fremdes Denken: Bemerkungen zum Stand der neueren Magieforschung seit Evans-Pritchard." In *Magie, Katastrophenreligion und Kritik des Glaubens*, edited by Hans-Günther Heimbrock and Heinz Streib, 61–103. Kampen: Kok, 1994.

Caldecott, Stratford. *Beauty for Truth's Sake: On the Re-Enchantment of Education*. Grand Rapids, MI: Brazos Press, 2009.

Callicott, J. Baird. "The Land Aesthetic." *Orion Nature Quarterly* 3 (summer 1984): 16–22.

Calloway, Katherine. *Natural Theology in the Scientific Revolution: God's Scientists*. London: Pickering & Chatto, 2014.

Calver, Neil. "Sir Peter Medawar: Science, Creativity and the Popularization of Karl Popper." *Notes and Records of the Royal Society* 67 (2013): 301–14.

Caputo, John D. "In Praise of Ambiguity." In *Ambiguity in the Western Mind*, edited by Craig J. N. de Paulo, Patrick Messina, and Marc Stier, 15–34. New York: Peter Lang, 2005.

Carey, Daniel. *Locke, Shaftesbury, and Hutcheson: Contesting Diversity in the Enlightenment and Beyond*. Cambridge: Cambridge University Press, 2006.

Carlson, Allen. *Aesthetics and the Environment: The Appreciation of Nature, Art, and Architecture*. London: Routledge, 2000.

Carlson, Allen, and Arnold Berleant, eds., *The Aesthetics of Natural Environments.* Peterborough, ON: Broadview Press, 2004.

Carnell, Corbin Scott. *Bright Shadow of Reality: Spiritual Longing in C. S. Lewis.* Grand Rapids, MI: Eerdmans, 1999.

Carraud, Vincent. "L'imaginer inimaginable: le Dieu de Montaigne." In *Montaigne: scepticisme, métaphysique, théologie,* edited by Vincent Carraud and Jean-Luc Marion, 137–71. Paris: Presses Universitaires de France, 2004.

Carroll, Anthony J. "Disenchantment, Rationality, and the Modernity of Max Weber." *Forum Philosophicum* 16, no. 1 (2011): 117–37.

Carroll, Anthony J. *Protestant Modernity: Weber, Secularisation, and Protestantism.* Scranton, PA: University of Scranton Press, 2007.

Carroll, Thomas D. "The Traditions of Fideism." *Religious Studies* 44, no. 1 (2008): 1–22.

Carroll, Thomas D. *Wittgenstein within the Philosophy of Religion.* Basingstoke: Palgrave Macmillan, 2014.

Cartwright, Nancy. *The Dappled World: A Study of the Boundaries of Science.* Cambridge: Cambridge University Press, 1999.

Cartwright, Nancy. "God's Order, Man's Order and the Order of Nature." *Euresis* 5 (2013): 99–108.

Cary, Philip. *Augustine's Invention of the Inner Self: The Legacy of a Christian Platonist.* Oxford: Oxford University Press, 2000.

Cashell, Kieran. "Reality, Representation and the Aesthetic Fallacy: Critical Realism and the Philosophy of C. S. Peirce." *Journal of Critical Realism* 8, no. 2 (2009): 135–71.

Casper, Bernhard. *Das dialogische Denken: Franz Rosenzweig, Ferdinand Ebner und Martin Buber.* 2nd edn. Freiburg: Alber, 2002.

Casserley, J. V. Langmead. *Graceful Reason: The Contribution of Reason to Theology.* London: Longmans, Green, 1955.

Castoriadis, Cornelius. *The Imaginary Institution of Society.* Cambridge, MA: MIT Press, 1987.

Castoriadis, Cornelius. *World in Fragments: Writings on Politics, Society, Psychoanalysis, and the Imagination.* Stanford, CA: Stanford University Press, 1997.

Cathey, Robert Andrew. *God in Postliberal Perspective: Between Realism and Non-Realism.* Farnham: Ashgate, 2009.

Cattell, Maria G., and Jacob J. Climo. "Meaning in Social Memory and History: Anthropological Perspectives." In *Social Memory and History: Anthropological Perspectives,* edited by Jacob J. Climo and Maria G. Cattell, 1–36. Walnut Creek, CA: AltaMira Press, 2002.

Chalmers, Thomas. *Works.* 7 vols. New York: Robert Carter, 1840.

Chandrasekhar, Subrahmanyan. *Truth and Beauty: Aesthetics and Motivations in Science.* Chicago: University of Chicago Press, 1990.

Chang, Hasok. *Inventing Temperature: Measurement and Scientific Progress.* Oxford Studies in Philosophy of Science. Oxford: Oxford University Press, 2007.

Chenu, M. D. "La nature et l'homme." In *La théologie au XIIe siècle,* 19–51. Paris: Vrin, 1957.

Chenu, M. D. *La théologie comme science au XIIIe siècle*. Paris: Vrin, 1969.

Chestnutt, Glenn A. *Challenging the Stereotype: The Theology of Karl Barth as a Resource for Inter-Religious Encounter in a European Context*. New York: Peter Lang, 2010.

Chidester, David. *Word and Light: Seeing, Hearing, and Religious Discourse*. Urbana. IL: University of Illinois Press, 1992.

Chihaia, Matei. "Das Imaginäre bei Cornelius Castoradis und seine Aufnahme durch Wolfgang Iser und Jean Marie Apostolidès." In *Literaturtheorie und sciences humaines: Frankreichs Beitrag zur Methodik der Literaturwissenschaft*, edited by Rainer Zaiser, 69–85. Berlin: Frank & Timme, 2008.

Childs, Elizabeth C. *Vanishing Paradise: Art and Exoticism in Colonial Tahiti*. Berkeley, CA: University of California Press, 2013.

Clark, Samantha. "Contemporary Art and Environmental Aesthetics." *Environmental Values* 19 (2010): 351–71.

Clarke, Elizabeth. *Theory and Theology in George Herbert's Poetry: "Divinitie and Poesy Met."* Oxford: Clarendon Press, 1997.

Claudel, Paul. "Introduction à un poème sur Dante." In *Oeuvres en prose*, 422–34. Paris: Gallimard, 1965.

Clavier, Paul. *Qu'est-ce que la théologie naturelle?* Paris: Vrin, 2004.

Clayton, Philip, and Steven Knapp *The Predicament of Belief: Science, Philosophy, Faith*. Oxford: Oxford University Press, 2011.

Cobb, John B. *A Christian Natural Theology, Based on the Thought of Alfred North Whitehead*. 2nd edn. Louisville, KY: Westminster John Knox Press, 2007.

Code, Murray. "On the Poverty of Scientism, Or: The Ineluctable Roughness of Rationality." *Metaphilosophy* 28 (1997): 102–22.

Cohen, Daniel J. *Equations from God: Pure Mathematics and Victorian Faith*. Baltimore, MD: Johns Hopkins University Press, 2007.

Colapietro, Vincent Michael. *Peirce's Approach to the Self: A Semiotic Perspective on Human Subjectivity*. Albany, NY: State University of New York Press, 1989.

Coleridge, Samuel Taylor. *Biographia Literaria*. 2 vols. Oxford: Clarendon Press, 1907.

Collicutt, Joanna. *The Psychology of Christian Character Formation*. Norwich: SCM Press, 2015.

Collier, Andrew. *Critical Realism: An Introduction to Roy Bhaskar's Philosophy*. London: Verso, 1994.

Collingwood, R. G. *An Essay on Metaphysics*. Oxford: Clarendon Press, 1998.

Collins, Christopher. *The Poetics of the Mind's Eye: Literature and the Psychology of Imagination*. Philadelphia: University of Pennsylvania Press, 1991.

Collins, John J. "The Biblical Precedent for Natural Theology." *Journal of the American Academy of Religion* 45 (1977): B35–B67.

Collins, John J. "Natural Theology and Biblical Tradition: The Case of Hellenistic Judaism." *Catholic Biblical Quarterly* 60 (1998): 1–15.

Colorado, Carlos D., and Justin D. Klassen, eds. *Aspiring to Fullness in a Secular Age: Essays on Religion and Theology in the Work of Charles Taylor*. Notre Dame, IN: University of Notre Dame Press, 2014.

Congar, Yves M.-J. *La foi et la théologie*. Tournai: Desclée, 1962.

Connelly, James. "R. G. Collingwood, Analytical Philosophy and Logical Positivism." *Baltic International Yearbook of Cognition, Logic and Communication* 4 (2009): 1–15.

Connolly, Patrick J. "Henry of Ghent's Argument for Divine Illumination Reconsidered." *American Catholic Philosophical Quarterly* 89 (2015): 47–68.

Conron, John. *American Picturesque*. University Park, PA: Pennsylvania State University Press, 2000.

Cooper, John M. "Socrates and Philosophy as a Way of Life." In *Maieusis: Essays in Ancient Philosophy in Honour of Myles Burnyeat*, edited by Dominic Scott, 20–43. Oxford: Oxford University Press, 2007.

Corbin, Alain. *The Lure of the Sea: The Discovery of the Seaside in the Western World, 1750–1840*. Berkeley, CA: University of California Press, 1994.

Corcho, Oscar. *A Layered Declarative Approach to Ontology Translation with Knowledge Preservation*. Washington, DC: IOS Press, 2005.

Corneanu, Sorana. *Regimens of the Mind: Boyle, Locke, and the Early Modern Cultura Animi Tradition*. Chicago: University of Chicago Press, 2011.

Corrington, Robert S. "A Comparison of Royce's Key Notion of the Community of Interpretation with the Hermeneutics of Gadamer and Heidegger." *Transactions of the Charles S. Peirce Society* 20, no. 3 (1984): 279–301.

Cottingham, John. "The Lessons of Life: Wittgenstein, Religion and Analytic Philosophy." In *Wittgenstein and Analytic Philosophy*, edited by Hans-Johann Glock and John Hyman, 203–27. Oxford: Oxford University Press, 2009.

Coudert, Allison P. "Forgottten Ways of Knowing." In *The Shapes of Knowledge from the Renaissance to the Enlightenment*, edited by Donald R. Kelley and Richard H. Popkin, 83–100. Dordrecht: Kluwer Academic Publishers, 1991.

Coudert, Allison P. *Religion, Magic, and Science in Early Modern Europe and America*. Santa Barbara, CA: Praeger, 2011.

Couenhoven, Jesse. *Stricken by Sin, Cured by Christ: Agency, Necessity, and Culpability in Augustinian Theology*. New York: Oxford University Press, 2013.

Coulombe, Joseph L. *Mark Twain and the American West*. Columbia, MO: University of Missouri Press, 2003.

Coyne, Jerry A. *Faith versus Fact: Why Science and Religion Are Incompatible*. New York: Viking, 2015.

Craig, William Lane, and James P. Moreland, eds. *The Blackwell Companion to Natural Theology*. Oxford: Wiley-Blackwell, 2009.

Crosby, Donald A. *Living with Ambiguity: Religious Naturalism and the Menace of Evil*. Albany, NY: State University of New York Press, 2008.

Cross, Richard. "Duns Scotus and Suarez at the Origins of Modernity." In *Deconstructing Radical Orthodoxy: Postmodern Theology, Rhetoric and Truth*, edited by Wayne J. Hankey and Douglas Hedley, 65–80. Aldershot: Ashgate, 2005.

Crowe, Benjamin Dillon. "On 'The Religion of the Visible Universe': Novalis and the Pantheism Controversy." *British Journal of the History of Philosophy* 16 (2008): 125–46.

Crowther-Heyck, Kathleen. "Wonderful Secrets of Nature: Natural Knowledge and Religious Piety in Reformation Germany." *Isis* 94 (2003): 253–73.

Cyrenne, Chad. "Is Thick Description Social Science?" *Anthropological Quarterly* 79, no. 2 (2006): 315–24.

Dafni, Evangelia G. "Natürliche Theologie im Lichte des hebräischen und griechischen Alten Testaments." *Theologische Zeitschrift* 57 (2001): 295–310.

Dahm, John J. "Science and Apologetics in the Early Boyle Lectures." *Church History* 39 (1970): 172–86.

D'Aniello, Giovanna. "Von der Religion zur Theologie: Schleiermacher als Schüler Eberhards?" In *Ein Antipode Kants? Johann August Eberhard im Spannungsfeld von spätaufklärerischer Philosophie und Theologie*, edited by Hans-Joachim Kertscher and Ernst Stöckmann, 165–84. Berlin: De Gruyter, 2012.

Darnton, Robert. "Intellectual and Cultural History." In *The Past before Us: Contemporary Historical Writing in the United States*, edited by Michael Kammen, 327–54. Ithaca, NY: Cornell University Press, 1980.

Darwin, Charles. *On the Origin of the Species by Means of Natural Selection*. London: John Murray, 1859.

Darwin, Francis, ed. *The Life and Letters of Charles Darwin*. 3 vols. London: John Murray, 1887.

Daston, Lorraine, and Katharine Park. *Wonders and the Order of Nature*. New York: Zone, 1998.

Davies, Sir John. *Complete Poems*. 2 vols. London: Chatto & Windus, 1876.

Davies, Sir John. *Orchestra: Or, a Poem of Dancing*. London: Chatto & Windus, 1946.

Davis, Martin M. "Kataphysical Inquiry, Onto-Relationality and Elemental Forms in T. F. Torrance's Doctrine of the Mediation of Jesus Christ." *In die Skriflig/In Luce Verbi* 47, no. 1 (2013): doi: 10.4102/ids.v47i1.100.

Dawes, Gregory, and James Maclaurin, eds. *A New Science of Religion*. London: Routledge, 2012.

Dawkins, Richard. *An Appetite for Wonder: The Making of a Scientist*. London: Bantam Press, 2013.

Dawkins, Richard. *The God Delusion*. London: Bantam, 2006.

Dawkins, Richard. *Unweaving the Rainbow: Science, Delusion and the Appetite for Wonder*. London: Penguin Books, 1998.

Deacon, Terrence W. *The Symbolic Species: The Co-Evolution of Language and the Brain*. New York: W. W. Norton, 1997.

Dean, Mitchell. *Critical and Effective Histories: Foucault's Methods and Historical Sociology*. London: Routledge, 2003.

Dear, Peter R. *The Intelligibility of Nature: How Science Makes Sense of the World*. Chicago: University of Chicago Press, 2006.

Dear, Peter R. *Revolutionizing the Sciences: European Knowledge and Its Ambitions, 1500–1700*. 2nd edn. Princeton, NJ: Princeton University Press, 2009.

Dearborn, Kerry. *Baptized Imagination: The Theology of George MacDonald*. Aldershot: Ashgate, 2006.

Dean, Mitchell. *Critical and Effective Histories: Foucault's Method and Historical Sociology*. London: Routledge, 1994.

Debray, Régis. *Vie et mort de l'image: Une histoire du regard en Occident*. Paris: Gallimard, 1992.

Debus, Allen G., and Michael Thomson Walton, eds. *Reading the Book of Nature: The Other Side of the Scientific Revolution*. Kirksville, MO: Sixteenth Century Journal Publishers, 1998.

De Cruz, Helen. "The Enduring Appeal of Natural Theological Arguments." *Philosophy Compass* 9, no. 2 (2014): 145–53.

De Cruz, Helen, and Johan de Smedt. "Delighting in Natural Beauty: Joint Attention and the Phenomenology of Nature Aesthetics." *European Journal for Philosophy of Religion* 5, no. 4 (2013): 167–86.

De Cruz, Helen, and Johan de Smedt. "Evolved Cognitive Biases and the Epistemic Status of Scientiific Beliefs." *Philosophical Studies* 157 (2012): 411–29.

De Cruz, Helen, and Johan de Smedt. *A Natural History of Natural Theology: The Cognitive Science of Theology and Philosophy of Religion*. Cambridge, MA: MIT Press, 2014.

DeHart, Paul J. *The Trial of the Witnesses: The Rise and Decline of Postliberal Theology*. Oxford: Blackwell, 2006.

Demeritt, David. "What Is the 'Social Construction of Nature'? A Typology and Sympathetic Critique." *Progress in Human Geography* 26, no. 6 (2002): 767–90.

Demeter, Tamás. *Conflicting Values of Inquiry: Ideologies of Epistemology in Early Modern Europe*. Leiden: Brill, 2015.

Demut, André. *Evangelium und Gesetz: Eine systematisch-theologische Reflexion zu Karl Barths Predigtwerk*. Berlin: De Gruyter, 2008.

Den Uyl, Douglas J. *God, Man, and Well-Being: Spinoza's Modern Humanism*. New York: Peter Lang, 2008.

Denzinger, Heinrich. *Enchiridion Symbolorum Definitionum et Declarationum de Rebus Fidei et Morum*. 39th edn. Freiburg-im-Briesgau: Herder, 2001.

Deonna, Waldemar. *Le symbolisme de l'oeil*. Paris: Broccard, 1965.

Derrida, Jacques. *La verité en peinture*. Paris: Flammarion, 1978.

Dihle, Albrecht. "Die *Theologia Tripertita* bei Augustin." In *Geschichte – Tradition – Reflexion: Festschrift für Martin Hengel zum 70. Geburtstag*, edited by Hubert Cancik, 183–202. Tübingen: Mohr Siebeck, 1996.

Diller, Kevin. "Does Contemporary Theology Require a Postfoundationalist Way of Knowing?" *Scottish Journal of Theology* 60, no. 3 (2007): 271–93.

Dinkler, Erich. *Im Zeichen des Kreuzes: Aufsätze*. Berlin: De Gruyter, 1992.

Dixon, Philip. *Nice and Hot Disputes: The Doctrine of the Trinity in the Seventeenth Century*. London: T. & T. Clark, 2003.

Dixon, Thomas. "Theology, Anti-Theology and Atheology: From Christian Passions to Secular Emotions." *Modern Theology* 15, no. 3 (1999): 297–330.

Donne, John. *The Epithalamions, Anniversaries, and Epicedes*. Oxford: Clarendon Press, 1978.

Donoghue, Denis. *Speaking of Beauty*. New Haven, CT: Yale University Press, 2003.

Dooley, Mark. *Roger Scruton: The Philosopher on Dover Beach*. London: Continuum, 2009.

Dorato, Mauro. "Why Is the Language of Nature Mathematical?" In *Galileo and the Renaissance Scientific Discourse*, edited by Aldo Altamore and Giovanni Antonini, 65–71. Rome: Edizioni Nuova Cultura, 2010.

Dougherty, Trent, ed. *Evidentialism and Its Discontents*. Oxford: Oxford University Press, 2011.

Dowey, Edward A. *The Knowledge of God in Calvin's Theology*. New York: Columbia University Press, 1952.

Downie, Robin. "Science and the Imagination in the Age of Reason." *Medical Humanities* 27 (2001): 58–63.

Draper, Paul R. "God, Science and Naturalism." In *The Oxford Handbook of Philosophy of Religion*, edited by William J. Wainwright, 272–303. Oxford: Oxford University Press, 2005.

Dubay, Thomas. *The Evidential Power of Beauty: Science and Theology Meet*. San Francisco: Ignatius Press, 1999.

Dulles, Avery. *A History of Apologetics*. 2nd edn. San Francisco: Ignatius Press, 2005.

Dürbeck, Gabriele. *Einbildungskraft und Aufklärung: Perspektiven der Philosophie, Anthropologie und Ästhetik um 1750*. Tübingen: Max Niemeyer Verlag, 1998.

Eagleton, Terry. *Reason, Faith, and Revolution: Reflections on the God Debate*. New Haven, CT: Yale University Press, 2009.

Echeverria, Eduardo J. "The Reformed Objection to Natural Theology: A Catholic Response to Herman Bavinck." *Calvin Theological Journal* 45, no. 1 (2010): 87–116.

Eckermann, Johann Peter. *Gespräche mit Goethe in den letzten Jahren seines Lebens*. 3 vols. Leipzig: F. A. Brockhaus, 1836.

Eco, Umberto. *Le signe*. Brussels: Labor, 1988.

Eddington, Arthur S. *The Nature of the Physical World*. New York: Macmillan 1929.

Eddy, Matthew D. "The Rhetoric and Science of William Paley's *Natural Theology*." *Theology and Literature* 18 (2004): 1–22.

Edwards, Jonathan. *Works*. 26 vols. New Haven, CT: Yale University Press, 1977–2009.

Edwards, Karen L. *Milton and the Natural World: Science and Poetry in Paradise Lost*. Cambridge: Cambridge University Press, 1999.

Edwards, L. Clifton. *Creation's Beauty as Revelation: Toward a Creational Theology of Natural Beauty*. Eugene, OR: Pickwick Publications, 2014.

Elder, Bruce. *Body of Vision: Representations of the Body in Recent Film and Poetry*. Waterloo, ON: Wilfrid Laurier University Press, 1997.

Elders, Leo. "Le rôle de la philosophie en théologie." *Nova et Vetera* 72, no. 2 (1997): 34–68.

Elias, Camelia. "Framing the Fragment: Epigraphic Writing in Gordon Lish and Jacques Derrida." *Oxford Literary Review* 25 (2003): 239–59.

Elliott, Anthony. "The Social Imaginary: A Critical Assessment of Castoriadis' Psychoanalytic Social Theory." *American Imago* 59, no. 2 (2002): 141–70.

Elshtain, Jean Bethke. *Sovereignty: God, State, and Self.* New York: Basic Books, 2008.

Eltester, Walter. "Schöpfungsoffenbarung und natürliche Theologie im frühen Christentum." *New Testament Studies* 3 (1957): 93–114.

Enders, Markus. *Natürliche Theologie im Denken der Griechen.* Frankfurt am Main: Josef Knecht, 2000.

Escobar, Arturo. "After Nature: Steps to an Anti-Essentialist Political Ecology." *Current Anthropology* 40, no. 1 (1999): 1–30.

Evans, C. Stephen. *Faith beyond Reason: A Kierkegaardian Account.* Grand Rapids, MI: Eerdmans, 1998.

Evans, C. Stephen. *Natural Signs and Knowledge of God: A New Look at Theistic Arguments.* Oxford: Oxford University Press, 2010.

Evans, C. Stephen. *Why Believe? Reason and Mystery as Pointers to God.* Grand Rapids, MI: Eerdmans, 1996.

Evernden, Neil. *The Social Creation of Nature.* Baltimore, MD: Johns Hopkins University Press, 1992.

Falardeau, Jean-Charles. "Le sens du merveilleux." In *Le merveilleux: Deuxième colloque sur les religions populaires,* edited by Fernand Dumont, Jean-Paul Montminy, and Michel Stein, 143–56. Québec: Presses de l'Université Laval, 1973.

Farber, Paul Lawrence. *Finding Order in Nature: The Naturalist Tradition from Linnaeus to E. O. Wilson.* Baltimore, MD: Johns Hopkins University Press, 2000.

Farley, Edward. *Faith and Beauty: A Theological Aesthetic.* Aldershot: Ashgate, 2001.

Farley, Edward. *Theologia: The Fragmentation and Unity of Theological Education.* Philadelphia: Fortress Press, 1983.

Farrer, Austin. "The Christian Apologist." In *Light on C. S. Lewis,* edited by Jocelyn Gibb, 23–43. London: Geoffrey Bles, 1965.

Farrer, Austin. *The Glass of Vision.* London: Dacre Press, 1948.

Feingold, Lawrence. *The Natural Desire to See God According to St. Thomas and His Interpreters.* Rome: Apollinare Studi, 2001.

Ferguson, Everett. *Baptism in the Early Church: History, Theology, and Liturgy in the First Five Centuries.* Grand Rapids, MI: Eerdmans, 2008.

Fergusson, David. "Types of Natural Theology." In *The Evolution of Rationality: Interdisciplinary Essays in Honor of J. Wentzel Van Huyssteen,* edited by F. LeRon Schults, 380–93. Grand Rapids, MI: Eerdmans, 2007.

Feynman, Richard P. *The Character of Physical Law.* Cambridge, MA: MIT Press, 1988.

Fiddes, Paul S. *Freedom and Limit: A Dialogue between Literature and Christian Doctrine.* Macon, GA: Mercer University Press, 1999.

Fiddes, Paul S. *Participating in God: A Pastoral Doctrine of the Trinity.* London: Darton, Longman, and Todd, 2000.

Fiddes, Paul S. *Seeing the World and Knowing God: Hebrew Wisdom and Christian Doctrine in a Late-Modern Context.* Oxford: Oxford University Press, 2013.

Finkelstein, David, and Alistair McCleery. *An Introduction to Book History*. 2nd edn. New York: Routledge, 2013.

Finley, C. Stephen. *Nature's Covenant: Figures of Landscape in Ruskin*. University Park, PA: Pennsylvania State University Press, 1992.

Fisch, Harold. "The Scientist as Priest: A Note on Robert Boyle's Natural Theology." *Isis* 44 (1953): 252–65.

Fisch, Menachem. "Whewell's Consilience of Inductions: An Evaluation." *Philosophy of Science* 52, no. 2 (1985): 239–55.

Fish, Stanley E. *Is There a Text in This Class? The Authority of Interpretive Communities*. Cambridge, MA: Harvard University Press, 1980.

Fisher, Philip. *Wonder, the Rainbow, and the Aesthetics of Rare Experiences*. Cambridge, MA: Harvard University Press, 1998.

Fitzgerald, Timothy. "Religion, Philosophy and Family Resemblances." *Religion* 26, no. 3 (1996): 215–36.

Fletcher, Angus. *Time, Space, and Motion in the Age of Shakespeare*. Cambridge, MA: Harvard University Press, 2007.

Florio, Lucio. "Las ciencias naturales en la elaboración de la teología. Algunas propuestas actuales." *Revista Teología* 44, no. 94 (2007): 551–78.

Fludernik, Monika. *Towards a "Natural" Narratology*. New York: Routledge, 1996.

Foot, Sarah. "Plenty, Portents, and Plague: Ecclesiastical Readings of the Natural World in Early Medieval Europe." In *God's Bounty? The Churches and the Natural World*, edited by Peter Clarke and Tony Claydon, 15–41. Woodbridge: Boydell Press, 2010.

Forbes, Eric G. "The Pre-Discovery Observations of Uranus." In *Uranus and the Outer Planets*, edited by Garry Hunt, 67–70. Cambridge: Cambridge University Press, 1983.

Force, James E. "Providence and Newton's Pantokrator: Natural Law, Miracles, and Newtonian Science." In *Newton and Newtonianism: New Essays*, edited by James E. Force and Sarah Hutton, 65–92. Dordrecht: Kluwer, 2004.

Ford, David F. "An Interfaith Wisdom: Scriptural Reasoning between Jews, Christians, and Muslims." *Modern Theology* 22, no. 3 (2006): 345–66.

Forde, Gerhard O. "The Word that Kills and Makes Alive." In *Marks of the Body of Christ*, edited by Carl E. Braaten and Robert W. Jenson, 1–12. Grand Rapids, MI: Eerdmans, 1999.

Foucault, Michel. *Du gouvernement des vivants: Cours au Collège de France*. Paris: Seuil, 2012.

Foucault, Michel. "Nietzsche, la généalogie, l'histoire." In *Hommage à Jean Hyppolite*, 145–72. Paris: Presses Universitaires de France, 1971.

Fouke, Daniel C. "Argument in Pascal's *Pensées*." *History of Philosophy Quarterly* 6 (1989): 57–68.

Fowl, Stephen E. *Engaging Scripture: A Model for Theological Interpretation*. Challenges in Contemporary Theology. Oxford: Blackwell, 1998.

Fowles, John. *The Tree*. London: Vintage, 2000.

Fraenkel, Carlos. "Maimonides' God and Spinoza's *Deus sive Natura*." *Journal of the History of Philosophy* 44, no. 2 (2006): 169–215.

Frank, Michael C. "Imaginative Geography as a Travelling Concept." *European Journal of English Studies* 13, no. 1 (2009): 61–77.

Frank, Roslyn M. "Sociocultural Situatedness: An Introduction." In *Sociocultural Situatedness*, edited by Roslyn M. Frank, René Dirven, Tom Ziemke, and Enrique Bernárdez, 1–18. Berlin: De Gruyter, 2008.

Franz, Michael, and Eleonore Kalisch. "Tertius Spectans: Die spektatorische Situation als spezifische Zeichensituation." *Weimärer Beiträge* 54, no. 3 (2008): 500–29.

Freedman, Joseph S. "'Professionalization' and 'Confessionalization': The Place of Physics, Philosophy, and Arts Instruction at Central European Academic Institutions during the Reformation Era." *Early Science and Medicine* 6, no. 4 (2001): 334–52.

Frigo, Alberto. "L'evidenza del Dio nascosto. Pascal e la critica della teologia naturale." *Rivista di Filosofia* 102, no. 2 (2011): 193–216.

Fulkerson, Laurel. *No Regrets: Remorse in Classical Antiquity*. Oxford: Oxford University Press, 2013.

Funkenstein, Amos. *Theology and the Scientific Imagination from the Middle Ages to the Seventeenth Century*. Princeton, NJ: Princeton University Press, 1986.

Furnish, Victor Paul. *Thessalonians*. Nashville, TN: Abingdon, 2007.

Fyfe, Aileen. "Publishing and the Classics: Paley's Natural Theology and the Nineteenth-Century Scientific Canon." *Studies in the History and Philosophy of Science* 33 (2002): 433–55.

Gadamer, Hans-Georg. *Gesammelte Werke*. 10 vols. Tübingen: J. C. B. Mohr, 1985–93.

Gagnon, Philippe. "Raymond Ruyer, la biologie et la théologie naturelle." *Chromatikon* 8 (2012): 157–76.

Galilei, Galileo. *Opere*. 20 vols. Florence: Barbèra, 1890–1909.

Gallagher, Michael Paul. "Newman on Imagination and Faith." *Milltown Studies* 49 (2002): 84–101.

Ganzevoort, R. Ruard. "The Social Construction of Revelation." *International Journal of Practical Theology* 8, no. 2 (2006): 1–14.

Gaonkar, Dilip. "Toward New Imaginaries: An Introduction." *Public Culture* 14, no. 1 (2002): 1–19.

Garber, Daniel. "What's Philosophical about the History of Philosophy?" In *Analytic Philosophy and History of Philosophy*, edited by Tom Sorell and G. A. J. Rogers, 129–46. Oxford: Clarendon Press, 2005.

García-Rivera, Alex, and Thomas J. Scirghi. *Living Beauty: The Art of Liturgy*. Lanham, MD: Rowman & Littlefield, 2008.

Gascoigne, John. "Ideas of Nature: Natural Philosophy." In *The Cambridge History of Science*, vol. 4: *Eighteenth-Century Science*, edited by Roy Porter, 285–304. Cambridge: Cambridge University Press, 2003.

Gates, Barbara T. *Kindred Nature: Victorian and Edwardian Women Embrace the Living World.* Chicago: University of Chicago Press, 1998.

Gaukroger, Stephen. "The Early Modern Idea of Scientific Doctrine and Its Early Christian Origins." *Journal of Medieval and Early Modern Studies* 44, no. 1 (2014): 95–112.

Gaukroger, Stephen. *The Emergence of a Scientific Culture: Science and the Shaping of Modernity 1210–1685.* Oxford: Oxford University Press, 2006.

Gaukroger, Stephen. "Science, Religion and Modernity." *Critical Quarterly* 47, no. 4 (2005): 1–31.

Gaver, William W., Jacob Beaver, and Steve Benford. "Ambiguity as a Resource for Design." *Proceedings of the SIGCHI Conference on Human Factors in Computing Systems* 5, no. 1 (2003): 233–40.

Gawronski, Raymond. "The Beauty of the Cross: The Theological Aesthetics of Hans Urs Von Balthasar." *Logos: A Journal of Catholic Thought and Culture* 5, no. 3 (2002): 185–206.

Geertz, Armin W. "How Not to Do the Cognitive Science of Religion Today." *Method and Theory in the Study of Religion* 20 (2008): 7–21.

Geertz, Clifford. "Thick Description: Toward an Interpretive Theory of Culture." In *The Interpretation of Cultures: Selected Essays*, 3–30. New York: Basic Books, 1973.

Geivett, R. Douglas. "David Hume and a Cumulative Case Argument." In *In Defense of Natural Theology: A Post-Humean Assessment*, edited by James F. Sennett and Douglas Groothuis, 297–329. Downers Grove, IL: InterVarsity Press, 2005.

Geldhof, Joris. "Romantische Metaphysik als natürliche Theologie? Franz von Baader über Gott, die Welt und den Menschen." In *Idealismus und natürliche Theologie*, edited by Margit Wasmaier-Sailer and Benedikt Paul Göcke, 213–37. Freiburg im Breisgau: Verlag Karl Alber, 2011.

Gendler, Tamar Szabó. "The Puzzle of Imaginative Resistance." *Journal of Philosophy* 97, no. 2 (2000): 55–81.

Genette, Gérard. *Palimpsestes: La littératur au second degré.* Paris: Éditions du Seuil, 1997.

Genette, Gérard. *Seuils.* Paris: Éditions du Seuil, 1987.

Gerber, Judith. "Beyond Dualism: The Social Construction of Nature and the Natural and Social Construction of Human Beings." *Progress in Human Geography* 21, no. 1 (1997): 1–17.

Gerson, Lloyd P. *God and Greek Philosophy: Studies in the Early History of Natural Theology.* London: Routledge, 1994.

Gerson, Lloyd P. "Metaphysics in Search of Theology." *Lyceum* 2, no. 2 (1990): 1–21.

Gestrich, Christof. *Neuzeitliches Denken und die Spaltung der dialektischen Theologie: Zur Frage der natürlichen Theologie.* Tübingen: Mohr, 1977.

Gestrich, Christof. "Die unbewältige natürliche Theologie." *Zeitschrift für Theologie und Kirche* 68 (1971): 82–120.

Gieryn, Thomas F. "Boundary-Work and the Demarcation of Science from Non-Science: Strains and Interests in Professional Ideologies of Scientists." *American Sociological Review* 48 (1983): 781–95.

Glacken, Clarence J. *Traces on the Rhodian Shore: Nature and Culture in Western Thought from Ancient Times to the End of the Eighteenth Century.* Berkeley, CA: University of California Press, 1973.

Glick, Thomas F. "Cultural Issues and the Reception of Relativity." In *The Comparative Reception of Relativity*, edited by Thomas F. Glick, 381–400. Dordrecht: Reidel, 1987.

Glynn, Ian. *Elegance in Science: The Beauty of Simplicity.* Oxford: Oxford University Press, 2010.

Godzieba, Anthony J. "God, the Luxury of Our Lives: Schillebeeckx and the Argument." In *Edward Schillebeeckx and Contemporary Theology*, edited by Lieven Boeve, Frederiek Depoortere, and Stephan van Erp, 25–35. London: T. & T. Clark, 2010.

Goffman, Erving. *Frame Analysis: An Essay on the Organization of Experience.* Boston: Northeastern University Press, 1986.

Goldman, Alvin I. *Epistemology and Cognition.* Cambridge, MA: Harvard University Press, 1986.

Gorringe, Timothy J. "The Decline of Nature: Natural Theology, Theology of Nature, and the Built Environment." In *Without Nature? A New Condition for Theology*, edited by David Albertson and Cabell King, 203–20. New York: Fordham University Press, 2010.

Gorringe, Timothy J. *Karl Barth: Against Hegemony.* Oxford: Oxford University Press, 1999.

Gouk, Penelope. *Music, Science, and Natural Magic in Seventeenth-Century England.* New Haven, CT: Yale University Press, 1999.

Grabill, Stephen John. *Rediscovering the Natural Law in Reformed Theological Ethics.* Grand Rapids, MI: Eerdmans, 2006.

Gray, John. *The Silence of Animals: On Progress and Other Modern Myths.* London: Allen Lane, 2013.

Grayling, A. C. *The God Argument.* London: Bloomsbury, 2013.

Green, Garrett. *Imagining God: Theology and the Religious Imagination.* Grand Rapids, MI: Eerdmans, 1998.

Greider, Thomas, and Lorraine Garkovich. "Landscapes: The Social Construction of Nature and the Environment." *Rural Sociology* 59, no. 1 (1994): 1–24.

Groh, Andreas C. *Die Gesellschaftskritik der politischen Romantik: Eine Neubewertung ihrer Auseinandersetzung mit den Vorboten von Industrialisierung und Modernisierung.* Bochum: Winkler Verlag, 2004.

Gross, Franz. *Relativistic Quantum Mechanics and Field Theory.* New York: Wiley, 1999.

Guerrini, Anita. *Obesity and Depression in the Enlightenment: The Life and Times of George Cheyne.* Norman, OK: University of Oklahoma Press, 2000.

Guite, Malcolm. "Through Literature." In *Beholding the Glory: Incarnation through the Arts*, 27–46. Grand Rapids, MI: Baker, 2001.

Gunton, Colin E. *The Promise of Trinitarian Theology*. Edinburgh: T. & T. Clark, 1991.

Gunton, Colin E. "The Trinity, Natural Theology, and a Theology of Nature." In *The Trinity in a Pluralistic Age*, edited by Kevin Vanhoozer, 88–103. Grand Rapids, MI: Eerdmans, 1997.

Gussow, Alan. "Beauty in the Landscape: An Ecological Viewpoint." In *Landscape in America*, edited by George F. Thompson, 223–40. Austin, TX: University of Texas Press, 1995.

Gustafson, James M. "The Sectarian Temptation: Reflections on Theology, the Church and the University." *Proceedings of the Catholic Theological Society of America* 40 (1985): 83–94.

Guy, Alain. "La *Theologia Naturalis* en son temps: Structure, portée, origines." In *Montaigne, Apologie de Raimond Sebond: De la theologia à la théologie*, edited by Claude Blum, 13–47. Paris: Honoré Champion, 1990.

Guy, Alain. "La *Theologia Naturalis*: Manuscrits, éditions, traductions." In *Montaigne, Apologie de Raimond Sebond: De la theologia à la théologie*, edited by Claude Blum, 301–19. Paris: Honoré Champion, 1990.

Haakonssen, Knud, ed. *The Cambridge History of Eighteenth-Century Philosophy*. 2 vols. Cambridge: Cambridge University Press, 2011.

Haakonssen, Knud, ed. *Enlightenment and Religion: Rational Dissent in Eighteenth-Century Britain*. Cambridge: Cambridge University Press, 1996.

Haase, Rudolf. *Aufsätze zur harmonikale Naturphilosophie*. Graz: Akademische Druck- und Verlangsanstalt, 1974.

Habermas, Jürgen. *Erkenntnis und Interesse*. Frankfurt am Main: Suhrkamp, 1968.

Habert, Mireille. *Montaigne traducteur de La Théologie Naturelle: Plaisantes et sainctes imaginations*. Paris: Classiques Garnier, 2010.

Hadot, Pierre. *Philosophy as a Way of Life: Spiritual Exercises from Socrates to Foucault*. Oxford: Blackwell, 1995.

Hadot, Pierre. *Plotinus, or, the Simplicity of Vision*. Chicago: University of Chicago Press, 1993.

Hadot, Pierre. *What Is Ancient Philosophy?* Cambridge, MA: Harvard University Press, 2002.

Haldane, John. "Philosophy, the Restless Heart, and the Meaning of Theism." *Ratio* 19 (2006): 421–40.

Hall, Stuart, ed. *Representation: Cultural Representations and Signifying Practices*. 2nd edn. London: Sage, 2013.

Hammond, David M. "Imagination in Newman's Phenomenology of Cognition." *Heythrop Journal* 29, no. 1 (1988): 21–32.

Hanegraaff, Wouter J. "How Magic Survived the Disenchantment of the World." *Religion* 33 (2003): 357–80.

Hanke, Thomas. "Kein Wunder und keine Instruktion: Kants Umgang mit dem Offenbarungsbegriff vor und in der *Religionsschrift* als Beitrag zu dessen diskreter Transformation." In *Kant und die biblische Offenbarungsreligion*, edited by Jakub Sirovátka and David Vopřada, 16–27. Prague: Karolinum, 2013.

Hanson, N. R. *Patterns of Discovery: An Inquiry into the Conceptual Foundations of Science.* Cambridge: Cambridge University Press, 1961.

Haralambous, Bronwen, and Thomas W. Nielsen. "Wonder as a Gateway Experience." In *Wonderful Education: The Centrality of Wonder in Teaching and Learning*, edited by Kieran Egan, Annabella Cant, and Gillian Judson, 219–38. London: Routledge, 2013.

Hardie, Philip R. *Virgil's Aeneid: Cosmos and Imperium.* Oxford: Clarendon Press, 1986.

Hargrove, Nancy D. "T. S. Eliot and the Dance." *Journal of Modern Literature* 21, no. 1 (1997): 61–88.

Harries, Richard. *Art and the Beauty of God: A Christian Understanding.* London: Continuum, 2005.

Harrington, Michael. "Creation and Natural Contemplation in Maximus the Confessor's *Ambiguum* 10: 19." In *Divine Creation in Ancient, Medieval, and Early Modern Thought*, edited by Willemien Otten, Walter Hannam, and Michael Treschow, 191–212. Leiden: Brill, 2007.

Harrison, Carol. *Beauty and Revelation in the Thought of Saint Augustine.* Oxford: Oxford University Press, 1992.

Harrison, Carol. "Typology of Listening: The Transformation of Scripture in Early Christian Preaching." In *Delivering the Word: Preaching and Exegesis in the Western Christian Tradition*, edited by William John Lyons and Isabella Sandwell, 62–79. New York: Routledge, 2014.

Harrison, C. M., and Burgess, J. "Social Constructions of Nature: A Case Study of Conflicts over the Development of Rainham Marshes SSSI." *Transactions of the Institute of British Geographers* 19 (1994): 291–310.

Harrison, Edward. "The Redshift-Distance and Velocity-Distance Laws." *Astrophysical Journal* 403, no. 1 (1993): 28–31.

Harrison, Peter. *The Bible, Protestantism, and the Rise of Natural Science.* Cambridge: Cambridge University Press, 1998.

Harrison, Peter. "The 'Book of Nature' and Early Modern Science." In *The Book of Nature in Early Modern and Modern History*, edited by Klaas van Berkel and Arie Johan Vanderjagt, 1–26. Louvain: Peeters, 2006.

Harrison, Peter. "The Development of the Concept of Laws of Nature." In *Creation: Law and Probability*, edited by Fraser Watts, 13–36. Aldershot: Ashgate, 2008.

Harrison, Peter. *The Fall of Man and the Foundations of Science.* Cambridge: Cambridge University Press, 2007.

Harrison, Peter. "Natural Theology, Deism, and Early Modern Science." In *Science, Religion, and Society: An Encyclopedia of History, Culture and Controversy*, edited by Arri Eisen and Gary Laderman, 426–33. New York: Sharp, 2006.

Harrison, Peter. "Original Sin and the Problem of Knowledge in Early Modern Europe." *Journal of the History of Ideas* 63, no. 2 (2002): 239–59.

Harrison, Peter. "Physico-Theology and the Mixed Sciences: The Role of Theology in Early Modern Natural Philosophy." In *The Science of Nature in the Seventeenth Century*, edited by Peter Anstey and John Schuster, 165–83. Dordrecht: Springer, 2005.

Harrison, Peter. "Sentiments of Devotion and Experimental Philosophy in Seventeenth-Century England." *Journal of Medieval and Early Modern Studies* 44, no. 1 (2014): 113–33.

Harrison, Peter. *The Territories of Science and Religion*. Chicago: University of Chicago Press, 2015.

Hart, David Bentley. *The Beauty of the Infinite: The Aesthetics of Christian Truth*. Grand Rapids, MI: Eerdmans, 2003.

Hart, Ray L. *Unfinished Man and the Imagination: Toward an Ontology and a Rhetoric of Revelation*. New York: Herder & Herder, 1968.

Harter, Joel. *Coleridge's Philosophy of Faith: Symbol, Allegory, and Hermeneutics*. Tübingen: Mohr Siebeck, 2011.

Hartle, Ann. *Michel de Montaigne: Accidental Philosopher*. Cambridge: Cambridge University Press, 2003.

Hauerwas, Stanley. "The Church in a Divided World. The Interpretative Power of the Christian Story." *Journal of Religious Ethics* 8, no. 1 (1980): 55–82.

Hauerwas, Stanley. "The Demands of a Truthful Story: Ethics and the Pastoral Task." *Chicago Studies* 21 (1982): 59–71.

Hauerwas, Stanley. *With the Grain of the Universe: The Church's Witness and Natural Theology*. London: SCM Press, 2002.

Hauerwas, Stanley. *The Peaceable Kingdom: A Primer in Christian Ethics*. Notre Dame, IN: University of Notre Dame Press, 1983.

Hauerwas, Stanley. *Performing the Faith: Bonhoeffer and the Practice of Nonviolence*. Grand Rapids, MI: Brazos Press, 2004.

Hauerwas, Stanley. *Vision and Virtue: Essays in Christian Ethical Reflection*. Notre Dame, IN: Fides Publishers, 1974.

Haught, John. *Is Nature Enough? Meaning and Truth in the Age of Science*. Cambridge: Cambridge University Press, 2006.

Hay, David. *Something There: The Biology of the Human Spirit*. London: Darton, Longman, and Todd, 2006.

Hayek, Friedrich August von. *Mißbrauch und Verfall der Vernunft*. Tübingen: Mohr Siebeck, 2004.

Hays, Richard B. *The Conversion of the Imagination: Paul as Interpreter of Israel's Scripture*. Grand Rapids, MI: Eerdmans, 2005.

Healey, Nicholas M. *Hauerwas: A (Very) Critical Introduction*. Grand Rapids, MI: Eerdmans, 2014.

Healy, Mary. "Knowledge of the Mystery: A Study of Pauline Epistemology." In *The Bible and Epistemology: Biblical Soundings on the Knowledge of God*, edited by Mary Healy and Robin Parry, 134–58. Milton Keynes: Paternoster, 2007.

Heaney, Seamus. *The Redress of Poetry: Oxford Lectures*. London: Faber, 1995.

Heidegger, Martin. *The Basic Problems of Phenomenology*. Bloomington, IN: Indiana University Press, 1988.

Heidegger, Martin. "Die Zeit des Weltbildes." In *Holzwege*, 75–95. Frankfurt am Main: Vittorio Klostermann, 1977.

Heinze, Richard. *Virgil's Epic Technique*. 2nd edn. London: Bristol Classical Press, 2004.

Heller-Andrist, Simone. *The Friction of the Frame: Derrida's Parergon in Literature*. Tübingen: Francke Verlag, 2012.

Hellwig, Harold H. *Mark Twain's Travel Literature: The Odyssey of a Mind*. Jefferson, NC: McFarland & Co., 2008.

Henrot Sostero, Geneviève. "La fabrique du pré-dire: Proust et la dédicace d'exemplaire." *Poétique* 175 (2014): 121–33.

Henry, John. "Metaphysics and the Origins of Modern Science: Descartes and the Importance of Laws of Nature." *Early Science and Medicine* 9 (2004): 73–114.

Henson, Shaun. *God and Natural Order: Physics, Philosophy, and Theology*. New York: Routledge, 2014.

Hepburn, Ronald W. "Aesthetic Appreciation of Nature." *British Journal of Aesthetics* 3, no. 3 (1963): 195–209.

Hepburn, Ronald W. "Contemporary Aesthetics and the Neglect of Natural Beauty." In *The Aesthetics of Natural Environments*, edited by Allen Carlson and Arnold Berleant, 43–62. Peterborough, ON: Broadview Press, 2004.

Herdt, Jennifer A. "Alasdair MacIntyre's 'Rationality of Traditions' and Tradition-Transcendental Standards of Justification." *Journal of Religion* 78 (1998): 524–46.

Herman, David. "Introduction: Narratologies." In *Narratologies: New Perspectives on Narrative Analysis*, edited by David Herman, 1–30. Columbus, OH: Ohio State University Press, 1999.

Hersey, George L. "Ruskin as an Optical Thinker." In *The Ruskin Polygon: Essays on the Imagination of John Ruskin*, edited by John Dixon Hunt and Faith M. Holland, 44–64. Manchester: Manchester University Press, 1982.

Hesse, Hermann. *"Mit dem Erstaunen fängt es an." Herkunft und Heimat; Natur und Kunst*. Frankfurt am Main: Suhrkamp Verlag, 1986.

Hesse, Hermann. "Die Sehnsucht unser Zeit nach einer Weltanschauung." *Uhu* 2 (1926): 3–14.

Heywood, Bethany T., and Jesse M. Bering. "'Meant to Be': How Religious Beliefs and Cultural Religiosity Affect the Implicit Bias to Think Teleologically." *Religion, Brain and Behavior* 4, no. 3 (2014): 183–201.

Hicks, Joshua A., and Laura A. King. "Meaning in Life and Seeing the Big Picture: Positive Affect and Global Focus." *Cognition and Emotion* 21, no. 7 (2007): 1577–84.

Himes, Brian. "Lonergan's Position on the Natural Desire to See God and Aquinas' Metaphysical Theology of Creation and Participation." *Heythrop Journal* 54, no. 5 (2013): 767–83.

Hitchens, Christopher. *God Is Not Great: How Religion Poisons Everything*. New York: Twelve, 2007.

Hitchin, Neil. "Probability and the Word of God: William Paley's Anglican Method and the Defense of the Scriptures." *Anglican Theological Review* 77 (1995): 302–407.

Hoffmeyer, Jesper. "A Biosemiotic Approach to the Question of Meaning." *Zygon* 45, no. 2 (2010): 367–90.

Hogeterp, Albert L. A. *Paul and God's Temple: A Historical Interpretation of Cultic Imagery in the Corinthian Correspondence.* Leuven: Peeters, 2006.

Holden, Thomas A. *Spectres of False Divinity: Hume's Moral Atheism.* Oxford: Oxford University Press, 2012.

Holder, Rodney D. "Hume on Miracles: Bayesian Interpretation, Multiple Testimony, and the Existence of God." *British Journal for the Philosophy of Science* 49, no. 1 (1998): 49–65.

Holder, Rodney D. "Thomas Torrance: 'Retreat to Commitment' or a New Place for Natural Theology?" *Theology and Science* 7 (2009): 275–96.

Holland, Margaret. "Social Convention and Neurosis as Obstacles to Moral Freedom." In *Iris Murdoch, Philosopher*, edited by Justin Broackes, 255–74. Oxford: Oxford University Press, 2012.

Hollander, Robert. "Dante's 'Paradiso' as Philosophical Poetry." *Italica* 86, no. 4 (2009): 571–82.

Holmes, Richard. *The Age of Wonder: How the Romantic Generation Discovered the Beauty and Terror of Science.* New York: Vintage Books, 2010.

Holyer, Robert. "C. S. Lewis on the Epistemic of the Imagination." *Soundings: An Interdisciplinary Journal* 74, no. 1/2 (1991): 215–41.

Honnefelder, Ludger. "Weisheit durch den Weg der Wissenschaft. Theologie und Philosophie bei Augustinus und Thomas von Aquin." In *Philosophie und Weisheit*, edited by Willi Oelmüller, 65–77. Paderborn: Schöningh, 1989.

Hooker, Morna D. "Chalcedon and the New Testament." In *The Making and Remaking of Christian Doctrine*, edited by Sarah Coakley and David A. Pailin, 73–93. Oxford: Clarendon Press, 1993.

Höpfl, Heather. "Frame." *Culture and Organization* 12, no. 1 (2006): 11–24.

Horton, Michael S. *The Christian Faith: A Systematic Theology for Pilgrims on the Way.* Grand Rapids, MI: Zondervan, 2011.

Hough, Adrian. "Not a Gap in Sight: Fifty Years of Charles Coulson's *Science and Christian Belief*." *Theology* 109 (2006): 21–7.

Hough, Graham. "The Natural Theology of *In Memoriam*." *Review of English Studies* 91 (1947): 244–56.

Howard, Donald R. "Renaissance World-Alienation." In *The Darker Vision of the Renaissance*, edited by Robert S. Kinsman, 47–76. Berkeley, CA: University of California Press, 1974.

Howell, Kenneth J. *God's Two Books: Copernican Cosmology and Biblical Interpretation in Early Modern Science.* Notre Dame, IN: University of Notre Dame Press, 2002.

Howson, Colin, and Peter Urbach. *Scientific Reasoning: The Bayesian Approach.* 3rd edn. Chicago: Open Court, 2005.

Hull, David L. "The God of the Galápagos." *Nature* 352, no. 6335 (1991): 485–6.

Hume, David. *Philosophical Works.* London: Fenton, 1828.

Hunter, Ian. *The Secularisation of the Confessional State: The Political Thought of Christian Thomasius.* Cambridge: Cambridge University Press, 2007.

Husbands, Mark. "Calvin on the Revelation of God in Creation and Scripture: Modern Reception and Contemporary Possibilities." In *Calvin's Theology and*

Its Reception: Disputes, Developments, and New Possibilities, edited by J. Todd Billings and I. John Hesselink, 25–48. Louisville, KY: Westminster John Knox Press, 2012.

Huston, Joseph P., Marcos Nadal, Francisco Mora, Luigi Francesco Agnati, and Camilo José Cela Conde, eds. *Art, Aesthetics, and the Brain*. Oxford: Oxford University Press, 2015.

Hutchinson, John. "The Uses of Natural Theology: An Essay in Redefinition." *Journal of Philosophy* 55, no. 22 (1958): 936–44.

Hütter, Reinhard. "*Desiderium naturale visionis Dei – est autem duplex hominis beatitudo sive felicitas:* Some Observations about Lawrence Feingold's and John Millbank's Recent Interventions in the Debate over the Natural Desire to See God." *Nova et Vetera* 5 (2007): 81–132.

Hütter, Reinhard. "University Education, the Unity of Knowledge – and (Natural) Theology: John Henry Newman's Provocative Vision." *Nova et Vetera* 11, no. 4 (2013): 1017–56.

Huxley, Aldous. *The Perennial Philosophy*. New York: Harper and Row, 1945.

Ilany, Bat-Sheva, and Bruria Margolin. "Language and Mathematics: Bridging between Natural Language and Mathematical Language in Solving Problems in Mathematics." *Creative Education* 1 (2010): 138–48.

Illanes, José Luis. "Teología y ciencias en una visión cristiana de la universidad." *Scripta Theologica* 14 (1982): 873–88.

Illich, Ivan. *In the Vineyard of the Text: A Commentary to Hugh's Didascalicon*. Chicago: University of Chicago Press, 1993.

Illiffe, Rob. "Newton, God, and the Mathematics of the Two Books." In *Mathematicians and Their Gods: Interactions between Mathematics and Religious Beliefs*, edited by Snezana Lawrence and Mark McCartney, 121–44. Oxford: Oxford University Press, 2015.

Imbach, Ruedi. "La philosophie comme exercice spirituel." *Critique* 41, no. 454 (1985): 275–83.

Inge, John. *A Christian Theology of Place*. Aldershot: Ashgate, 2003.

Inge, William Ralph. *Faith and Its Psychology*. New York: Charles Scribner's Sons, 1910.

Iranzo, Valeriano. "Bayesianism and Inference to the Best Explanation." *Theoria* 61 (2008): 89–106.

Irlenborn, Bernd. "Abschied von der 'natürlichen Theologie'? Eine sprachphilosophische Standortbestimmung." *Theologie und Philosophie* 78 (2003): 545–57.

Irlenborn, Bernd. "Konsonanz von Theologie und Naturwissenschaft? Fundamentaltheologische Bemerkungen zum interdisziplinären Ansatz von John Polkinghorne." *Trierer Theologische Zeitung* 113 (2004): 98–117.

Irving, Sarah. "Public Knowledge, Natural Philosophy, and the Eighteenth-Century Republic of Letters." *Early American Literature* 49, no. 1 (2014): 67–88.

Isambert, François-André. "Le 'désenchantement' du monde: non sens ou renouveau du sens?" *Archives de Sciences Religieuses* 61, no. 1 (1986): 83–103.

Israel, Jonathan I. *Enlightenment Contested: Philosophy, Modernity, and the Emancipation of Man, 1670–1752*. Oxford: Oxford University Press, 2008.

Jackson, Myles W. "Music and Science during the Scientific Revolution." *Perspectives on Science* 9, no. 1 (2001): 106–15.

Jager, Colin. "*Mansfield Park* and the End of Natural Theology." *MLQ: Modern Language Quarterly* 63 (2002): 31–63.

Jaki, Stanley L. *The Origin of Science and the Science of Its Origin.* Edinburgh: Scottish Academic Press, 1978.

James, William. "On a Certain Blindness in Human Beings." In *Talks to Teachers on Psychology*, 149–69. New York: Norton, 1958.

James, William. *The Principles of Psychology.* New York: Holt, 1890.

James, William. *The Varieties of Religious Experience.* London: Longmans, Green, & Co., 1902.

James, William. *The Will to Believe.* New York: Dover Publications, 1956.

Jarvis, Simon. *Adorno: A Critical Introduction.* Cambridge: Polity Press, 1998.

Jay, Martin. *Downcast Eyes: The Denigration of Vision in Twentieth-Century French Thought.* Berkeley, CA: University of California Press, 1993.

Jay, Martin. "Scopic Regimes of Modernity." In *Vision and Visuality*, edited by Hal Foster, 3–28. Seattle: Bay Press, 1988.

Jehle, Frank. *Emil Brunner: Theologe im 20. Jahrhundert.* Zurich: Theologischer Verlag, 2006.

Johansen, Jørgen Dines. "Let Sleeping Signs Lie: On Signs, Objects, and Communication." *Semiotica* 97, no. 3 (1993): 271–95.

Johnson, Nuala C. "Grand Design(er)s: David Moore, Natural Theology and the Royal Botanic Gardens in Glasnevin, Dublin, 1838–1879." *Cultural Geographies* 14, no. 1 (2007): 29–55.

Johnson, Samuel. *Works.* 17 vols. New Haven, CT: Yale University Press, 1958–78.

Johnston, Hank. "A Methodology for Frame Analysis." In *Social Movements and Culture*, edited by Hank Johnston and Bert Klandermans, 217–46. Minneapolis, MN: University of Minnesota Press, 1995.

Jonas, Hans. "The Nobility of Sight: A Study in the Phenomenology of the Senses." *Philosophy and Phenomenological Research* 14, no. 4 (1954): 507–19.

Jones, Matthew L. "Descartes's Geometry as Spiritual Exercise." *Critical Inquiry* 28, no. 1 (2001): 40–71.

Jones, Matthew L. *The Good Life in the Scientific Revolution: Descartes, Pascal, Leibniz, and the Cultivation of Virtue.* Chicago: University of Chicago Press, 2006.

Jones, Susan. "'At the Still Point': T. S. Eliot, Dance, and Modernism." *Dance Research Journal* 41, no. 2 (2009): 31–51.

Jong, Jonathan, and Aku Visala. "Evolutionary Debunking Arguments against Theism Reconsidered." *International Journal for Philosophy of Religion* 76, no. 3 (2014): 243–58.

Jong, Jonathan, Christopher Kavanagh, and Aku Visala. "Born Idolaters: The Limits of the Philosophical Implications of the Cognitive Science of Religion." *Neue Zeitschrift für systematische Theologie und Religionsphilosophie* 57, no. 2 (2015): 244–66.

Joyce, George Hayward. *Principles of Natural Theology.* London: Longmans, Green, and Co., 1922.

Jüngel, Eberhard. "Das Dilemma der natürlichen Theologie und die Wahrheit ihres Problems. Überlegungen für ein Gespräch mit Wolfhart Pannenberg." In *Entsprechungen: Gott – Wahrheit – Mensch*, 158–77. Tübingen: Mohr Siebeck, 2002.

Jüngel, Eberhard. "Unterbrechung des Weltlebens: Eberhard Jüngel über 'Gottes Sein ist im Werden'." In *Werksbesichtigung Geisteswissenschaften: Fünfundzwanzig Bücher von ihren Autoren gelesen*, edited by Henning Ritter, 131–8. Frankfurt am Main: Insel Verlag, 1990.

Kaiser, Christopher B. *Toward a Theology of Scientific Endeavour: The Descent of Science.* Aldershot: Ashgate, 2007.

Kant, Immanuel. *Gesammelte Schriften.* 30 vols. Berlin: Reimer, 1902.

Kapper, Michael. "'Natürliche Theologie' als innerprotestantisches und ökumenisches Problem? Die Kontroverse zwischen Eberhard Jüngel und Wolfhart Pannenberg und ihr ökumenischer Ertrag." *Catholica* 49 (1995): 276–309.

Kareem, Sarah Tindal. *Eighteenth-Century Fiction and the Reinvention of Wonder.* Oxford: Oxford University Press, 2014.

Kärkkäinen, Veli-Matti. *Trinity and Revelation.* Grand Rapids, MI: Eerdmans, 2014.

Karnes, Michelle. *Imagination, Meditation, and Cognition in the Middle Ages.* Chicago: University of Chicago Press, 2011.

Kastanakis, Minas N., and Benjamin G. Voyer. "The Effect of Culture on Perception and Cognition: A Conceptual Framework." *Journal of Business Research* 67, no. 4 (2014): 425–33.

Kavanagh, Donncha. "The Limits of Visualization: Ocularcentrism and Organization." In *Routledge Companion to Visual Organization*, edited by Emma Bell, Samantha Warren, and Jonathan E. Schroeder, 64–76. London: Routledge, 2014.

Keats, John. *Letters*, edited by M. B. Forman. Oxford: Oxford University Press, 1947.

Kekes, John. *Moral Wisdom and Good Lives.* Ithaca, NY: Cornell University Press, 1995.

Kelemen, Deborah. "Are Children 'Intuitive Theists'? Reasoning about Purpose and Design in Nature." *Psychological Science* 15, no. 5 (2004): 295–301.

Kelemen, Deborah, Joshua Rottman, and Rebecca Seston. "Professional Physical Scientists Display Tenacious Teleological Tendencies: Purpose-Based Reasoning as a Cognitive Default." *Journal of Experimental Psychology* 142, no. 4 (2013): 1074–83.

Kelly, Robert A. "Public Theology and the Modern Social Imaginary." *Dialog: A Journal of Theology* 50, no. 2 (2011): 162–73.

Keltner, Dacher, and Jonathan Haidt. "Approaching Awe: A Moral, Spiritual and Aesthetic Emotion." *Cognition and Emotion* 17 (2003): 297–314.

Kepler, Johann. *Gesammelte Werke.* 22 vols. Munich: C. H. Beck, 1937–83.

Kerr, Fergus. *Immortal Longings: Versions of Transcending Humanity.* London: SPCK, 1997.

Kerr, Fergus. "Knowing God by Reason Alone: What Vatican I Never Said." *New Blackfriars* 91, no. 1033 (2010): 215–28.

Kertelge, Karl. "'Natürliche Theologie' und Rechtfertigung aus dem Glauben bei Paulus." In *Grundthemen Paulinischer Theologie*, 148–60. Freiburg: Herder, 1991.

Khamara, Edward J. "Hume versus Clarke on the Cosmological Argument." *Philosophical Quarterly* 42, no. 1 (1992): 34–55.

Kieran, Matthew. "Art, Imagination, and the Cultivation of Morals." *Journal of Aesthetics and Art Criticism* 54, no. 4 (1996): 337–51.

Kim, Young Yun. "Ideology, Identity, and Intercultural Communication: An Analysis of Differing Academic Conceptions of Cultural Identity." *Journal of Intercultural Communication Research* 36, no. 3 (2007): 237–53.

Kimmel, Michael. "Properties of Cultural Embodiment: Lessons from the Anthropology of the Body." In *Sociocultural Situatedness*, edited by Roslyn M. Frank, René Dirven, Tom Ziemke, and Enrique Bernárdez, 77–108. Berlin: De Gruyter, 2008.

King, Anna S. "Spirituality: Transformation and Metamorphosis." *Religion* 26 (1996): 343–51.

King, Anthony. "Thinking with Bourdieu against Bourdieu: A 'Practical' Critique of the Habitus." *Sociological Theory* 18, no. 3 (2000): 417–33.

Kirshenblatt-Gimblett, Barbara. *Destination Culture: Tourism, Museums, and Heritage*. Berkeley, CA: University of California Press, 1998.

Kitayama, Shinobu, Sean Duffy, Tadashi Kawamura, and Jeff T. Larsen. "Perceiving an Object and Its Context in Different Cultures: A Cultural Look at New Look." *Psychological Science* 14, no. 3 (2003): 201–6.

Klauber, Martin. *Between Reformed Scholasticism and Pan-Protestantism: Jean-Alphonse Turretin (1671–1737) and Enlightened Orthodoxy at the Academy of Geneva*. Cranbury, NJ: Associated University Presses, 1994.

Klauber, Martin. "Jean-Alphonse Turrettini (1671–1737) on Natural Theology: The Triumph of Reason over Revelation at the Academy of Geneva." *Scottish Journal of Theology* 47 (1994): 301–25.

Klauck, Hans-Josef. "Nature, Art, and Thought: Dio Chrysostom and the *Theologia Tripertita*." *Journal of Religion* 87 (2007): 333–54.

Kleeberg, Bernard. "God–Nature Progressing: Natural Theology in German Monism." *Science in Context* 20 (2007): 537–69.

Kleiner, Scott A. "Explanatory Coherence and Empirical Adequacy: The Problem of Abduction, and the Justification of Evolutionary Models." *Biology and Philosophy* 18 (2003): 513–27.

Kloos, Kari. *Christ, Creation, and the Vision of God: Augustine's Transformation of Early Christian Theophany Interpretation*. Leiden: Brill, 2011.

Knauer, Peter. "Natürliche Gotteserkenntnis." In *Verifikationen, Festschrift für Gerhard Ebeling zum 70. Geburtstag*, edited by Eberhard Jüngel, Johannes Wallmann, and Wilfried Werbeck, 275–94. Tübingen: Mohr Siebeck, 1982.

Kneller, Jane. *Kant and the Power of Imagination*. Cambridge: Cambridge University Press, 2007.

Knight, Kathleen. "Transformations of the Concept of Ideology in the Twentieth Century." *American Political Science Review* 100, no. 4 (2006): 619–26.

Knoepflmacher, U. C., and G. B. Tennyson, eds. *Nature and the Victorian Imagination.* Berkeley, CA: University of California Press, 1977.

Knuuttila, Simo, and Pekka Kärkkäinen, eds. *Theories of Perception in Medieval and Early Modern Philosophy.* Dordrecht: Springer, 2008.

Kock, Christoph. *Natürliche Theologie: Ein evangelischer Streitbegriff.* Neukirchen-Vluyn: Neukirchener, 2001.

Koestler, Arthur. *The God that Failed.* New York: Columbia University Press, 2001.

Koestler, Arthur. *The Invisible Writing.* Boston: Beacon Press, 1954.

Kolakowski, Leszek. "Concern about God in an Apparently Godless Age." In *My Correct Views on Everything,* edited by Zbigniew Janowski, 173–83. South Bend, IN: St. Augustine's Press, 2005.

Komonchak, Joseph A. "The Future of Theology in the Church." In *New Horizons in Theology,* edited by Terrence W. Tilley, 16–39. Maryknoll, NY: Orbis Books, 2005.

Koons, Robert C. "A New Look at the Cosmological Argument." *American Philosophical Quarterly* 34, no. 2 (1997): 193–211.

Kooten, Geurt Hendrik van. *Cosmic Christology in Paul and the Pauline School: Colossians and Ephesians in the Context of Graeco-Roman Cosmology.* Tübingen: Mohr Siebeck, 2003.

Kornblith, Hilary. "Justified Belief and Epistemically Responsible Action." *Philosophical Review* 92 (1983): 33–48.

Kors, Alan C. "Theology and Atheism in Early Modern France." In *The Transmission of Culture in Early Modern Europe,* edited by Ann Blair and Anthony Grafton, 238–75. Philadelphia: University of Pennsylvania Press, 1990.

Kort, Wesley A. *C. S. Lewis Then and Now.* New York: Oxford University Press, 2001.

Kramer, Werner. "'Die andere Aufgabe der Theologie.' Ein bleibendes Anliegen Emil Brunners im Briefwechsel mit Karl Barth." *Theologische Zeitschrift* 57 (2001): 363–79.

Kraus, Georg. *Gotteserkenntnis ohne Offenbarung und Glaube? Natürliche Theologie als ökumenisches Problem.* Paderborn: Verlag Bonifatius-Druckerei, 1987.

Kretzmann, Norman. *The Metaphysics of Creation: Aquinas's Natural Theology in Summa Contra Gentiles II.* Oxford: Clarendon Press, 1999.

Kretzmann, Norman. *The Metaphysics of Theism: Aquinas's Natural Theology in Summa Contra Gentiles I.* Oxford: Clarendon Press, 1997.

Kreuzer, Johann. "'Die Sphäre die Höher ist, als die des Menschen: Diese ist der Gott.' Hölderlin und die natürliche Theologie." In *Idealismus und natürliche Theologie,* edited by Margit Wasmaier-Sailer and Benedikt Paul Göcke, 238–57. Freiburg im Breisgau: Verlag Karl Alber, 2011.

Krüger, Klaus. *Das Bild als Schleier des Unsichtbaren: Ästhetische Illusion in der Kunst der frühen Neuzeit in Italien.* Munich: Fink, 2001.

Kulp, Christopher B. "Dewey, the Spectator Theory of Knowledge, and Internalism/ Externalism." *Modern Schoolman* 87, no. 1 (2009): 67–77.

Kulp, Christopher B. *The End of Epistemology: Dewey and His Current Allies on the Spectator Theory of Knowledge.* Westport, CT: Greenwood Press, 1992.

Lalor, Brendan J. "The Classification of Peirce's Interpretants." *Semiotica* 114, no. 1 (1997): 31–40.

Landsman, N. P. *Mathematical Topics between Classical and Quantum Mechanics.* New York: Springer, 1998.

Lane, Belden C. "Jonathan Edwards on Beauty, Desire and the Sensory World." *Theological Studies* 65, no. 1 (2004): 44–68.

Lane, Belden C. "Thomas Traherne and the Awakening of Want." *Anglican Theological Review* 81, no. 4 (1999): 651–64.

Lane, William C. "Leibniz's Best World Claim Restructured." *American Philosophical Journal* 47, no. 1 (2010): 57–84.

Langtry, Bruce. "Richard Swinburne." In *Twentieth-Century Philosophy of Religion*, edited by Graham Oppy and N. N. Trakakis, 285–300. London: Routledge, 2014.

Larmer, Robert. "Is There Anything Wrong with 'God of the Gaps' Reasoning?" *International Journal for the Philosophy of Religion* 52 (2002): 129–42.

Larrain, Jorge. *Ideology and Cultural Identity.* Cambridge: Polity Press, 1994.

Lasher, Connie. "Dialogue with Nature and Interreligious Encounter: Toward a Comparative Theology of the Sense of Wonder." *Journal of Oriental Studies* 21 (2011): 187–209.

Lawrence, D. H. *Lady Chatterley's Lover.* London: Penguin Books, 1993.

Lefebvre, Martin. "Peirce's Esthetics: A Taste for Signs in Art." *Transactions of the Charles S. Peirce Society* 43, no. 2 (2007): 319–44.

Leib, Ethan J. "On the Difficulty of Imagining an Aesthetic Politics." *Yale Journal of Law and the Humanities* 12, no. 1 (2000): 151–68.

Lemeni, Adrian. "The Rationality of the World and Human Reason as Expressed in the Theology of Father Dumitru Stăniloae: Points of Connection in the Dialogue between Theology and Science." *International Journal of Orthodox Theology* 3, no. 4 (2012): 89–101.

Lesher, James H. *Xenophanes of Colophon: A Text and Translation.* Toronto: University of Toronto Press, 1992.

Leslie, Charles Robert. *Memoirs of the Life of John Constable, Esq., R.A., composed chiefly of his Letters.* London: Longman, Brown, Green, and Longmans, 1845.

Levering, Matthew. *Scripture and Metaphysics: Aquinas and the Renewal of Trinitarian Theology.* Oxford: Blackwell, 2004.

Levin, David M. "Decline and Fall: Ocularcentrism in Heidegger's Reading of the History of Metaphysics." In *Modernity and the Hegemony of Vision*, edited by David M. Levin, 186–217. Berkeley, CA: University of California Press, 1993.

Levy, Sandra M. *Imagination and the Journey of Faith.* Grand Rapids, MI: Eerdmans, 2008.

Lewis, C. S. *The Abolition of Man.* London: Oxford University Press, 1943.

Lewis, C. S. *The Allegory of Love: A Study in Medieval Tradition.* Oxford: Clarendon Press, 1936.

Lewis, C. S. *Christian Reflections.* Grand Rapids, MI: Eerdmans, 1967.

Lewis, C. S. *The Discarded Image: An Introduction to Medieval and Renaissance Literature*. Cambridge: Cambridge University Press, 1964.

Lewis, C. S. *Essay Collection*. London: HarperCollins, 2002.

Lewis, C. S. *The Four Loves*. London: Geoffrey Bles, 1960.

Lewis, C. S. *Perelandra*. London: HarperCollins, 2005.

Lewis, C. S. *Surprised by Joy*. London: HarperCollins, 2002.

Lewis, C. S. *The Pilgrim's Regress*. London: Geoffrey Bles, 1950.

Liao, Shen-yi, Nina Strohminger, and Chandra Sekhar Sripada. "Empirically Investigating Imaginative Resistance." *British Journal of Aesthetics* 54, no. 3 (2014): 339–55.

Librett, Jeffrey S. "Aesthetics in Deconstruction: Derrida's Reception of Kant's Critique of Judgment." *Philosophical Forum* 43, no. 3 (2012): 327–44.

Liere, Franciscus A. van. *An Introduction to the Medieval Bible*. Cambridge: Cambridge University Press, 2014.

Lightbody, Brian. *Philosophical Genealogy: An Epistemological Reconstruction of Nietzsche and Foucault's Genealogical Method*. New York: Peter Lang, 2010.

Lillard, Angeline S. "Ethnopsychologies: Cultural Variations in Theory of Mind." *Psychological Bulletin* 123 (1998): 2–32.

Lim, Paul Chang-Ha. *Mystery Unveiled: The Crisis of the Trinity in Early Modern England*. New York: Oxford University Press, 2012.

Lindbeck, George. *The Nature of Doctrine*. Philadelphia: Westminster, 1984.

Lindberg, David C. "The Genesis of Kepler's Theory of Light: Light Metaphysics from Plotinus to Kepler." *Osiris* 2 (1986): 5–42.

Lipton, Peter. *Inference to the Best Explanation*. 2nd edn. London: Routledge, 2004.

Liszka, James. "Peirce's Interpretant." *Transactions of the Charles Sanders Peirce Society* 26, no. 1 (1990): 17–62.

Livesey, Graham. "Assemblage Theory, Gardens and the Legacy of the Early Garden City Movement." *Architectural Research Quarterly* 15, no. 3 (2011): 271–8.

Livingstone, David N. *Dealing with Darwin: Place, Politics, and Rhetoric in Religious Engagements with Evolution*. Baltimore, MD: Johns Hopkins University Press, 2014.

Livingstone, David N. "Science, Text, and Space: Thoughts on the Geography of Reading." *Transactions of the Institute of British Geographers* 35 (2005): 391–401.

Livio, Mario. *Is God a Mathematician?* New York: Simon & Schuster, 2009.

Lohr, Charles. "Metaphysics and Natural Philosophy as Sciences: The Catholic and Protestant Views in the Sixteenth and Seventeenth Centuries." In *Philosophy in the Sixteenth and Seventeenth Centuries: Conversations with Aristotle*, edited by Constance Blackwell and Sachiko Kusukawa, 280–95. Aldershot: Ashgate, 1999.

Löhr, Katja. *Sehnsucht als poetisches Prinzip bei Joseph von Eichendorff*. Würzburg: Königshausen & Neumann, 2003.

Lonergan, Bernard J. F. "The General Character of the Natural Theology of Insight." In *Collected Works of Bernard Lonergan*, 3–9. Toronto: University of Toronto Press, 2004.

Lonergan, Bernard J. F. *Insight: A Study of Human Understanding*. 3rd edn. New York: Philosophical Library, 1970.

Long, D. Stephen. *Speaking of God: Theology, Language, and Truth*. Grand Rapids, MI: Eerdmans, 2009.

Loo, Stephanie van de. *Versöhnungsarbeit: Kriterien, theologischer Rahmen, Praxis-perspektiven*. Stuttgart: Kohlhammer, 2009.

Losee, John. *Theories of Scientific Progress: An Introduction*. New York: Routledge, 2004.

Louth, Andrew. "Light, Vision, and Religious Experience in Byzantium." In *The Presence of Light: Divine Radiance and Religious Experience*, edited by Matthew Kapstein, 85–104. Chicago: University of Chicago Press, 2004.

Lovibond, Sabina. *Iris Murdoch, Gender and Philosophy*. New York: Routledge, 2011.

Lundberg, Matthew D. "Echoes of Barth in Jon Sobrino's Critique of Natural Theology: A Dialogue in the Context of Post-Colonial Theology." In *Theology as Conversation: The Significance of Dialogue in Historical and Contemporary Theology*, edited by Bruce L. McCormack and Kimlyn J. Bender, 82–100. Grand Rapids, MI: Eerdmans, 2009.

Lustig, Abigail. "Natural Atheology." In *Darwinian Heresies*, edited by Abigail Lustig, Robert J. Richards, and Michael Ruse, 69–83. Cambridge: Cambridge University Press, 2004.

Luy, David. "The Aesthetic Collision: Hans Urs Von Balthasar on the Trinity and the Cross." *International Journal of Systematic Theology* 13, no. 2 (2011): 154–69.

Luz, Ulrich. "*Theologia Crucis* als Mitte der Theologie im Neuen Testament." *Evangelische Theologie* 34 (1974): 141–75.

Lynch, William F. *Christ and Apollo: The Dimensions of the Literary Imagination*. 2nd edn. New York: New American Library, 1975.

Lyons, John D. *Before Imagination: Embodied Thought from Montaigne to Rousseau*. Stanford, CA: Stanford University Press, 2005.

Machamer, Peter K. "Feyerabend and Galileo: The Interaction of Theories, and the Reinterpretation of Experience." *Studies in History and Philosophy of Science* 4 (1973): 1–46.

MacIntosh, J. J. "Robert Boyle's Epistemology: The Interaction between Scientific and Religious Knowledge." *International Studies in the Philosophy of Science* 6 (1992): 91–121.

MacIntyre, Alasdair. *Whose Justice? Which Rationality?* London: Duckworth, 1988.

Macken, John. *The Autonomy Theme in the Church Dogmatics: Karl Barth and His Critics*. Cambridge: Cambridge University Press, 1990.

Mackey, Louis. *Faith – Order – Understanding: Natural Theology in the Augustinian Tradition*. Toronto: Pontifical Institute of Mediaeval Studies, 2011.

Maclean, Ian. *Logic, Signs, and Nature in the Renaissance: The Case of Learned Medicine*. Cambridge: Cambridge University Press, 2002.

Maclean, Marie. "Pretexts and Paratexts: The Art of the Peripheral." *New Literary History* 22, no. 2 (1991): 273–9.

Macquarrie, John. "The Idea of a Theology of Nature." *Union Seminary Quarterly Review* 30 (1975): 69–75.

Macquarrie, John. *In Search of Deity: An Essay in Dialectical Theism*. London: SCM Press, 1985.

Maffie, James. "Naturalism, Scientism and the Independence of Epistemology." *Erkenntnis* 43 (1995): 1–27.

Maguire, Matthew W. *The Conversion of Imagination: From Pascal through Rousseau to Tocqueville*. Cambridge, MA: Harvard University Press, 2006.

Makuchowska, Ludmila. *Scientific Discourse in John Donne's Eschatological Poetry*. Newcastle: Cambridge Scholars Publishing, 2014.

Malet, Antoni. "Isaac Barrow on the Mathematization of Nature: Theological Voluntarism and the Rise of Geometrical Optics." *Journal of the History of Ideas* 58, no. 2 (1997): 265–87.

Mancini, Italo. *Filosofia della religione*. 3rd edn. Genoa: Editrice Marietti, 1991.

Mandelbrote, Scott. "Eighteenth-Century Reactions to Newton's Anti-Trinitarianism." In *Newton and Newtonianism: New Studies*, edited by J. E. Force and S. Hutton, 93–112. Dordrecht: Kluwer, 2004.

Mandelbrote, Scott. "The Uses of Natural Theology in Seventeenth-Century England." *Science in Context* 20 (2007): 451–80.

Marcolungo, Ferdinando Luigi. "Christian Wolff und der physiko-theologische Beweis." In *Die natürliche Theologie bei Christian Wolff*, edited by Michael Albrecht, 147–62. Hamburg: Meiner Felix Verlag, 2012.

Markham, Ian. *Truth and the Reality of God: An Essay in Natural Theology*. Edinburgh: T. & T. Clark, 1998.

Markley, Robert. "Representing Order: Natural Philosophy, Mathematics, and Theology in the Newtonian Revolution." In *Chaos and Order: Complex Dynamics in Literature and Science*, edited by Katherine Hayles, 125–48. Chicago: University of Chicago Press, 1991.

Marquardt, Friedrich-Wilhelm. *Theologie und Sozialismus: Das Beispiel Karl Barths*. 3rd edn. Munich: Kaiser, 1985.

Marrone, Steven. *The Light of Thy Countenance: Science and Knowledge of God in the Thirteenth Century*. 2 vols. Leiden: Brill, 2001.

Martinengo, Alberto. "From the Linguistic Turn to the Pictorial Turn: Hermeneutics Facing the 'Third Copernican Revolution'." *Proceedings of the European Society for Aesthetics* 5 (2013): 302–12.

Mascall, E. L. *The Openness of Being: Natural Theology Today*. London: Darton Longman and Todd, 1971.

Masuzawa, Tomoko. *The Invention of World Religions, or, How European Universalism Was Preserved in the Language of Pluralism*. Chicago: University of Chicago Press, 2005.

Matczak, S. A. "Fideism." In *The New Catholic Encyclopedia*. 2nd edn, vol. 5, 711–13. Washington, DC: Catholic University of America, 2003.

Mathews, William A. *Lonergan's Quest: A Study of Desire in the Authoring of Insight*. Toronto: University of Toronto Press, 2005.

Matsuda, Matt K. *Empire of Love: Histories of France and the Pacific*. New York: Oxford University Press, 2005.

Matthias, Marcus. "Bekehrung und Wiedergeburt." In *Geschichte der Pietismus*, edited by Ulrich Gäbler, Martin Sallmann, Martin Brecht, Klaus Deppermann, and Hartmut Lehmann, vol. 4, 49–79. Göttingen: Vandenhoeck & Ruprecht, 2004.

Mattison, Andrew. "Sweet Imperfection: Milton and the Troubled Metaphor of Harmony." *Modern Philology* 106, no. 4 (2009): 617–47.

Maurer, Dominique. "Warum wie alle das Heidi lieben." *Journal Franz Weber* 97 (2011): 8–11.

Mayne, Michael. *This Sunrise of Wonder: Letters for the Journey.* London: Fount, 1995.

Mazis, Glen A. "Merleau-Ponty's Artist of Depth: Exploring 'Eye and Mind' and the Works of Art Chosen by Merleau-Ponty as Preface." *Phaenex* 7, no. 1 (2012): 244–74.

McAllister, James W. *Beauty and Revolution in Science.* Ithaca, NY: Cornell University Press, 1996.

McCabe, Herbert. *Faith within Reason.* London: Continuum, 2007.

McCabe, Herbert. *God Still Matters.* London: Continuum, 2002.

McCauley, Robert N. *Why Religion Is Natural and Science Is Not.* New York: Oxford University Press, 2011.

McClymond, Michael James, and Gerald R. McDermott. *The Theology of Jonathan Edwards.* New York: Oxford University Press, 2012.

McCrea, Brian. "The Hermeutics of Deliverance: *Robinson Crusoe* and the Problem of Witnessing." In *Hermeneutics at the Crossroads*, edited by Kevin J. Vanhoozer, James K. A. Smith, and Bruce Ellis Benson, 150–63. Bloomington, IN: Indiana University Press, 2006.

McFarland, Ian A. *From Nothing: A Theology of Creation.* Louisville, KY: Westminster John Knox Press, 2014.

McGrath, Alister E. "Arrows of Joy: Lewis's Argument from Desire." In *The Intellectual World of C. S. Lewis*, 105–28. Oxford: Wiley-Blackwell, 2013.

McGrath, Alister E. "Chance and Providence in the Thought of William Paley." In *Abraham's Dice: Chance and Providence in the Monotheistic Traditions*, edited by Karl Giberson. Oxford: Oxford University Press, 2016.

McGrath, Alister E. *Darwinism and the Divine: Evolutionary Thought and Natural Theology.* Oxford: Wiley-Blackwell, 2011.

McGrath, Alister E. *Emil Brunner: A Reappraisal.* Oxford: Wiley-Blackwell, 2014.

McGrath, Alister E. "An Enhanced Vision of Rationality: C. S. Lewis on the Reasonableness of Christian Faith." *Theology* 116, no. 6 (2013): 410–17.

McGrath, Alister E. *A Fine-Tuned Universe: The Quest for God in Science and Theology.* Louisville, KY: Westminster John Knox Press, 2009.

McGrath, Alister E. *The Genesis of Doctrine: A Study in the Foundations of Doctrinal Criticism.* Oxford: Blackwell, 1990.

McGrath, Alister E. *Inventing the Universe: Why We Can't Stop Talking about God, Science, and Faith.* London: Hodder & Stoughton, 2015.

McGrath, Alister E. *Luther's Theology of the Cross: Martin Luther's Theological Breakthrough.* 2nd edn. Oxford: Wiley-Blackwell, 2011.

McGrath, Alister E. "New Atheism – New Apologetics: The Use of Science in Recent Christian Apologetic Writings." *Science and Christian Belief* 26, no. 2 (2014): 99–113.

McGrath, Alister E. *The Open Secret: A New Vision for Natural Theology.* Oxford: Wiley-Blackwell, 2008.

McGrath, Alister E. *The Passionate Intellect: Christian Faith and the Discipleship of the Mind.* Downers Grove, IL: InterVarsity Press, 2010.

McGrath, Alister E. "The Privileging of Vision: Lewis's Metaphors of Light, Sun, and Sight." In *The Intellectual World of C. S. Lewis*, 83–104. Oxford: Wiley-Blackwell, 2013.

McGrath, Alister E. "'Schläft ein Lied in allen Dingen'? Gedanken über die Zukunft der natürlichen Theologie." *Theologische Zeitschrift* 65 (2009): 246–60.

McGrath, Alister E. *A Scientific Theology.* 3 vols. London: T. & T. Clark, 2001–3.

McGrath, Alister E. "Theologie als Mathesis Universalis? Heinrich Scholz, Karl Barth, und der wissenschaftliche Status der christlichen Theologie." *Theologische Zeitschrift* 62 (2007): 44–57.

McGrath, Sean. "Heidegger's Approach to Aquinas." In *Belief and Metaphysics*, edited by Peter M. Chandler and Conor Cunningham, 260–90. London: SCM Press, 2007.

McGrew, Timothy J., and John M. DePoe. "Natural Theology and the Uses of Argument." *Philosophia Christi* 15, no. 2 (2013): 299–309.

McGuire, James E. "The Rhetoric of Sprat's Defence of the Royal Society." *Archives internationals d'histoire des sciences* 55 (2005): 203–10.

McGuire, James E., and P. M. Rattansi. "Newton and the Pipes of Pan." *Notes and Records of the Royal Society* 21, no. 2 (1966): 104–43.

McMahon, Darrin M. "The Return of the History of Ideas?" In *Rethinking Modern European Intellectual History*, edited by Darrin M. McMahon and Samuel Moyn, 13–31. Oxford: Oxford University Press, 2014.

McMaken, W. Travis. "The Impossibility of Natural Knowledge of God in T. F. Torrance's Reformulated Natural Theology." *International Journal of Systematic Theology* 12, no. 3 (2010): 319–40.

McShane, Katie. "Rolston's Theory of Value." In *Nature, Value, Duty: Life on Earth with Holmes Rolston III*, edited by Christopher J. Preston and Wayne Ouderkirk, 1–15. Dordrecht: Springer, 2007.

Meacham, Standish. *Regaining Paradise: Englishness and the Early Garden City Movement.* New Haven, CT: Yale University Press, 1999.

Medawar, Peter B. *The Limits of Science.* Oxford: Oxford University Press, 1985.

Medawar, Peter B. "Science and Literature." *Encounter* 32, no. 1 (1969): 15–23.

Meier, Christel. "Malerei des Unsichtbaren. Über den Zusammenhang von Erkenntnistheorie und Bildstruktur im Mittelalter." In *Text und Bild, Bild und Text*, edited by Wolfgang Harms, 35–65. Stuttgart: Metzler, 1990.

Meier-Oeser, Stephan. *Die Spur des Zeichens: Das Zeichen und seine Funktion in der Philosophie des Mittelalters und der frühen Neuzeit.* Berlin: De Gruyter, 1997.

Menninghaus, Winfried "Biology à la Mode: Charles Darwin's Aesthetics of 'Ornament'." *History and Philosophy of the Life Sciences* 31, no. 2 (2009): 263–78.

Menozzi, Daniele. "Antimodernismo, secolarizzazione e cristianità." In *Il modernismo tra cristianità e secolarizzazione*, edited by Alfonso Botti and Rocco Cerrato, 53–82. Urbino: Quattro Venti, 2000.

Messer, Neil. "Natural Evil after Darwin." In *Theology after Darwin*, edited by Michael Northcote and R. J. Berry, 139–54. Carlisle: Paternoster Press, 2009.

Methuen, Charlotte. "On the Threshold of a New Age: Expanding Horizons as the Broader Context of Scriptural Interpretation." In *Hebrew Bible, Old Testament: The History of Its Interpretation from the Renaissance to the Enlightenment*, edited by Magne Sæbø, 665–90. Göttingen: Vandenhoeck & Ruprecht, 1996.

Metz, Christian. *Le signifiant imaginaire: psychanalyse et cinéma*. Paris: Christian Bourgois, 2002.

Mews, Constant J. "The World as Text: The Bible and the Book of Nature in Twelfth-Century Theology." In *Scripture and Pluralism: Reading the Bible in the Religiously Plural Worlds of the Middle Ages and Renaissance*, edited by Thomas J. Heffernan and Thomas E. Burman, 95–122. Leiden: Brill, 2005.

Miall, David S., and Don Kuiken. "Foregrounding, Defamiliarization, and Affect: Response to Literary Stories." *Poetics* 22, no. 5 (1994): 389–407.

Micheletti, Mario. "Analisi filosofica e teologia naturale." In *Teologia Naturale e Teologia Filosofica*, 43–79. Rome: Aracne, 2006.

Micheletti, Mario. "La rinascita della teologia naturale nella filosofia analitica." In *Hermeneutica 2005: Quale Metafisica?* 53–85. Brescia: Morcelliana, 2005.

Micheletti, Mario. "'Some interpreter within': l'ermeneutica religiosa di John Smith, platonico di Cambridge." In *Metodo della filosofia della religione* 2, 29–68. Padua: Editrice La Garangola, 1975.

Midgley, Mary. *Are You an Illusion?* Durham: Acumen, 2014.

Midgley, Mary. *The Myths We Live By*. London: Routledge, 2004.

Midgley, Mary. *Science and Poetry*. London: Routledge, 2001.

Midgley, Mary. *Wisdom, Information, and Wonder: What Is Knowledge For?* London: Routledge, 1995.

Milbank, Alison. "Apologetics and the Imagination: Making Strange." In *Imaginative Apologetics: Theology, Philosophy and the Catholic Tradition*, edited by Andrew Davison, 31–45. London: SCM Press, 2011.

Milbank, John. "Only Theology Saves Metaphysics: On the Modalities of Terror." In *Belief and Metaphysics*, edited by Connor Cunningham and Peter M. Chandler, 452–500. London: SCM Press, 2007.

Miles, Margaret. "Vision: The Eye of the Body and the Eye of the Mind in Saint Augustine's *De Trinitate* and *Confessions*." *Journal of Religion* 63, no. 2 (1983): 125–42.

Millay, Edna St. Vincent. *Collected Sonnets*. New York: Harper, 1988.

Miller, Arthur I. *Einstein, Picasso: Space, Time, and Beauty that Causes Havoc*. New York: Basic Books, 2001.

Miller, Henry. *Big Sur and the Oranges of Hieronymus Bosch*. New York: New Directions, 1957.

Miller, Jerome. *In the Throe of Wonder*. Albany, NY: State University of New York Press, 1992.

Millican, Peter J. R. "Hume's Sceptical Doubts Concerning Induction." In *Reading Hume on Human Understanding*, edited by P. J. R. Millican, 107–73. Oxford: Clarendon Press, 2002.

Milz, Bernhard. *Der gesuchte Widerstreit: Die Antinomie in Kants Kritik der praktischen Vernunft*. Berlin: De Gruyter, 2002.

Mitchell, Basil. *The Justification of Religious Belief*. London: Macmillan, 1973.

Molnar, Paul D. "Natural Theology Revisited: A Comparison of T. F. Torrance and Karl Barth." *Zeitschrift für dialektische Theologie* 21, no. 1 (2005): 53–83.

Mongrain, Kevin. "The Eyes of Faith: Newman's Critique of Arguments from Design." *Newman Studies Journal* 6 (2009): 68–86.

Monti, Anthony. *A Natural Theology of the Arts: Imprint of the Spirit*. Aldershot: Ashgate, 2003.

Moore, Andrew. "Should Christians Do Natural Theology?" *Scottish Journal of Theology* 63, no. 2 (2010): 127–45.

Moore, Ronald. *Natural Beauty: A Theory of Aesthetics Beyond the Arts*. Peterborough, ON: Broadview Press, 2008.

Moran, Dermot. "The Destruction of the Destruction: Heidegger's Versions of the History of Philosophy." In *Martin Heidegger: Politics, Art, and Technology*, edited by Karsten Harries and Christoph Jamme, 176–96. New York: Holmes & Meier, 1994.

Morgan, Vance G. "Humility and the Transcendent." *Faith and Philosophy* 18, no. 3 (2001): 306–22.

Morley, Georgina. *John Macquarrie's Natural Theology: The Grace of Being*. Aldershot: Ashgate, 2003.

Moroney, Stephen K. *The Noetic Effects of Sin: A Historical and Contemporary Exploration of How Sin Affects Our Thinking*. Lanham, MD: Lexington Books, 2000.

Morrison, Margaret. *Unifying Scientific Theories: Physical Concepts and Mathematical Structures*. Cambridge: Cambridge University Press, 2000.

Morrison, Robert G. "Natural Theology and the Qur'an." *Journal of Qur'anic Studies* 15, no. 1 (2013): 1–22.

Mortimore, G. W., and J. B. Maund. "Rationality in Belief." In *Rationality and the Social Sciences*, edited by S. I. Benn and G. W. Mortimore, 11–33. London: Routledge, 1976.

Motion, Andrew. *Keats*. Chicago: University of Chicago Press, 1998.

Müller, Jan-Dirk. "Writing – Speech – Image: The Competition of Signs." In *Visual Culture and the German Middle Ages*, edited by Kathryn Starkey and Horst Wenzel, 35–52. New York: Palgrave Macmillan, 2005.

Muller, Richard A. *Post-Reformation Reformed Dogmatics: The Rise and Development of Reformed Orthodoxy, ca. 1520 to ca. 1725*. 4 vols. Grand Rapids, MI: Baker Academic, 2003.

Munck, Thomas. *The Enlightenment: A Comparative Social History 1721–1794*. New York: Oxford University Press, 2000.

Murdoch, Iris. *The Fire and the Sun: Why Plato Banished the Artists*. Oxford: Clarendon Press, 1977.

Murdoch, Iris. *Metaphysics as a Guide to Morals*. London: Penguin, 1992.

Murdoch, Iris. *The Sovereignty of Good*. London: Macmillan, 1970.

Murdoch, Iris. "Vision and Choice in Morality." *Proceedings of the Aristotelian Society*, Supplementary Volume 30 (1956): 32–58.

Murphy, George L. *The Cosmos in the Light of the Cross*. Harrisburg, PA: Trinity Press International, 2003.

Murphy, Nancey. "MacIntyre, Tradition-Dependent Rationality, and the End of Philosophy of Religion." In *Contemporary Practice and Method in the Philosophy of Religion: New Essays*, edited by David Cheetham and Rolfe King, 32–44. London: Continuum, 2008.

Murray, Michael. *Nature Red in Tooth and Claw: Theism and the Problem of Animal Suffering*. Oxford: Oxford University Press, 2011.

Myers, Benjamin. "The Stratification of Knowledge in the Thought of T. F. Torrance." *Scottish Journal of Theology* 61 (2008): 1–15.

Naddaf, Gerard. *The Greek Concept of Nature*. Albany, NY: State University of New York Press, 2005.

Naddaf, Gerard. "Plato: The Creator of Natural Theology." *International Studies in Philosophy* 36, no. 1 (2004): 129–50.

Nagel, Thomas. *The View from Nowhere*. New York: Oxford University Press, 1986.

Naranch, Laurie E. "The Imaginary and a Political Quest for Freedom." *différences* 13, no. 3 (2002): 64–82.

Nebelsick, Harold P. "Karl Barth's Understanding of Science." In *Theology beyond Christendom: Essays on the Centenary of the Birth of Karl Barth*, edited by John Thompson, 165–214. Allison Park, PA: Pickwick Publications, 1986.

Nehamas, Alexander. "The Return of the Beautiful: Morality, Pleasure, and the Value of Uncertainty." *Journal of Aesthetics and Art Criticism* 58, no. 4 (2000): 393–403.

Neville, Jennifer. *Representations of the Natural World in Old English Poetry*. Cambridge: Cambridge University Press, 1999.

Newman, John Henry. *Fifteen Sermons Preached before the University of Oxford*. London: Rivingtons, 1880.

Newman, John Henry. *The Letters and Diaries of John Henry Newman*. edited by Charles Stephen Dessain and Thomas Gornall. 31 vols. Oxford: Clarendon Press, 1963–2006.

Nicolson, Marjorie Hope. *Mountain Gloom and Mountain Glory: The Development of the Aesthetics of the Infinite*. Ithaca, NY: Cornell University Press, 1959.

Niebuhr, Reinhold. *Leaves from the Notebook of a Tamed Cynic*. Chicago: Willett, Clark & Colby, 1929.

Nielsen, Marie Vejrup. *Sin and Selfish Genes: Christian and Biological Narratives*. Leuven: Peeters, 2010.

Nightingale, Andrea Wilson. *Spectacles of Truth in Classical Greek Philosophy: Theoria in Its Cultural Context*. Cambridge: Cambridge University Press, 2004.

Nisbet, Matthew C. "Communicating Climate Change: Why Frames Matter to Public Engagement." *Environment* 51, no. 2 (2009): 12–23.

Nisbett, Richard E. *The Geography of Thought: How Asians and Westerners Think Differently – and Why.* New York: Free Press, 2003.

Nobis, Heribert Maria. "Buch der Natur." In *Historisches Wörterbuch der Philosophie*, edited by Joachim Ritter, Karlfried Gründer, and Gottfried Gabriel, vol. 1, 957–9. Basle: Schwabe, 1971.

Noble, T. F. X. "The Vocabulary of Vision and Worship in the Early Carolingian Period." In *Seeing the Invisible in Late Antiquity and the Early Middle Ages*, edited by G. de Nie, K. F. Morrison, H. L. Kessler, and M. Mostert, 215–39. Turnhout: Brepols, 2004.

Nongbri, Brent. *Before Religion: A History of a Modern Concept.* New Haven, CT: Yale University Press, 2013.

Norris, Kathleen. *Dakota: A Spiritual Geography.* New York: Houghton Mifflin, 2001.

Nöth, Winfried "The Criterion of Habit in Peirce's Definitions of the Symbol." *Transactions of the Charles S. Peirce Society* 46, no. 2 (2010): 82–93.

Novak, David. *Natural Law in Judaism.* Cambridge: Cambridge University Press, 1998.

Nünning, Ansgar. "Narratology or Narratologies? Taking Stock of Recent Developments, Critique and Modest Proposals for Future Usages of the Term." In *What Is Narratology? Questions and Answers Regarding the Status of a Theory*, edited by Tom Kindt and Hans-Harald Müller, 239–75. Berlin: De Gruyter, 2003.

Nussbaum, Martha C. *Upheavals of Thought: The Intelligence of Emotions.* Cambridge: Cambridge University Press, 2001.

O'Connor, David. *Routledge Philosophy Guidebook to Hume on Religion.* London: Routledge, 2001.

Oddie, William. *Chesterton and the Romance of Orthodoxy: The Making of GKC, 1874–1908.* Oxford: Oxford University Press, 2008.

Odom, Herbert H. "The Estrangement of Celestial Mechanics and Religion." *Journal of the History of Ideas* 27 (1966): 533–58.

Ogilvie, Brian W. "Natural History, Ethics, and Physico-Theology." In *Historia. Empiricism and Erudition in Early Modern Europe*, edited by Gianna Pomata and Nancy G. Siraisi, 75–103. Cambridge, MA: MIT Press, 2005.

Ogilvie, Brian W. *The Science of Describing.* Chicago: University of Chicago Press, 2006.

O'Gorman, Frank. *The Long Eighteenth Century: British Political and Social History, 1688–1832.* London: Arnold, 1997.

Ohly, Friedrich. "Neue Zeugen des 'Buchs der Natur' aus dem Mittelalter." In *Iconologia sacra. Mythos, Bildkunst und Dichtung in der Religions- und Sozialgeschichte Alteuropas*, edited by Hagen Keller and Nikolaus Staubach, 546–68. Berlin: Arbeiten zur Frühmittelalterforschung, 1994.

Olafson, Frederick A. *Naturalism and the Human Condition: Against Scientism.* London: Routledge, 2001.

Oliver, Simon. "Analytic Theology." *International Journal for Systematic Theology* 12, no. 4 (2010): 464–75.

Olivier, Bert. "Derrida, Art and Truth." *Journal of Literary Studies* 1, no. 3 (1985): 27–38.

Olk, Claudia. *Virginia Woolf and the Aesthetics of Vision.* Berlin: De Gruyter, 2014.

Ollman, Bertell. *Alienation: Marx's Conception of Man in Capitalist Society.* 2nd edn. Cambridge: Cambridge University Press, 1976.

Onega, Susana. "Self, World and Art in the Fiction of John Fowles." *Twentieth Century Literature* 42 (1996): 29–56.

Ong, Walter J. "The Shifting Sensorium." In *The Varieties of Sensory Experience,* edited by David Howes, 47–60. Toronto: University of Toronto Press, 1991.

Oppy, Graham R. *Arguing about Gods.* Cambridge: Cambridge University Press, 2006.

Oppy, Graham R. "Natural Theology." In *Alvin Plantinga,* edited by Deane-Peter Baker, 15–47. Cambridge: Cambridge University Press, 2007.

Ormerod, Neil. "Charles Taylor and Bernard Lonergan on Natural Theology." *Irish Theological Quarterly* 74 (2009): 419–33.

Ormerod, Neil. "In Defence of Natural Theology: Bringing God into the Public Realm." *Irish Theological Quarterly* 72, no. 3 (2007): 227–41.

Ormerod, Neil. "Preliminary Steps Towards a Natural Theology." *Irish Theological Quarterly* 76 (2011): 115–27.

Ormerod, Neil. *A Public God: Natural Theology Reconsidered.* Minneapolis, MN: Fortress Press, 2015.

Ormerod, Neil, and Cynthia S. W. Crysdale. *Creator God, Evolving World.* Minneapolis, MN: Fortress Press, 2013.

Ortega y Gasset, José. "El origen deportivo del estado." *Citius, Altius, Fortius* 9, no. 1–4 (1967): 259–76.

Osborn, Eric. *Tertullian: First Theologian of the West.* Cambridge: Cambridge University Press, 1997.

Oster, Patricia. *Der Schleier im Text: Funktionsgeschichte eines Bildes für die neuzeitliche Erfahrung des Imaginären.* Munich: Fink, 2002.

Otto, Rudolf. *The Idea of the Holy.* London: Oxford University Press, 1977.

Owen, David. "Criticism and Captivity: On Genealogy and Critical Theory." *European Journal of Philosophy* 10, no. 2 (2002): 216–30.

Paden, Roger. "A Defense of the Picturesque." *Environmental Philosophy,* 10 (2013): 1–21.

Paden, Roger, Laurlyn K. Harmon, and Charles R. Milling. "Ecology, Evolution, and Aesthetics: Towards an Evolutionary Aesthetics of Nature." *British Journal of Aesthetics* 52 (2012): 124–39.

Padgett, Alan G. "*Theologia Naturalis:* Philosophy of Religion or Doctrine of Creation?" *Faith and Philosophy* 21 (2004): 493–502.

Pailin, David. "The Confused and Confusing Story of Natural Religion." *Religion* 24, no. 3 (1994): 199–212.

Pais, Abraham. *Niels Bohr's Times, in Physics, Philosophy and Polity.* Oxford: Clarendon Press, 1991.

Palmerino, Carla Rita. "The Mathematical Characters of Galileo's Book of Nature." In *The Book of Nature in Early Modern and Modern History*, edited by Klaas van Berkel and Arie Johan Vanderjagt, 27–44. Louvain: Peeters, 2006.

Pangritz, Andreas. "'Natürliche Theologie' als Grundlage für den interreligiösen Dialog heute?" *Zeitschrift für Dialektische Theologie* 26, no. 1 (2010): 88–111.

Pannenberg, Wolfhart. *Analogie und Offenbarung: Eine kritische Untersuchung zur Geschichte des Analogiebegriffs in der Lehre von der Gotteserkenntnis.* Göttingen: Vandenhoeck & Ruprecht, 2007.

Pannenberg, Wolfhart. *Systematische Theologie.* 3 vols. Göttingen: Vandenhoeck & Ruprecht, 1988–91.

Park, Crystal L. "Religion as a Meaning-Making Framework in Coping with Life Stress." *Journal of Social Issues* 61, no. 4 (2005): 707–29.

Parsons, Glenn. *Aesthetics and Nature.* London: Continuum, 2008.

Partee, Charles. *The Theology of John Calvin.* Louisville, KY: Westminster John Knox Press, 2008.

Pasnau, Robert. *Theories of Cognition in the Later Middle Ages.* Cambridge: Cambridge University Press, 1997.

Patey, Douglas. *Probability and Literary Form: Philosophic Theory and Literary Practice in the Augustan Age.* Cambridge: Cambridge University Press, 1984.

Peirce, Charles S. *Collected Papers*, edited by Charles Hartshorne and Paul Weiss. 8 vols. Cambridge, MA: Harvard University Press, 1960.

Pelikan, Jaroslav. *Christianity and Classical Culture: The Metamorphosis of Natural Theology in the Christian Encounter with Hellenism.* New Haven, CT: Yale University Press, 1993.

Pellerey, Roberto. "Thomas Aquinas: Natural Semiotics and the Epistemological Process." In *On the Medieval Theory of Signs*, edited by Umberto Eco and Costantino Marmo, 81–106. Amsterdam: Benjamins, 1989.

Penelhum, Terence. *Butler.* London: Routledge, 1999.

Penrose, Roger. *The Road to Reality: A Complete Guide to the Laws of the Universe.* London: Jonathan Cape, 2004.

Perry, Seamus. *Coleridge and the Uses of Division.* Oxford: Clarendon Press, 1999.

Peterfreund, Stuart. "Robert Browning's Decoding of Natural Theology in 'Caliban upon Setebos'." *Victorian Poetry* 43 (2005): 317–31.

Peterfreund, Stuart. *Turning Points in Natural Theology from Bacon to Darwin: The Way of the Argument from Design.* New York: Palgrave Macmillan, 2012.

Peters, James R. *The Logic of the Heart: Augustine, Pascal, and the Rationality of Faith.* Grand Rapids, MI: Baker Academic, 2009.

Peters, Ted. "Evolution, Evil, and the Theology of the Cross." *Svensk Teologisk Kvartalskrift* 83 (2007): 98–120.

Peters, Ted. "Robert John Russell's Contribution to the Theology and Science Dialogue." In *God's Action in Nature's World: Essays in Honour of Robert John Russell*, edited by Ted Peters and Nathan Hallanger, 1–18. Aldershot: Ashgate, 2006.

Peterson, Eugene H. *Christ Plays in Ten Thousand Places: A Conversation in Spiritual Theology.* Grand Rapids, MI: Eerdmans, 2005.

Pettet, E. C. *Of Paradise and Light: A Study of Vaughan's Silex Scintillans.* Cambridge: Cambridge University Press, 1960.

Pfizenmaier, Thomas C. *The Trinitarian Theology of Dr. Samuel Clarke (1675–1729): Context, Sources, and Controversy.* Leiden: Brill, 1997.

Pfizenmaier, Thomas C. "Was Isaac Newton an Arian?" *Journal of the History of Ideas* 58, no. 1 (1997): 57–80.

Phillips, D. Z. *Faith and Philosophical Enquiry.* London: Routledge & Kegan Paul, 1970.

Piattelli-Palmarini, Massimo. *Inevitable Illusions: How Mistakes of Reason Rule Our Minds.* New York: Wiley, 1994.

Picciotto, Joanna. *Labors of Innocence in Early Modern England.* Cambridge, MA: Harvard University Press, 2010.

Pick, John. *Building Jerusalem: Art, Industry, and the British Millennium.* Amsterdam: Harwood Academic, 1999.

Pieper, Josef. *Was heißt Philosophieren?* 4th edn. Munich: Kösel, 1959.

Pier, John. "Gérard Genette's Evolving Narrative Poetics." *Narrative* 18, no. 1 (2010): 8–18.

Pigliucci, Massimo. "New Atheism and the Scientistic Turn in the Atheism Movement." *Midwest Studies in Philosophy* 37, no. 1 (2013): 142–53.

Pigliucci, Massimo, and Maarten Boudry, eds. *Philosophy of Pseudoscience: Reconsidering the Demarcation Problem.* Chicago: University of Chicago Press, 2013.

Pilkuhn, Hartmut M. *Relativistic Quantum Mechanics.* 2nd edn. Berlin: Springer, 2005.

Pirinen, Mikko. "Parergon, Paratext, and Title on the Context of Visual Art." In *Picturing the Language of Images*, edited by Nancy Pedri and Laurence Petit, 241–51. Newcastle: Cambridge Scholars Publishing, 2013.

Plantinga, Alvin J. "Reason and Belief in God." In *Faith and Philosophy: Reason and Belief in God*, edited by Alvin Plantinga and Nicholas Wolterstorff, 16–93. Notre Dame, IN: University of Notre Dame, 1983.

Plantinga, Alvin J. "The Reformed Objection to Natural Theology." *Proceedings of the American Catholic Philosophical Association* 54 (1980): 49–62.

Plantinga, Alvin J. *Warranted Christian Belief.* New York: Oxford University Press, 2000.

Plantinga, Alvin J. *Where the Conflict Really Lies: Science, Religion, and Naturalism.* New York: Oxford University Press, 2011.

Plett, Heinrich F. *Rhetoric and Renaissance Culture.* Berlin: De Gruyter, 2004.

Polanyi, Michael. *Personal Knowledge: Towards a Post-Critical Philosophy.* Chicago: University of Chicago Press, 1962.

Polkinghorne, John. "The New Natural Theology." *Studies in World Christianity* 1, no. 1 (1995): 41–50.

Polkinghorne, John. "Physics and Metaphysics in a Trinitarian Perspective." *Theology and Science* 1 (2003): 33–49.

Polkinghorne, John. *Quantum Physics and Theology: An Unexpected Kinship.* London: SPCK, 2007.

Polkinghorne, John. *Science and Creation: The Search for Understanding.* London: SPCK, 1988.

Polkinghorne, John. "Where Is Natural Theology Today?" *Science and Christian Belief* 18 (2006): 169–79.

Popper, Karl R. "Natural Selection and the Emergence of Mind." *Dialectica* 32 (1978): 339–55.

Porteous, J. Douglas. *Environmental Aesthetics: Ideas, Politics and Planning.* London: Routledge, 1996.

Porter, Jean. "Tradition in the Recent Work of Alasdair MacIntyre." In *Alasdair MacIntyre,* edited by Mark C. Murphy, 38–69. Cambridge: Cambridge University Press, 2003.

Potestà, Paola. *Gli occhi, il sole, la luce: Metafore sulla visione tra scienza e arte dall'antichità greca al '400.* Florence: Fondazione Giorgi Ronchi, 2002.

Power, William L. "Peircian Semiotics, Religion, and Theological Realism." In *New Essays in Religious Naturalism,* edited by Creighton Peden and Larry E. Axel, 211–24. Macon, GA: Mercer University Press, 1993.

Pratt, L. Scott. "Two Cases against Spectator Theories of Knowledge." *Southwest Philosophy Review* 10 (1994): 105–15.

Preller, Victor. *Divine Science and the Science of God: A Reformulation of Thomas Aquinas.* Princeton, NJ: Princeton University Press, 1967.

Prenter, Regin. "Das Problem der natürlichen Theologie bei Karl Barth." *Theologische Literaturzeitung* 77 (1952): 607–11.

Preston, Claire. *Thomas Browne and the Writing of Early Modern Science.* Cambridge: Cambridge University Press, 2005.

Prickett, Stephen. *Words and the Word: Language, Poetics, and Biblical Interpretation.* Cambridge: Cambridge University Press, 1986.

Prins, Jacomien. *Echoes of an Invisible World: Marsilio Ficino and Francesco Patrizi on Cosmic Order and Music Theory.* Leiden: Brill, 2015.

Proust, Marcel. *La prisonnière.* Paris: Gallimard, 1925.

Ramelli, Ilaria L. E. "Forgiveness in Patristic Philosophy: The Importance of Repentance and the Centrality of Grace." In *Ancient Forgiveness: Classical, Judaic, and Christian,* edited by Charles L. Griswold and David Konstan, 195–215. Cambridge: Cambridge University Press, 2012.

Rapport, Nigel. "'Imagination Is the Barest Reality:' On the Universal Human Imagining of the World." In *Reflections on Imagination: Human Capacity and Ethnographic Method,* edited by Mark Harris and Nigel Rapport, 3–22. Farnham: Ashgate, 2015.

Rasmusson, Arne. *The Church as Polis: From Political Theology to Theological Politics as Exemplified by Jürgen Moltmann and Stanley Hauerwas.* Lund: Lund University Press, 1994.

Ratzsch, Del. "Natural Theology, Methodological Naturalism, and 'Turtles All the Way Down'." *Faith and Philosophy* 21 (2004): 436–55.

Rausch, Hannelore. *Theoria: Von ihrer sakralen zur philosophischen Bedeutung.* Munich: Fink, 1982.

Re Manning, Russell, ed. *The Oxford Handbook of Natural Theology*. Oxford: Oxford University Press, 2013.

Read, Sophie. *Eucharist and the Poetic Imagination in Early Modern England*. Cambridge: Cambridge University Press, 2013.

Rehnman, Sebastian. "Natural Theology and Epistemic Justification." *Heythrop Journal* 48 (2010): 1017–22.

Reill, Peter Hanns. *Vitalizing Nature in the Enlightenment*. Berkeley, CA: University of California Press, 2005.

Reimer, Maria Hellström. "Whose Goodness? Ethics and Aesthetics in Landscapes of Dissensus." *Journal of Landscape Architecture* 7, no. 3 (2012): 76–81.

Reinhardt, Carsten. "Disciplines, Research Fields, and Their Boundaries." In *Chemical Sciences in the 20th Century: Bridging Boundaries*, edited by Carsten Reinhardt, 1–13. Chichester: Wiley, 2001.

Révah, I. S. *Une source de la spiritualité péninsulaire au XVIe siècle: la "théologie naturelle" de Raymond Sebond*. Lisbon: Academia das Ciências de Lisboa, 1953.

Ribeiro, Sidarta, Angelo Loula, Ivan de Araujo, Ricardo Gudwin, and Joao Queiroz. "Symbols Are Not Uniquely Human." *BioSystems* 90 (2007): 263–72.

Richards, Alison. "Shaking the Frame: Erving Goffman and Performance Studies." *Australasian Drama Studies* 39 (2001): 58–73.

Ricœur, Paul. *From Text to Action*. Evanston, IL: Northwestern University Press, 2007.

Rivera, Nelson. *The Earth is Our Home: Mary Midgley's Critique and Reconstruction of Evolution and Its Meanings*. Exeter: Imprint Academic, 2010.

Robbins, Jeffrey W. "The Problem of Ontotheology: Complicating the Divide between Philosophy and Theology." *Heythrop Journal* 43, no. 2 (2002): 139–51.

Roberts, Noel K. "Newman on the Argument from Design." *New Blackfriars* 88 (2007): 56–66.

Robinson, Andrew. *God and the World of Signs: Trinity, Evolution, and the Metaphysical Semiotics of C. S. Peirce*. Leiden: Brill, 2010.

Robinson, Andrew, and Christopher Southgate. "Semiotics as a Metaphysical Framework for Christian Theology." *Zygon* 45, no. 3 (2010): 689–712.

Robinson, Daniel N., and Richard N. Williams, eds. *Scientism: The New Orthodoxy*. London: Bloomsbury, 2014.

Robson, Jon M. "The Fiat and the Finger of God: The Bridgewater Treatises." In *Victorian Faith in Crisis: Essays on Continuity and Change in Nineteenth-Century Religious Belief*, edited by Richard J. Helmstadter and Bernard Lightman, 71–125. London: Macmillan, 1990.

Rohls, Jan. *Offenbarung, Vernunft und Religion: Ideengeschichte des Christentums*. Tübingen: Mohr Siebeck, 2012.

Rolf, Sybille. "*Crux sola est nostra theologia*: Die Bedeutung der Kreuzestheologie für die Theodizeefrage." *Neue Zeitschrift für systematische Theologie und Religionsphilosophie* 49, no. 2 (2007): 223–40.

Rolston, Holmes. "Does Aesthetic Appreciation of Landscapes Need to Be Science-Based?" *British Journal of Aesthetics* 33 (1995): 374–86.

Rolston, Holmes. *Environmental Ethics: Duties to and in the Natural World.* Philadelphia: Temple University Press, 1988.

Rosenberg, Alexander. *The Atheist's Guide to Reality: Enjoying Life without Illusions.* New York: W. W. Norton, 2011.

Rosenberg, Jay F. *One World and Our Knowledge of It: The Problematic of Realism in Post-Kantian Perspective.* Dordrecht: Reidel, 2012.

Rosenberg, Stanley P. "Forming the *Saeculum*: The Desacralization of Nature and the Ability to Understand It in Augustine's *Literal Commentary on Genesis.*" In *God's Bounty? The Churches and the Natural World,* edited by Peter Clarke and Tony Claydon, 1–14. Woodbridge: Boydell Press, 2010.

Ross, Stephanie. "Landscape Perception: Theory-Laden, Emotionally Resonant, Politically Correct." *Environmental Ethics* 27, no. 3 (2005): 245–63.

Roszak, Theodore. *Where the Wasteland Ends: Politics and Transcendence in Post-industrial Society.* Garden City, NY: Doubleday, 1972.

Roth, Michael. *Gott im Widerspruch? Möglichkeiten und Grenzen der theologischen Apologetik.* Berlin: De Gruyter, 2002.

Roy, Louis. *Transcendent Experiences: Phenomenology and Critique.* Toronto: University of Toronto Press, 2001.

Royce, Josiah. *The Problem of Christianity.* Washington, DC: Catholic University of America Press, 2001.

Rüpke, Jörg. *Die Religion der Römer: Eine Einführung.* Munich: C. H. Beck, 2001.

Rupke, Nicholas. "A Geography of Enlightenment." In *Geography and Enlightenment,* edited by David N. Livingstone and Charles W. J. Withers, 319–38. Chicago: University of Chicago Press, 1999.

Rurak, James. "Butler's *Analogy*: A Still Interesting Synthesis of Reason and Revelation." *Anglican Theological Review* 62, no. 2 (1980): 365–81.

Rushdie, Salman. *Is Nothing Sacred? The Herbert Read Memorial Lecture 1990.* Cambridge: Granta, 1990.

Ruskin, John. *Complete Works.* 39 vols. London: George Allen, 1903.

Russell, Bertrand. *The History of Western Philosophy.* London: Routledge, 2004.

Russell, John Malcolm. *From Nineveh to New York: The Strange Story of the Assyrian Reliefs in the Metropolitan Museum and the Hidden Masterpiece at Canford School.* New Haven, CT: Yale University Press, 1997.

Russell, Paul. *The Riddle of Hume's Treatise: Skepticism, Naturalism, and Irreligion.* Oxford: Oxford University Press, 2008.

Russell, Robert J. "Special Providence and Genetic Mutation." In *Evolutionary and Molecular Biology: Scientific Perspectives on Divine Action,* edited by Robert J. Russell, William R. Stoeger, and Francisco J. Ayala, 191–223. Vatican City: Vatican Observatory, 1998.

Ruster, Thomas. *Der verwechselbare Gott: Theologie nach der Entflechtung von Christentum und Religion.* Freiburg: Herder, 2000.

Ryle, Gilbert. *"The Thinking of Thoughts: What Is 'Le Penseur' Doing?"* In *Collected Essays 1929–1968,* 494–510. New York: Routledge, 2009.

Sagan, Carl. *The Demon-Haunted World: Science as a Candle in the Dark.* New York: Ballantine Books, 1997.

Said, Edward. *The World, the Text, and the Critic.* Cambridge, MA: Harvard University Press, 1982.

Saito, Yuriko. "The Aesthetics of Unscenic Nature." *Journal of Aesthetics and Art Criticism* 56, no. 2 (1998): 101–11.

Saler, Benson. "The Definition of Religion in the Context of Social-Scientific Study." *Historical Reflections/Réflexions Historiques* 25, no. 2 (1999): 391–404.

Saler, Michael T. "Modernity, Disenchantment, and the Ironic Imagination." *Philosophy and Literature* 28 (2004): 137–49.

Sallis, John. *Delimitations: Phenomenology and the End of Metaphysics.* 2nd edn. Bloomington, IN: Indiana University Press, 1995.

Sallis, John. *Force of Imagination: The Sense of the Elemental.* Bloomington, IN: Indiana University Press, 2000.

Sallis, John. *Logic of Imagination: The Expanse of the Elemental.* Bloomington, IN: Indiana University Press, 2012.

Santmire, H. Paul. *Before Nature: A Christian Spirituality.* Minneapolis, MN: Fortress Press, 2014.

Santmire, H. Paul. "A Reformation Theology of Nature Transfigured: Joseph Sittler's Invitation to See as Well as to Hear." *Theology Today* 61 (2005): 509–27.

Sapiro, Gisèle. "La formation de l'habitus scientifique." In *Pierre Bourdieu, sociologue,* edited by Louis Pinto, Gisèle Sapiro, and Patrick Champagne, 319–25. Paris: Fayard, 2004.

Sauer-Thompson, Gary, and Joseph Wayne Smith. *The Unreasonable Silence of the World: Universal Reason and the Wreck of the Enlightenment Project.* Aldershot: Ashgate, 1997.

Sauter, Gerhard. "Theologisch miteinander Streiten: Karl Barths Auseinandersetzung mit Emil Brunner." In *Karl Barth in Deutschland (1921–1935): Aufbruch – Klärung – Widerstand,* edited by Michael Beintker, Christian Link, and Michael Trowitzsch, 267–84. Zurich: Theologischer Verlag, 2005.

Saye, Scott C. "The Wild and Crooked Tree: Barth, Fish and Interpretative Communities." *Modern Theology* 12, no. 4 (1996): 435–58.

Scarry, Elaine. *On Beauty and Being Just.* Princeton, NJ: Princeton University Press, 1999.

Schapiro, Meyer. "On Some Problems in the Semiotics of Visual Art: Field and Vehicle in Image-Signs." *Simiolus: Netherlands Quarterly for the History of Art* 6, no. 1 (1972): 9–19.

Schifferdecker, Kathryn. *Out of the Whirlwind: Creation Theology in the Book of Job.* Cambridge. MA: Harvard University Press, 2008.

Schindler, D. C. *The Catholicity of Reason.* Grand Rapids, MI: Eerdmans, 2013.

Schindler, Samuel. "Model, Theory, and Evidence in the Discovery of the DNA Structure." *British Journal for Philosophy of Science* 59, no. 4 (2008): 619–58.

Schleusener-Eichholz, Gudrun. *Das Auge im Mittelalter.* 2 vols. Munich: Fink, 1985.

Schloss, Jeffrey, and Michael Murray, eds. *The Believing Primate: Scientific, Philosophical and Theological Reflections on the Origin of Religion.* Oxford: Oxford University Press, 2009.

Schluchter, Wolfgang. *Die Entstehungsgeschichte des modernen Rationalismus.* Frankfurt am Main: Suhrkamp, 1998.

Schmidt, James. *What Is Enlightenment? Eighteenth-Century Answers and Twentieth-Century Questions.* Berkeley, CA: University of California Press, 1996.

Schmidt, M. A. "Der Ort der Trinitätslehre bei Emil Brunner." *Theologische Zeitschrift* 59, no. 1 (1949): 46–66.

Schnall, Ira M. "Constancy, Coherence, and Causality." *Hume Studies* 30, no. 1 (2004): 33–50.

Schneiders, Sandra M. "Religion vs. Spirituality: A Contemporary Conundrum." *Spiritus: A Journal of Christian Spirituality* 3, no. 2 (2003): 163–85.

Scholes, Robert. *Protocols of Reading.* New Haven, CT: Yale University Press, 1991.

Schoot, Albert van der. "Kepler's Search for Form and Proportion." *Renaissance Studies* 15 (2001): 59–78.

Schreiner, Susan Elizabeth. *The Theater of His Glory: Nature and the Natural Order in the Thought of John Calvin.* Durham, NC: Labyrinth Press, 1991.

Schroeder, Rossitza. "Looking with Words and Images: Staging Monastic Contemplation in a Late Byzantine Church." *Word & Image: A Journal of Verbal/Visual Enquiry* 28, no. 2 (2012): 117–34.

Schults, F. LeRon. "The Role of Trinitarian Reflection in the Religion-Science Dialogue." In *Preparing for the Future: The Role of Theology in the Science–Religion Dialogue,* edited by Niels Henrik Gregersen and Marie Vejrup Nielsen, 27–40. Aarhus: Teologiske Fakultet, 2004.

Schults, F. LeRon. "Wising Up: The Evolution of Natural Theology." *Zygon* 47, no. 3 (2012): 542–8.

Schumacher, Lydia. *Divine Illumination: The History and Future of Augustine's Theory of Knowledge.* Challenges in Contemporary Theology. Oxford: Wiley-Blackwell, 2011.

Schumacher, Lydia. "The Logic of Faith: Prolegomena to a Theological Theory of Knowledge." *New Blackfriars* 92, no. 1042 (2011): 664–77.

Schumacher, Lydia. "The Lost Legacy of Anselm's Argument: Rethinking the Purpose of Proofs for the Existence of God." *Modern Theology* 27, no. 1 (2011): 87–101.

Schuppisser, Fritz Oskar. "Schauen mit den Augen des Herzens: Zur Methodik der spätmittelalterlichen Passionsmeditationen, besonders in der *Devotio Moderna* und bei den Augustinern." In *Die Passion Christi in Literatur und Kunst des Spätmittelalters,* edited by Walter Haug and Burghart Wachtinger, 169–210. Tübingen: Mohr, 1993.

Scruton, Roger. *The Aesthetics of Music.* Oxford: Clarendon Press, 1997.

Scruton, Roger. "Scientism in the Arts and Humanities." *New Atlantis* 40 (fall, 2013): 33–46.

Sebonde, Raymond de. *Theologia naturalis seu Liber creaturarum.* Stuttgart-Bad Cannstatt: Frommann Verlag, 1966.

Secord, James A. "Knowledge in Transit." *Isis* 95 (2004): 654–72.

Seeskin, Kenneth. *Searching for a Distant God: The Legacy of Maimonides.* New York: Oxford University Press, 2000.

Séguy, Jean. "Rationalisation, modernité et avenir de la religion." *Archives de Sciences Sociales des Religions* 61, no. 1 (1986): 127–38.

Sennett, James. "Hume's Stopper and the Natural Theology Project." In *In Defense of Natural Theology: A Post-Humean Assessment*, edited by James F. Sennett and Douglas Groothuis, 82–104. Downers Grove, IL: InterVarsity Press, 2005.

Serjeantson, Richard. "Francis Bacon and the 'Interpretation of Nature' in the Late Renaissance." *Isis* 105, no. 4 (2014): 681–705.

Sheldrake, Philip F. *Spaces for the Sacred: Place, Memory and Identity.* Baltimore, MD: Johns Hopkins University Press, 2001.

Sherry, Patrick J. "The Sacramentality of Things." *New Blackfriars* 89, no. 1023 (2009): 575–90.

Shiota, Michelle N., Dacher Keltner, and Amanda Mossman. "The Nature of Awe: Elicitors, Appraisals, and Effects on Self-Concept." *Cognition and Emotion* 21, no. 5 (2007): 944–63.

Shore, Bradd. *Culture in Mind: Cognition, Culture, and the Problem of Meaning.* New York: Oxford University Press, 1998.

Short, Thomas L. *Peirce's Theory of Signs.* Cambridge: Cambridge University Press, 2007.

Sikka, Sonia. "On the Truth of Beauty: Nietzsche, Heidegger, Keats." *Heythrop Journal* 39 (1998): 243–63.

Sim, Lorraine. *Virginia Woolf: The Patterns of Ordinary Experience.* Farnham: Ashgate, 2010.

Simon, Gérard. *Le regard, l'être et l'apparence dans l'optique de l'Antiquité.* Paris: Edition du Seuil, 1988.

Simonin, Michel. "La préhistoire de l'Apologie de Raimond Sebond." In *Montaigne, Apologie de Raimond Sebond: De la theologia à la théologie*, edited by Claude Blum, 85–116. Paris: Honoré Champion, 1990.

Simonson, Harold P. "Typology, Imagination, and Jonathan Edwards." In *Radical Discontinuities: American Romanticism and Christian Consciousness*, 19–43. Rutherford, NJ: Fairleigh Dickinson University Press, 1983.

Singer, Thomas C. "Hieroglyphs, Real Characters, and the Idea of Natural Language in English Seventeenth-Century Thought." In *Language and the History of Thought*, edited by Nancy S. Struever, 61–82. Rochester, NY: University of Rochester Press, 1995.

Sittler, Joseph. *Essays on Nature and Grace.* Philadelphia: Fortress Press, 1972.

Smith, A. Mark. "Saving the Appearances of the Appearances: The Foundations of Classical Geometrical Optics." *Archive for History of Exact Sciences* 24, no. 2 (1981): 73–99.

Smith, Barbara Herrnstein. *Natural Reflections: Human Cognition at the Nexus of Science and Religion.* New Haven, CT: Yale University Press, 2009.

Smith, Christian. *Moral, Believing Animals: Human Personhood and Culture.* Oxford: Oxford University Press, 2009.

Smith, Grover. "Memory and Desire in *The Waste Land*." In *Critical Essays on T. S. Eliot's The Waste Land*, edited by Lois Cuddy and David Hirsh, 122–40. Boston: G. K. Hall, 1991.

Smith, James K. A. *Desiring the Kingdom: Worship, Worldview, and Cultural Formation*. Grand Rapids, MI: Baker Academic, 2009.

Smith, James K. A. *Imagining the Kingdom: How Worship Works*. Grand Rapids, MI: Baker Academic, 2013.

Smith, Janet E. "Come and See." In *Reading John with St. Thomas Aquinas: Theological Exegesis and Speculative Theology*, edited by Michael Dauphinais and Matthew Levering, 194–211. Washington, DC: Catholic University of America Press, 2005.

Smith, John. *Select Discourses*. 3rd edn. London: Rivingtons and Cochran, 1821.

Smith, John E. "The Present Status of Natural Theology." *Journal of Philosophy* 55, no. 22 (1958): 925–36.

Smith, John E. *Royce's Social Infinite: The Community of Interpretation*. Hamden, CT: Archon Books, 1969.

Smith, Kurt. "A General Theory of Cartesian Clarity and Distinctness Based on the Theory of Enumeration in the *Rules*." *Dialogue* 40, no. 2 (2001): 279–310.

Smith, Philip. *Cultural Theory: An Introduction*. Oxford: Blackwell, 2001.

Smoller, Laura Ackerman. "Astrology and the Sibyls: John of Legnano's *De Adventu Christi* and the Natural Theology of the Later Middle Ages." *Science in Context* 20 (2007): 423–50.

Snobelen, Stephen D. "To Discourse of God: Isaac Newton's Heterodox Theology and His Natural Philosophy." In *Science and Dissent in England, 1688–1945*, edited by Paul B. Wood, 39–65. Aldershot: Ashgate, 2004.

Snobelen, Stephen D. "The Myth of the Clockwork Universe: Newton, Newtonianism, the the Enlightenment." In *The Persistence of the Sacred in Modern Thought*, edited by Chris L. Firestone and Nathan Jacobs, 149–84. Notre Dame, IN: University of Notre Dame Press, 2012.

Sobel, Jordan Howard. *Logic and Theism: Arguments for and against Beliefs in God*. Cambridge: Cambridge University Press, 2004.

Sosa, Ernest. "Natural Theology and Naturalist Atheology: Plantinga's Evolutionary Argument against Naturalism." In *Alvin Plantinga*, edited by Deane-Peter Baker, 93–106. Cambridge: Cambridge University Press, 2007.

Sosis, Richard, and Jordan Kiper. "Religion Is More Than Belief: What Evolutionary Theories of Religion Tell Us About Religious Commitment." In *Challenges to Moral and Religious Belief: Disagreement and Evolution*, edited by Michael Bergmann and Patrick Kain, 256–76. Oxford: Oxford University Press, 2014.

Southgate, Christopher. *The Groaning of Creation: God, Evolution, and the Problem of Evil*. Louisville, KY: Westminster John Knox Press, 2008.

Spangler, David, and William Irwin Thompson. *Reimagination of the World: A Critique of the New Age, Science, and Popular Culture*. Santa Fe, NM: Bear & Company Publishing, 1991.

Speer, Andreas. *Die entdeckte Natur: Untersuchungen zu Begründungsversuchen einer "Scientia Naturalis" im 12. Jahrhundert*. Leiden: Brill, 1995.

Spencer, Stephen R. "Is Natural Theology Biblical?" *Grace Theological Journal* 9, no. 1 (1988): 59–72.

Spitzer, Leo. "Classical and Christian Ideas of World Harmony." *Traditio* 2 (1944): 409–64; 3 (1945): 307–64.

Sprat, Thomas. *History of the Royal Society of London, for the Improving of Natural Knowledge.* London: Martyn & Allestry, 1667.

Spyri, Johanna. *Heidis Lehr- und Wanderjahre.* Villingen: Nexx Verlag, 2014.

Stackelberg, Jürgen von. *Jean-Jacques Rousseau. Der Weg zurück zur Natur.* Munich: Fink, 1999.

Stanbury, Sarah. *The Visual Object of Desire in Late Medieval England.* Philadelphia: University of Pennsylvania Press, 2008.

Stăniloae, Dumitru. *The Experience of God: Orthodox Dogmatic Theology. Revelation and Knowledge of the Triune God.* Brookline, MA: Holy Cross Orthodox Press, 1998.

Stanovich, Keith E. *Rationality and the Reflective Mind.* New York: Oxford University Press, 2011.

Stanovich, Keith E., and Richard F. West. "Individual Differences in Reasoning: Implications for the Rationality Debate?" *Behavioral and Brain Sciences* 23 (2000): 645–726.

Starr, G. Gabrielle. *Feeling Beauty: The Neuroscience of Aesthetic Experience.* Cambridge, MA: MIT Press, 2013.

Stebbins, J. Michael. *The Divine Initiative: Grace, World-Order, and Human Freedom in the Early Writings of Bernard Lonergan.* Toronto: Toronto University Press, 1995.

Steiner, George. *Nostalgia for the Absolute.* Toronto: Anansi, 2004.

Steinke, Johannes Maria. *John Polkinghorne: Konsonanz von Theologie und Naturwissenschaft.* Göttingen: Vandenhoeck & Ruprecht, 2006.

Stenmark, Mikael. *Scientism: Science, Ethics and Religion.* Aldershot: Ashgate, 2001.

Stephenson, Bruce. *The Music of the Heavens: Kepler's Harmonic Astronomy.* Princeton, NJ: Princeton University Press, 1994.

Stevenson, Leslie. "Twelve Conceptions of Imagination." *British Journal of Aesthetics* 43, no. 3 (2003): 238–59.

Stikkers, Kenneth W. "Royce and Gadamer on Interpretation as the Constitution of Community." *Journal of Speculative Philosophy* 15, no. 1 (2001): 14–19.

Stolnitz, Jerome. *Aesthetics and Philosophy of Art Criticism.* Boston: Houghton Mifflin, 1960.

Stone, Alison. "Adorno and the Disenchantment of Nature." *Philosophy and Social Criticism* 32 (2006): 231–53.

Stone, Gregory B. "Dante and the 'Falasifa': Religion as Imagination." *Dante Studies, Annual Report of the Dante Society* 125 (2007): 133–56.

Stone, Lawrence. "Literacy and Education in England, 1640–1900." *Past & Present* 42, no. 1 (1969): 67–139.

Stout, Jeffrey. *The Flight from Authority: Religion, Morality and the Quest for Autonomy.* Notre Dame, IN: University of Notre Dame Press, 1981.

Strandberg, Hugo. *The Possibility of Discussion: Relativism, Truth and Criticism of Religious Beliefs.* Aldershot: Ashgate, 2006.

Straus, Nina Pelikan. "Grand Theory on Trial: Kafka, Derrida, and the Will to Power." *Philosophy and Literature* 31, no. 2 (2007): 378–93.

Strobel, Kyle C. "Theology in the Gaze of the Father: Retrieving Jonathan Edwards's Trinitarian Aesthetics." In *Advancing Trinitarian Theology: Explorations in Constructive Dogmatics*, edited by Oliver Crisp and Fred Sanders, 147–70. Grand Rapids, MI: Zondervan, 2014.

Styles, Elizabeth A. *The Psychology of Attention*. 2nd edn. New York: Psychology Press, 2006.

Suárez, Mauricio. "Experimental Realism Reconsidered: How Inference to the Most Likely Cause Might Be Sound." In *Nancy Cartwright's Philosophy of Science*, edited by Stephan Hartmann, Carl Hoefer, and Luc Bovens, 137–63. New York: Routledge, 2008.

Sudduth, Michael. *The Reformed Objection to Natural Theology*. Farnham: Ashgate, 2009.

Sweetman, Brendan. "Commitment, Justification, and the Rejection of Natural Theology." *American Catholic Philosophical Quarterly* 77, no. 3 (2003): 417–36.

Swinburne, Richard. *The Existence of God*. 2nd edn. Oxford: Clarendon Press, 2004.

Swinburne, Richard. "Natural Theology, Its 'Dwindling Probabilities' and 'Lack of Rapport'." *Faith and Philosophy* 21 (2004): 533–46.

Swinburne, Richard. *The Resurrection of God Incarnate*. Oxford: Clarendon Press, 2003.

Swinburne, Richard. "Sobel on Arguments from Design." *Philosophia Christi* 8, no. 2 (2006): 227–34.

Szekeres, Attila. "Karl Barth und die natürliche Theologie." *Evangelische Theologie* 24 (1964): 229–42.

Tabarasi, Ana-Stanca. *Der Landschaftsgarten als Lebensmodell: Zur Symbolik der "Gartenrevolution" in Europa*. Würzburg: Königshausen & Neumann, 2007.

Tallis, Raymond. *In Defence of Wonder and Other Philosophical Reflections*. Durham: Acumen, 2012.

Tang, C. L. *Fundamentals of Quantum Mechanics*. Cambridge: Cambridge University Press, 2005.

Tanner, Kathryn. *God and Creation in Christian Theology*. Minneapolis, MN: Fortress Press, 2005.

Tanzella-Nitti, Giuseppe. "The Book of Nature and the God of Scientists According to the Encyclical 'Fides et Ratio'." In *The Human Search for Truth: Philosophy, Science, Faith. The Outlook for the Third Millennium*, 82–90. Philadelphia: St Joseph's University Press, 2001.

Tanzella-Nitti, Giuseppe. "La dimensione cristologica dell'intelligibilità del reale." In *L'intelligibilità del Reale: Natura, Uomo, Macchina*, edited by Sergio Rondinara, 213–25. Rome: Città Nuova, 1999.

Tanzella-Nitti, Giuseppe. "Le rôle des sciences naturelles dans le travail du théologien." *Revue des Questions Scientifiques* 170 (1999): 25–39.

Tanzella-Nitti, Giuseppe. "The Two Books Prior to the Scientific Revolution." *Annales Theologici* 18 (2004): 51–83.

Taylor, Charles. "Geschlossene Weltstruktur in der Moderne." In *Wissen und Weisheit: Zwei Symposien zu Ehre von Josef Pieper*, edited by Hermann Fechtrup, Friedbert Schulze, and Thomas Sternberg, 137–69. Münster: LIT Verlag, 2005.

Taylor, Charles. *Modern Social Imaginaries*. Durham, NC: Duke University Press, 2002.

Taylor, Charles. *Philosophical Arguments*. Cambridge, MA: Harvard University Press, 1995.

Taylor, Charles. *A Secular Age*. Cambridge, MA: Belknap Press, 2007.

Taylor, Charles. *Sources of the Self: The Making of the Modern Identity*. Cambridge, MA: Harvard University Press, 1992.

Taylor, Stephen A. "The Vision Quest in the West, or What the Mind's Eye Sees." *Journal of Anthropological Research* 40, no. 1 (1984): 23–39.

Tegtmeyer, Henning. *Gott, Geist, Vernunft: Prinzipien und Probleme der natürlichen Theologie*. Tübingen: Mohr Siebeck, 2013.

Tennant, F. R. *Philosophical Theology*. 2 vols. Cambridge: Cambridge University Press, 1930.

Terrall, Mary. "Metaphysics, Mathematics, and the Gendering of Science in Eighteenth-Century France." In *The Sciences in Enlightened Europe*, edited by William Clark, Jan Golinski, and Simon Schaffer, 246–71. Chicago: University of Chicago Press, 1999.

Teske, Roland J. "Augustine of Hippo on Seeing with the Eyes of the Mind." In *Ambiguity in the Western Mind*, edited by Craig J. N. de Paulo, Patrick Messina, and Marc Stier, 72–87. New York: Peter Lang, 2005.

Thagard, Paul. "The Emotional Coherence of Religion." *Journal of Cognition and Culture* 5 (2005): 58–74.

Thesiger, Sarah. "The *Orchestra* of Sir John Davies and the Image of the Dance." *Journal of the Warburg and Courtauld Institutes* 36 (1973): 277–304.

Thomson, Iain. "Ontotheology? Understanding Heidegger's *Destruktion* of Metaphysics." *International Journal of Philosophical Studies* 8, no. 3 (2000): 297–327.

Thornes, John E. *John Constable's Skies: A Fusion of Art and Science*. Birmingham: University of Birmingham Press, 1999.

Tingey, David L. *Seeing Jaakob: The Poetics of Visuality in Thomas Mann's Die Geschichten Jaakobs*. New York: Peter Lang, 2010.

Todd, Richard. *The Opacity of Signs: Acts of Interpretation in George Herbert's The Temple*. Columbia, MO: University of Missouri Press, 1986.

Tolkien, J. R. R. *Tree and Leaf*. London: HarperCollins, 2001.

Tomasello, Michael. *The Cultural Origins of Human Cognition*. Cambridge, MA: Harvard University Press, 2000.

Topham, Jonathan R. "Biology in the Service of Natural Theology: Darwin, Paley, and the Bridgewater Treatises." In *Biology and Ideology: From Descartes to Dawkins*, edited by Denis R. Alexander and Ronald Numbers, 88–113. Chicago: University of Chicago Press, 2010.

Topham, Jonathan R. "Natural Theology and the Sciences." In *The Cambridge Companion to Science and Religion*, edited by Peter Harrison, 59–79. Cambridge: Cambridge University Press, 2010.

Torrance, Thomas F. *The Christian Doctrine of God: One Being, Three Persons*. Edinburgh: T. & T. Clark, 1996.

Torrance, Thomas F. *God and Rationality*. London: Oxford University Press, 1971.

Torrance, Thomas F. *The Ground and Grammar of Theology*. Charlottesville, VA: University of Virginia Press, 1980.

Torrance, Thomas F. *Karl Barth: Biblical and Evangelical Theologian*. Edinburgh: T. & T. Clark, 1990.

Torrance, Thomas F. *The Mediation of Christ*. Colorado Springs, CO: Helmers & Howard, 1992.

Torrance, Thomas F. "The Problem of Natural Theology in the Thought of Karl Barth." *Religious Studies* 6 (1970): 121–35.

Torrance, Thomas F. *Reality and Evangelical Theology: The Realism of Christian Revelation*. Eugene, OR: Wipf & Stock, 2003.

Torrance, Thomas F. "Reason in Christian Theology." *Evangelical Quarterly* 14, no. 1 (1942): 22–41.

Torrance, Thomas F. *Space, Time and Incarnation*. London: Oxford University Press, 1969.

Torrance, Thomas F. *Theological Science*. London: Oxford University Press, 1969.

Toulmin, Stephen. *The Uses of Argument*. Cambridge: Cambridge University Press, 2003.

Tracy, David. *The Analogical Imagination: Christian Theology and the Culture of Pluralism*. New York: Crossroad, 1981.

Trigg, Roger, and Justin Barrett, eds. *The Roots of Religion: Exploring the Cognitive Science of Religion*. Aldershot: Ashgate, 2014.

Turner, Denys. *Faith, Reason, and the Existence of God*. New York: Cambridge University Press, 2004.

Turner, Frank M. "The Secularization of the Social Vision of British Natural Theology." In *Contesting Cultural Authority: Essays in Victorian Intellectual Life*, 101–27. Cambridge: Cambridge University Press, 1993.

Turner, Jonathan H., and David E. Boyns. "The Return of Grand Theory." In *Handbook of Sociological Theory*, edited by Jonathan H. Turner, 353–78. New York: Springer, 2001.

Twain, Mark. *Life on the Mississippi*. New York: Penguin, 1986.

Tyson, Paul. *Returning to Reality: Christian Platonism for Our Times*. Cambridge: Lutterworth Press, 2014.

Umbach, Maiken. *Federalism and Enlightenment in Germany, 1740–1806*. London: Hambledon Press, 2000.

Utzschneider, Helmut. *Gottes Vorstellung: Untersuchungen zur literarischen Ästhetik und ästhetischen Theologie des Alten Testaments*. Stuttgart: Kohlhammer, 2007.

Vainio, Olli-Pekka. *Beyond Fideism: Negotiable Religious Identities*. Farnham: Ashgate, 2010.

Vallins, David. *Coleridge and the Psychology of Romanticism: Feeling and Thought.* New York: St Martin's Press, 1999.

van den Berge, Luc, and Stefan Ramaekers. "Figures of Disengagement: Charles Taylor, Scientific Parenting, and the Paradox of Late Modernity." *Educational Philosophy and Theory* 64 (2014): 607–25.

Vance, Eugene. "Seeing God: Augustine, Sensation, and the Mind's Eye." In *Rethinking the Medieval Senses: Heritage, Fascinations, Frames,* edited by Stephen G. Nichols, Andreas Kablitz, and Alison Calhoun, 13–29. Baltimore, MD: Johns Hopkins University Press, 2008.

VanDrunen, David. "Wisdom and the Natural Moral Order: The Contribution of Proverbs to a Christian Theology of Natural Law." *Journal of the Society of Christian Ethics* 33, no. 1 (2013): 153–68.

Vanhoozer, Kevin J. *Is There a Meaning in This Text? The Bible, the Reader, and the Morality of Literary Knowledge.* Grand Rapids, MI: Zondervan, 1998.

Varnelis, Kazys. "The Education of the Innocent Eye." *Journal of Architectural Education* 51, no. 4 (1998): 212–23.

Veldhuis, Henri. *Ein versiegeltes Buch: Der Naturbegriff in der Theologie J. G. Hamanns (1730–1788).* Berlin: De Gruyter, 1994.

Vidal, Fernando. "Extraordinary Bodies and the Physicotheological Imagination." In *The Face of Nature in Enlightenment Europe,* edited by Lorraine Daston and Gianna Pomata, 61–96. Berlin: Berliner Wissenschafts-Verlag, 2003.

Vidal, Fernando, and Bernard Kleeberg. "Knowledge, Belief, and the Impulse to Natural Theology." *Science in Context* 20 (2007): 381–400.

Viladesau, Richard. "Natural Theology and Aesthetics: An Approach to the Existence of God from the Beautiful?" *Philosophy & Theology* 3 (1988): 145–60.

Viladesau, Richard. *Theological Aesthetics: God in Imagination, Beauty and Art.* New York: Oxford University Press, 1999.

Visala, Aku. *Naturalism, Theism and the Cognitive Study of Religion: Religion Explained?* Aldershot: Ashgate, 2011.

Vitiis, Pietro de. "La problematica dell'ontoteologia e la filosofia teologica." In *Teologia naturale e teologia filosofica,* 113–32. Rome: Aracne, 2006.

Vogelsanger, Peter. "Theologie als Apologie des Glaubens: Ein Anliegen Emil Brunners." In *Der Auftrag der Kirche in der modernen Welt,* edited by Peter Vogelsanger, 75–88. Zurich: Zwingli-Verlag, 1959.

Volpe, Medi Ann. *Rethinking Christian Identity: Doctrine and Discipleship.* Oxford: Wiley-Blackwell, 2013.

Voltolini, Alberto. "The Content of a Seeing-as Experience." *Aisthesis: Pratiche, linguaggi e saperi dell'estetico* 6, no. 1 (2013): 215–37.

Wachter, Armin. *Relativistic Quantum Mechanics.* New York: Springer, 2011.

Wall, Kathleen. "Ethics, Knowledge, and the Need for Beauty: Zadie Smith's *On Beauty* and Ian McEwan's *Saturday.*" *University of Toronto Quarterly* 77, no. 2 (2008): 757–88.

Wang, Stephen. "Aquinas on Human Happiness and the Natural Desire for God." *New Blackfriars* 88, no. 1015 (2007): 322–34.

Ward, Graham. *Cultural Transformation and Religious Practice*. Cambridge: Cambridge University Press, 2005.

Ward, Timothy. *Word and Supplement: Speech Acts, Biblical Texts, and the Sufficiency of Scripture*. Oxford: Oxford University Press, 2002.

Warner, Michael, Jonathan VanAntwerpen, and Craig J. Calhoun, eds. *Varieties of Secularism in a Secular Age*. Cambridge, MA: Harvard University Press, 2010.

Wasmaier-Sailer, Margit, and Benedikt Paul Göcke. "Idealismus als Chance für die natürliche Theologie." In *Idealismus und natürliche Theologie*, edited by Margit Wasmaier-Sailer and Benedikt Paul Göcke, 9–28. Freiburg im Breisgau: Verlag Karl Alber, 2011.

Waters, Brent. *Christian Moral Theology in an Emerging Technoculture: From Posthuman back to Human*. Farnham: Ashgate, 2012.

Watts, Fraser, and Léon P. Turner, eds. *Evolution, Religion, and Cognitive Science: Critical and Constructive Essays*. Oxford: Oxford University Press, 2014.

Webb, Clement Charles Julian. *Studies in the History of Natural Theology*. Oxford: Clarendon Press, 1915.

Weber, Max. *Gesammelte Aufsätze zur Religionssoziologie*. 3 vols. Tübingen: Mohr, 1988.

Weber, Max. *Gesammelte Aufsätze zur Wissenschaftslehre*. Tübingen: J. C. B. Mohr, 1922.

Weidemann, Christian. *Die Unverzichtbarkeit natürlicher Theologie*. Munich: Karl Alber, 2007.

Welker, Michael. *Schöpfung und Wirklichkeit*. Neukirchen-Vluyn: Neukirchener Verlag, 1995.

Weinstein, Philip. "The View from Somewhere." *Raritan* 32, no. 4 (2013): 85–101.

Weissmann, Gerald. "Ecosentimentalism: The Summer Dream beneath the Tamarind Tree." In *The Flight from Science and Reason*, edited by Paul R. Gross, Norman Levitt, and Martin W. Lewis, 483–89. New York: New York Academy of Sciences, 1996.

Wells, Samuel. *Into Destiny: The Theological Ethics of Stanley Hauerwas*. Eugene, OR: Cascade Books, 1998.

Werner, Ilka. "'Die Reformation geht noch fort!' Friedrich Schleiermacher und Johannes Calvins." In *Calvins Erbe: Beiträge zur Wirkungsgeschichte Johannes Calvins*, edited by Marco Hofheinz, Wolfgang Lienemann, and Martin Sallmann, 182–203. Göttingen: Vandenhoeck & Ruprecht, 2011.

Westfall, Richard S. "The Scientific Revolution of the Seventeenth Century: A New World View." In *The Concept of Nature*, edited by John Torrance, 63–93. Oxford: Oxford University Press, 1992.

Westphal, Merold. *Overcoming Onto-Theology: Toward a Postmodern Christian Faith*. New York: Fordham University Press, 2001.

Wettlaufer, Alexandra. *In the Mind's Eye: The Visual Impulse in Diderot, Baudelaire and Ruskin*. New York: Rodopi, 2003.

Wheat, Andrew. "The Road before Him: Allegory, Reason, and Romanticism in C. S. Lewis' *The Pilgrim's Regress*." *Renascence: Essays on Values in Literature* 51, no. 1 (1998): 21–39.

Wheeler, Kathleen. "Romanticism's Fragmentary Unities: Melville, Faulkner, and Lessing." In *Romantic Presences in the Twentieth Century*, edited by Mark Sandy, 133–48. Farnham: Ashgate, 2012.

Whewell, William. *Astronomy and General Physics Considered with Reference to Natural Theology*. 5th edn. London: William Pickering, 1836.

Whewell, William. *The Philosophy of the Inductive Sciences*. 2 vols. 2nd edn. London: John W. Parker, 1847.

White, Thomas Joseph. *Wisdom in the Face of Modernity: A Study in Thomistic Natural Theology*. Ave Maria, FL: Sapientia Press, 2009.

Whitehead, Alfred North. *Science and the Modern World*. New York: Free Press, 1967.

Wielenberg, Erik J. *God and the Reach of Reason: C. S. Lewis, David Hume, and Bertrand Russell*. Cambridge: Cambridge University Press, 2008.

Wigner, Eugene. "The Unreasonable Effectiveness of Mathematics." *Communications on Pure and Applied Mathematics* 13 (1960): 1–14.

Wilcox, Miranda. "Alfred's Epistemological Metaphors: *Eagan Modes* and *Scip Modes*." *Anglo-Saxon England* 35 (2006): 179–217.

Wildman, Wesley J. "Comparative Natural Theology." *American Journal of Theology and Philosophy* 27, no. 2–3 (2006): 173–90.

Wiles, Maurice. *Archetypal Heresy: Arianism through the Centuries*. Oxford: Clarendon Press, 1996.

Williams, Anna N. *The Architecture of Theology: Structure, System, and Ratio*. Oxford: Oxford University Press, 2011.

Williams, Rowan. "Barth on the Triune God." In *Karl Barth: Studies of His Theological Method*, edited by S. W. Sykes, 147–93. Oxford: Clarendon Press, 1979.

Williams, Rowan. *On Christian Theology*. Oxford: Blackwell, 2000.

Williams, Rowan. *The Edge of Words: God and the Habits of Language*. London: Bloomsbury, 2014.

Williams, Rowan. *A Ray of Darkness*. Lanham, MD: Cowley, 1995.

Williams, Rowan. *Resurrection: Interpreting the Easter Gospel*. 2nd edn. London: Darton, Longman & Todd, 2002.

Williams, Rowan. "Teaching the Truth." In *Living Tradition: Affirming Catholicism in the Anglican Church*, edited by Jeffrey John, 29–43. London: DLT, 1991.

Wilson, Ross. *Shelley and the Apprehension of Life*. Cambridge: Cambridge University Press, 2013.

Wiseman, James A. *Theology and Modern Science: Quest for Coherence*. New York: Continuum, 2002.

Wisse, Maarten. "*Habitus Fidei*: An Essay on the History of a Concept." *Scottish Journal of Theology* 56, no. 2 (2003): 172–89.

Wissink, Jozef. *De Inzet van de Theologie: Een Onderzoek naar de Motieven en de Geldigheid van Karl Barths Strijd tegen de natuurlijke Theologie*. Amersfoort: De Horstink, 1983.

Withers, Charles W. J. *Placing the Enlightenment: Thinking Geographically about the Age of Reason*. Chicago: University of Chicago Press, 2007.

Wittgenstein, Ludwig. *Culture and Value: A Selection from the Posthumous Remains.* Oxford: Blackwell, 1998.

Wolfson, Elliott R. "Hermeneutics of Light in Medieval Kabbalah." In *The Presence of Light: Divine Radiance and Religious Experience*, edited by Matthew Kapstein, 105–18. Chicago: University of Chicago Press, 2004.

Wolfson, Elliott R. *Through a Speculum that Shines: Vision and Imagination in Medieval Jewish Mysticism.* Princeton, NJ: Princeton University Press, 1997.

Wolin, Sheldon S. *Democracy Incorporated: Managed Democracy and the Specter of Inverted Totalitarianism.* Princeton, NJ: Princeton University Press, 2008.

Wolloch, Nathaniel. *History and Nature in the Enlightenment: Praise of the Mastery of Nature in Eighteenth-Century Historical Literature.* Farnham: Ashgate, 2011.

Wolterstorff, Nicholas. "Entitlement to Believe and Practices of Inquiry." In *Practices of Belief: Selected Essays*, edited by Terence Cuneo, vol. 2, 86–117. Cambridge: Cambridge University Press, 2010.

Wolterstorff, Nicholas. "The Migration of the Theistic Arguments: From Natural Theology to Evidentialist Apologetics." In *Rationality, Religious Belief, and Moral Commitment*, edited by Robert Audi and William J. Wainwright, 38–80. Ithaca, NY: Cornell University Press, 1986.

Wood, William. "Thomas Aquinas on the Claim that God is Truth." *Journal of the History of Philosophy* 51 (2013): 21–47.

Wordsworth, William. *Lyrical Ballads: 1798 and 1802.* Oxford: Oxford University Press, 2013.

Wright, William M. *Rhetoric and Theology: Figural Reading of John 9.* Berlin: De Gruyter, 2009.

Wüthrich, Matthias Dominique. *Gott und das Nichtige: Eine Untersuchung zur Rede vom Nichtigen.* Zurich: Theologischer Verlag Zürich.

Wynn, Mark. "Beauty, Providence and the Biophilia Hypothesis." *Heythrop Journal* 38, no. 3 (1997): 283–99.

Wynn, Mark R. *Renewing the Senses: A Study of the Philosophy and Theology of the Spiritual Life.* Oxford: Oxford University Press, 2013.

Yamazaki, Tatsuya. "Leben ohne Warum: Der Ursprung des Lebens in der Theologie Meister Eckharts." *Journal of Oriental Studies* 18 (2008): 169–79.

Yeo, Richard R. *Defining Science: William Whewell, Natural Knowledge, and Public Debate in Early Victorian Britain.* Cambridge: Cambridge University Press, 1993.

Yoder, Joella G. *Unrolling Time: Christiaan Huygens and the Mathematization of Nature.* Cambridge: Cambridge University Press, 1988.

Young, Davis A. *John Calvin and the Natural World.* Lanham, MD: University Press of America, 2007.

Zachhuber, Johannes. *Theology as Science in Nineteenth-Century Germany: From F. C. Baur to Ernst Troeltsch.* Oxford: Oxford University Press, 2013.

Zachman, Randall C. "The Universe as the Living Image of God: Calvin's Doctrine of Creation Reconsidered." *Concordia Theological Monthly* 61 (1997): 299–312.

Zahl, Simeon. "On the Affective Salience of Doctrines." *Modern Theology* 31, no. 3 (2015): 428–44.

Zeitz, Lisa M. "Addison's 'Imagination' Papers and the Design Argument." *English Studies* 73 (1992): 493–502.

Zeki, Semir. "The Neurology of Ambiguity." *Consciousness and Cognition* 13, no. 1 (2004): 173–96.

Index

Re-Imagining Nature: The Promise of a Christian Natural Theology, First Edition.
Alister E. McGrath.
© 2017 John Wiley & Sons, Ltd. Published 2017 by John Wiley & Sons, Ltd.